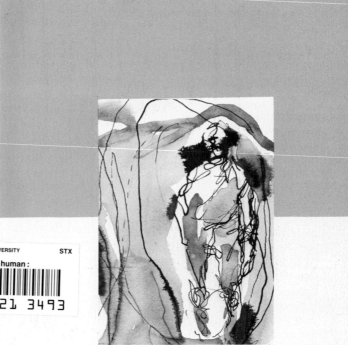

THE ART OF BEING HUMAN

Humanities as a Technique for Living

Richard Paul Janaro
Miami Dade Community College

Thelma C. Altshuler
Miami Dade Community College

HARPER & ROW, PUBLISHERS
SAN FRANCISCO

Cambridge   London
Philadelphia   Mexico City
New York   Sao Paolo
                 Sydney

1817

Sponsoring Editor
Earl Shepard

Project Editor
Carol Pritchard-Martinez

Production Coordinator
Marian Hartsough

Designer
Dare Porter

Illustrator
Marcia Murray

Cover Artist
Dare Porter

Compositor
ComCom, Division of Haddon
Craftsmen

Printer and Binder
R. R. Donnelley & Sons
Company

Four color separator
Focus 4

Typeface
CRT Asler $^{11}/_{13}$

Display type
Optima

The Art of Being Human: The Humanities as a Technique for Living

Additional credits for color art are located on page xi.

Library of Congress Cataloging in Publication Data

Janaro, Richard Paul.
  The art of being human.

  Includes index.
  1. Conduct of life. 2. Humanities. I. Altshuler, Thelma C., joint author. II. Title.
  BJ1581.2.J36 170'.202 79-13491
  ISBN 0-06-044427-4

Acknowledgments

Few books ever spring directly from their authors' heads into a typesetter's machine without requiring a great deal of help from a variety of experts. It is doubtful that any interdisciplinary text such as this could be so presumptuous. The authors have been especially fortunate in having received invaluable feedback from a number of colleagues, who were generous with their time and comments. We should like to extend our heartfelt thanks to the following, who provided overall suggestions or read very carefully specific sections within their fields of expertise: Marjorie Buhr, Joan Cronin, Patrick DeLong, Donald Early, and David Spitzer, of Miami-Dade Community College; and Joshua Zim and Eric Weiss of Vajradhatu, an Association of Buddhist Meditation Centers, with main offices in Boulder, Colorado.

PREFACE

This book is designed to be an introduction to the humanities, and a glance at the table of contents will show how we the authors view its mission. Clearly, we believe another look at the history of Western culture is not needed. The chronology of Western civilization is profusely available to the reader who wants historical perspective.

On the other hand, the chronology of Western civilization is only part of a much larger area of concern, one that the humanities in all cultures and periods of time have professed to: *the conduct of human life.* What makes life good, enriched, ennobled; in short, worth living?

It has always been an assumption of books about the humanities that art, music, philosophy, dance, literature, religion, and so on are indispensable because they do make life worth living. Just *how* they do is not, however, always apparent. As often as not, humanists decide to write about the humanities not in the springtime burst of excitement over newfound joys, but in the more deliberate, well-ordered zeniths of their academic careers. They write long after they suppose there can be any question about the need for, about the intrinsic down-to-earth *caring* for the humanities. Both of us have been teaching the humanities for many years, and yes, there was indeed a time when we painstakingly covered the march of Western culture from Socrates to Shaw—always caring, you understand, but sometimes not having the time to let it show. So now, when we are entitled to be deliberate and well-ordered, we have decided to open the windows and let the spring back in. This is a book about the whole of living, about being as fully human as each individual can possibly be. It has plenty to say about art and music and philosophy, but as they pertain to each of us— now. Here.

The humanities, in our opinion, are not limited to just those disciplines which people used to say comprised human culture. Functions of the humanist include noticing one's surroundings, looking at other people, being willing to change one's image every so often, learning how to grow old with grace and dignity and still stay young.

This book is not designed as impersonal instruction. It is addressed to you the reader, not merely to relay the names and achievements of celebrated human beings, but to recommend that you too become involved in some of the concerns which led to those achievements. Like the "celebrated" people who wanted to do more with their lives than they really had to, you can decide that minimum *surviving* is not enough. And that, briefly, is the underlying idea of this book.

Richard Paul Janaro
Thelma C. Altshuler

We are also indebted to the following individuals who reviewed and responded to our manuscript prior to publication: Lawrence S. Cunningham, **Florida State University at Tallahassee;** Gene R. Duckworth, **Delta College, Michigan;** Myron Marty, **St. Louis Community College at Florissant Valley;** Ed Parks, **Diablo Valley College;** James Zigerell, **(formerly) City Colleges of Chicago.**

CONTENTS

COLOR PLATES

Plate I	**upper left**	Marble statue of Christ, Coventry Cathedral, England, by Jacob Epstein (1880–1959).
		The sensitive eye can readily detect what deserves to be called art and what does not.
	bottom	Stonehenge, England.
		Stonehenge remains a symbol of the human mystery.
	upper right	A page from the Book of Kells, an illuminated manuscript (ninth century), which illustrates the pervasive use of the Golden Rectangle.
Plate II	**top**	An arrangement of Pottery by Henri Matisse (1869–1954), illustrating the Apollonian principle of order.
		. . . connections which make sense out of apparently unrelated phenomena.
	lower left	*Mythology can really be called the cumulative wisdom of the human race.*
	lower right	Marble statue, "Victory at Samothrace"; 8' high; the Louvre, Paris.
		Beautiful works conceived in a mode no longer current are still products of human minds and feelings.
Plate III		*The way people use lines in buildings tells us much about them and their times.*

upper left	Side wall of Chartres Cathedral, France, twelfth century: a supreme example of Gothic architecture.
middle left	The Schönbrunn Palace in Vienna, built in the seventeenth century as the royal residence of the Hapsburgs: one of the world's most notable examples of the high Baroque style.
lower left	An office building in Denver, Colorado.

The Dionysian and Apollion spirits in art can readily be seen in a comparison of these two statues of David.

upper right	The work of Donatello (1386–1466), circa 1430, bronze, 62¼" high, National Museum, Florence.
lower right	Michelangelo's (1475–1564) *David,* 1501–1504, marble, 13'5" high, The Academy, Florence.

Plate IV	**top**	The paintings of Marc Chagall (b. 1887) stand as vivid examples of the artist's need to retain a childlike sense of wonder and love of color.
	lower left	Passers-by taking a few moments to enjoy the sidewalk art always on display in New Orleans' Pirates Alley. (Photo by Lloyd Madansky)
	lower right	Design for a wall mural in a community center. Many communities include such art projects in their budgets as "essentials." (Courtesy of the artist, Patricia Roberts)

Plate V	**full page**	Francisco Goya (1746–1828), "Saturn Devouring His Son," 1820. Copyright © Prado Museum, Madrid. All rights reserved. Total or partial reproduction prohibited.

Raises the question of whether evident unpleasantness in subject matter and execution detracts from a work of art.

Plate VI	**full page**	Pablo Picasso (1881–1974), "The Actor," 1904–1905. The Metropolitan Museum of Art, Gift of Thelma Chrysler Foy, 1952. All rights reserved.

The best known work of Picasso's "Rose Period" in which he confined his subjects to circus performers. Contradicts an often-made charge—namely that artists who become famous for non-objective works are secretly unable to handle recognizable subjects.

Plate VII	**top**	Vincent Van Gogh (1853–1890), "The Starry Night," 1889. Oil on canvas, 29 × 36¼". Collection, The Museum of Modern Art, New York. Acquired through the Lillie P. Bliss Bequest. All rights reserved.

. . . a short, stabbing technique, throbbing with energy.

	bottom	August Renoir (1841–1919), "Madame Monet and Her Son," 18—/ National Gallery of Art, Washington. Ailsa Mellon Bruce Collection. All rights reserved.

Impressionism: A painting is something to experience totally for itself; it is an event, not something meant to call to mind something else.

Plate VIII	**full page**	Mary Cassatt, "The Bath." Collection of The Art Institute of Chicago. All rights reserved.

1

TO BE HUMAN

Overview

If everything could be as educational psychology would wish: if the most skillful educational theorists could design the perfect environment, hire an ideal staff who could make it function flawlessly, with society offering jobs to match everyone's qualifications; then, one would suppose, we should enjoy a highly advanced civilization—a utopia.

In such a society, however, there would still be people who marry the wrong people, and people who feel sorry for themselves because something they can't define is still missing from their lives. There would be people who sit around on a Sunday afternoon and wonder what to do with themselves, who have not opened a book in years, and people who sit and stare at each other without wanting to or being able to start an interesting conversation.

There would be others who take long walks, visit art galleries, enjoy attending symphony concerts, or just sit on a rock to watch the waves breaking. While some would get together and start a community theater, others would prefer to be by themselves and think—not to solve the world's overwhelming problems,—but because they had discovered that the mind, like the body, needs exercise and feels good when it has been challenged and when it has made some connections it hadn't made before.

Computers have no official name for what might be after all the most important skill anyone can acquire. But we all know what it is—we talk about it all the time. Sometimes we just call it *living.* We may say of a person, "He has a great deal of money, but does he really know how to live?" or "She died without ever having lived."

The distance that lies between us has been shrunken, and in certain ways annihilated. What takes place in Delhi, in Peking, in Tokyo, is known the same day in London, in Paris, in New York. A continuous stream of images and sounds comes from thence to eddy about our heads. It is an inevitable coming together . . . Mechanical coming together would be nothing if it did not prepare the way for an exchange of secret treasures.

A new humanism is on the horizon. This time it will take in humanity entire.
Paul-Louis Couchoud

We can say, "They don't know how to live," of just about everyone, even of a president of the United States, an actress whose permanent address is Paris, or of the person who scoops out ice cream at a corner stand. We can say the opposite of someone who never earned an enormous salary, or of someone who did. To have life—to breathe, to have a heartbeat, to have operating senses, to possess motor skills —is not what constitutes *living,* nor is it a matter either of having wealth, fame, or good fortune. Living is more than a skill: it is an art. It is not inborn, but the art is not necessarily taught either. At some point it is acquired.

At some point you know that you are living more effectively or less effectively. No amount of rationalizing, no amount of taking inventory of your possessions, degrees,

---

Eve's Daughter

When my eyes turn skyward,
I am aware that I
see the moon that Adam saw
lighting up the sky.

When my eyes turn downward
and measure fields of grass,
I am mindful then that Eve
saw each season pass.

But when my eyes turn inward
then I truly know
that what I am and what I feel
happened long ago.[1]

Hannah Kahn

---

powers, and friends can convince you that you are living effectively if inwardly you do not believe it.

People who live effectively are those who:

make the most of their potential
make the most of their environment
reexamine their beliefs periodically
change their life styles when necessary
find new friends when necessary
never stop thinking
are not afraid to feel and show emotion

Such people are called humanists throughout this book. And the assumption behind this book is, that while almost anyone *can become* a humanist, you must first deliberately *choose* to be one. In fact, for the humanist, life is strictly a matter of the willingness, the desire, to make intelligent choices among significant alternatives. Humanists do not believe that every choice is determined by some external condition, nor that it is easier to accept rather than change a less-than-satisfying life.

The basic aptitudes a humanist needs are those capacities given to all of us at birth: the capacity for thinking, feeling, and having sensory experiences. An individual may feel most alive when captivated by an exciting idea, when expressing emotions that will not be denied, or when indulging in the senses, as when inhaling a delicious odor. A person's sensitivity will vary with given conditions: a pleasant sensation may come in the sudden absence of pain, as when a headache goes away; or as when anger or grief passes, and a person then feels tranquility. No matter what the nature of the sensation, the humanist experiences it totally.

Humanism: Old and New

The pursuit of an ideal life style ought to be the concern of each of us. Unfortunately, many of us never get around to thinking about it. Perhaps most people do what they can, supposing it to be *all* they can do. Later in life they sometimes pause, looking back regretfully and blaming circumstances for their lot in life.

The Humanist as Anti-Social

Over the centuries there developed a particular breed of human beings whose primary concern was the quality of living, as opposed to the basic necessities of living. They acquired the designation of humanists and at one time encouraged a sharp distinction between themselves and people concerned with such "practical" matters as military strategies, scientific discoveries, and just plain earning a living.

Socrates enjoys the enduring reputation of having been one of the first truly dedicated humanists. He appears to have spent much of his life in the company of young intellectuals, who followed him everywhere and engaged him in profound discussions about beauty, justice, and virtue, and not for any immediate gain, but for the joy of using the mind as it was meant to be used. In other words, Socrates and his group enriched their lives and practiced the art of being human by discovering that it was both possible and pleasurable to talk about profound and puzzling subjects.

On the other hand, Xantippe, the wife of Socrates, "enjoys" the reputation of having been a rather unpleasant shrew, continually getting after her lazy, good-for-nothing husband for not doing something more profitable with his

George Horace Lorimer

Back of every noble life there are principles that fashioned it.

life. For centuries Xantippe represented all that was antihumanistic. A modern play, *Barefoot in Athens,* attempts to show both sides. In this play, Socrates is witty and sympathetic, but Xantippe can be forgiven for being somewhat irked by his never staying home and remaining such a poor breadwinner.

Humanists have always been set apart from "practical" people, an unfortunate distinction. The practical were supposed to be concerned with the here-and-now, the humanists with the past. Finding much of society uncongenial, the humanist took revenge by scoffing at the present and the domain of the practical, and finding enrichment only in the noble thoughts and emotions of persons long since gone.

"Humanities" courses in schools and colleges were often equated with extremes of impracticality. The artists and philosophers who were the object of the humanists' study were often found guilty by association. Thus the entire field of the humanities—referring to both the creative minds and the audience who read, listened, or looked at their works—became separated from the mainstream of everyday life as well as from the realm of scientific thought. This distinction is highly regrettable since one of the enduring humanistic ideals has been the importance of achieving wholeness, of seeing and participating in all the aspects of human existence.

The Humanist as Mr. Chips

Nonetheless, humanists have been laughed at, or treated with gentle condescension, as in James Hilton's famous novelette *Goodbye, Mr. Chips.* Mr. Chips, beloved though eccentric master of generations of English schoolboys, was always seen mince-stepping his way penguin-like across the campus, his frail body shrouded in a black robe, hat and tassel bobbing uncertainly atop his pure white hair.

Mr. Chips was a stern taskmaster. He required long hours of study and absolutely accurate recitations from his students. What he taught had no relevance to the practical world of human affairs, but this dissociation supposedly made Mr. Chips even more lovable, even if terribly forgetful and careless about his personal effects. No doubt he dropped coins from his pocket, and his clothes were never completely clean or pressed.

Yet Mr. Chips's creator, James Hilton, had no trouble accepting his character as basically fine, noble, and spiritual. Having spent his life in the company of great minds, he cannot have failed to absorb some of their fervor and glow. This attitude, again, was well within the humanist tradition, which had always viewed humankind as being spiritual and thus a far cry from simple animal life. While not having a strictly religious point of view, humanism had nonetheless agreed with the Judeo-Christian belief in man as the lord of creation. Of course, Darwin's theory of evolution, published in 1859, did some damage to the humanist ideal.

But not completely. Humanism in the traditional sense managed to survive. In the early post-Darwin days, survival often meant outright denial of evolutionary theory, as when the aristocratic lady at the dinner table is reported to have put a halt to a long discussion of the pros and cons of Darwinism by saying to the most enthusiastic spokesman for evolution: "Perhaps your family is descended from the apes, but mine certainly is not!"

To survive in what often seemed an increasingly hostile world—a world of science and technology and less and less of true culture—humanists often did resemble Mr. Chips. And often humanism *was* a very upper class phenomenon, because it was the people who did not have to struggle for economic survival in the early years of this century who believed they had a responsibility to be the guardians of culture. Humanism became elitist and not very liberal. Mr. Chips may have been lovable, but he was also a white, Anglo-Saxon male. He may not have received a large salary, but he devoted his life to the training of those who would. In this elitism, one achieved humanistic status either through wealth or education.

It takes more than rationality to be a full human being

But humanism has changed dramatically. The change was inevitable. There was never a profound reason that humanism should have been the exclusive property of the wealthy classes and the academic elite. Humanists' snobbishness was a reaction against the unfamiliar twentieth-century world of machines, labor unions, and the threat they thought science posed to the human spirit.

Today we witness a return to non-elitist humanism, to the original proposition that to achieve the human potential takes some doing, but is within everyone's grasp. After all, the human beings most revered by Mr. Chips—Shakespeare or Michelangelo—were not distinctly aristocratic, but ordinary mortals with extraordinary passions, who insisted upon making their presence felt and leaving their mark. It is they—not the gentle Mr. Chips—we want to emulate. For, whether they wanted to or not, the turn-of-century humanists often gave the impression that the humanist's role was to admire, not to emulate; that the great things of this world had already been done and there was nothing left to do in the uncultured present but for the sensitive few to keep alive the memory of past achievements.

But today, there is a deeper awareness of the full significance of the term *human.* It does not refer only to past greatness, but to the present and future potential of every man, woman, and child. Where once it tended to mean only the intellectual and artistic best of what a gifted few could achieve, the word now connotes a much wider range of sensibilities. Creativity and rationality were once abstracted from the people they characterized, and were worshipped as entities in themselves, beyond the reach of plain folk. Humanists today realize how dangerous it can be to rationally segregate the human ideal from the human context. It takes more than rationality to achieve the full human potential. Hitler and his followers may be said to have been skilled at rational organization, and surely they represented an elite group. But they were *not* humanists.

Profile of the Modern Humanist

Above talent, genius, creativity, intellect, or any of the most revered human traits the humanist values freedom. In a very real sense, this is a book about freedom as much as it is a presentation of the humanist viewpoint. For if the art of being human consists of making responsible choices, there must be a context of freedom within which to choose.

On the other hand, the humanist's understanding of freedom may be considerably different from the casual definition of the term. That one lives in a free society does not make one free. Nor does imprisonment (while surely not a goal of life) necessarily mean a total absence of freedom. For the humanist, freedom is a state of mind, a disposition to discover what alternatives exist, what choices can be made, a willingness to act upon the profound conviction that a

---

Robert Benchley

The world is divided into two kinds of people —those who divide the world into two kinds of people and those who don't.

The humanist values freedom.

given choice is the right one, *and* the courage to accept responsibility for the results of one's actions.

Humanism today receives some support from gestalt psychology, a form of therapy in which patients are restored to an inner state of well-being by taking full responsibility for what has happened to them.

Then there is also existential philosophy, prophetically called a humanism by Jean-Paul Sartre, its leading exponent. Existentialists hold that "man is nothing but what he makes of himself." Further, they find that life taken out of a human context has no meaning or purpose, and since people come in and go out of this world by sheer accident, the emphasis people give their existence is an absurdity. The meaning of life, so believe the existential philosophers, is something each of us is free to determine.

According to the existentialists, freedom is measured only in terms of what we actually do. You might say that conditioning factors bring us to the crossroads many times a day, but this does not alter the immediate consciousness of having a choice. Is it not better, say the existentialists, to be cognizant of making free choices and to take responsibility for them than to insist one is not and can never be free? In other words, freedom—like motion—is measured against a fixed point. At any given moment of time one knows oneself to be here, rather than there, and before changing position, one may recognize the choice: "I am free to take this step or that one, or to take no steps at all."

Today's humanists stress freedom because once the decision to be free is made, the individual suddenly finds doors opening in all directions. There are no blind alleys, no dead ends. One finds the strength to change old routines, to leave tiresome jobs, to go back to school and learn new skills. The way of nature, says the humanist, is growth and change, and it is only in a free context that people can live in harmony with the nature of things. But freedom is something we are free to *not* accept. In a way, freedom can be a burden, forcing us to move away from familiar, even if stifling, environments and to wander, uncertainly at first, through unfamiliar landscapes. Many people prefer to lock themselves into dull routines and to blame others (the government, the weather, the company, the times) for their unhappiness.

After the decision to accept freedom comes *critical detachment.* It is hard to separate the two. Critical detachment is

George Bernard Shaw

Liberty means responsibility. That is why men dread it.

standing back and seeing oneself and others in action. It is being sensitive to the shape of events. The humanist believes unhappiness and frustration often stem from finding oneself caught up in the stream of events and losing one's perspective. Thinking about what is happening is much more difficult for some people than just drifting with the current and surrendering their human capacity for thought.

Without thought, feelings lose perspective

Much is made today of feeling. Psychologists warn of the dangers of suppressing emotion, and it is true that it is seldom wise to deny what you are feeling. (Of course, there are limits to any course of action. Does one give free play to a strong urge to kill someone else?) But feelings are not the extent of our make-up. Humankind has developed a brain for some good reason. Thought *can* be used to manipulate one's environment, to control others, to maneuver one's way up the ladder of success; it can become a survival skill, detached from self-awareness. Yet thought is the instrument through which we come to observe ourselves, the life around us, and our relationship to it. Thought is the fixed point against which we can measure the motion of life, though the point should not *stay* fixed. Feeling can be a counter motion to thought—like two trains moving along together, thought and feeling may simultaneously cover great distances. But without thought, feeling loses perspective; we may even say that without feelings, thought can lose its humanity. The thinking person needs to be able to empathize with—to put himself in the place of—others, to have some idea of where the fixed points of other people are located.

The skill of empathy is greatly enhanced by the activity of *noticing.* You can be so lost in both thought and feeling that you fail to see changes that are taking place. It is like pulling down the shades inside your train and not knowing where you are or where you are going. Your fixed point disappears. Humanists take the time to look, listen, and touch before thinking, before feeling. They need the data from experience to help them grow. They know they are not free unless they are free to act, and they know they must have something clearly before them to act *upon.* There are people who go through life never really seeing what others are doing, hearing what others are saying, never noticing the looks people exchange. There are people who never notice what effect they are having upon others.

To notice, you must stay closely anchored to the present reality. Doing this is problematic for humanists, for they know you can lose perspective by becoming too involved with specific sensations in the moment-by-moment flow of time. For example, a person will go to a movie and when asked what it was all about will answer, "It's about a man who builds a cabin and marries a lady from Boston, who has never been in the West before, and then the cabin burns down and they lose everything." Another person, having witnessed the same events on the screen, will answer, "The film deals with the conflict between man and nature and with the human will to survive." The humanist has the ability to see enduring principles at work behind concrete events.

The critical facility also enables us to see through some exceedingly large and not always tenable abstractions. Abstractions like "material rewards" and "getting ahead" serve to condition us, but if we would be truly be free, we must develop the ability to determine what these things really mean from our fixed points, from our own frames of reference. We must subject some of the traditional goals of our society to careful scrutiny: power, prestige, status, wealth, and, of course, those ever-present opposites, success and failure. How many suicides have been the result of a too-ready and uncritical willingness to admit an abstraction like failure?

As you read through this book, you will become aware of many other dimensions of the humanist life style. This chapter intended only to introduce the subject, to indicate that, from this modern perspective, humanism is not something we can afford to tuck away on the other side of the campus. Humanism now means doing the most you can with all of your human capacities. Yet even prominent political figures, famous movie stars, and best-selling authors may not necessarily be utilizing all of these capacities. But it is possible that someone whose name has never been in the news may well be doing just that.

Under the terms of the new humanism, no one is excluded or automatically included. Mr. Chips may not be a humanist at all! There may be many roads he has never taken, many choices he refused to make and now regrets not having made. At the same time, a person who has devoted his life to laboratory research can exemplify every ideal humanists

---

Goethe

Everybody wants to be somebody: nobody wants to grow.

cherish. In a recent TV interview the Nobel prize-winning scientist Albert Szent-Gyorgyi, who discovered Vitamin C in 1937 and who in his 80s is actively engaged in cancer research, summed up the meaning of science: "You see, in my idea, scientific research, essentially, is seeing what everybody has seen but then to think what nobody has thought." Is this not growth? Is this not freedom itself? Is this not humanism?

Chapter 1 Footnote

[1]Hannah Kahn, "Eve's Daughter," *Eve's Daughter.* Copyright by Hannah Kahn, and reprinted with permission of the author.

2

THE ESTHETIC SENSE

Overview

One of the most common, yet least understood, aspects of human existence is what has been variously defined as esthetic experience.

It makes a difference whether we say that we are having an esthetic *kind* of experience or that we are experiencing *something* that *is* esthetic. In the first case we are *describing* an experience; in the other, the esthetic becomes an object, an entity, a *thing* of some kind. The assumption in the latter case is that an esthetic something is out there on the side of the road, waiting for someone to pass by and find it.

In addition to a glowing sunset or the statue of the Milo Venus, the taste of champagne can be esthetic, as can the feeling of soft velvet and the sound of water lapping against our canoe, or a Schubert quartet.

Even so, when we say that the sight of someone's face provides an esthetic experience, we are not saying that any sight will do the same thing. Certain faces affect us in ways we would never describe as "esthetic." Some tastes seem unpleasant. Obviously some other factor enters the picture —some factor which is not always present when we depend on only our five senses.

It is simpler to imagine the existence of another kind of sense—one that becomes activated in the presence of certain stimuli and stays dormant in the presence of others. Precisely *where* this sense is "located" is less important than the probability that it works in conjunction with the other senses whenever it is awakened.

We walk along a crowded street. We are late for an engagement. Nothing of great moment occupies our mind, except the need to move as rapidly as possible. Questions of esthetics are far away. Yet all of a sudden, we stop. Behind a lace curtain in the window of a small house we are passing, we glimpse the shape of a human being and a face peeking through the curtain. It is a certain kind of face—yet which kind? It reminds us of—or does it? There is just something about that face—but what? For a long time afterwards— long after the reason for our appointment is forgotten—we remember the incident. We think about the face. It cannot possibly matter. The moment has nothing to do with the conduct of our lives, with earning a living, real estate transactions, finding a job, shopping for dinner, cleaning the house, causes, movements, revolutions, wars, the march of history. Yet it may be that some time in the distant future, in the middle of a heated discussion on some very urgent piece of business, we will think back to that slight moment —and smile.

There exists a sense—call it the seventh, since the possibility of a sixth has also been considered—by which we do more than see or hear or touch and which sends back a message to the pleasure center located in the brain—a message that everything is suddenly very much all right. The esthetic sense tells us that seeing, hearing, and touching are sometimes worth doing for their own sake, in precisely the same way that delicious food is worth eating for more than our basic survival needs.

No doubt the most widely experienced use of this seventh sense occurs when the body has just regained its health after

*Every moment some form grows perfect in hand or face; some tone on
the hills or sea is choicer than the rest . . . that moment only. Not
the fruit of experience, but experience itself is the end. . . . To burn
always with this hard gemlike flame, to maintain this ecstasy is
success in life. . . . While all melts under our feet, we may well catch
at any exquisite passion . . . that seems, by a lifted horizon, to set
the spirit free for a moment, or any stirring of the senses, strange
dyes, strange flowers, curious odors, or work of the artist's hands, or
the face of one's friend.*
Walter Pater

an illness. The aches are gone, the fever has vanished, the
wound has healed, the broken limb has mended. Mental
health has its parallels. The depression we haven't been able
to explain or control suddenly lifts one morning like pre-
dawn fog. Or we have forgiven ourselves for some long
forgotten transgression, and we see the world with new
eyes: there is a tiny bird perched on the windowsill; the sun
is warm and friendly; from down the street comes the reassuring purr of somebody's lawn mower. Who does not know
what it is like to sink back into the pillow and just lie there,
feeling good? Who believes that such a sensation has any
other purpose except to be enjoyed?

Now, esthetic experience in general has implications for
both physical and mental well-being, and in this respect it
may be said to have a purpose. To activate the brain's pleasure center without bringing guilt feelings can be said to have
a purpose (except for such instances as when the overweight person goes right on enjoying delicious food). The
esthetic sense is unrelated to the quest of financial success,
of power, or status. In the frantic rush of living in this
society, the esthetic sense is therefore likely to be pushed to
one side. The pleasure center is likely to get along with
enjoying new automobiles, new clothes, and the uninspired
products of fast-food chains. The solitary bird on the windowsill usually has to wait long months for our notice and
response.

This chapter will try to give the esthetic sense its rightful
place in our lives. The discussions of esthetics need not be
restricted to the arts. The stimulus to the esthetic sense can
be something that happens to us, something we touch, the

sight of the bird on the windowsill, or an original Van Gogh. Artists, after all, derive their inspiration from the sights and sounds of the world; such inspiration need not be denied to others. But whether it is art or a natural object which provokes the esthetic reaction, there has to be something about the stimulus that makes it different from things to which an individual has either a negative reaction or no reaction at all.

For centuries people have disagreed over what this "something" should be called and how it should be described. It would be impossible to deal with all of the theories that have been advanced. It seems wiser to limit our discussion to three very broad concepts which have always been central to esthetic matters: the concepts of form, beauty, and taste.

Form

A pile of rocks accidentally thrown together in the back yard can be viewed as a "formless mess." (The same can be said of the living room after last night's party.) But the very same rocks can be used to make a Japanese rock garden and the results judged almost immediately as having or not having the form one has attempted to create.

Form and shape are not the same, though surely they are related. When we speak of the shape of a statue, for example, we refer to its outward contour, the way it cuts into the space around it. We speak of a building's shape in the same terms. But shape in this sense is not the same thing as form; shape is what is plainly visible. The shape is an outward component of the total form. Poems and musical compositions also have form, without having shapes in the same sense that solid, three-dimensional objects have shapes.

Forms are basic ingredients of our lives. In fact, we speak of our lives *in general,* as having or not having form. We talk of the need to "get it all together," which is another way of saying that form is necessary. We show decided preference for certain kinds of forms in our environments. The forms we select are therefore reflections of our inner natures, our deeper selves.

Form as Arrangement

Arrangements or systematic relationships are fundamental to the workings of the universe, to society, to the human organism. In fact, all three probably *are* arrangements. Though to be sure there is no complete understanding of what constitutes THE universe, Einstein suspected the universe was an integral whole, governed by potentially discoverable laws. Others postulate it is an infinite series of explosions or other kinds of cosmic activities without laws to govern all of its events. Although there is much disagreement about how the universe functions, the belief is nonetheless very strong that such a thing as a universe does exist. As for society and human relationships, there is little doubt that they are systems of one sort or another, and that their many different components relate to each other, governed by certain laws or principles.

Arrangements	Accidents
the family	residents of an apartment house
a floral display	weeds
a three-act play	things that happened yesterday

What About:

a traffic jam

a flight crew

a tennis match

a religion

a poker hand

It seems only natural that we should be arrangement-conscious. The law of existence, as we know it, provides that things do not work by themselves but in conjunction with other things. There is balance in nature *(homeostasis);* there is alternation in the seasons; and there is the principle identified in ancient Chinese philosophy as the *yin* and the *yang,* one active, the other passive, one positive, the other negative. This principle corresponds in some respects to that of magnetic fields, in which negative poles are attracted by their opposites, thus achieving stability.

While the Judeo-Christian view of the universe is centered on the idea that it was created out of nothing by God, the Greeks, notably Aristotle, entertained the belief that the universe was an orderly arrangement and had been that way without beginning; that arrangement was inherent in the nature of things.

Whichever view you accept, it is undeniable that all the basic units of life function as arrangements. The way the body and mind operate is crucial to us, as is the predictable operation of natural law. Why is it that the pollution of the environment is so disturbing to so many people? Or the suspected "tampering" with the atmosphere, which seems to be an inevitable result of continued nuclear testing? Why do people spend thousands of dollars consulting psychiatrists if it were not that possessing a sense of inner wholeness is imperative? And why has society labeled as mental illness any number of inner disorders that cause people to behave in antisocial (that is, system-destroying) ways?

We reach out for forms because all life exists as part of some arrangement or other.

Leonard Bernstein

Beethoven broke all the rules, and turned out pieces of breathtaking rightness. Rightness— that's the word.

The present concern over the possible destruction—or near-destruction—of nature's ecological system may reflect an unconscious anxiety over taking something away from a complete, unified whole as well as reflecting a fear that humanity may soon be extinct. The point is that anything stable and enduring requires systematic arrangement, and however much humanity may pretend to be separate from or superior to the natural world, we remain biologically and psychologically tuned in to its way of being. We are *naturally* desirous of maintaining, creating, and experiencing systems —from the great ecological systems of nature to the tiny brush strokes on a hand-painted ivory ring.

The analogy that can be drawn between natural systems and man-made arrangements (art, architecture, music, social institutions, and so on) seems inevitable. Our responsiveness in each case appears to have the same motivation: *We need the sense of completeness.* If spring were not to follow winter, there would be a disastrous interruption of an arrangement—a sudden, unexplained incompleteness. We wait throughout our lives for the dropping of the second shoe, and we are frustrated when it does not happen on schedule.

As a matter of fact, because there is so little completeness in our lives, we hunger for arrangements. Internal incompleteness is felt whenever an idea will not fall into place, even if it is only the missing word in the "across" column of a crossword puzzle or the last verse of an almost-remembered song. External incompleteness surrounds us: families that break up; a promising peace treaty that fails; an unfinished overpass. Our frustrations spring from a desire for wholeness and permanence. Completeness is the vital entity in human life. All natural things, including us, need completeness to exist.

People enjoy artistic designs because they are designs, not because they like art. As a matter of fact, something does not become art unless it *first* becomes a design. The difference between those designs which are designated "art" and those which are not, is the difference between complete and incomplete arrangements.

An obvious question at this point: who decides when an arrangement is complete, and how? Very likely intuition tells us. And why not? If, as has been suggested, we need arrangements in order to live, must we not possess that "seventh" sense to recognize them? In science there are experiments and there are results. No need for a seventh sense there. But outside of science—when it is a question of whether a room is arranged just right or a painting represents exactly what is intended—there is something which whispers the verdict. That the verdict is variable, that it may differ from period to period and culture to culture is undeniable. But it does not appear to be wildly, irresponsibly variable.

There are whole traditions of forms in art which constitute the heritage of a given culture. Critical agreements about art exist in African culture as well as in Hindu or European cultures. All cultures have buildings, dances, dramas, etc., which are held in esteem. Such forms give a people continuity, a hold on the earth. They learn quickly to establish formal standards in order to guarantee this continuity.

If establishing forms makes us human, the continuity of forms makes us this people or that people. And if we would aspire to a more universal humanity, we must look beyond the forms to which we respond most readily, and involve ourselves in less familiar forms.

It is dehumanizing to regard the forms of one's own culture as the standard of civilization and others as quaint or primitive. Even the label "prehistoric" can be patronizing, unless one means a reference to cultures which existed before either oral or written history, and calls "history" a record of those cultures whose people have interested us.

The Japanese Zen painting on the next page, lies outside the formal tradition of most people in the West. Like all Zen paintings, it occupies only a very small portion of the canvas. A typical Western response might be: "Where's the rest of it?" Or "Why do they use up so much canvas for such a small design?" What Westerners often do not realize, however, is the importance of space to the Zen mind. In Zen meditation one sits until one is aware of nothingness, emotions, ego, vacillating thoughts—all of the things which Zen Buddhism believes bring us suffering and despair—are gone. Thus in Zen art it is *significant absence* that makes an arrangement complete.

In sharp contrast is an altar from a Baroque church. The Baroque movement in Western art was associated with the

Counter Reformation of the seventeenth century, a reaction of Catholicism against Protestant austerity. Churches built in the period, especially in Germany, Poland, and Austria, are highly ornate. Almost every available space is filled with a picture or a statue. Trumpeting cherubs hang from the ceilings, which are usually painted in brilliant colors to represent heaven. A Zen practitioner, coming to the West for the first time and encountering a Baroque church, might well consider the arrangements *over*done: not form at all, but formlessness; over-completeness to the point at which system disappears. "I want," the practioner might think, "as little stimulation as possible. This gives me far too much."

At the same time, one hardly doubts that some forms unite us all in a universal abstraction called humanity. Michelangelo's *David* may well represent such an arrangement. Surely the thousands of persons who visit the Academy in Florence are not all members of Western culture. The artist conceived of *David* as the universal man, the marble embodiment of the human potential, demanding to be free, hand forever poised, ready to seize the weapon hanging from his shoulder and use it against tyranny and oppression.

In Zen art it is significant absence that makes an arrangement complete.

The size, the contour, the pose, the noble features—all of

the elements—of the *David* seem to come together; and it happens over and over again, mysteriously, through the act of human creativity. *David* meant Florence to the Florentines, but he clearly belongs now to all people, everywhere.

Forms Are Part of Us

Even within their own culture there are people who believe the forms which have created their tradition are somehow remote and irrelevant. Not everyone born or raised in Western society wants to travel to Greece, where that society had its origins, nor to Western Europe, where it rose to world preeminence. Not everyone wants to make the pilgrimage to see the original *David* or the *Mona Lisa* or Shakespeare performed at Stratford. Similarly, not every person with an Afro-American background wants to visit the countries of his or her ancestors for their sculpture, their dances, their music. It is one of the ironies of our complex nature that, while form is at once so crucial to our being, it often seems to be dispensable.

But the very fact that we can take form or leave it gives us a clue to what we are all about as people.

Forms do not just happen. They are projections of an inner need for completeness. Without them we would inhabit lonely wastelands with only natural forms for companions, but we could never count on natural forms to be complete. So we have been putting our own forms around us for thousands of years: stone circles, buildings, monuments, statues, gardens. They were not imposed upon the earth by the gods. They are closely tied in with human nature; therefore studying our forms will enable us to understand ourselves better.

The fact that some belong to seemingly remote periods of history may partially explain our frequent indifference to forms, but it seems clear that the history of no culture is long enough to justify a lack of curiosity. Sometimes it is a simple matter of reminding ourselves that a temple, no matter how "ancient," is a human response to a need to relate to a higher force; that the carving on a column is the result of a human judgment that straight lines seem more complete than wavy ones.

In Western society—as in others—a broad distinction can be made between forms: some can be called *classical* and others can be called *modern.* That is, we can spread the mantle of cultural history out like a timeline and look at it from end to end and see certain types of forms emerging at the beginning and contemporary and even futuristic forms emerging today. Taking liberties with time and space and compressing cultural history into the territory of a glance, we can see ourselves reflected at both ends. *We* are both classical and modern by nature, at least in terms of our particular culture.

If anything can be said to characterize the human being of the West, it is a desire for motion. The West got to be as expansive as it is *because* of this desire. The Greeks were a collection of tribes that swept down from the north and settled throughout the Balkan peninsula. No sooner had Athens attained its cultural preeminence than it opened trade routes with the East. Then came the Romans with a positive obsession for spreading out and annexing territories. When Constantine turned Rome into a Christian empire, church and state teamed up to embark upon an epic case of cultural expansion. Eventually what we know as Europe emerged. Europeans spread to America. Americans in turn could not be happy confined to the eastern shore when there was a continent of unimagined vastness to be explored. We know the rest.

The rest is a story of restlessness. It describes what each of us is like deep down. We cannot stay put. We never seem to know what we want. We want a home, a family, job security. But we also want to travel, to see new places and have new experiences. We want love, friendship, stable relationships; but we never miss an opportunity to seek out the company of unfamiliar, potentially more exciting companions.

Still, in casting aside—or wishing to cast aside—the tried and true; in peering over our neighbor's fence at his always greener grass; in finally leaving home and striking out on our own; we inevitably reach a point at which where we were seems more inviting than where we are going. If we return and stay where we were once comfortable, we are often sorry we did and begin once again to change our minds. In some moments we scoff at our nostalgia and keep on going; in others we wish we could go home.

In this restlessness, Western people are probably not basically different from people everywhere else. The fluctuation in attitude appears to be a fundamental pattern of human nature. Various cultures have various ways of manifesting this pattern. In Buddhism, for example, meditation serves to break apart the inner forms of intellect and ego. The difficulty many people have in meditating is in trying to achieve an extreme state, void of forms, without thinking of forms. As one attempts to sit and think of nothing at all, the mind works furiously, generating idea after idea. At length, meditation calms the mind's processes, and the inner forms temporarily vanish.

Western culture's classical Greek and Roman forms seem to be projections of our deeper selves' hungers for stability, oneness, wholeness. These classical forms are geometrical, with an abundant use of Golden Rectangles, a phenomenon we will consider later, in this chapter's section on beauty. The artists of the classical world worked in stone, as did the artists of the Middle Ages and the Renaissance. They wanted their forms to be around for a while.

The modern world (defined as beginning in the seventeenth century) has seen a gradual and deepening understanding of nature's way, the way of change. Forms have gradually come to reflect change rather than the need for permanence. To be sure, the eighteenth century witnessed a classical revival, a return to geometrical forms, a return to balance and precision in architectural, musical, and literary arrangements; but this revival can be understood in relation to the steady rise of modern science and the fears some experienced that science might mean an end to a stable culture.

Even today, surrounded as we are by non-geometrical, fluid forms, suggestive of nature's dynamics rather than of stability, we find people building stately homes with Greek columns and going in for heavy, solid furniture instead of floating water beds and modular furniture that can be put together, separated, stood on its side, and its function changed from one week to the next. There must have been some Greeks who despised the omnipresent stone and the symmetry of the buildings around them. Just as Aeschylus and Sophocles were building up the structural tradition of Greek tragedy, Euripides was tearing it to shreds with a throbbing, psychological kind of drama which must have both thrilled and horrified his audience. Medieval stone masons "sneaked in" some obscenities and a good deal of irreverence in the dark corners of the cathedrals they built.

The classical part of us tries to pull it all together; the

modern part of us wants to blast it apart. These impulses don't appear to be very compatible, but then neither do positive and negative electrical poles, or winter and summer. Yet neither could exist without the other. *The modern world was already implied in the classical world.*

Many people exhibit apathy toward the forms of their culture. They may lack concern over whether a house is "done" in any particular style or whether there are paintings on the wall; they have a distaste for the forms of the past as well as the present. Perhaps such disdain stems from a *fear of form;* for, although arrangements are needed, they suggest a stability which is threatening to our need for change. The important thing to recognize is not to visualize the path of change as a straight line. You cannot go from here to there directly.

Einstein has shown us how the universe which appears to go on into infinity, containing billions of galaxies, any one of which is of unfathomable size, is *not only infinite but curved!* The magnetic forces of all the stars and planets would keep any trajectory curving back upon its own path, so that a *straight* voyage "out" would be impossible. Maybe infinity scares nature itself—the idea of things just exploding forever and ever, world without end—so that a built-in conservatism has developed, a tendency to curve back upon roads already taken before spurting ahead again into the unknown.

The glory of human existence is that both Greece and the spaced-out architecture of the next World's Fair not only can co-exist, but probably must. We impoverish ourselves by turning our backs on either.

The "classical" self likes:

permanence

identity

support

immortality

heirs

financial security

slow change

solid possessions

and

-
-
-

-
-
-

The "modern" self likes:

new experiences

experimentation

change

the occult

free expression

being off-center

different personalities

Beauty

Some define beauty as being something about a *particular* form which makes us want to hold onto it, which makes us lose our apathy. Some say that beauty is something which lifts a form above others, making it art. This is a limited view since it rules out the innumerable forms we find in nature to which the adjective "beautiful" is eminently suited. Though there cannot be one everlasting definition of beauty, there are many ways to think or talk about it.

*Physical Beauty
and Cultural Relativity*

The title of Anita Loos' novel *Gentlemen Prefer Blondes* is an example of a statement about beauty that has underlying cultural bias. The belief that blond hair—and its counterpart, blue eyes—is an indispensable element in physical beauty is common among people who descend from or who in some way have been influenced by northern European culture. Since the British Isles were invaded and occupied at various times by Angles, Saxons, Jutes, and Vikings, blond hair and blue eyes are important in the English and, by emigration, the American traditions.

Thorstein Veblen in his *Theory of the Leisure Class* (1899), (which will be further discussed in this chapter's section on taste) pointed out that since there are economic factors influencing most preferences in beauty, there is nothing *absolutely* beautiful about blond hair and blue eyes. It has been observed that these features remind middle to lower middle-class Americans of the Anglo-Saxon aristocracy which once ruled their country and which continue to dictate standards of taste. Perhaps immigrants and children of immigrants from *non-* northern countries were envious of those with a "Mayflower background," and appreciated blond hair and blue eyes in order to identify with such status-raising characteristics. Many northern European settlers may have sought spouses with these characteristics and passed them down to their own progeny, and so perpetuated a taste for them.

On the other hand, Western culture has often associated dark hair and eyes of southern European cultures with forbidden pleasures and dangerous liaisons. The silent film idol of millions, Rudolf Valentino, must surely have altered people's thinking about the blond monopoly of beauty. It is not improbable that personal preferences crossed over the picket lines, so to speak, with Northern Europeans hankering after alluring dark features and and black-haired settlers identifying with the nobility of blondness.

Along with blond hair, fine, straight hair was associated with the landed gentry of this country rather than with the later arrivals. Straight silky hair was for a long time associated with beauty, influencing many blacks to cut their hair very close to the scalp or have it straightened—anything to conceal the natural tendency of the hair to grow out in the curly, fluffy appearance of what we now call the "Afro" or "natural." So beautiful has the "natural" now come to seem that many whites are getting permanents to achieve a similar hairstyle.

Beauty in facial elements appears to be just as relative, and as cultural, as beauty in hair. No statistics are available, but it is quite likely that in bygone days, before television and other media shrank the world's size, people tended to prefer the facial characteristics of their immediate cultures. Political events also influenced people's tastes. During World War II, Japanese features no doubt struck few Americans as esthetically appealing, while the fair-skinned Germanic look, once

Disorder

so desirable, no doubt acquired a somewhat sinister cast.

American and international beauty pageants continue to reflect the prejudices of earlier times, though both blacks and Orientals appear to be gaining in popularity. Even so, nothing seems so absurd as a panel of so-called experts adding up the "scores" and emerging with numerical figures which are supposed to represent some universal index of beauty.

A slight flurry of evidence has recently appeared to indicate that responsiveness to facial beauty (or lack of it) may be intuitive and innate, rather than culturally acquired, but this evidence is far from conclusive. For what it is worth, three behavioral psychologists recently conducted an experiment in which 700 college students were asked to rank drawings of infant faces in order of their appeal. It was found that in nearly every instance babies with large eyes and small chins outranked babies with other kinds of features. Since infants have fewer pronounced cultural characteristics, it would seem that such preferences *could* be universal. At any rate, it seems clear that beyond the infant stage standards of physical beauty change and display considerable cultural variety.

When it comes to the depiction of the human face in art,

Standards of physical beauty change and display considerable cultural variety.

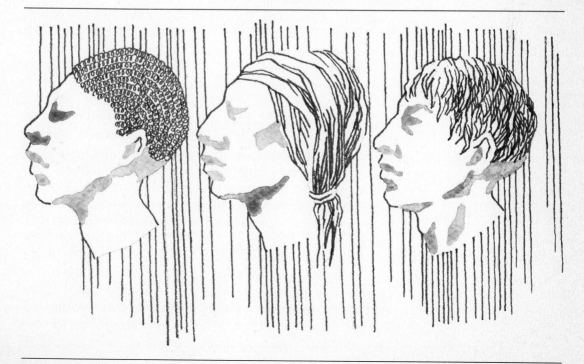

however, it is hard to say just how significant cultural preferences are, for the dimension of *artistic craft* is also an element of the beautiful.

Beauty and Historical Periods

Even if the classicist and the modernist were both inside each of us, it we wouldn't be responsive to *every* manifestation of beauty of *every* historical period. The well proportioned nude form idealized by the Greeks becomes much fleshier, even flabbier, in the Italian Renaissance and among the French Impressionists. We can find portraits of early nineteenth-century aristocrats painted to flatter their subjects, but whose "beauty" is often obscure now. Some are short and squat; some have cold-looking, angular faces; and some look downright unpleasant.

You can visit famous royal residences like Escorial, Versailles, and the Schönbrunn, and ask yourself how anyone could ever have been comfortable amid such austere, impersonal surroundings. There are chairs no one could actually have used, beds far too small for human beings, and long hallways guarded by the oppressive stare of generations of ancestors. Surely people could have chosen their furnishings more wisely than that!

On the other hand, the need for beauty does not equate with the external arrangements which satisfy that need. The need is no doubt universal, no doubt basic to human beings. But we are limited by what is available. The beautiful may be found in nature, but more often it is a legacy of the artist (in the broadest sense of that term). Artists are people like us, existing in specific times and places, motivated by certain kinds of stimuli which produce certain kinds of responses. Nobody writes music like Mozart anymore. Nobody *could*. Therefore, the complaint that a painting or a building is "old fashioned," hence not beautiful, may be a meaningless one.

The main question is this: In what sense is something *no longer beautiful?* A secondary question: What is one's responsibility to that which has historical, but not contemporary, beauty? If you visit Vienna, you may well see one Baroque church too many. A four-hour stay in the Louvre may make you wish never to see another eighteenth-century French painting. People who avoid the Louvre altogether on the grounds that it will be "probably very dull" are sometimes scorned as being devoid of "culture." Yet they may be extremely responsive to other manifestations of beauty.

There is no easy answer. It makes sense to recognize that the past has its rights too. Beautiful works conceived in a mode no longer current are still products of human minds and feelings. People who make the effort to reenter the past through conscious acts of empathy enrich their own storehouses of beautiful moments. More important, such acts probably expand each individual's own humanity, increasing the potential for extending sympathetic concern to others.

Yet some works, like the *David* and the *Mona Lisa,* have undoubtedly earned the right to be *always current.* If they transcend cultures, they can transcend history. Michelangelo's intention, to freeze for eternity the readiness of humankind to defend itself against oppression, is one that has been and no doubt always will be shared by artists and appreciators of art. It speaks to basic concerns.

Leonardo's masterpiece gives us a more-than-realistic portrait of a merchant's wife of the Florence of four centuries ago. It has more than the famous smile and the mysterious gaze. The lady's face is a marvel of *ambiguity,* containing both sensuality and coldness, warmth and distance. She is at once a dream image and an earthy, attainable woman. If you were to meet her in real life, you would be hard pressed to open the conversation. There would be too many mysteries about her. But, when you think about it, when you *really* look into anybody's face, do you not find ambiguity? We generally see only as much as we need to of anybody's face. We see the part that reassures us; we ignore the part that might baffle us. Our general perception of reality is often as limited as this. Leonardo awakens our sensibilities and raises our consciousness.

Walt Whitman

The smallest sprout shows there is really no death.

Beauty:
Simplicity versus Grandeur

Everyone has probably watched an ice-skating show or Olympic figure skaters on television, but many of us have never worn a pair of skates and never intend to. Yet the sight of a lean figure gliding effortlessly across the ice is undeniably fascinating; we are thrilled with the execution of a leap at precisely the right moment, followed by a rapid spin.

A flawless performance on ice offers a good example of the

creation of the beautiful through simplicity. The better the skater, the more viewers are apt to believe that they themselves could go on next and do the very same routine—at least the glides, if not the leaps. The trick of highly accomplished bodily performances requiring perfect coordination, is to seem unaccomplished, to seem natural.

The same holds true in acting. There are performances we applaud *as* performances. Often, while listening to a Hamlet or a Lear or a long exit speech in which a character denounces tyranny in sweeping sentences of poly-syllabled rhetoric, we cannot wait to cheer, to show admiration for the virtuosity thus displayed. But we may not have been moved; we may not have surrendered completely to the illusion. In contrast, the archives of theater are filled with famous moments of sheer simplicity which, if reports can be trusted, have lifted audiences to the heights.

One of the peak moments of contemporary American drama occurs in the trial scene of Arthur Miller's *The Crucible.* The author presumably wrote the play, first presented in 1953, to vent his anger over the Washington "witch hunts," when Senator Joseph McCarthy and his associates in the Un-American Affairs Committee were accusing hundreds of well known persons of covert communist sympathies. Included were many from the entertainment world, even Miller himself. What angered Miller more than anything else was the offer made by the Committee to suspend charges if an accused person were willing to testify against others.

To dramatize the horrifying injustice of these trials, Miller wrote a play about America's first witch hunts—those which had taken place in seventeenth-century Salem. The hero, John Proctor, must stand by helplessly as his wife Elizabeth is taken off to prison, accused of consorting with the devil. Her accuser is the Proctors' former house servant, a vain and seductive young lady who had tried unsuccessfully to estrange Proctor from his wife. In revenge, the girl has concocted a monstrous lie about Elizabeth's witchcraft.

Outraged that the court is willing to believe the girl's unsubstantiated testimony, Proctor rises from his seat and denounces her, disclosing his own terrible secret, that he had committed adultery with her. After the furor dies down, the judge announces that, should Proctor's wife confirm the story, the court would have no choice but to believe that the girl has lied.

Shakespeare

Now boast thee, Death, in thy possession lies a lass unparalleled.

Lines spoken of the great queen in *Antony and Cleopatra*

In Miller's *The Crucible* the simple word "no" has a breathtaking effect. A lesser playwright would have written more.

Elizabeth is sent for. The judge instructs Proctor not to try in any fashion to influence his wife's testimony; he must not even look in her direction. No one in the courtroom must make a sound. The door opens, and the woman steps onto an absolutely silent stage. (Even the theater audience is abnormally quiet; no one dares stir in his seat!) The judge puts the question very directly: did Mr. Proctor ever, to her knowledge, commit adultery?

Now, Elizabeth has no idea of the events which preceded her appearance. She has no idea why such an appalling question has been asked. But we can easily understand what is running through her mind. Her dear husband must have been accused by that vicious schemer. What on earth is she up to now? In any event, it is clear that her husband's reputation must be spared. After a very long and very agonizing pause, Elizabeth looks straight into the judge's eyes and answers, "No."

She thus has unknowingly condemned herself to the gallows, and, after Proctor screams his protest, accusing the court of deliberate, inhuman deceit, he too is sentenced to death. There are very few works of literature, drama, or fiction, in which one small word is able to produce such a mighty, devastating impact. Carefully building up to it, Miller created a moment of authentic beauty in theater.

In contrast are those beautiful works which sweep over us like tidal waves. Simplicity is hardly the major ingredient. Instead, we are overwhelmed by grandeur, by monumentality. It is impossible to imagine that the human mind was able to carry off so awesome a project. St. Peter's in Rome was conceived in the imagination of Michelangelo who had already spent four years lying on his back to paint the complex wonders of the Sistine Chapel ceiling. Beethoven's final symphony, his ninth, was given its first performance under the baton of the totally deaf composer, who must indeed have pulled the extraordinary sounds right out of the stars, making them audible (or partially audible) to a stunned audience. The symphony was longer than any in the history of music, and after three movements in which the orchestra's entire range was explored and exhausted, there burst forth the final movement in which a hundred or more human voices become another kind of orchestra. Legend has it that Beethoven stood there, head down, after the last note had been played, certain that he had failed and not daring to face the audience, which, unknown to him, was already on its feet shouting its raptured appreciation.

One theory of simplicity's appeal is that it is easy for us to identify with it. The sense of completeness is so readily *there* that we are astonished at how "little" effort it took. We sense we could go out and do very much the same thing tomorrow. No matter that we cannot, or do not even try. We secretly understand that the simple stroke can be the hardest of all. But we have shared the completeness, participated in the experience *as though* we had created it.

On the other hand, grandeur and monumentality seldom, if ever, inspire such identification. We feel humbled. We feel dazed. The heavens have opened before our very eyes, permitting glimpses of wonders we did not know existed. Keats's sonnet, "On First Looking into Chapman's Homer," describes the experience for all of us.

On First Looking into Chapman's Homer

Much have I travell'd in the realms of gold,
*   And many goodly states and kingdoms seen;*
*   Round many western islands have I been*
Which bards in fealty to Apollo hold.
Oft of one wide expanse had I been told
*   That deep-brow'd Homer ruled as his demesne;*
*   Yet did I never breathe its pure serene*
Till I heard Chapman speak out loud and bold:
Then felt I like some watcher of the skies
*   When a new planet swims into his ken;*
Or like stout Cortez when with eagle eyes
*   He star'd at the Pacific—and all his men*
Look'd at each other with a wild surmise—
*   Silent, upon a peak in Darien.*

The monumental in nature is especially important to us: the fjords of Norway, Mount Everest, the Grand Canyon, Niagara Falls. It is impossible to stand there and identify personally with these things. Rather, we renew our feelings of awe at the immensity and power of natural, or supernatural, forces.

But why such a need? If it is imperative that we create or sympathetically project ourselves into arrangements, if we labor so to pull it all together inside us, so that we have things pretty much under control, why do we want to suddenly blow our security apart and be overwhelmed by vast arrangements over which we have *no* control whatever? The answer appears to be that the process of going back and forth from the simple to the grand is very much analogous to the process of going back and forth from classicism to modernism. We like to stay put, but we also have to grow, to change, to become other than what we have been. The creation or experience of the monumental is part of the human strategy of change. Once our identity has been devastated by what Abraham Maslow, a contemporary psychologist, calls *peak experience,* it is hard to go backwards. We *must* grow. It is dangerous to stay indoors and become comfortable in one's quarters. It is necessary from time to time to go outside and feel the exhilarating loneliness of space.

The Golden Section: Beauty and Geometry

The classical artists of Greece were looking for the eternal, mainly in the medium of stone. But stone by itself could not produce beauty. Another element was needed, and they *did* find it. This other element was geometry, and it is with us still. The classical atmosphere is one of straight lines, squares, and rectangles. We accept this unquestioningly, yet, stop to consider: did it *have* to be that way? The Greeks made the discovery that to be surrounded by art and buildings created out of geometric principles was to walk in an urban paradise, to always be in the presence of beauty.

The Egyptians had used geometric shapes, most impressively, of course, in the Great Pyramids. But the evidence indicates that the pyramids got their shape from practical solutions to engineering problems, not from the infatuation with geometry common among the Greeks. In addition, Egyptian art and architecture was imperial, connected with the gods and the pharaohs, meant to humble and impress, not clearly to be enjoyed for its own sake as a general enhancement of urban life. Much Egyptian art was locked inside the tombs, for the pharaoh's pleasure after death.

In the sixth century before Christ, the mathematician Pythagoras was enamored of numbers, numerical sequences, geometric ratios, and mathematical laws; he developed many geometrical principles such as his famous theorem concerning the hypotenuse of a right triangle. He kept making discovery after discovery, and the regularity, the absolute *dependability* of mathematics, led him to the conclusion that the eternal, spiritual, world was composed of nothing but mathematical principles and that the greatest human achievements were those in which such principles were manifest.

Yet, almost every beginning student in a geometry class today wonders why it is necessary to learn how to make isosceles triangles and polygons. What has geometry to do with anything? The answer is, that if the Greeks were right, there is an enduring beauty to these shapes. Geometric proportion seems to appeal to our esthetic sense. (Unfortunately, geometry is seldom taught from this viewpoint.)

One geometric proportion in particular seemed to stand out from all the rest. It was undoubtedly known before his time, but the fifth-century (B.C.) mathematician Euclid formulated a principle concerning it, calling it the "Golden Section." It was later elaborated by the Roman architect Vitruvius (first century, B.C.) and called the "Golden Mean."

Simply stated, the law of the Golden Section is this: the ratio between two dimensions of a plane figure must be such that the smaller segment is to the larger what the larger is to the whole. The numerical value of the ratio is approximately 1 to 1.618. Thus in the Golden Rectangle if the width is 1, the length must be 1.618. And the length will have the same relationship to the sum of width *and* length.

The so-called Golden Rectangle is probably the most pervasive man-made example of the Golden Section, but the Greek mathematicians felt that the ratio was intrinsic to the order of things and was found (as indeed it is) throughout nature. In other words, the shapes in a geometry textbook may not be found in nature, but the relationship of 1 to 1.68 that exists between two dimensions of a thing really *is.* Students of esthetics have discovered the Golden Section in seashells, for example, as well as in microscopic cell structures.

Among Greek mathematicians there was a popular belief, apparently borne out in actual experiments, that, if asked to divide a stick at the most pleasing point, people would invariably mark the division at the point of the Golden Section.

That the esthetic appeal of this ratio was not the result of

Euclid discovered the ratio, but whoever designed the Parthenon 200 years earlier had known about it too.

Euclid's having set down the principle seems to be indicated by recent blueprints of the probable floor plan of the Parthenon, constructed two centuries before Euclid. These show conclusively that the architects incorporated the Golden Section into the Parthenon.

The Greek mathematicians believed the Golden Rectangle was found throughout nature.

It is also found throughout Roman ruins, in Medieval cathedrals, on the pages of illuminated manuscripts from the Middle Ages, and almost everywhere in Renaissance art and architecture. The Italians renamed the principle the Divine Proportion. Its appeal has never been really explained—only confirmed.

Plato's Theory:
Beauty is Objective

The adage "Beauty is in the eye of the beholder" may not be entirely true, if the judgment of the ages concerning the Golden Section still holds. That is to say, since that geometric principle is clearly external to the viewer and since it is supposed to evoke a sense of the beautiful, it becomes tempting to believe that the beauty is actually contained *within* the ratio itself.

This would mean that if human beings did not exist on earth to perceive them, objects with dimensions having this ratio would still be beautiful. To many, the argument might resemble the one about the tree falling in the forest. Does it make a noise if no one is around?

Plato's theory of beauty is an extreme one—that beauty is objective, that we come *upon* it instead of *putting* it somewhere. For Plato all knowledge—including the awareness of beauty—exists apart from individual experience.

Plato was fascinated with the subject of knowledge: not just the content of knowledge, but the fact that it could exist, that it was an entity. How was it to be defined? More particularly: where did it come from? What could be known, and what was the act of knowing comprised of?

It is one thing to say knowledge is the sum total of ideas in the mind, but then what is an idea? In looking into this intriguing question, Plato came to a very important realization: namely, that we have two different kinds of thoughts inside us. One kind he called *belief* or *opinion.* Suppose it is raining heavily. You need the water for your garden. You think, "How nice that it is raining." The person riding next to you on the bus does not have a garden; all the rain means to *him* is that he will have to slosh through puddles to get to his job, ruin the shine on his shoes, and possibly catch a cold. He thinks, "Just my luck that it's raining!"

As opinions, both thoughts are valid. It makes no sense to tell the man who has no garden that he is wrong, that the rain is really quite wonderful. Yet we can hardly say that his thoughts about the rain constitute "knowledge," for they are not shared by his seatmate. Knowledge has to be something universal, and for Plato, something timeless.

Knowledge consists of the other kinds of thoughts, different from opinions. Plato called them ideas. Plato thought of an idea as a thought which is independent of subjective judgment and personal opinions. For example, the convenience or inconvenience of the rain are subjective matters; the *wetness* of the rain is not. Whether rain is welcomed or despised, it is always going to be wet. Hence the idea of wetness is not dependent upon subjectivity. To recognize wetness is to have knowledge.

It could be argued that wetness *is* subjective, that the number of people able to experience wetness does not really *prove* it really exists, external to all of them. The contemporary philosopher C. E. M. Joad explains Plato's view in a provocative passage dealing with the whiteness of cream:

> *If it were true that whiteness were a concept in the mind, then if all minds were abolished, cream would cease to be white. Let us consider a hypothetical case in which the last human being possessing consciousness is engaged in thinking . . . about the whiteness of cream. . . . As he contemplates the white cream, the vividness of his sensation grows fainter and fainter, until, finally he ceases to be able to see it at all. Are we, then, to suppose that during this process the cream* itself *grows gradually less and less white, until eventually, as the last human consciousness fades out of the universe, it ceases to be altogether white?[1]*

In this example, whiteness can be taken as an absolute—something that really and truly exists independent of our thoughts and sensations. The name given by Plato to those absolutes which we think *about* but which are not solely subjective the way opinions are, is *Form*.

> *Plato concludes that whiteness is what he calls a Form—something, that is to say, which is not* in *the mind, but is recognized and thought about by the mind. This Form, whiteness, manifests itself in all white things, and, by virtue of its manifestation, bestows upon them that quality by reason of which we call them white.[2]*

Forms represent true knowledge because, without them, we would have no proper understanding of objects and

If human beings did not exist on earth, would a sunset or autumn forest still be beautiful?

Plato says yes. For Plato, the beautiful "exists apart from individual experience."

events external to us. We know a tree when we see one because of its "treeness"; a human being, because of humanness, and so on. Wet things are wet because we know wetness.

Plato followed this line of thinking all the way up to huge abstractions like the good, the true, and the beautiful. We recognize a good deed because in the act goodness is manifested; we recognize a true statement because truth is manifested; the same can be said for beautiful objects and beautiful people: we respond to the beauty which is absolutely there. A beautiful person is one in whom beauty is present.

Like all Forms, beauty exists apart not only from the mind but from the person or object which is *called* beautiful. Consider the case of someone you knew in high school, someone everybody agreed was beautiful to look at. You meet this person 25 years later. Surely much change will have taken place. You may still decide the person possesses beauty but then again you may not. There is a distinct chance that the Form will have disappeared from that person. But most importantly, beauty continues to exist in other people and objects. In Plato's philosophy, the Forms participate in people, objects, and events. In Joad's example, whiteness participates in the cream.

It is also asserted that the whiteness of cream is separate from the cream itself. If it is absurd to suppose that cream would grow less white if human consciousness were to fade from the world, it is equally absurd to say that if there were no cream left in the world, there would be no whiteness.

The crucial aspect of this theory is that *even if all white things were to disappear, it could not be said that whiteness had also gone.* Since whiteness is separate from things that are white, it cannot depend upon *them* for its existence.

Similarly, for Plato, beauty would still exist even if no beautiful objects or people could be found. The Form is always there, ready for participation. It is manifested through an event, but it does not vanish when the event does.

But what does happen to beauty when not manifested, when no one is around to participate in it? What is beauty if nothing is beautiful? Or truth if nothing is true? Or goodness if the whole world is corrupt and no good deed or good person can be found?

Plato's answer is that Forms are real but immaterial. They

belong to a dimension the mind can apprehend but the senses cannot observe. Though Plato's metaphysics are not always clear, it seems he understood Forms to have always existed, without beginning or end, and that they constitute the universal soul, or universal mind. In a myth about the birth of the material world, Plato maintained that God (or god—in any case, not in the Judeo-Christian sense) joined matter to form, but that matter, being an inferior substance, could never quite make the purity of the Form entirely shine through. Thus no object or person could ever be *absolutely* beautiful, could never reach the perfection of pure beauty. Pure beauty could be contemplated as an idea, but never experienced in the material world.

While the Platonic concept of beauty is subject to debate, it is hard to dismiss altogether, to say, for example, that there is nothing at all objective about beauty. In that case, there would be no artistic traditions of any kind. Even taking into consideration cultural and historical relativity, even making allowances for wide discrepancies in the way people variously respond to works which are assumed beautiful, much evidence exists to support the belief that *there are a good many commonalities in people's standards of beauty.*

In Plato's philosophy, Forms are with us from the time we are born, in the same sense that photographs are with an undeveloped roll of film. There is no other *place* in which they could be; it is foolish to say that the photographs do not exist at all until they are developed. Where would they come from? Forms, we might say, are "undeveloped" ideas: that is, we do not know we have them until we run across objects, persons, or events which participate in them.

As simply as possible: we recognize a tree as a tree because we have prior knowledge of the Form *treeness.* Plato believed the mind and soul (these seem to be interchangeable terms) to be immortal, entering the temporary house of the body when a person is born. Hence the body too is immaterial; it too belongs to the dimension of Forms.

It is difficult to reconcile the Platonic theory of beauty with the phenomenon of cultural relativity. If a person from the West, for example, were to look at a Zen painting and see no beauty in it, would this viewer be insensitive to the form that is in fact present? Do people from the East necessarily experience a form of beauty in Western buildings or faces?

> **For Plato, the Forms are always there, but not in the material world.**

One must, however, be careful not to go to an extreme in believing that beauty is totally subjective, or that for those who find beauty irrelevant in their lives, beauty does not in fact exist. Many persons pretend to an insensitivity, hiding a sensitivity they are afraid to disclose. If Plato is right, there is no human being on earth who does not hunger for beauty, no matter how much importance is put on other aspects of life.

Taste

Taste is one of the five senses. If a person were to lack taste, people would have sympathy for such a medical condition. But if a person were to lack taste in art, music, or films, the same people's reactions would have any number of overtones. Maybe psychological: "There is something abnormal about him", sociological: "He is from a disadvantaged background"; economic: "He is obviously middle-class, so what can you expect?"; cultural: "He belongs to an ethnic group which is lacking in the refinements of civilization"; and, of course, esthetic: "He is lacking in true sensitivity."

Similarly, the charge of "bad" taste can stay with a person throughout a lifetime. It is expected that the clothing of people with "bad taste" will be uncoordinated and obviously inexpensive, that their home surroundings will have clashing colors and be generally lacking in style, that they spend most of their time watching sex and violence on television, never read books, that they put mass reproductions on their walls, and so on.

The fact is that esthetic taste is seldom investigated *solely* in terms of the real issues, namely, what it is that constitutes the beautiful and whether responses to the beautiful are indeed universal and absolute. If they are not, then the charge of "bad" taste cannot make as much total sense as the accusers suppose.

On the other hand, can we say that good and bad taste have no meaning as points of reference? Can we never say to a friend that his new apartment is tastefully done? Can we not look back at all the critics who despised *Moby Dick* when it was first published in 1851 and wonder how they could have been so insensitive to a masterpiece

John W. Gardner

There is a way of measuring excellence that involves comparison between people—some are musical geniuses and some are not.

when they no doubt heaped praise upon inferior works?

Standards or canons of taste, whether universal or not, seem to exist in all cultures. The hula dance of Polynesian islanders, for example, is not simply a matter of wiggling one's hips in time to the music. It is an ancient, narrative dance telling a complex story and for centuries constituted an important means of preserving and passing along island literature. Very subtle hand movements carry or change meanings. It is absurd to think that the Polynesians regarded or continue to regard the hula as a dance that "just anyone" could perform.

While the untrained eye of a casual visitor to the islands might observe light, fluffy entertainment suited to accompany a luau, a native might find himself transported beyond words. People accustomed to Bach and Beethoven might consider a rock concert nothing but offensive noise, while rock enthusiasts hear intricate patterns of sound.

The issue of taste must be confronted, even if there is no general agreement.

Kitsch or Bad Taste

The term "kitsch" is gaining stature as a convenient label for a broad variety of what are assumed to be monstrous sins against esthetic decency.

You can opens a magazine which caters to people of comfortable means. There are ads for Waterford crystal and mountain acreage in North Carolina, "ideal for getaway weekends." There is a picture of a toilet bowl out of which a huge bouquet of flowers seems to be growing. The caption says that such-and-such a toilet bowl cleaner is like a "burst of spring."

Such ads typify kitsch. It is not bad taste to advertise a toilet bowl cleaner, but it is kitsch to pretend you are doing something else. For it was the flower, not the cleaner, that was intended to capture attention. In this context kitsch means esthetic dishonesty. A painting of a nude woman playing a violin, in which the music is supposed to "elevate" the tone, might also be kitschy while the graphic display of the human body is used to arouse feelings that are not especially musical.

Seashells, bright paint, and gold glitter can be components of kitsch, particularly when accompanied by a lofty theme

Herbert Read

And so art for the sake of decoration—what does it matter, as long as it is art?

(for instance a plastic crucifix and a picture of The Pope). A similar piece may have the shells and the crucifix, no Pope, but instead proclaims itself a SOUVENIR OF MIAMI BEACH.

Souvenirs, says the anti-kitsch contingent, should be personal, tied to particular memories, not commercially generated by the thousands.

In the case of the seashell arrangement, kitsch occurs because the designers are playing on sure-fire religious sentiments instead of creating a design which affected *them* esthetically and which might then have been expected to do the same for the viewer. Of course, it cannot be proved that the designers were really *not* so affected. It is just a pretty good bet that nobody would have thought seriously of mixing shells, plastic, the Resurrection, and the Vatican.

It is kitschy to use a large photograph of a popular actress in a provocative outfit with a sultry smile in a public-service ad warning people about signals of cancer. It is kitschy because the designers, afraid that the subject would distress too many people and cause them not to read the danger signals, have introduced both sex and glowing health motifs to lure the viewers, thus misleading them.

Kitsch tends to cheapen its respective subjects. Religion can hardly be well served by gold glitter, and our trust in cancer prevention research could be a mite shaken by the ad's trickery.

The observation arises: Is it not insulting to the general public to point out, on the one hand, these prime examples of kitsch, while on the other hand designers cater to a big market for them? What is being said here about this market? Is it that people in general have poor taste?

What seems to be unfortunately true of the vast public is its susceptibility to sentiments: religion, admiration for success, patriotism, conformity, etc. The shell pieces and the ads all *dare* you to be detached from sentiment. Red, white, and blue color schemes defy you to turn away, as if indifference equals lack of patriotism. A cross defies you to scorn any arrangement in which it appears. A picture of a smiling, gurgling, happy infant can sell the Brooklyn Bridge. People have always known how to use sentiment to their own advantage. A popular novelist of the nineteenth century gave this advice to all writers aspiring to make money with their craft: "When in doubt, kill a child."

When lofty sentiments of patriotism, piety, and affection, are mixed with the garish, sensational, and inappropriately inexpensive, they turn into kitsch. But sometimes kitsch involves legitimate art and motifs that, under other circumstances, belong to esthetic experience of a very high order: the opening bars of Beethoven's Fifth Symphony, for example, or the cosmic opening strains from Strauss's *Thus Spake Zarathustra.* When during World War II Beethoven's Fifth supplied the dit-dit-dit-dah of the Morse Code "V for Victory," it effectively aroused the multitudes in a worthwhile cause. When Strauss's crescendos were adapted by Stanley Kubrick for his *2001: A Space Odyssey,* they heralded a new form of being in the universe, a new stage in evolution. But these two heroic musical fragments have since been used to sell everything from used cars to salad dressing and have thus been debased into kitsch.

It is not that people in general lack taste, but that they lack the proper defense against the exploitation of emotion. With sentiment rolling over them, people seldom have the time to locate form and beauty, to recognize an artist's intentions, and to evaluate them accordingly. Sentiment is cheap when it is too easily come by. Beautiful things take more effort to produce, and often require careful study before they can be recognized for what they are.

This is not to say that kitsch is necessarily absolute and universal. As one writer put it: "One man's kitsch is another man's living room." There are times when a pure intention on someone's part is construed as poor taste by someone else. This is a problem without solution. All one can say is that *within a given culture it is possible to pinpoint certain sentiments and to use them for ulterior purposes.* The notion of kitsch, or extremely bad taste, is probably best limited to instances in which exploitation seems to be clearly involved.

An in-group, elitist, offshoot of kitsch is *camp,* a knowing putdown of culture or exaggeration of bad taste, such as in jigsaw puzzles which form painters' masterpieces, absurd parodies of Shakespeare plays, and oil lamps with Da Vinci's *Last Supper* wrapped around the base. Such camp jokes are really saying: "We've all had introductory courses in the arts. We know the prescribed responses, and now we move a step beyond to separate ourselves from the earnest folk who don't even know what to do."

Often only a thin line exists between kitsch and camp.

"Camp" Is

Serious old movies with outdated techniques

A folk singer doing a serious protest song without a good voice

Wearing a stylish outfit from the 1920's which has not come back into vogue

Intent and audience are important factors in the distinction. Few people buy oil lamps except as decorations or for emergency use. Since it is highly unlikely that one would bother with an expensively dressed-up lamp as an emergency source of light, the manufacturers of the *Last Supper* "Special" were no doubt aiming at a knowledgeable crowd, willing to pay money for a joke to be shared with friends. Hence the article qualifies as camp. Much kitsch turns into camp when it becomes vogue to be mediocre, and of course the prices also rise. In summary, camp is bad taste deliberately sought and cultivated.

Economic Standards of Taste

At the turn of the century the economist Thorstein Veblen began to study American economic patterns, especially consumer buying habits. *The Theory of the Leisure Class* was the result of his study, and many decades after its initial publication, the work still seems to have much validity.

Veblen's central thesis is that in the United States the moneyed class is the aristocracy, imitated by all of the other classes. How does one imitate a moneyed aristocracy? Why, by *seeming* to have money, of course. People in the United States who are not rich, says Veblen, try to live as if they *were*. Those not rich try to impress their neighbors with nonexistent wealth, by wasting money conspicuously. The need to buy excessively and to make a public display of nonessentials is, in Veblen's term, conspicuous consumption.

In a chapter entitled "Pecuniary Canons of Taste," Veblen points out that esthetic considerations in the United States are fundamentally economic and follow the principle of conspicuous consumption. Thus one seeks to buy original paintings not for their intrinsic esthetic worth, but for what they say about the collector's ability to pay outlandish prices. People flock to see the *Mona Lisa* less for the actual esthetic experience than to be able to boast that they have seen the world's most expensive work of art.

Veblen's theory, however questionable as a universal description of esthetic motivation, may help to explain why some artists have difficulty finding recognition in their lifetime. Van Gogh, for example, sold only one painting while he was alive, and, with his general lack of recognition from

---

Thorstein Veblen

. . . any valuable object in order to appeal to our sense of beauty must conform to the requirements of beauty and of expensiveness both.

any art critics, it is not surprising that few people were impressed by his work.

When one comes upon "Starry Night," "Sunflowers," "Wheatfield with Crows," or the self-portraits in museums throughout the world, one is devastated by the colors and dynamics of Van Gogh. But it is not always easy to separate the response from the basic recognition that Van Gogh is *now* an acknowledged great master. Thus fame *and* economic value do enter into the experience at some point. In a society such as ours, in which pecuniary canons are omnipresent, there is little reason to believe they are missing from esthetic matters.

> **Veblen believed new works could be recognized provided they were full of "puzzling contrivances" and suggested a wasteful expenditure of time and energy.**

Attending the opera, the theater, or concerts is increasingly a luxury. Esthetic experience is becoming very expensive; moreover, there must be many who have the funds to belong to an elite group practicing *conspicuous esthetics* night after night in the glittering art centers of the country without necessarily enjoying what they see and hear.

The cost of art need not be a problem, however. One need not belong to an elite circle which practices conspicuous esthetics. Esthetic experience can be but does not *have* to be expensive. Recordings are cheaper than concerts, books are always available, and walking and noticing are absolutely free.

> **Conspicuous Esthetics Might Involve:**
>
> Membership in a private club
>
> Making highly visible donations of large sums to an art gallery
>
> Using objects of art as interior decoration
>
> Deliberately *avoiding* color and style matching

To Sum It Up: What Is Taste?

Taste can best be defined as the capacity for distinguishing among forms, for separating those which seem complete and honest from those which seem incomplete or dishonest. Taste is not the sole prerogative of a dominant culture or moneyed elite, though it is often invoked by such groups as a means of reinforcing their claim to superiority.

The fact that taste has cultural, historical, and ethnic aspects does not rule out the possibility that *certain* forms may possess a universal appeal. On the other hand, it is folly to insist that only those forms constitute the "true" human culture.

When all is said and done, it is far better to enjoy what can be enjoyed than to split hairs over which artist is greater or which kind of music is more "significant."

Still, one should recognize that taste is probably acquired after considerable exposure to many possible sources of esthetic experience. To scorn the quest of beauty because it seems to be the exclusive pursuit of an elite group with which one would prefer not to be associated is to deny oneself much that makes life satisfying.

Taste can be acquired but should not be imposed. It is possible to learn about the things that can evoke esthetic response, to be open to such growth. But one should never forget that what matters in the long run is the experience itself, and this is, at its best, a private and pure thing.

Chapter 2 Footnote

[1]C. E. M. Joad, *Philosophy* (New York: Fawcett, 1966), p. 44.

[2]*Ibid.,* p. 45.

3

THE WAY OF
THE ARTIST

I have wanted to give the impression of a way of life quite different from that of us civilized people. Therefore I am not at all anxious for everyone to like it or to admire it at once.
Vincent Van Gogh, to his brother Theo in reference to "The Potato Eaters"

You're no good except as a decorator! All right, that's perfectly true. But my intelligence and my will create a reality for themselves, by showing that they want to go beyond the talents that fell to my lot.
André Derain

Learn by heart the forms to be found in nature, so that you can use them like the notes in a musical composition. That is what these forms are for. Nature is a marvellous chaos, and it is our job and our duty to bring order into that chaos and—to perfect it.
Max Beckmann

Art is what the artist does.
Robert Thiele

Overview

The people quoted above are all artists, and their sentiments allow for a wide range of definitions on the subject of art. Note, however, that only one—the last artist cited—makes a direct definition *statement;* and note that this statement seems deliberately, almost coyly, to be begging the question. But that, we might as well recognize, is the right of artists, who take it anyway, so why resist? They are never going to come clean and tell us what *really* goes on inside their minds—why one insists on stretching an enormous curtain from one mountain to another in Colorado and audaciously calls it art, why another spends months working on a sculpture he calls *Giant Ice Bag,* which looks like nothing else but a—giant ice bag!

The most precise and memorable definitions of art usually come from those who teach but do not create art. This pattern is hardly unique; we seldom find composers clearly defining music or poets stating categorically that "a poem is...." Most creators—not just those in the visual arts—seem to shy away from analysis, interpretation, and in some extreme cases, even praise. Artists either know (like Michelangelo) that they are titans and will be remembered for all time, or else they find (like Van Gogh) that the question of fame is a matter of indifference to them. Artists who have completely revolutionized the form and scope of art (like Picasso) may nod politely in the direction of public taste, but in their hearts they know the public is going to have to catch up with what they are doing—and will someday be able to appreciate their work.

This chapter is less concerned with the content of art or the elements of art (balance, composition, texture, and so on) than with some other more compelling and mysterious factors: the wonders of the creative process itself and the personality of the artist as a model for a humanistic existence.

The model we shall use is not found in any book on art history nor in the letters of any artist. It is found in a most unexpected source: *the observation of children.*

Walt Whitman

There was a child went forth every day,
And the first object he look'd upon, that object he became,

And that object became part of him for the day
  or a certain part of the day,
Or for many years or stretching cycles of years.

In these amazing lines from *Leaves of Grass* Walt Whitman totally enters the mind and world of the child, and also provides us with a clue to the onset of creativity. Creativity, if it is to "happen" at all, starts in childhood. It has something to do with the child's unquestioning delight in things, his reaching out not only to make contact but to live and breathe inside the soul of things. Adults learn how to pull back, recoil, to hide like turtles. They learn how not to show their feelings, how to lie, and how to ignore almost anything that is not absolutely essential to the business at hand.

But children have no business at hand. They can easily drop what they are doing and do something else that looks eminently more exciting. Children—especially very small ones—are almost always wide-eyed and enthusiastic. They have not yet learned how to be bored. They become irritated and cranky only when over-tired or when grown-ups are not smart enough to understand what they are trying to say.

Children have an amazing affinity for things. The gift-balloons at a birthday party are likely to engage their attention more than the expensive gifts they give. Being in an airplane may excite a child more than the journey itself.

In the wide-eyed dawning of a child's world lies the core of the artist's nature and personality. It matters not what period of history or style of art we are talking about. The creative urge is the same as that which drives the child from phase to phase, for the child knows, and does not need to be taught, how to be that astonishing creature: a creative human being.

Standing Up and Reaching Out

"A man's reach should exceed his grasp," wrote Robert Browning. No doubt the poet believed people needed to be reminded of a fundamental fact of human existence—one that comes very naturally to children, and of course to the artist. To want what one is not supposed to have and to seek to do what is supposed to be impossible are fundamental human urges. Every small child reaffirms a miracle of human nature in deciding one day to stand up. Something deep inside tells him he is meant to walk on two legs.

If and when the "missing link" of human evolution is discovered and defined to everyone's satisfaction, it is highly likely that the turning point from animal to human will prove to be an *event:* the first time a primate had the urge to stand on two feet. Some theories have already been advanced. One recent theory postulates that a female primate, trying to protect her offspring from flood waters was the first to stand. When they saw that it could be done, the other females in the vicinity followed suit, and soon the males joined the trend. Some anthropologists (mostly men) have seriously challenged this theory.

A romantic notion is that of a woebegone primate (either sex) who was not very successful in hunting for food or battling other primates and who decided one day to show his/her superiority by standing higher than all the others. And lo! the others were aghast and fell to their knees in wonderment.

In any case, the need to stand up was the first and crucial test of humanness. And most artists have experienced the need to go beyond the familiar domain, to reach up further than anyone had before, to make themselves taller (hence nobler) still by finding ways of extending themselves, projecting themselves—to find *ways of soaring.*

Lifting Stones

Art may have begun as architecture, who knows? All of us think of cave drawings, but the cave dwellers may well have been busy outside before they started interior decorating. Outside there may have been stone mounds, early temples, places of ritual. The urge to build things that rose vertically from the ground may have been an inevitable extension of the childhood need to stand up. Self-assertion in terms of height. It *sounds* reasonable, does it not?

Few structures from the remote past survive except in sparse fragments. But both the great pyramids of Egypt and that incredible collection of carefully placed stones known as Stonehenge still remain as breathtaking reminders of the creative genius of people who should not have had the ability to do what they did. That is, they should have been far more modest in their aims considering the limitations of

Picasso

Every child is an artist. The problem is how to remain an artist once he grows up.

The Dejection of the Adult Poet:

There was a time when, though my path was rough,
This joy within me dallied with distress . . .
But now afflictions bow me down to earth;
Nor care I that they rob me of my mirth.
                    Samuel Taylor Coleridge

their technology. But it must have been the very impossibility of the task that drove them to the achievement.

The pyramids are directly linked to the need for extending the self and for attaining majesty through height. From the very beginning, some thirty centuries before the birth of Christ, they held tombs for the Pharaohs, who were considered gods and therefore immortal. The earliest pyramids were not in themselves tombs. The homes for the dead were underground, as might be expected. A large, hollow space was constructed and filled with the furniture and playthings of the departed Pharaoh for his eternal amusement in the next life. Jutting far above the ground, however, was the pyramid, a solid triangular construction with steps, permitting the priests to climb to the top for ritual services. In other words, while the tombs below related to the Egyptian belief in an after-life, the step pyramids above related to the need of the living to extend their range, to be closer, if you will, to the gods.

The three great pyramids, which still dominate the surrounding desert, date from the Fourth Dynasty—some twenty-five centuries B.C.—as does the Great Sphinx, hand carved from rock by who knows how many craftsmen and rising to a height of 65 feet. All four structures represent an incredible feat of "standing up," of an early civilization's insistence upon making contact with the very heavens.

The possibility that slavery paid for the Great Pyramids tends to diminish the magnificence of the architectural feats, but it is virtually impossible to say where myth ends and historical fact begins. According to art historian H. W. Janson, some records exist which indicate that the laborers on these structures were paid, "so that we are probably nearer the truth if we regard these monuments as vast public works providing economic security for a good part of the population."[1]

It scarcely matters whether the pyramids and the Great Sphinx represent the work of a few architects or a great number of persons. The fact remains that huge amounts of stone were collected, cut into the proper shapes, and hauled enormous distances before being hoisted into place in an ever more perilous endeavor.

The stone circle known as Stonehenge, much of which still holds forth majestically on the Salisbury plain in southwestern England, represents a feat of both height and science. Dating possibly back as far as 2000 B.C., the stones were once thought to be an enclosure marking a sacred, possibly sacrificial, place in the ancient Druid religion. Current opinion, however, sees Stonehenge as a remarkably early computer, a means of measuring the seasons and perhaps predicting eclipses of the sun. Whatever the practical necessities for its erection, Stonehenge is without precedent for its time. It consists of a circular series of two upright stone slabs joined together on top by a horizontal slab, or lintel stone. The type of stone used for the project is not found anywhere close to the Salisbury plain and may have been hauled from as far away as what is now Wales. How, no one actually knows. Nor does anyone know exactly how the lintel stones were hoisted into place. There are many theories, but the scientific facts are perhaps not as important as the still living evidence of the basic human creative drive expressing vertical importance. What lures thousands of tourists to the Salisbury plain each year is not only the pleasing shape of the circle —surrounded as it is by empty space—but the sheer wonder of seeing this altogether foreign entity, which in no way matches the local geography. Stonehenge remains a symbol of human mystery.

Churches

Equally symbolic are the many edifices constructed for religious worship throughout the world. Whether one is praying to God or Allah or sitting at meditation in a Buddhist temple, the surroundings are likely to be an important part of the total experience. The further back into the past you go, when gold and marble and other now hyper-expensive materials were more abundant, the more ornate the edifice is likely to be. But, as with the pyramids and Stonehenge, height is frequently the crucial factor.

The medieval Gothic[2] cathedral is without peer when it comes to engineering marvels, especially in its sharply pointed spire. Visitors to Paris today may be less impressed by the spire of Notre Dame than Parisians of the twelfth century, for the much grander Eiffel Tower, erected for a World's Fair in the 1890s, looms awesomely just down the river.

Nevertheless, when we consider that Notre Dame precedes the Eiffel Tower and other soaring achievements of the modern era by about seven hundred years, we might look upon the Gothic cathedral with a proper amount of respect. The edifice was designed to honor the Virgin Mary, but this fact alone does not account for the dramatic architectural advance it represents. It was the work of artists applying all of their ingenuity to a new kind of design.

It had no doubt occurred to church architects before the twelfth century that a religious experience ought to be ethereal and joyous, but because of the weight of stones and the difficulty in getting high enough into the air without a drastic stress problem, churches had been lower structures with a sense of massive solidity about them. The Gothic architects sought, quite literally, to "raise the roof."

The invention of the flying buttress, a stone semi-arc holding up a side wall of the church from the outside, was one advance which allowed for greater height. The pointed arch, while not exclusively a Gothic invention, was perfected between the twelfth and fifteenth centuries, the heyday of Gothic architecture. A mathematical principle of stress and balance made it possible to keep gaining greater and greater height in the arch without widening the base. The spire itself, because of its narrowness, posed no great architectural problem, but this feature, rising as it did from the top of an already incredibly high building, proved to be the proper finishing touch. A sense of awesome height was thus affected.

Freudian interpreters of human culture are found of reiterating Freud's basic view that the art and architecture of civilization are infallible signs of humankind's essential neurosis, its suppressed sexuality, which seeks expression in symbolic terms. Thus, in Freudian terms, a Gothic spire becomes obvious phallic symbolism. The creative mind, unable to fully realize its sexual desires, finds in certain shapes an almost satisfying alternative to the sexual encounters forbidden by the prevailing moral code, or by a long standing sense of guilt. Whether or not Freud is accurate in his analysis of the *origins* of creative activity, the creative act is worth considering by itself. Gothic architects wanted to create height. Later architects wanted to outdo their Gothic predecessors.

The Renaissance church, as typified by the Duomo (Cathedral) of Florence and St. Peter's of Rome, differed from the Gothic cathedral in many aspects, not the least of which was its substitution of a dome of vast proportions for the traditional spire. The dome was able to soar heavenwards on the outside, but at the same time to open up heavenly vistas to the worshipper inside. The Gothic spire was narrow, so it could not assist the worshipper in reaching upwards toward God. The dome was wide and was painted on the inside with heavenly scenes and angelic hosts, giving an *interior sense of height* which went beyond that of the Gothic cathedral.

Filippo Brunelleschi (1377–1446) designed the dome for the cathedral of Florence (Santa Maria del Fiore) with a clear sense of wanting to eclipse the dome of the Pantheon, a Roman temple dating back to 27 B.C. Michelangelo (1475–1564) grew up in a Florence that had become the artistic capital of the world, but with all the stimuli the young Florentine received, with all the incentives provided by masters like Donatello and Da Vinci, Michelangelo never lost his admiration for Brunelleschi's dome.

Perhaps because he was below average in height, Michelangelo aspired to gigantic art as a compensation. First there was the gargantuan (for its time) sculpture, the *David*, rising over thirteen feet from its pedestal. Then, much later, Michelangelo accepted the challenge of the Sistine Chapel ceiling, spending four agonizing years lying on a scaffold to complete a series of biblical paintings any other artist would have called impossible. Finally, he became the architect of Saint Peter's, designing a dome intended to be the most massive of all time.

There is a legend that Michelangelo, inspired in his youth by the dome of the Florentine cathedral, vowed out of deference to the earlier work that the dome of St. Peter's should be four inches smaller in diameter, but with Michelangelo's death intervening before the work could be completed, the artist's successors changed the plans. St. Peter's still boasts of the largest dome of any edifice.

The Love of Heights

You need not be an artist to share the universal need to extend yourself. Rents are higher on the top floors of apartment houses. Property is more expensive if located in the mountains. People almost always prefer to live, if not in the mountains, then surely with a hilltop view. Flat country tends to be depressing, and those who live in such surroundings tend to long for even "rolling" land.

Ranch-type (one story) houses proved popular some years back, as a comfortable alternative to the tiresome climbing of stairs. But the ranch-house trend has become so common (and widespread) that many people are seeking to live in homes, even townhouses and apartments, with staircases leading to a second or third story. Modern convenience, for them, is less important than style with a sense of the past.

Most of the world's population finds pleasure in climbing —from the thousands of tourists each day who climb the winding stairs leading to the crown of the Statue of Liberty, to the rare but universally admired adventurer whose lifelong ambition it is to reach the top of Mount Everest. It is almost impossible to visit the Aztec pyramids near Mexico City and not want to climb all of the steps on the Pyramid of the Sun. Many people go hang-gliding and ballooning and, for the same thrill in reverse, free-falling from airplanes. The highest paid circus performers are generally those who can perform daring stunts high in the air, without reliance on a safety net. The rest of us must be content with the more ordinary pleasure of soaring through the clouds in a jet airplane.

Climbing takes internal as well as external forms. Since the urge to stand marks our earliest assertion of an independent self, vertical images are no doubt among our earliest abstractions; and they stay with us throughout our lives, influencing thought and behavior in thousands of ways. We indulge in vertical fantasies of all sorts. How else did Leonardo Da Vinci come up with the earliest known blueprint for the airplane?

More than imagining actual feats of climbing, building, or flying, we tend to impose vertical imagery upon our thinking about our lives. Songs urge us to climb every mountain, to reach for the stars, and to hit the heights. More prosaically, we associate the "goal" of success with a climb upward:

I'm going to make it to the top—just watch!

He's a young man on the way up.

Be nice to the people you meet on the way up; you may run into them on the way down.

She's tops in her field.

But how high can I go in this corporation?

Well, my dear, looks like you're over the hill.

The natural height of a

mountain

pyramid

penthouse

airplane

trapeze

•

•

•

•

•

•

becomes the vertical symbolism of an upward climb to success and happiness

---

The drug culture in recent years, while in one sense objecting to the materialism of older generations, nonetheless borrows vertical imagery to identify its purposes. Thus a "high" becomes one of the great experiences life can offer, while a "low" is to be avoided. People are said to "crash" after the "high" has run its course. Drugs which "elevate" the spirits, leading to a temporary state of euphoria, are called "uppers." But such over stimulation can be bad, so people then have to seek "downers" to achieve tranquil, passive states. Often those who find themselves on an unending seesaw, imprisoned between the only set of alternatives they know —uppers and downers—have been led to the drug culture by disappointments experienced over earlier unsuccessful efforts to "make the grade" either in business or in the creative arts. Thus they remain solidly bound by the vertical symbolism which has been with them since childhood.

Vertical images, at their best, serve the interest of humanity by driving people to tackle one seemingly impossible task after another. The Gothic cathedral was designed in such a way that it could have remained standing without the use of mortar between the stones. There were probably scoffers who predicted that no such mathematical monstrosity could possibly work. For a long time Everest was supposed to be unconquerable. It is exhilarating to know that challenges can be made and overcome. We exhibit strength and ingenuity by doing so.

But vertical images can also depress, can provide a profound sense of failure. "I'm way down here; my classmates at college are way up there." It is essential to the art of being human that we notice the internal images which are not serving a useful purpose if they inhibit rather than enhance our self-esteem. The essence of human creativity is not in the direction it takes, but in the fact that it may go in more than one direction. The flowchart of corporate structure is usually vertical, with one executive clearly in command at the top with various workers filtering down to the bottom. To believe the chart is sometimes to believe one has an "inferior" job even though common sense may indicate it is preferable to the job "above" it.

Circular images may be substituted for vertical images: "I enjoy the work I do and have no desire to manage or supervise those beneath me"; "I see myself as a point on a circle, equidistant with all other points from the center"; "I am as I am, whatever that may be and whatever benefit the world may derive from my existence." Such attitudes are well within the individual's control. There are no statistics which say that the driving power of verticality is in the end any more effective for the development of a fully realized human being than other approaches to living, which may be expressed through other kinds of dominant inner imagery.

Filling Space with Oneself

After the child stands up, the child reaches out. It is not enough to have become vertical. It is now imperative to move to another point. In the beginning it is usually in the trusted hand of father or mother. Later, the child becomes more adventurous and reaches out when the parent is not present. The crashing starts then, accompanied at first by the bruised head, and later by the bruised ego. Human creativity begins with the vertical impulse, and is soon joined by a need to extend oneself to the spaces where one is not.

The child who will one day be the artist goes through the usual phases: leaning toward something; managing to reach and hence to possess it; losing interest in it and reaching, even further this time, for something else. Eventually he or she learns it is not necessary to depend upon something external to the self to reach toward, that it is humanly possible to put something out there in space, *something that means him- or herself!* In the beginning the child may be content with a collection of toys stacked in a corner in a certain way. But as the childhood years pass, the room is rearranged, filled with new images representing the new, older individual, an atmosphere that is a total extension of self.

All cultures, especially in the formative stages, share this same *urge toward horizontal extension:* this need to be enveloped by an atmosphere that says the culture back to itself. Hence there are not only buildings (for the standing-up need) but pieces of sculpture and places mapped out for certain activities, such as religious rituals or, as with the Greeks and Romans, intellectual conversation and debate. It is astonishing how deep-rooted is the spatial sense: how, for example, one may visit the country of one's ancestors, never having felt before the slightest twinge of ethnic feeling, only to experience a very definite inner spark of recognition. "This is me. I belong here. The atmosphere is part of me."

If it were not for the urge toward horizontal extension, many cultures would now be totally forgotten. The Mayan civilization of Mexico, for example, lives on only through the art by which it filled the spaces surrounding it. Who would speak of the Aztecs or the Incas if nothing remained of their art? Would anyone wonder about the inhabitants of Easter Island if it were not for those fantastic carved heads which make the landscape unique in all the world?

The need to extend oneself into space is integral to the human quest of immortality. For most of us a simple tombstone will serve as a modest-enough extension, but for entire groups, not to mention creative geniuses like Michelangelo, the filling of many spaces has been essential.

But throughout our lives it is important to be surrounded by ourselves. Alas, too many of us fail to make the first moves, and so we find ourselves at the mercy of atmospheres created (or thrown together) by others. We live in rented apartments or buy pre-built homes we did not design. We live amidst furniture supplied by landlords, or purchased from big-name outfits. We buy what we can afford, not what tells us who we are.

Small wonder, then, that ownership begins to mean so much. Whether it is a little piece of property somewhere, or a boat, or some rare roses in the backyard, we compensate for the passive roles we play by accumulating a few possessions. They are likely to be modest in cost. Even the automobiles we drive, which we would like to be extensions of ourselves, are often purchased for other reasons. We compromise, accepting less than first choice.

But then, it may not matter, if we hold fast to the imaginations we owned as children. Who does not remember special affection for an empty shoe box? A torn and stained "security blanket"? As adults we can continue the pleasure by choosing carefully among possibilities, accumulating special "things." Some people spend hours browsing through second-hand stores, thrift shops, swap meets, even white elephant sales.

Too many of us limit our observations of objects; we accumulate only souvenirs of happy occasions, like the high school prom or a wedding anniversary. Nostalgia has its place, but one's identity should be broader than selected memories. One becomes too quickly a creature of times past. No one wants to end up alone and lonely in a tiny room, with nothing left to do but to gaze upon his "things" each day.

A reason for this "limited" kind of self-extension is that most people fail to take advantage of leisure-time browsing. The items of nostalgia have been accidents of time and circumstances, not usually the result of deliberate choice. You cannot have art on the walls which reflects yourself without going out and looking for it. You cannot fill a corner in the most pleasing possible way without spending some time searching.

The reader is invited to look up from the page at this instant and gaze about at his surroundings. If they are your own home, there are some obvious questions you can ask:

What part did I play in the design of this room?

If it were up to me, what would I change? Why?

What would I not change? Why?

What object do I seem to like the most?

What does this object tell me about myself?

What object do I like the least?

What does this disdain tell me about myself?

Not everyone, of course, can design his own home. But one *may* be able to choose from among the habitats available at a price one can afford, choose in accordance with the personal tastes one has carefully examined. If such selection is not possible, then the next best thing is gathering a few meaningful possessions—art pieces, end tables, ashtrays—which can be arranged in some pleasing pattern.

Often a major source of depression is an atmosphere that

is dead to the observation or touch, that fails to reflect even the most superficial aspect of ourselves. How many people simply move in and live from day to day without carefully dressing their walls or furnishing the corners of their rooms? How many people live amidst a conglomeration of junk, thrown together by friends, relatives, and Goodwill Industries? Very often the "excuse" is not money, but laziness or fear: "I'd like to live otherwise, but I wouldn't know how to begin picking things out."

The first human being who ever reached out and put something of him- or herself in an empty space did not know how to begin either. But it happened.

Getting into Things: Mysteries of the Medium

In order to create one's own atmosphere, in order for an artist or a culture to extend into space, there must occur an interaction between the creative being and something material (a medium). Both the joy and the frustration of the creative act involve the nature of the medium and the challenge it poses. To look past the materials of art, going directly to content, is to miss a good deal of the point. It is therefore worthwhile to be conscious of the various materials available to artists and to think of art in terms of what happens to these materials.

The Resistance of the Medium

The medium does not surrender willingly to the hands of the artist. If it did, if the art were right there on the surface, requiring only slight encouragement to make its presence known, then the artist could not honestly say that he had extended himself into space. He would be accommodating the material, but *art happens when the material is forced to accommodate the artist.*

Human art is thought to date back over 30 thousand years, to the Stone Age. Not only cave paintings but stone carvings and engravings on cave walls have been discovered from this period, as well as small objects, such as a horse, carved from either stone or animal bones. There is much speculation over the purpose served by this early art. It is unlikely the result of a need to decorate the caves or an artist's *conscious* desire to extend himself into space. More probably the cave paintings were tied in with religious or hunting rituals and the carved objects were connected with the attainment or exercise of magic powers. But even at this stage of human society, those whose job it was to "make things happen" or to carve the stone must have experienced sensations that were clearly different from all others.

By the time of the Egyptians, stone art had reached monumental proportions. Egyptian artists not only designed the massive pyramids, but transferred the pharaohs and their queens to immortality as in the form of statues. True, the statues lack the fine detail, such as the flowing lines of a robe, which distinguish Greek statuary, but the sculptors must have experienced the keen excitement of doing something that had never been done so well: making blocks of stone actually resemble real people.

In the golden ages of Greece and Rome—during the fifth century B.C. for Greece, and in the centuries just before and after the birth of Christ, for Rome—artists continued to use stone as the major medium. *Possibly* stone was used because it was profusely available; *possibly* because it was so durable; and *possibly* because it was resistant and challenging. Limestone, a hard stone for sculpture, was popular, as was marble, harder still and destined to become the imperial stone medium.

Once again we mention the artist of major importance, Michelangelo, whose career and personality beautifully illustrate the concept of the artist as one who must be extended into space, and especially as one who must be challenged by his materials. After Michelangelo, the art of fashioning marble into forms would never again be the same. Works like the *David,* the *Moses,* and the Vatican Pietà became, and remain, the standard by which marble sculpture is judged.

One strong motivation driving the young Michelangelo must have been the low esteem into which sculpture had fallen. For centuries, churches had been filled with marble statues. Every important churchman, every aristocrat, was memorialized in a statue. Statues were to be found at every turn, on every street in Florence. So "common" had statuary become that Leonardo da Vinci, Michelangelo's contemporary and fellow genius, said condescendingly that sculptors were craftsmen, not true artists. And it was indeed as an

---

A dead space reflecting the taste of others

•

•

•

•

•

•

A live space, beginning with a few meaningful possessions

apprentice craftsman that Michelangelo began his career.

It did not take long, however, for the boy's massive talents with a chisel to be discovered. Most amazing was his ability to make marble seem soft, to make human figures look as if they were just about to move or stand. As he grew older and matured, this talent deepened until the figures not only suggested energy in temporary repose, but, what was unprecedented in sculpture, served as external signs of the strong emotions within. It is one thing to transfer emotion to music, but quite another to carve emotion into marble.

But with Michelangelo, we are speaking about an artist's interaction with his medium that few can fully comprehend. Michelangelo had an affinity for marble that defies words to explain. One can imagine him walking about the quarries at Carrara, on the western coast of Italy, home of the finest marble deposits in all the world. One can imagine his restless eyes continually searching for just the right block, almost as though he could see into the heart of the stone, perceiving the figures inside waiting to be liberated.

But the marble out of which Michelangelo carved the colossal *David* had not been precisely of his own choosing. It was a seventeen-foot block considered flawed and inferior. Da Vinci himself, offered the chance to carve his way into immortality with the tallest statue ever executed, rejected the very notion. Michelangelo, a lesser choice, agreed first, then began to wonder what he would do with the enormous stone. There are many tales of how *David* evolved —some highly romantic. One theory is that Michelangelo wanted to create an awesome symbol of Florence itself, small compared to Goliath (Rome, and the Vatican perhaps?) but huge in spirit, dignity, and the burning desire for freedom. Whatever the reason for the choice of subject matter, the *David* has come to be a symbol not only of Florence, but of the whole Renaissance ideal of the fully actualized human being. The human form is exalted as perhaps never before or since. But surely the hugeness of the stone, the seeming impossibility of the project, must have been the real source of inspiration.

Success has its price, however. Acclaimed far and wide as the ultimate genius, Michelangelo found the challenges becoming stronger. Each task appeared more superhuman than the one before. The media in which he worked—paint as well as stone—appeared to grow more, not less, resistant

Kenneth Clark

. . . we must recognize the emergence of Michelangelo as one of the great events in the history of western man

to his will. Why? The reason is obviously that the will demanded more and more of the artist. What do you do to top perfection, if indeed the *David were* perfection? Answer: you do even more with the same medium, or else you find even unlikelier materials.

If Leonardo had considered him, like all sculptors, a mere craftsman, then there remained the challenge of making paint do all that Leonardo had achieved—and more. The opportunity came when Pope Julius II, who had already commissioned Michelangelo to carve figures for his own tomb (a tomb that was never to be really completed), challenged the artist to paint the ceiling of the Vatican's Sistine Chapel. A number of things appealed to the artist: the location itself, as close to heaven as one might be; the huge expanse of ceiling, allowing for a series of paintings on religious themes that would at the same time present to the viewer a totally unified effect; and finally, the challenge of fresco, a technique of painting in water colors on wet plaster that, when dry, combines with the paints to form a wholly new kind of material, one whose texture creates a vivid and lifelike sense of immediacy.

It took Michelangelo four years to finish the ceiling, and, though millions of visitors have passed below it, gazing up in awe at the incredible number of human and divine figures, dominated by the central piece, "The Creation of Adam," one wonders whether the artist himself ever experienced a true sense of profound satisfaction. The sheer physical beating which the medium gave the artist has been recreated in a biographical novel:

For thirty days he painted from light to darkness, completing the Sacrifice of Noah, the four titanic male nudes surrounding it, the Erythraean Sibyl on her throne, and the Prophet Isaiah in the pendentive opposite, returning home at night to enlarge the cartoon of the Garden of Eden. For thirty days he slept in his clothes, without taking off even his boots; and when at the completion of the section, utterly spent, he had Michi pull his boots off for him, the skin came away with them.

He fed off himself. When he grew dizzy from standing and painting with his head and shoulders thrown back, his neck arched so that he could peer straight upward, his arms aching in every joint from the vertical effort, his eyes blurred from the dripping paint even though he had learned to paint through slits and to blink them shut with each brush stroke, as he did against flying marble chips, he had Roselli make him a still higher platform, the fourth on top of the scaffolding. He painted sitting down, his thighs drawn up tight against his belly for balance, his eyes a few inches from the ceiling, until the unpadded bones of his buttocks became so bruised and sore he could no longer endure the agony. Then he lay flat on his back, his knees in the air, doubled over as tightly as possible against his chest to steady his painting arm. Since he no longer bothered to shave, his beard became an excellent catchall for the constant drip of paint and water. No matter which way he leaned, crouched, lay or knelt, on his feet, knees or back, it was always in strain.[3]

A commitment to fresco is a drastic thing under even ideal conditions, since the paint must be applied before the plaster dries. But under the extremes of physical pain Michelangelo endured, the commitment would have taxed the dedication of all but one who could not live with himself if he failed to accept this supreme challenge of all art media.

Still, Michelangelo was seldom finished with a work—in his own mind. The Vatican Pietà (an extraordinary work of the artist at twenty-one, with the grieving Mary supporting the dead Christ on her lap) is the only work he ever signed. Many believe the reason he never signed his work was that he was confident that his masterly style needed no identification. But an equally possible reason may well be that Michelangelo never really "signed off" or gave his final approval, especially as his work became more complex.

He lived to be eighty-nine and continued working virtually up until the moment of death. Why shouldn't he have? He had already destroyed, or nearly so, many of his later works, including the *Pietà Rondanini,* an old man's version of the agony of the Holy Family, except that this time the emphasis is on Christ's face, no longer the youthful, serene, almost feminine Christ of the Vatican Pietà, but a man who has, like the figure's creator, suffered greatly. In his declining years he worked feverishly on the plans for Saint Peter's. A brief remark written in a 1557 letter is most illuminating: ". . . neither do I wish to fail the fabric of St. Peter's here, nor do I wish to fail myself."

In many of his letters and in his poetry the artist continually expresses the conviction that his work is not for the multitude, not for the critics, but for God Himself. There is little reason to doubt Michelangelo believed this implicitly, but it also seems clear that he himself attempted to judge his work as though to determine its worthiness for God. The ultimate medium—and the ultimate resistance—was the artist's own creative genius.

Creating the World Again—on a Flat Surface

Challenging as stone and marble must be as media, there at least exists for the sculptor the three-dimensionality of his material. The illusion of depth is not something that has to be somehow added. But this is precisely the challenge posed by the flat surface: from the walls of 30-thousand-year-old caves, to the vases on which Greek artists so patiently and delicately applied their paints, to the stretched canvas of artists today. It must remain one of the many tantalizing mysteries of human existence that the thought ever occurred to anyone to attempt to transfer reality to flat surfaces.

Apparently transference of reality *was* the original intention, rather than decoration or esthetic design. Cave paintings are in many cases unbelievably lifelike. Even though the motive for the transference is not exactly clear, most likely it was not so that the cave artist could point with pride to his artistic accomplishment, urging the others to "see what I've been able to do." If the paintings were connected with hunting rituals, as is currently believed—"To possess the image of the beast is to control it"—the talent for transferring must have been with the artists from the outset. But from what external source would it have come?

While cave paintings exhibit a surprising realism, it is limited to the general shape and some of the details of an animal's appearance. What is lacking is something that did not come into flat-surface art until the Renaissance: perspective. Greek vase painters, however, ingeniously used two sharply contrasting colors to create an illusion of depth. Often the figures are entirely black, while the background is red. Sometimes the reverse is true.

The scenes painted on Greek vases are usually mythological, showing the feats of Hercules or Theseus or one of the gods. The need for realism seems apparent. People wanted to see what their heroes actually looked like, just as today people who read best sellers demand that the stories and characters be transferred to the screen.

Medieval painting, which is always religious in theme, is not realistic because Christians supposedly had little interest in the material world. The medieval artist was supposedly aiming at spiritual realities. Yet the statuary art of the Middle Ages attempts to be lifelike. If one examines carefully the pages of illuminated manuscripts—that wonderful art which flourished in the monasteries during the seventh and eighth centuries with its brilliantly colored lettering and designs—one will find many strokes of attempted realism. The most famous and treasured of these manuscripts, the Irish *Book of Kells,* contains tiny scenes from everyday life in the monasteries, including a picture of a mouse gnawing on a piece of cheese in the monks' kitchen!

The sense of perspective lacking in flat-surface art became an exciting new technique for Italian artists in the early Renaissance. It is one thing to paint or draw real-looking figures, but quite another to correctly size them relative to each other and to a background which approximates what the eye sees when it looks at the real world. The artist who pioneered in creating the sense of depth is Giotto (1266–1337), a Florentine who made the two-dimensional medium look like three when he started placing foreground figures at the bottom of the painting—at eye level with the viewer—and putting background figures and objects in diminishing sizes at the top of the painting.

> Philip Rawson
>
> **All human experience of visual reality, to which art ultimately appeals, has been gained through eyes which move continually in all directions, located in a head which constantly changes its height above ground and its angle of tilt.**

After Giotto, artists kept improving the technique, largely through the painstaking care with which they were able to make background objects smaller, thus getting greater depth. They introduced a brand new element into the medium: the *central vanishing point,* a spot in the center of the flat surface at which the background literally disappears, as it does for the naked eye. They also introduced *chiaroscuro,* a technique of having some figures in light and some in darkness and obscuring the distinctions between them, for artists realized that the eye does not view all figures under the same light conditions or as sharply defined forms.

No doubt the triumphant Renaissance painting is Leonardo's *The Last Supper,* a mural for which the artist was commissioned by the church of Santa Maria del Grazie in Milan, in 1495. It was to occupy the entire far wall of the refectory, and, though the paint is fading and the entire work has become fragile, visitors continue to be astonished when they enter the refectory today and experience the

illusion that the room extends *into* the painting and continues on to the wall behind Christ and the disciples!

But perspective is only one of the work's extraordinary
features. Leonardo also uses the chiaroscuro effect to
heighten the realism of the scene. The interplay of light and
shadow is haunting to behold, as are the faces of the twelve
disciples, who have just heard Christ's words: "One of you
will betray me."

Each disciple can be studied separately as a psychological
portrait, and dominating the entire scene is the figure of
Christ himself with a face that defies precise verbal description. Certainly Leonardo has put sadness into it, but also
resignation, and a transcendent beauty. In fact, with this
work and the equally famous *Mona Lisa,* the artist uses his
art to capture and crystallize the mysterious complexity of
the human face. Art has gone beyond realism. It has become
a way of looking into the soul. Leonardo makes us see what
we normally miss when we look at people, *because we do not
look long enough or closely enough.*

One other artist was to do equally as well by the human
face, and that was Rembrandt (1606–1669), who especially
found beauty in the careworn lines of aged subjects and who
refined the technique of chiaroscuro to such an extent that
it became the single most identifying element in his work.
To look at a Rembrandt painting is to see such a contrast
between light and dark that one is tempted to believe the
source of light must be external to the painting. With Rembrandt one no longer speaks of the resistance of the medium,
for it seems impossible to believe that paints applied to a flat
surface could have created the intensity of the light and the
profundity of the shadows. In the massive *Night Watch,* a
canvas of more than 168 square feet in size, the artist has
painted an entire military company in full regalia as well as
the onlookers, creating a unity of light, shadow, and faces
that can occupy the attention of visitors to Amsterdam's
Rijksmuseum for hours.

With the flowering of European art throughout the seventeenth and eighteenth centuries, portrait and landscape
painting reached near perfection. The subtleties of human
vision were thoroughly explored, as was a greater range of
color. Artists found special blends of colors that seemed to
suit their needs, to express their particular vision of the
world. Some "did" skies better than others; some, trees;

The Art of Leonardo:

Art beyond realism—a way of looking into the soul.

•

•

•

•

•

•

The Art of Rembrandt:

Impossible to believe that paints applied to a flat surface could have created the intensity of the light and the profundity of the shadows.

some, water, and so on. In truth there seemed little challenge left in the medium. It could no longer resist the artist's ability to transfer reality from three dimensions to two without sacrificing the whole range of visual experience.

When people first become interested in the world of modern art, a frequent question is "Why doesn't it *look* like something?" At an exhibition of the works of Kandinsky, an abstractionist who strikes the unprepared as alarmingly radical, a young lady was overheard asking what a certain painting was supposed to be representing. Her friend seemed suddenly to have had a divine inspiration and cried: "Why, it's two electric light bulbs!" The previously baffled lady then smiled, nodded, and voiced high level approval of the painting. The idea for many viewers is that "It's good if you know what it is and bad if you don't"—as if the artist were forever committed to the same motivation that underlies the work of artists who lived centuries ago.

The imitation of reality is only one of the things art can do and does. After all, imitation is only one of the things the *child* does. Certainly it is basic to the humanizing process. The child learns to smile and laugh and use language as he observes and listens to the people around him. Whether he wants to or not, he picks up traits from his parents, brothers, and sisters. He may imitate so effectively that he will grow up to outdo his model in a particular respect: in writing, playing ball, or in mechanical skills. But sooner or later he will need to assert himself in some way that is distinctive. He will have imitated as much as he can, and now he feels the desire to be the bearer of something new, the speaker of a different word, the singer of a song no one has ever heard before.

The same thing happened in art.

Altering

When people like the young lady at the Kandinsky exhibition are satisfied that they know what a painting "is supposed to be," they derive a comfort baffling to most contemporary artists. They are likely to be the same people who "like" a play or a poem after they have determined in their own minds "what the author is trying to say." And the contemporary poet or dramatist is just as likely as the artist to ask why the presence of identifiable visual or intellectual content makes something worthwhile.

The artist of today is quick to point out, not that art has a right to be whatever it is, but that the whole point of art during most of its history has been transformation and alteration, not realism. If cave paintings or Greek statues can be described as lifelike, it is also true that they are not faithful reproductions of what existed in reality. No animal could have been exactly like a cave artist's representation, nor could the average human being have looked exactly like the Greek sculptor's idealization of the human form. What we might call photographic realism in painting flourished during the seventeenth and eighteenth centuries about as well as it ever could, and artists began to realize it was possible to look inward rather than outward for inspiration. They went back again to the transformation and alteration of reality. They brought something new into being.

Goya: A Case History

Spain's major artist of the late eighteenth and early nineteenth century was Francisco Goya (1746–1828), whose work provides an almost perfect model of the phases of an artist. His early works are realistic—landscapes depicting the natural beauty of the Aragon countryside in which the artist was nurtured, and portraits of astonishing vitality, with finely detailed photographic likenesses of his subjects. Though Goya was little known when he came to Madrid, the cultural center of Spain, he soon grew in popularity among the aristocrats, largely because of his skill in portraiture. But after a time, he risked his fame and fortune in the name of a far more compelling drive: his own needs as an artist.

Since portrait and landscape painting had reached a peak of sophistication before Goya's time, both kinds of art were fashionable and economically rewarding. An artist had only to study the techniques carefully, spend a few years in apprentice work, copying the style of a master he admired, and then begin to develop a style and manner of his own. Little of his own self needed to go into the work. After a time, mastery of technique failed to suffice for Goya. His eyes turned inward, and he began to paint what he saw and felt

---

Clive Bell

... to appreciate a work of art we need bring with us nothing from life, no knowledge of its ideas and affairs, no familiarity with its emotions.

as a unique human being. Goya introduced the element of personal psychology into his art.

The person he discovered through his paints was essentially a cynic. Goya found himself out of tune with the life of polite society—the superficial manners, the idle conversation, and worse, the continual intrigues of people driven by the need for power and position—and he was unable to keep his cynicism out of his works. His portrait of royalty, *The Family of Charles IV,* completed in 1800, best illustrates Goya's mood at the time when his motivation as an artist was beginning to change.

The family is standing in a gallery: the king, the queen, and young aristocrats of varying ages and sizes. In Rembrandtian style, there is light coming into the gallery from some undefined source beyond the canvas. There is just enough light to illuminate the faces. Certainly they do not represent the idealization of royalty that artists were normally paid to create. Goya shows the family not at its best, but at its worst. The youngest children have bizarre, almost paranoiac expressions. Perhaps for the very first time an artist has captured the less-than-enviable life style of children who are not so much spoiled and pampered as enslaved to certain behaviors. The queen seems insensitive to them, indeed to just about everything. She is posing foolishly, as though she were not very bright and has a naive conception of what regal bearing is all about. The king is equally silly-looking, and there is also a trace of sadness in his face, a sense of now unremembered, occasional happy times in a youth he never really had. We know that the children will grow up and be very much like their father.

The fact that the royal family must have been pleased with the portrait—after all, they did accept it and did not throw the artist out of the palace—remains one of the ironies in art history. Were the king and queen so vain or so blind to reality that they never noticed Goya's insulting approach? If so, then the artist was probably right in his assessment of the court of Madrid. In any case, his style became even darker, more pessimistic.

The invasion of Spain by Napoleon during the first decade of the nineteenth century did not help Goya's disposition much. The ravages of war, the inhumanities human beings were capable of inflicting on each other, depressed him further. In two of his masterpieces, *The Second of May* and *The*

The imitation of reality is only one of the things art can do.

•

•

•

Art during most of its history has been transformation and alteration.

Third of May, Goya dramatizes the theme of war's cruelty. In the latter painting we see the execution of several Spaniards by Napoleon's firing squad. Realistic detail has been minimized. There is pure fear on the faces of the condemned men, and those who are about to fire the guns are lacking in any expression. One could expect no mercy from such a crew.

Like Beethoven, Goya became deaf during the high period of his artistic career. One would imagine that deafness could only have added to the depression of his spirit. Surely most of his later work is an expression of anger, directed perhaps at both the way life treated him and the society from which the artist had by this point become totally alienated. And there may be more reasons for his anger than these. Having become introspective in his work, Goya allowed his unconscious free reign to surface and find visual embodiment in the deformed shapes and grinning faces of his final paintings.

Because of Goya's originality, innovative artistic techniques, and the total range of his work, his significance in the history of art is assured. However, his later paintings seem sometimes unpleasant, if not hideous, to many viewers. So the time has come to confront the question which—next to "What is it supposed to be?"—is most frequently asked about paintings and sculptures: "Yes, but is it art?" There is a widespread belief that art and beauty mean the same thing and that if a particular work appears grotesque, violent, or expressive of a neurotic mental state, it has no right to be called art.

An answer given by some artists is that any work is beautiful which seems to hold together for any reason—design, theme, or their need to express a particular feeling or an intricate complex of feelings. Beauty, in this instance, is defined as artistry itself. It is a beautiful experience to observe the creative personality in the act of self-assertion. To insist that beauty in art must be limited to pleasing combinations of colors or landscape vistas is, they believe, inhibiting to the viewer's personal growth and degrading to them. Above all, they insist, it is their right to be what they are and to let the canvases be as they must. Theirs is the gift. Ours is the privilege of sharing it.

Goya was unable to keep his cynicism out of his works.

Thomas Craven

I have no use for an art that is founded upon the limited attention of specialists, or upon the eccentricities of monomaniacs; I ask that art contain meanings which may be verified, shared and enjoyed by a large and intelligent audience.

Art as Sensuous Experience

Before the middle of the nineteenth century there occurred a milestone event in technology which was to divert art "officially" into the new paths already cleared by Goya and others: the invention of photography. Artists recognized that, even if they wanted to continue developing the techniques of ultra-lifelike representations, they would be no match for the camera. If people wanted to collect nostalgic memories of places they had been, the camera could provide hundreds of pictures for the price of one painting. If people want portraits of themselves, why not hire a photographer?

The French artist Edouard Manet (1832–1883) provided an anti-photography rationale for art. A painting, he said, is something to experience totally for itself; it is an *event*, not something meant to call to mind something else. Manet and some of his colleagues began working in a new style, which, for a number of years, had no name. Their aim was to project onto the canvas subjective visions of people and places—to show *how* life is experienced, not *what* is experienced.

The new style found a name when a painting appeared by Claude Monet (1840–1926) entitled *Impression: Sunrise.* Exponents of Impressionism contended that earlier, realistic painters had not been faithful to the true nature of consciousness, that so-called "realistic" landscapes and finely detailed portraits did not represent reality at all. In fact, they said, no one knew what reality was—only what it seemed to be. Artists like Goya had already shown how important it was to make art the objectification of subjective states of mind and feelings.

The subjective states which dominated the work of the Impressionists were mainly the excitement and enticement of sensuous experience: an abandonment to the joy of color and form, even as the composer sometimes abandons himself to the joy of sound and rhythm. Color burst upon canvas in a profusion never before known. Artists experimented feverishly with new combinations of colors and new brushstroke techniques. The race was on to see who could approximate ever more closely the subtleties of visual consciousness.

The Impressionists were obsessed with their mission: to reeducate the art-viewing public. No work must be analyzed, interpreted, or enjoyed because of its resemblance to the locale which may have inspired it.

The foremost American Impressionist was James McNeill Whistler (1834–1903), who painted the famous portrait of his mother in 1871. Though the work is universally admired for the subject matter, though reproductions have sold in the millions and are probably as omnipresent as "Home Sweet Home" embroidery samplers, most people are unaware that the painting's full title is *Arrangement in Black and Gray: The Artist's Mother.* Whistler simply used his mother as a subject —a woman in a setting, to be experienced as a study in both form and color. Far from willfully having created a masterpiece of sentimentality, Whistler is well on the way to what happened to art *after* the Impressionists: there is a gradual shift in emphasis from indulgence in the sensuous pleasures of form and color to the conscious creation of a formal experience which takes place as the interaction between viewer and canvas.

During the last quarter of the nineteenth century artists on both sides of the Atlantic who had been profoundly influenced by the Impressionists began to resist slavish imitation and to go their own ways. The label Post-Impressionism has been coined as a convenient way of referring to the innovators, but there is no concise definition of the term. What these artists had in common was the conviction that they needed to please themselves first, to use their medium as a way of defining their own identities and projecting them onto the canvas. Of this group Vincent Van Gogh (1853–1890) was perhaps the most intense.

Van Gogh remains the prototype of the artist who creates entirely for himself. His style was so strange in its time that the few critics who ever took notice of his work were generally baffled, having nothing with which to compare or contrast it. He lived most of his life in abject poverty, supported in part by his brother Theo, who believed in Van Gogh's genius and stood by him even when his work was denounced and ridiculed. Only one of the artist's paintings was ever sold in his lifetime, which he himself tragically terminated before his fortieth birthday.

In fact, Van Gogh is the prototype of the artist for whom art becomes the last outpost of being itself. Totally alienated in this world, totally misunderstood by almost everyone except his brother, rejected twice as a suitor (once with a

John Ruskin

He is the greatest artist who has embodied, in the sum of his works, the greatest number of the greatest ideas.

vehement cry of "No, never, never!"), hovering much of the time on the thin border between functional rationality and insanity (eventually to cross the border, never to return), he survived as long as he did mainly because of his work. Small wonder that the viewer of his paintings finds himself enveloped in a completed altered version of reality. What obligation did the artist feel toward an everyday world through which he passed as a stranger?

In works such as *Sunflowers, Wheatfield with Crows,* and *Starry Night,* which have become priceless since Van Gogh's death, the viewer witnesses a brushstroke method that has become utterly identified with its creator: a short, stabbing technique, as opposed to the flowing line, that makes the entire canvas appear to be throbbing with energy. His rational mind seldom under control, Van Gogh abandoned himself to the sensuous impact of life's forms and colors, absorbing them fully and converting them into a heightened reality— an explosion of pure feeling transferred to color, shapes, and paint textures. The one critic who within Van Gogh's lifetime found the work praiseworthy used a singularly appropriate term to describe it: *insolent.* Van Gogh's lines and bright colors virtually scream from the canvas. His art comes as close to sound as is possible in a silent medium.

If children pass through the creative phases recognizable in all artistic endeavor, Van Gogh's art never lost the intensity with which the child reaches out, touches, and then alters his reality. The child who colors the sky purple and gives the postman an orange face would probably respond immediately to Van Gogh if only adults were far-sighted enough to provide the exposure.

One last comment about Van Gogh: there was never any doubt that he must paint as he did, never any question about changing his style to suit prevailing tastes, never a thought of compromise or trying to earn money first, then doing as he wished. His total absorption in his own way has a purity of intention about it that still compels admiration. Despite its tragic ending, one suspects that a life so devoted to creativity must have had its moments of joy.

With Van Gogh and other turn-of-the-century artists the means were increasingly at hand to allow the inner self to unfold with a depth not possible in earlier times. The reason is that artists of our age (which includes the whole twentieth century) are accustomed to insisting on the right not only to retain the purity of their intentions, but to determine their own standards, techniques, even materials. Where artists like Michelangelo had labored to overcome the resistance of the medium, modern artists will alter the medium if necessary. Fitting in successfully, distinguishing oneself with respect to past traditions, is less important for the contemporary artist, who often revels in—or else is utterly indifferent to—being controversial, shocking, even offensive.

The important thing for the rest of us is to see the creative child's play still there behind the sometimes baffling products of artists' imagination; to view modern art not as a collection of increasingly uncommunicative oddities but as an exciting phase of the same phenomenon which first manifested itself thousands and thousands of years ago in the caves.

Vincent Van Gogh

As to the market value of my pictures, I should be very much surprised if, in time, they did not sell as well as other people's.

Picasso: A Summing Up

A prominent historian has observed that when the twentieth century is evaluated, two specific persons will prove to have had a shattering impact on the nature and direction of modern life. One of these was Sigmund Freud, whose discovery of the unconscious mind must rank among the most important advances ever made in human knowledge. The other was Pablo Picasso (1881–1974), an authentic master easily on a par with Leonardo and Michelangelo, a genius of sublime proportions who has influenced not only the direction of art and sculpture, but architecture, drama, literature, and philosophy as well. It is not too much to say that had Picasso never existed, the modern world would not look or "feel" quite as it does.

That we have lost the art of spontaneous vision is not surprising, for from adolescence we tend to use our eyes generally for intellectual perception, to qualify what we see with reservations formed by acquired knowledge and to restrict our view of the outside world to things of practical interest and immediate necessity.
Peter Owen

The reader is encouraged to experience as much Picasso as possible, for no verbal description of the artist's work can possibly do justice to what "altering" means in this instance.

The viewer, seeing a typical Picasso for the first time, with its angular shapes, its disembodied parts of the human anatomy—a head here, an arm there—is likely to be confused, even incensed. The old question "But is it art?" rings out once more, with special vehemence.

But the viewer needs to know that Picasso is equally at home in the realistic tradition. By the 1920s the artist had acquired an international reputation for abstractionism—a technique whereby real-life shapes are reduced to their simplest essences—and cubism—a technique whereby real-life people and objects become mere geometrical forms and are put on the canvas for design, not representation. Some of his severest critics were charging that Picasso painted as he did because he could not master traditional forms. To show them up, he produced a series of realistic masterpieces, thereby *proving* that, when he presented a startlingly different view of reality on his canvas, the artist was doing so *because he wanted to!*

Whether Picasso is being realistic or whether he is indulging in abstractionism or cubism, the emphasis is on the viewing experience as a self-contained complex of thought and feeling. The experience of art really always *has* been such a phenomenon. Whereas in the past, viewers (even in the case of the Impressionists) were able to recognize the "familiar" context of a work, what it was "supposed to look like," Picasso made the question "What is it?" far less meaningful than "What has the artist done?"

For the question "What is it?" can be answered with, "I have no idea," and many people at that point are likely to drop the matter. The question "What has the artist done?" can be answered—*should* be answered—by a discussion of the kind of alteration that has taken place. For example, in responding to what may well emerge as Picasso's single greatest work, the mural *Guernica* painted in 1937 for the Spanish pavilion at the Paris World's Fair, one can make the following observations about what the artist has done:

He has expressed himself about a particular atrocity (the bombing of the city of Guernica by terrorist guerillas).

He has expressed universally shared feelings about the inhumanity of war in general.

He has abstracted from the original event shapes which come to symbolize elements in the human tragedy of war.

He has utilized elements of the cubist style to *show* the disintegration of civilization which happens in war.

By fusing isolated details into an original unity, he has telescoped more into one visual experience than can happen over a period of days to a participant in the actual event.

In Picasso we have the triumph of alteration, the vindication of the artist's right to unfold his profoundest being and give it objective, external shape. In so doing, he does indeed adorn nature with new things and pounds an unmistakable human stamp on the face of the earth. As one walks through the streets of the world's major cities, noticing the new architecture, the murals, the sculptures, one should keep reminding oneself that people like Picasso, in their unfoldings, have helped to create the environment within which we live.

Epilogue

Though one doubts whether the twentieth century will prove to have nurtured an artist more deserving of the label "titan" than Picasso, the reader should not suppose that Picasso's innovations reflect the whole scene of modern art. Today's artists tend to admire Picasso enormously, recognize the debt they owe him for opening so many doors of creativity, but at the same time believe that his work is by now "traditional" and altogether "safe."

This is a time of feverish experimentation in art. Almost anything is possible. Visitors to the United States Pavilion at the 1970 World's Fair in Osaka, Japan, for example, gathered around in amazement to watch a sculpture that moved. It was not only shaped like, it *was* a giant ice bag, with some kind of machine inside that caused it to breathe in and out and otherwise go through a series of contortions. The artist, Claes Oldenburg (b. 1929), seeing no reason to struggle for the illusion of softness in sculpture, simply decided to use soft material. Nor did he see any reason to create the illusion of motion when we have the technology to cause *real* movement.

We are living at a time when an artist

can put himself on videotape, moving a chair, sitting in it, rising, moving it again for what seems an interminable period.

can call a six-foot block of wood a self-portrait because it is his
own height and weighs as much as he does

can find a piece of fiberglass that captures his fancy and hang
it up in his studio as a work of his own art, though he has done
nothing to it

can hold a memorial service for a deceased friend in an art
gallery into which he had dumped four truckloads of dirt and
in which he has lit seventy-five votive candles, and claim the
event to be a piece of art

If you ask a contemporary artist why he is hanging an
enormous curtain between two Colorado mountains, he is
likely to tell you it belongs there.

If you ask a contemporary artist why anyone should not,
without any previous training, paint an abstract picture and
have it hailed as a masterpiece, he is likely to say that you
must first establish your credentials as an artist before you
can shock, offend, or bewilder your public.

But many quite serious people challenge the label "art"
when it is applied to some of the products. There are oddities
in museums and galleries today which make Picasso's *Guernica* look like an eighteenth-century landscape painting.
There is a mural executed entirely in butcher's wrapping
paper and bits of broken glass. There is a sculpture of an
aborted fetus wrapped in bandages and lying inside a tiny
coffin: meaningful, say some critics; sensationalistic and ugly,
say others. There are sculptures made of automobile rem-
nants picked up in junkyards: beautiful? ask some critics.

On the other hand, in his eighties, Henri Matisse (1869–
1954) was doing collages some claim could have been done
just as well by a seven-year-old child. The defense has been
that Matisse had already proven himself as a master, had
already exhibited a supreme control of style and technique;
that, once an artist has become established, he may then
look deep within himself for the bizarre, often inexplicable,
sometimes childlike shapes and designs which seem to require projection.

The defenders of modernism are quick to point out that
the sensitive eye can readily detect what deserves to be
called art and what does not. There is, they observe, an
underlying discipline which cannot be forged. Those whose
style appears unfamiliar, sometimes downright unpleasant,
may yet be recognized as titans, as Vincent Van Gogh was
finally so recognized.

Picasso. Guernica. *1937, May–early June. Oil on canvas, 11'-1/2" x 25'-3/4" Collection, The Museum of Modern Art, New York. On extended loan from the artist's estate.*

"Had Picasso never existed, the modern world would not look nor feel quite as it does."

There are, for the defenders of modern art, only art and non-art. And today's artists are only repeating the eternal cycle: seeking to stand up and be noticed, to reach out and touch, to get their hands on things in space, and to leave space quite altered for their having been around.

Chapter 3 Footnotes

[1]*History of Art* (Englewood Cliffs, N.J.: Prentice-Hall, and New York: Harry N. Abrams, 1977), p. 59.

[2]The term *Gothic* has a very complicated history. Originally it was a reference to the culture of the Goths, a warlike Germanic tribe that over-ran the Roman Empire early in the fifth century A.D. During the post-Roman period, which ushered in the medieval world, the Christian Church spread throughout Europe, creating a new style of civilization. The term *Gothic* gradually became a designation for the art and architecture of the later Middle Ages. The Gothic cathedral (for example, Notre Dame and Chartres) is perhaps the outstanding single example of this movement. But the term, *un*capitalized, can also be used in something like its original sense, as a synonym for wild or barbaric.

[3]Excerpted from Irving Stone, *The Agony and The Ecstasy,* pp. 529–530. Copyright © 1961 by Doubleday & Company, Inc. Reprinted by permission of the publisher.

4

MUSIC: SOUND AND SILENCE

Overview

Musicians tell us music is necessary not because it is an added treat, a pleasant way to spend time, or even a beautiful enrichment of life. It is needed *because it is not possible to be human without it.* Music is as necessary for human survival as language, breathing, or taking in food.

There are, of course, different *kinds* of music, serving a variety of human functions. There is concert or "serious" (an unfortunate label!) music; jazz; folk music; standard popular music; and the multiple categories of rock, from the songs of Elvis Presley to punk rock and disco.

This chapter attempts to understand music as a human strategy, as a phenomenon essential to humanization. The main premise behind this chapter is that one comes a little closer to oneself by considering what kinds of music one enjoys and what kinds one tends to avoid. No effort is made here to persuade the reader to single out concert music as the only kind worth supporting. If a bias exists at all, it is surely that the well-rounded person, the human being able to celebrate his humanness in the fullest manner, probably opens himself to more than one form of musical expression. The concert buff ought to drop in and hear a session of blue grass music sometimes, and the ardent rock fan might profit from a Verdi aria.

The reason seems clear. The spectrum of musical forms exists not because there are enormous differences in kinds of people, but because people have so many different *needs.* To limit oneself musically is to take care of fewer needs than is necessary—to leave many needs unexamined and unfilled. It is with music as it is with other human habits and patterns of living: too often we stay with what is comfortable and familiar, unwilling to stray into alien territories.

The Need for Silence

It is traditional to introduce a discussion of music by talking about sound. But we may perhaps find ourselves more enlightened on the subject if we first consider silence—the absence of sound. The mystery and mystique of silence hold the secret of all music. It stands to reason, does it not, that if musical notes were played continuously, with no pauses in between—that is, without silences—there could be no such thing as a musical form. Melody and rhythm, two of the basic elements in music, are made possible by silence in the same way that a piece of sculpture engages us because of the empty space around it.

Since music is one of the oldest expressions of humanity, since its exact origins are lost in prehistory, we shall never know whether the need for silence or the need for significant sound came first. The order may not be important. It is tempting, however, to construct a hypothetical profile of the very first human being to identify both.

> **Too often we stay with what is comfortable and familiar, unwilling to stray into alien territories.**

Noise and the Hunter's Wife

Snakes do not unwind seductively in their baskets and perform slow dances to the charmer's reed. They cannot hear any sounds at all. Many other creatures also seem to get along without hearing. Human beings apparently required a highly complex auditory system, a sensitivity to a broad range of decibels.

One disadvantage with the senses—especially those of sight and hearing—is that they keep on working whether needed or not. People with sight are always looking, except when they are asleep. Anyone who tries to concentrate on a particularly demanding task knows how readily the eye can be distracted by the slightest movement. It is impossible to see only what one wishes, though people *do* exercise a certain degree of selectivity. Nonetheless, extraneous objects are continually parading across the field of vision. We might use the phrase *unplanned visual environment* for the range of the eye with all the things which can possibly be seen at any given moment.

By the same token we live in the midst of an unplanned audio environment, and this is possibly more distracting than the other. People in rural areas may be less oppressed by unplanned sounds than people living in crowded cities, but by far the majority of the world's population exists at the mercy of street cries, transportation screeching, jet plane roars, and construction drilling. Add to these police whistles, ambulance sirens, a roller-skating child's "harmless" dragging of a stick along a wrought-iron fence, the barking of dogs, the sudden thud delivery doors make when someone closes them—and you have at best the continual blare of unwanted sound. People who can afford to live in well-insulated, air-conditioned buildings may be somewhat exempt, but everyone has to venture into the unplanned audio world many times a day.

Our hypothetical first—a hunter's wife, let us say—finds herself caught up in an unexplained depression. Each morning the hunter girds himself with loin cloth and spear and goes forth for the day's hunting. The wife is left behind to care for the little ones and prepare the food killed the day before. One morning she realizes a major reason for her depression: noise. Birds are cawing, little ones are screaming, rocks keep sliding down the mountain. Escape! But where? Is there in all the world a tiny spot where one may sit very quietly and simply hear nothing?

The first person to need refuge from noise may well deserve the honor of being called the first humanist. It is easy

We live in the midst of an unplanned audio environment.

to imagine this need's having come before the need to put pictures on stone walls, for example, or make the wheel or sophisticated eating utensils. One begins to change the environment when one feels comfortable within it. The hunter's wife is not yet at ease. Her head is splitting.

At length she can bear the noise no longer. Making certain that the little ones are engaged in some nonviolent game, well within earshot if need be, she tiptoes softly into the wooded area nearby. She is amazed at how the leaves filter out much of the harshness of the noise, though she is still aware of the children's playing. She sinks to the cool ground, leans her head against the trunk of a tree, closes her eyes, and, for the first time in human history, listens to silence.

Several days pass. The wife's secret hiding place becomes sacred to her. She does not reveal it to anyone, not even her husband. What could she say she was doing? Little by little the experience becomes more complicated. At first the absence of grating noise was reward enough. Now she is not so sure. Continuous silence soon loses its appeal. There is no way to measure it. Five hours of silence are no more silent than five minutes. It is necessary to find a way to keep silence vivid, alive, meaningful.

Soon she learns that, in addition to the reassuring, distant sounds of the children at play, there are other sounds she had not noticed before: the leaves rustling, for example; a waterfall; far-off hunting calls made by blowing softly into a hollow shell. These sounds have a soothing effect on her and also serve *to heighten the silences between them.* Music is born.

The Unplanned Audio Environment

Like the rustling of leaves or the sound of a waterfall in the hypothetical case of the hunter's wife, musical experience needs to be surrounded on all sides by silence if it is to do a proper job for us. Concert music owes almost as much to the atmosphere of the concert hall as it does to the notes written down by the composer and played by the orchestra. The hush that covers the audience like a mantle after the conductor has tapped his baton is absolutely a part of the symphony which follows.

In contrast, the ceaseless blasting of popular music from transistor radios or the record shops along the street surely represents a cultural phenomenon quite different from the

Publius Syrus

I have often regretted my speech, never my silence.

Skip Lowery

Poor Wordsworth. Poor Thoreau. What would such seekers of isolated streams and wildflowers say today . . .

simple experiencing of a piece of music. There can be no question that this phenomenon fills *some* needs at least which have little to do with music by itself.

Is silence feared more than it used to be? Perhaps people are not being exposed to silence at an early enough age. Almost every home contains at least one electronic stimulus: television. Millions of homes contain stereo equipment. Transistor radios cost next-to-nothing to buy. Have parents been guilty of using loud music as a numbing agent, an audio tranquilizer that simply smashes juvenile aggressiveness into passive submission?

Silence is conducive to serious thought, especially introspection. Loud music renders introspection unnecessary. Is looking inward also something to be feared? Perhaps human beings have always had some difficulty with silence. Perhaps it has always been something of a challenge. Introspection is not necessarily a joyous experience. One is sometimes faced with embarrassing truths about oneself. The presence of loudness in the audio environment gives one an excuse not to look too closely inside.

The resistance to silence is also a result of what Alvin Toffler (in *Future Shock,* 1970) has labeled "information overload." The electronic media are continually communicating, as are purely visual media like newspapers, magazines, ads on buses and waiting benches, billboards, and the like. More information is available than anyone really wants, but in our society, who can escape it? Hence people become overstimulated. If over-stimulation persists over many years, as of course it does, a curious phenomenon occurs. Instead of wanting nothing so much as solitude and silence, people tend to require more and more stimulation. It becomes impossible to function unless one is being bombarded on all sides by messages, regardless of content.

The continuing need for stimulation frequently takes the form of *noise addiction,* for loud sounds probably affect us more rapidly than any other stimulus. Thus we are faced with a frightening paradox. In a society notable for its rapid pace and rate of change, a society of blare and blast, one becomes conditioned to require *more* of the same, not a peaceful alternative.

Loud music—especially rock—has other functions, as shall be seen. It *is* music, after all, and as such it must perform some of the tasks of music. The issue here is not

David Riesman

. . . in the field of popular music . . . The music industry, with its song pluggers, its juke-box outlets, its radio grip, seems to be able to mold popular taste and to eliminate free choice by consumers.

that medium itself, but the addiction many people develop for its loudness. In the throes of such an addiction one is often indifferent to the source of the loudness, so that the musicality of rock becomes a secondary consideration.

We are not to understand from the foregoing that everyone becomes a noise addict in this society. The noise-battered hunter's wife is still around. Every year more and more people who can afford the move are fleeing the noise-polluted metropolitan areas for suburban, if not rural, quiet. Concert music, while favored by only a small percentage of the population, is nonetheless enjoying considerable popularity. Ever since the late '50s, there has been widespread interest in the folk tradition, a great willingness to listen to fragile voices accompanied by a solitary guitar. The need for silence *does* manifest itself as a reaction to information overload, overstimulation, and noise pollution. As always, the delights of music are rediscovered as the possibilities of silence are reexplored.

The Controlled Audio Environment

There seems to be no question that music originated out of the need for human control of the audio environment. Either human beings accidentally found they could attain such control—perhaps by striking rocks against each other or beating sticks against hard objects for want of something to do—or they tried consciously to imitate attractive sounds provided in nature. No one is ever going to know precisely *how* the making of music began. Nor does it much matter. The fact that all signs point to the omnipresence of some kind of music in every early culture indicates a strong, basic urge for music in the very nature of humankind.

Rhythmic dance may have preceded the discovery of melody. Anthropologists know that even the most remote civilizations punctuate the milestones and rites of time's passage in some rhythmic manner. The attainment of puberty, marriage, religious occasions, seasonal changes, planting and harvesting, births, and deaths seem to have been rhythmically observed almost from the beginning.

That rhythm—as well as whatever other aspects of music may have existed—could be used to influence human behavior may also be an early discovery. It's easy to imagine parties of hunters being worked into a frenzy of excitement

---

Skip Lowery

One of the first things a visitor to a London park notices, for example . . . is the sign at the entrance which prohibits transistor radios from the area.

Alvin Toffler

. . . we note the glazed stares and numb, expressionless faces of youthful dancers at the great rock music auditoriums where light shows, split screen movies, high decibel screams, shouts and moans . . . create a sensory environment characterized by . . . extreme unpredictability.

and enthusiasm for the kill by the steady beating of sticks and rocks, and by rhythmic sounds uttered by the human voice. One can imagine the rite of human sacrifice made "easier" (or was it more pleasurable?) through rhythmic acceleration, the gradual working up to the actual moment of death, which could conceivably have been a moment of ecstasy for mesmerized victim as well as rhythm-intoxicated priests. More advanced societies undoubtedly sent their men off to war in some rhythmic way.

World Wars I and II saw troops marching on and off transports, almost always with bands playing. The Korean and Vietnam Wars appear to have abandoned rhythmic leave-takings and arrivals, and who can say what effect such non-rhythm may have had on those who participated?

Rhythm and spectacle are closely related. Stylized walking or dancing lends itself to further elaboration, such as bodily adornments. All have played their part in affecting human behavior in ways that were and are essential to the family, community, or nation. We know that sacrificial and fertility rites were almost always performed with body paint, extraordinary clothes and accessories, and bizarre masks. Though the separate elements differ in their nature, they all seem to share the ability to induce people to behave in ways that are not typical of them as private individuals or of everyday life.

To test the instantaneous effect of rhythm on a mass of people, one need only stage a curtain call for an indifferent musical comedy. It does not matter in the least how tedious or banal the piece has been up to the final curtain. If there is a highly rhythmic tune in the score, the orchestra must play it now, as raucously as possible, exaggerating and punctuating the rhythm with drums and cymbals. At once the audience applause will adopt the same rhythm as the tune, and it can continue indefinitely. Not only will the amount and volume of applause give the impression that the show is a "smash hit," but the majority of those present will be convinced—at least for a time—that they have thoroughly enjoyed themselves.

To the early Greeks has sometimes gone the credit for having discovered—or is it invented?—melody. No Greek music survives, so we cannot know for sure what Plato or Aristotle listened to during their off-hours. But we *do* know about the monochord, an extremely early version of a

Walter Breen

[A] psychedelic component in music is variously called *assault* or *impact*. Music . . . emphasizing this aspect . . . insists on a rhythm extremely compelling . . . matching one's heartbeat and alpha rhythms.

stringed instrument which existed at the time of Pythagoras, the philosopher/mathematician of the sixth century B.C. The monochord was a simple, rectangular wooden box with an opening on top, much like the guitar. Tightly strung across this opening was a single string, similar to the strings on a violin. To produce a variety of sounds on this string the Greeks used a moveable bridge.

Tradition insists it was Pythagoras himself who, fascinated by the whole phenomenon of sound, especially the change in vibrations as the monochord's bridge was moved from point to point along the string, discovered that all such strings produced exactly the same graduated rate of vibrations.

With this basic and simple scale, the Greeks must have constructed melodic lines, no doubt predicated on mathematical principles. The Greeks were enraptured by the notion of numerical schemes that repeated themselves everywhere. (See Chapter 2's discussion of the Golden Section.) Pythagoras believed the entire universe had been put together according to precise mathematical formulas and that musical intervals—the "distance" between one sound and another in terms of vibrations—were outward signs of this mathematical order. Pythagoras believed that if one could somehow ascend to the heavens for a closer observance of the planets, one would hear glorious music as the planets moved in their orbits.

In any event, melody *is* significant repetition of sounds, whether or not based on mathematical principles. It *does* make possible the controlled audio environment, because, like rhythm, it is clearly distinguishable from random, unplanned sounds.

Also, like rhythm, melody is shaped by silence. To have musical notes one must have silent intervals in between. Early composers of melody may have been preoccupied with the joy of seeing what happened when notes succeeded each other in certain patterns and may have done less with silence than the great composers would eventually do. But from the very beginning music was *significant sound floating in silences.* This alternation between sound and silence gave humankind its power to control the audio environment, however much some are now allowing themselves to be controlled by *it.*

Walter Breen

[Through music one tunes into] the overriding pattern of order and design unfolding in the universe . . . the embracing of something exquisitely beautiful and worth knowing.

Music and Personality

If music developed out of a human need, it follows that music tells us something about ourselves. If music results from the artful interplay of sound and silence, it follows that human beings also exist partly in sound and partly in silence. An analogy could be drawn between music and the human personality.

Some people are more random and less selective in their "soundings" than others. That is, they scream, shout, and babble on, much in the manner of children, all of whom begin their human careers as sources of unplanned sounds. In other words, some people do far less with silence than others, and as a result they do not take the time, or have the inclination, to "shape" the sounds they make in between silences. They open their mouths whenever the impulse is there, often interrupting others attempting to make their own sounds.

Such people may be said *to lack melody.* Not taking advantage of the opportunity for self-examination that silence gives, they fail to develop significant patterns of thought and behavior that are *under control.* They have the potential for melody—the notes—but this potential is forever wasted, forever being drowned in the general noise of unreflective human interaction.

As to rhythm, nothing is easier than to critique one's demeanor, one's bearing—one's way of walking, sitting, rising, asking, answering, and thinking—and determine how rhythmic it is. Unmelodious people usually exist unrhythmically. They sprawl, slump, slink, stoop, jiggle, and jangle. In a book called *The Zen of Running* unmelodious people are referred to as being "ahead of," never "within" their breath.

All you have to do is take your pulse to recognize how fundamental rhythm is. Irregular heart rhythm is a dangerous sign. Irregular breathing is an abnormality. When the breath is soft and regular, when the pulse is slow and steady, you feel tuned into the proper way of being. You know when you're there. No one has to tell you. When you're arhythmic, no one has to tell you either.

The "musical" people of this world are always clearly identifiable. They are obviously in control of things; they are people we most eagerly trust to do difficult creative tasks.

For in nearly every instance the appropriate action cannot be conceived accidentally, *noisily.* It requires both silence and music.

Music Tells Us What We Are

Thus far in this chapter the concern has been with identifying music as a certain kind of phenomenon. The term *significant* has been used more than once to distinguish musical sound and its intervening silences from unplanned noise. We know the sound between silences affects us in many ways, otherwise we should not want to hear it. But now we must come a little closer to understanding what the effect actually is and how music achieves it.

Feelings

It almost goes without saying that music is somehow involved with feelings. We say that a piece of music is "full of feeling" or that it "works on" our feelings. We are not always sure what we mean, however, for feelings are difficult to isolate and define.

The need to know what we are feeling is part of the general human need to be located in time and space. Music tells us what we are feeling, what we are capable of feeling—in short, it reveals our emotional make-up.

As a matter of fact, much of our emotional life is no doubt inseparable from—would not exist without—music. The differentiation between a loving person, for example, as opposed to someone who is "in" love may find no expression other than through certain types of music which embody the loving state. Tchaikovsky's *Romeo and Juliet* Overture is surely one of the world's most enduring works because it gratifies the listener to be identified with the sound of rapturous love. Wagner's *Liebestod,* or *Love-Death,* composed for the grieving Isolde as a final expression of her passion for Tristan before she too dies, takes the listener spiritually out of this world, carries him to places where love can be so total and all-engulfing that, having once experienced such a thing, one dies joyfully. It is such music which makes us know we can understand such feeling, such music that tells us we share in its idealism.

Music is what emotions sound like

Music does more than *identify* emotion. It is our souls' ideal listener. In a sense we give the music back to the music. It speaks, we answer. With whom can we share profound feelings that cannot be expressed *except* through music? We and the music enjoy a private conversation from which all others are excluded.

We also turn to music when we have specific feelings we *can* identify. Music is a reinforcement. If we are feeling sorrow over the loss of a friendship, the end of a romance, or a failure to achieve a certain goal, the sad music helps us to experience the emotion more completely. Happy music simply does not suffice for unhappy moods. Again the music is an ideal listener. It both speaks and hears our unhappiness. Music allows us to be as miserable as we need to be, and by granting emotion full range, music provides a release and establishes inner balance.

Yet sad music always seems somehow pleasant. Who does not like the slow movement of the symphony or the mournful ballad of a love forsaken and betrayed? As a matter of fact, if you were to collect every song that had ever been written and were to study the lyrics, you would doubtless discover that the vast majority deal with broken hearts, loneliness, even death. If it is true, as the poets tell us, that life is inevitably tragic, perhaps sad music is one way of adapting to tragedy. And perhaps the beauty of sad music is the compensation.

But, of course, there is a place for happy, light-hearted music. There are times when everything seems to be going just right for us, when we can identify no discord in our lives. At such moments, the feelings they inspire need reinforcement as much as sorrow. "Toe-tapping" musical comedy tunes, brisk marches, frantic rock, or the scherzo movements of symphonies can answer our call. In moments of happiness, it is often difficult to communicate even with our closest friends. Friends—even lovers—like to be needed, like to comfort and console, like to be understanding and provide shoulders to lean on. When you have no need of anyone, to whom do you turn to express yourself? "Up" music is there to say "I know how you feel."

Beyond light moments one may ascend through music to feelings of ecstatic joy, feelings which virtually defy any verbal parallels. The final movement of Beethoven's Ninth (Choral) Symphony (in which the composer, having exhausted the possibilities of instruments, explored the full range of the human voice) unfolds inner emotional horizons nobody knew to exist until surrendering to its tidal wave of sound. The music, set appropriately enough to Schiller's "Ode to Joy," does more than reinforce feeling—it defies one not to share its ecstasy. Whatever mood one has at the onset of the music, in the end a profound, responsive chord is struck within one's soul. Such music as this causes us to understand our full capacity for feeling.

Nostalgia is yet another emotion which is reinforced and experienced through music. If one is in a remembering mood —say while looking through the high-school yearbook— appropriate music (the alma mater, the "fight song," the last tune in the prom orchestra's last set) bolsters the feelings and permits them to run their course.

Nostalgia is, however, mostly a vague emotion, a bitter-sweet collage of sound in which we float midway between conscious memory and unconscious echoes of the past. Frequently we have no idea why we experience this feeling. One theory is that nostalgia is the organism's way of readjusting, of restoring inner equilibrium in the face of rapid change. Nostalgia often comes upon us unawares, when we have no specific past memories in our minds.

Some music, for reasons no one quite understands, speaks directly to this emotion. It enables us to lie back and allow a procession of memories, often unrelated, to wander back and forth along the surrealistic landscape of the mind. Nostalgic music tends to be slow and lyrical; perhaps it's because we need to revisit the past in slow motion.

We periodically need to live at an abnormally slow pace. Nostalgia can sometimes be a pure experience, unrelated to *any* need to glance backwards. Sometimes we need to stop changing for a little while, and with certain music we imagine we are revisiting our past. Perhaps we are only slowing down, permitting our emotional heart beat and breathing to return to normal.

Some "lyrical" music no doubt belongs in the category of nostalgia, as here defined. You may just have returned to the safety of your home after a near disaster; you may have received chilling, shocking, deplorable news that causes your heart to pound frantically; you may just have thrown a tantrum after discovering a chartreuse carpet has been installed by mistake. But just play the second movement of

Romain Rolland

At the moment when the theme of joy appears for the first time, the orchestra stops abruptly, thus giving a sudden unexpected character to the entrance of the song. And this is a true touch; the theme is rightly divine. Joy descends from heaven enveloped in a supernatural calm.

Beethoven's *Emperor* Concerto or the Grieg Piano Concerto, and you your muscles begin to relax and the pounding in the temples slowly subsides. Add a Chopin etude, and you may feel completely restored, at least temporarily capable of handling new disasters.

Another feeling to which music allows full identification is sensuousness. Human beings possess senses not only for taking care of minimum survival needs but for esthetic pleasure as well. So far as we can tell, humanity is the only species that takes the time to enjoy the colors of a sunset, the sound of a mountain brook, or the way a shiny red apple looks and feels to the touch. Music, with its variety of sounds, permits us to indulge in sense experience for its own sake, permits us to exercise a purely human capacity.

With the coming of the electronic era, the sense of vision has become part of the total experience. Listening to the stereo is usually more effective at night, with dim lights or perhaps candles. The different colored lights in the equipment are all part of the scene: the illuminated dial of the stereo receiver or the tiny red light on the pre-amplifier, even the faint light under the turntable. A phonograph disc in itself is not without sensuous appeal; there is a certain fascination in watching it spin, all shiny black, light bouncing lightly on its fragile surface.

The ideal place for hearing music is the concert hall, especially if it is relatively new or has been renovated according to updated acoustical principles. There is something about the live music, directionally experienced, which cannot quite be duplicated in one's own living room, though highly discriminating stereo speakers *can* produce the illusion of three-dimensionality in the sound.

In the concert hall there can be a maximum of concentration on the sound with a minimum of distraction. Many people resist attending concerts of baroque, classical, romantic, or contemporary music on the grounds that the experience will be dull, incomprehensible, and/or lacking in clearly identifiable melodies. But precisely the reverse is the case. The concert hall experience of so-called "serious" music (as opposed to what is hard to say) is essentially no different from the concert hall experience of rock or folk or jazz. The works of music themselves represent only part of the total experience. The dimensionality, the all-pervasiveness of the sound—so that all traces of the unplanned audio environment are eliminated—adds as much to the experience as the actual notes played. If one is open to sound experience, there is no musical form which, in the concert hall, fails to provide some degree of emotional identification.

As well as sensuousness there is sensuality—two terms which are often confused. Sensuality is probably limited to the human species, for while other animals experience sexual desires at the appropriate season, humankind is capable of experiencing erotic feelings almost any time. Such feelings are not necessarily aroused by another person. They can be stimulated by colors, objects, and sounds.

Musical structures are prime sources of erotic feelings, as will be discussed in the next section. For now it is only necessary to point out that certain instruments inspire erotic responses: percussion instruments, for example, especially tympani and cymbals; and clarinets, saxophones, and French horns.

While we humans *are* sensual creatures, we do not usually take the time to exercise this aspect of our natures: that is, apart from sexual experience itself. All manner of outside pressures conspire to prevent us from allowing sensuality to manifest itself and be identified. No doubt for some, such experience is unthinkable, a source of private embarrassment, tied in with guilt.

Guilt happens to be one emotion which is never experienced in and for itself; hence is never really let go. Instead, it serves to suppress other feelings, such as sensuality. Whether it is desirable to suppress sensuality aroused by the presence of another *person,* can be debated. The individual's conscience must be his or her guide on that score. Indulgence in erotic feelings, when the object of one's desires is present, can lead to all manner of acts, some of which may not have the consent of the other person. But to *never* indulge in sensual feelings can be far more harmful, certainly to oneself, and perhaps to others in the long run. Music enjoyed for its sensuality may well be the ideal catharsis, allowing the emotion full range *without causing any harm.*

Most Japanese music appears to exist for its sensuality. The music which accompanies Geisha dancing is one example. But even music heard in authentic Japanese dining places in this country exemplifies true sensuality in music. Unlike Western music, in which the "main melody" is usually clearly separate from the other musical notes, Japanese

Shakespeare

That strain again! It had a
  dying fall.
O, it came o'er my ear
  like the sweet sound
that breathes upon a bank
  of violets,
stealing and giving odour.

As You Like It

music exists in and for the individual note. No note seems more important than another. Hence the music invites full participation on a note-to-note basis. The effect of such intense concentration is bound to be sensual, to the degree that all profound involvement in musical experience ends up being sensual, whatever else it may be. (The element of sensuality is not missing even from religious music and hymns, when these invite similar *total* involvement. Many who attend the Easter High Mass at Saint Patrick's Cathedral in New York, when members of the New York Philharmonic join forces with the Westminster Choir, have an experience that is deeply spiritual *and* deeply sensual.)

To sum up: we need music to help identify our emotions for us or to reinforce those we have identified but which need externalization. Music helps us keep in touch with our emotional make-up, which is an essential part of our identity. It also helps us to express certain feelings such as sensuality without the problems that such feelings can bring about when other people are involved.

Musical Structures

Musical experience does not take place until musical sounds come to us in some sort of sequence or arrangement. Not notes, but structures (forms), lie at the heart of the experience. One note, even one chord, repeated endlessly, would hardly be music.

When we deal with musical structures, we are facing the same esthetic phenomenon involved when we talk about the human response to form (see Chapter Two). No doubt this response has much to do with the discontinuity, the fragmentary nature, of inner consciousness, and the human need for some anchor in the external environment.

The house, apartment, or room in which one lives—one's immediate residential environment—the familiar "four walls"—probably represents the basic anchor, the basic form of one's life. A person who lives nowhere, who wanders perpetually from one place to another, might well experience profound identity problems, though there surely are many other kinds of external forms to which one can relate. Some people even refuse to remain in one environment on the grounds that relating each day to the same walls, the same objects—not to mention the same

Western music:
A main melody separate from other musical notes.
•
•
•

Japanese music:
No note seems more important than another.

people—is too confining, too stifling to one's growth.

Whatever your preference in the matter of external forms, the fact remains that they are necessary. We cannot turn our eyes inside out, and if it were not for our forms—pictures, sculptures, furniture arrangement, landscaping, music and so on—we would not have a true sense of how we exist as conscious beings.

There are two major categories of external forms, hence two major ways of anchoring ourselves. One is the category of stable, unchanging, "frozen" forms such as public buildings, statues, museums, and houses (others' as well as our own). These external forms can be experienced all at once, if they are small enough, or in part, if they are large. In either case, the entire form is there before us.

The other category is that of linear forms, which can only be experienced sequentially. A play, a movie, a novel, a journey, and, of course, a musical piece, all make themselves known to us one moment at a time. You can look at a building from the back and then walk around to the front without disturbing or changing what the building is. But if you begin watching the movie halfway through, leaving at the finish and never seeing the part you missed, you could not in good conscience venture a critical opinion. You have *not* experienced the film.

Both frozen and linear forms appear to be necessary as anchors of our inner beings. The frozen forms may appeal to our need for a sense of total identification. The linear forms may appeal to our need for a sense of becoming, of growth.

No one likes to think that he or she is this or that and can never be anything else. No one likes to be "pegged" once and for all. Whenever anyone looks at us and says, "Let me tell you what you are," the tendency is to recoil inwardly and resist any such feedback. This part of us feels quite comfortable with fluid (as opposed to frozen) linear forms. This part of us does not need the answer right away. Linear forms provide an exercise in change, in development.

Few people can identify comfortably with only fluid forms. Everyone needs to come home at night and rest. At such times one wants plants, vases, paintings, ash trays, lamps, chairs; one wants the mementos of his own permanence. The frozen forms are quick identification cards. They are silent mirrors, reflecting back our identities at a glance. They tell others much about us, also at a glance.

Now the less urgent your need for instant and total iden-tification, the more casual you may be about your frozen forms. The painting may hang crooked on the wall for months at a time. The lampshade may stay there lopsided. On the other hand, you may have a passion for keeping your frozen forms "just so," and this passion could indicate a person with a strong, assertive sense of self, or one with a desperate desire for a recognizable self.

During the 1960s—an era of great social change which witnessed a considerable decline in the family circle and a pervasive rebellion against authoritative systems—the pop-ular life style was characterized by casualness in dress, in sexual relationships, and in almost all social dealings; by a love of mobility; and by a preference for fluidity in the arts. The value system and tastes of the 1960s reflected a great emphasis on *becoming.* Tired of the war in Vietnam, tired of the "same old" social institutions, people clamored for vast and sweeping changes. It was an exciting period for music, drama, and poetry—all linear forms. Even the frozen arts took on fluid qualities as artists worked in media such as plastic or created "happenings" that were intended to re-place formal art.

Within either category—frozen or linear—one finds great variety. Some frozen forms, as we have just seen, aspire to fluidity, while some fluid forms—a Haydn symphony, for example—try to achieve a sense of wholeness through brev-ity and symmetry. Beethoven is far more fluid than Haydn and was at one time considered a dangerous radical by the conservatives in his audience. But today it is customary to think of Beethoven as a "classical" composer and to equate his music with all that is proper and decent and acceptable —hardly shocking!

From the start, the creators of linear forms probably recog-nized the difficulties under which they labored. In music, for example, repetition may have been a compensation for fluidity. Perhaps melody originated in just such a way.

While music is a linear form and appeals on this basis, it should be noted that not all linear forms are the same. They differ according to structure. In music, as in poetry, some structures seem to go on endlessly in no definite pattern, thus carrying linearity to its extreme, while others seem to keep backtracking on themselves, the end always near the beginning, giving a sense of the whole. Let us briefly look at four types of musical structure and see what they tell us about ourselves.

A Bach Toccata and Fugue
(With a Footnote on Jazz)

Frozen forms:

buildings

statues

museums

paintings

•

•

•

•

•

•

Linear forms:

movies

novels

journeys

musical pieces

The seventeenth and eighteenth centuries were times of tremendous musical advances in Western society. In the seventeenth century there developed a style of music—associated with religion as much earlier music had been, but going beyond the church in its impact. It was the music of the *Baroque era.*

The Baroque period was characterized by an architectural grandeur and an excessive use of color and ornamentation. Civic buildings, such as those which line the Ringstrasse in Vienna, had much gilt, statuary, and other forms of embellishment, none of it intended to be purely functional. Baroque buildings were to be enjoyed as objects of vision, not simply as places in which certain tasks were accomplished.

The churches of the period tended to follow the style. Throughout Germany, Austria, and Poland, in particular, you'll find places of worship dating from the seventeenth century, with flying angels suspended from painted ceilings and smiling cherubs peeking out from behind the tops of marble columns. These churches, many of which are Catholic, are the last word in opulence, and belong to a time when religion could be a sensuous experience without apology.

Catholicism, recovering from the impact of the Protestant Reformation of the early 1500s, found in Baroque splendor one way of bringing defectors back to the fold. Many of the more austere Protestant sects, such as that of Puritanism, critical of the sensuous extremism of the Catholic mass and the economic wastefulness of the older cathedrals, offered their worshippers unadorned walls and ceilings, simple wooden pews, and a complete absence of paintings or statues.

But the Baroque period touched both Protestants and Catholics, and its music was inspired by the same need for embellishment and sensuous appeal. Baroque music is far from simple. Indeed, as the era progressed, composers, especially in Italy, sought to outdo one another in the complexity of melodic lines, the intricacy of counterpoint, and the sheer size of their compositions.

The high point in Baroque music was achieved, by Bach. Beginning his musical career as a church organist in Arnstadt, Germany, Bach had no expectation of achieving greatness. Music in early eighteenth-century Germany was hardly considered an art form. The Italians to the south appeared to have a monopoly on musical art. Bach was hired to play the organ at Neue Kirche and to compose music for the mass, and that was all.

Thus confined—both geographically and professionally—Bach found liberation in exploring the possibilities of the music. The Baroque style called for long, highly fluid melodies and counter-melodies, but also for *improvisation*—a spontaneous variation or set of variations on a stated musical theme (melody). Through improvisation the composer/organist could take wings and soar into the endless skies of inner space.

One must listen to a Bach composition wholeheartedly. The great *Toccata and Fugue* in D Minor is a good introduction for the reader who has yet to enjoy the many subtle pleasures provided by Bach as well as for those who need to renew an old acquaintance.

Bach's music parallels in sound the richness of the whole Baroque period. It is elaborate, embellished, and complicated. Indeed one sometimes suspects that music, rather than art or architecture, served as the ideal expression of Baroque tastes, because its linear form makes it possible to experience complexities little by little, point by point, rather than to have them overwhelm one's vision as many Baroque interiors do.

A *toccata* is a free-style musical form designed to allow the performer of Bach's day to display his virtuosity and is frequently, as in the case of the D Minor work, followed by a *fugue*, which is more strictly controlled by preestablished musical laws.

In the toccata the composer or performer may improvise on the stated themes, taking them in virtually any direction. This practice has definite counterparts in jazz, often said to be the one true contribution of American musicians to the world. It is no coincidence that jazz players often acknowledge a strong debt to Bach, particularly for his genius at improvisation, and often include variations on Bach melodies in their repertoire.

The Baroque tradition in music—like jazz itself—produces a rich psychological experience; the inner self is *also* ornate, complicated, and abundant with thoughts (themes) running in all directions. The free-form segments of Baroque compositions, as in the toccata section of the D Minor, allow us to use the music to explore the moment-by-moment stream of consciousness. We seldom get the chance to participate fully in the free flow of our thoughts because the practical necessities of everyday life continually force us to focus on details, decisions, and specific recollections. On other occasions we are likely to be watching television or conversing with friends, so that a significant portion—indeed the greater portion—of our inner lives remains hidden and unexpressed. Listening to a Bach toccata is a little like having our brain waves suddenly converted into rich sounds.

The fugue section begins to exercise the control that is necessary if you are to function sensibly as a human being. To remain engulfed in your stream of consciousness is to run the risk of becoming dangerously confused. The fugue allows for the simultaneous hearing of different melodies; it is a highly fluid, usually rapid form, which is stabilized by the laws of counterpoint. That is, the melodic lines heard simultaneously must complement, not conflict with, each other. Since the Bach fugue was written to be performed by one musician and since the melodies are played by the left and right hands of the performer, the body's own limits of coordination really keep the lines in contact with each other.

You need only listen to the D Minor work to be astounded that one pair of hands could engage in so difficult a task. The idea behind the fugue is to demonstrate that what should *not* be a coordinated effort (that is, what for the average person would be an impossibility) is indeed well within the capabilities of the performer. Thus the Bach fugue in particular satisfies (harmonizes) two of our needs which at first seem to be in conflict—the need for total freedom (or the lack of coordination) and the need for some principle of control. It offers an experience continually on the brink of getting beyond control, but which always stays within its form.

Jazz works are very, very similar to those of the Baroque period. The composer/performer will take a theme and appear to be running away with it, never to return to the point of origin. But jazz musicians will tell you the flight is never

---

In Baroque music one experiences the complexities little by little, point by point.

•

•

•

•

•

•

In jazz improvisation each person seems to be going his own way . . . a strange, mystic unity.

wild or directionless. It is always within striking distance of the theme. When a jazz combo improvises together, a strange, perhaps even mystic, unity is always there, hovering over the notes.

Neither Bach nor jazz can compete for the attention of the majority of listeners. Popular songs, rock, and country-and-western music outsell both by a considerable margin. The reason may be not that Bach and jazz are "hard" to listen to, but that the beginner approaches both with the wrong expectations. The most readily accessible music permits identification only with our superficial beings. If you seldom look deeper, you'll miss many stimuli worthy of reflection, ignoring a great deal of self-exploration. You must *want* such exploration. It is the first step in broadening your range of musical experience.

The Folk Song

A wry lecturer on the college circuit once observed that the reason folk music is so bad is that "it is written by the folks." One presumes that the gentleman was a purist, unable to take folk music seriously as a significant form of human expression. Frequently the dedicated concert-goer and collector of "serious" music considers folk music altogether too haphazard in its origins and careless in its execution. But music which springs so naturally from its source cannot be so easily dismissed.

Unlike concert music, jazz and a good deal of rock, folk music was not intended to be solely a listening experience. It is rewarding as such, but it was meant to be danced to or sung. Folk music also has strong sociological functions. It serves as an external anchor not so much for one's personal self, but for one's group or ethnic identity. It is, to use Carson McCullers's memorable phrase, the "we of me." There are so many categories of folk music that wholesale generalizations are difficult to make. But a few examples can illustrate the function of this very spontaneous art.

The *commemorative song* is one of the oldest categories, deriving from times before people started keeping written records of important events. During the Middle Ages, for example, minstrels and troubadours kept people informed of battles and skirmishes. But even after historical records came into being, the habit persisted of crystallizing special happenings in words and music. Maritime folk music abounds with such songs, often because the remembered event took place far out at sea, such as an atrocity committed by a pirate captain or the plunging of a ship to a lonely, watery grave.

Of particular interest is that the narrator of the commemorative song seldom if ever identifies himself. The opening words are likely to be something like this: "My name is nothing extra / So that I will not tell. . . ." One song winds up in this self-effacing manner: "Now to conclude and finish, too far my lines have run. . . ." The focus is clearly the event itself, and the obscurity of the balladier makes possible an easy transfer to the group. It is always *our* song, never *his* song.

The *work song* is highly durable, for it is hard to imagine a time when the job will not be central in most people's lives. In some cases the work song reflects great hardship and a state of tension between management and labor. Often, however, the music is jolly and the words are full of bounce and nonsense.

> *I've been workin' on the railroad*
> *All the livelong day;*
> *I've been workin' on the railroad*
> *Just to pass the time away.*

No one who hears or sings this old favorite believes that anybody ever worked hard all day long just for the fun of it. But the humorous approach to the job, transferred from the song to the consciousness of the group singing it, continues to perform a valuable psychological function.

What probably makes this particular folk song so popular, however, is its structure. It continues beyond a meaningful stopping point—several times.

> *Can't you hear the whistle blowing,*
> *"Rise up so early in the morn!"*
> *Can't you hear the captain shouting,*
> *"Dinah, blow your horn!"*

The two stanzas conclude what should be a little vignette of railroad life. But there follows a sing-a-long refrain common in folk music.

Dinah, won't you blow?
Dinah, won't you blow?
Dinah, won't you blow your ho—o—orn?
Dinah, won't you blow?
Dinah, won't you blow?
Dinah, won't you blow your horn?

We can imagine the singing group clinging to the song, not wanting it to end, not wanting to have to disperse and go separate ways. So the song obliges.

Someone's in the kitchen with Dinah,
Someone's in the kitchen I know—ho—ho—ho,
Someone's in the kitchen with Dinaaah,
Strumming on the old banjo.

Once again the song appears to have come to an end, and once again picks itself up and keeps going, only this time with typical nonsense syllables: "Fee, fi, fiddle—ee—ay—o," etc.

"I've Been Working on the Railroad" is an excellent example of folk tradition. It relates that the survival of the *group* that matters first, and *then* one's personal survival within the group. Even in our own somewhat fragmented times—when few groups remain together a whole lifetime—people on buses or stuck in an airport waiting room during a blizzard, can quite suddenly turn into a temporary family group by singing such songs. If someone begins to sing "I've," the spark has been struck. There are times when even the most alienated loner finds it absolutely essential to be safe in the enfolding arms of the group, and folk songs make it happen naturally and easily.

During the 1960s, a period of wholesale fragmentation and alienation in the United States, a significant revival of folk music took place. Young people, often far from home, got together for the night around a Colorado campfire and became instant—if temporary—friends through the common bond of singing.

Sophisticated performers like Bob Dylan, Joan Baez, Phil Ochs, and Judy Collins sang new folk songs, using the familiar structures of the past, to make statements against war, pollution, and the corrupt establishment; and, if their listeners did not always sing along, the words of the songs usually reflected the audience's own feelings. But often—with such songs as "We Shall Overcome" and "Amazing Grace"—the solo performer might be joined by as many as ten thousand voices.

The *spiritual* had its special beginnings and appealed to blacks' need for a cosmic identity. Taken—stolen—away from their homeland, blacks in the United States with no future except slavery, pain, and death, concentrated on a relationship with God. While much nineteenth-century literature depicts the slave as happy-go-lucky, just bubbling over with exuberance, black songs of the period suggest a very different consciousness.

The spiritual allows for the release of the most profound kind of religious feeling, as religion proved to be the major solace for a suppressed and shackled people. The spiritual places the singer—and, through identification, the group—into a direct relationship with God and heaven.

Emphasis is on God's personal awareness of each person, however obscure he may be in the eyes of other mortals.

> *I sing because I'm happy,*
> *I sing because I'm free,*
> *For his eye is on the sparrow,*
> *And I know he watches me.*

Emphasis is on the ultimate release from pain and the coming of everlasting joy.

> *Swing low, sweet chariot,*
> *Coming for to carry me home;*
> *Swing low, sweet chariot,*
> *Coming for to carry me home.*

How music becomes the external anchor of our deepest feelings is beautifully illustrated by this spiritual. In the first line "chariot," a three syllable word, is stretched to four in the singing, as "swing" is stretched to two syllables in the third line. To liberate themselves, feelings need space, breathing room. A note-for-syllable correspondence is too regular, too confining.

In the black *gospel* songs, the liberation becomes even more pronounced. The singer—as well as the group—soon leaves the stated theme and takes flight, allowing the musical pattern to serve as guide, to keep the emotions from becoming overwhelming and uncontrollable. But gospel allows for emotional release not readily found in any other musical form. It is, of course, the wellspring of contemporary *soul* music, which often applies the gospel approach to more secular themes, but which still has emotional liberation as its aim.

But neither gospel nor any other kind of true folk music occupies the majority's musical attention. It is the Top Forty, coming at us from transistor radios and record shops at every turn, which obviously fulfills the most immediate needs of the young. And it is probably the slow fox-trot ballads played by large, heavily stringed orchestras, which fulfill the musical needs of their parents.

Those whose job it is to fill time capsules with the essence of our age may well overload their cylinders with rock records—and so overstate their case. While Elvis Presley may have been the most popular performer of the mid-century, one cannot be certain that rock music per se really sums up contemporary consciousness.

Rock is good for dancing of course, and dancing—especially the free-style, do-your-own-moves dancing of the present—has something to do with the need for being free from authority. But in disco or college prom dancing, it's the *motion* of the music that's important, not necessarily the melody and lyrics. Rock may be far more a dancing, rather than listening, phenomenon.

The rock concert—immortalized by Woodstock, *the* rock concert of all rock concerts, where in 1969 over a quarter of a million rock enthusiasts experienced not only music but monsoon-like rains and mud—has become a sociological if not purely musical phenomenon. The rock concert has been a gathering of forces, a show of organized defiance, a modern version of Dionysian revelry (see Chapter 6). If the inner self needs an external anchor—frequently a sense of belonging —then the rock concert, even without music, would satisfy many, especially those who are lonely and cut off from family bonds, seeking a temporary circle of friends.

The words of popular songs—from as far back as five decades ago to the present time—have changed surprisingly little in intent and function over the years. Perhaps the needs to which such music speaks have not altered either. It seems likely, as the popular songs of virtually all countries

B. B. King

The blues is feeling low, missing a woman, needing a job, wanting to move on to a better place.

generally have two revealing themes: (1) a lost romance, which was once perfect but has run its inevitable course, and (2) a found romance, which *is* quite perfect and will go on forever.

Who cannot identify with the theme of lost love, and who does not have deep feelings on that score which need to be expressed? Who does not dream of a perfect relationship or need such a fantasy? The young in particular, who buy most of the Top Forty records, continue to nourish expectations that the fantasy will become a reality one day.

Popular songs, then, identify and reinforce the idealism of the listener. Some changes, however, can be noted during the past, say, thirty years, since ideals reflect the influence of their times. The changes are not so much in the character of romantic love, but in the role of the participants. Women used to be the tender and fragile objects of men's affections; women used to be the ones who needed and gave love the most. A good many "lost love" songs were written from the point of view of the forsaken female. Today it is just as acceptable for a man to be deserted and to admit to shedding tears and spending lonely nights.

The country-and-western tradition generally deals much more realistically with human problems than do other popular songs. Typical country-and-western themes are adultery (either sex), suicide, murder, and, of late, even the boredom (from the woman's viewpoint) of middle-class domestic life. Of course, we also find the "perfect love" idealism, but this probably stems from Nashville's desire to capture its share of Top Forty income.

True country-and-western springs directly from the folk tradition, and carries on the tragic themes especially common in the Appalachian/Blue Grass regions, whose folk are heirs to the Anglo-Irish sorrowful ballad. This particular music literature abounds with songs of unrequited love ending in death and in cruel murders, often to keep an unwanted pregnancy from becoming known. Just why such themes are so prevalent is hard to say. We note, however, that the sadness of the songs matches the brooding countrysides of both Britain the southern mountains of the U.S.A. As to the love tragedy, we are reminded that the earliest dramas were tragic. If people need a release for their emotions, tragic stories can hardly be surpassed for that purpose.

A Beethoven Symphony

There appears to be a tremendous leap from a tragic country-and-western song to Beethoven, but the arrangement of
subject matter has been quite deliberate. The music of Lud-
wig van Beethoven (1770–1827) performs many of the same
functions, but probably in a much more overwhelming way
than a plaintive ballad of passion gone wrong. Beethoven
seems a fitting summation for this chapter.

In the Baroque musical tradition, epitomized by Bach, improvisation was the key. The composer worked through a
limited range of musical forms to find his own way through
the music. Bach managed to make the forms express his own
inner needs, but Beethoven added substantially to the available repertoire of musical forms, placing his own needs
ahead of the requirements of the music. We must remember
that Bach, as a church composer/performer, was committed
to religious music. Beethoven composed for church, concert
hall, small salons, private performances, and, above all else,
purely for himself. When he completely lost his hearing
during the peak of his musical career, Beethoven turned
inward, and out of his complex and anguished soul came
sounds no one had ever heard before. Even today, a century
and a half after Beethoven's death, when every note written
by him has been played and interpreted by thousands upon
thousands of musicians, and heard by millions of listeners,
each new listener can find in the music some as yet undisclosed aspect of the composer's personality as well as some
unexplored region of his own inner space.

Beethoven built upon the new expansive tradition in German music established before him by Franz Josef Haydn
(1732–1809) and Wolfgang Amadeus Mozart (1756–1791). It
was a secular, religious, nationalistic tradition rolled into
one. It declared that the music of northern Europe was every
bit the equal of Italian music—indeed would become supreme in all the world. The last quarter of the eighteenth
century was a time of great musical excitement in Germany,
as the range of instruments and the size of orchestras increased to permit exploration and experimentation. Of special importance was the development of the piano as we
know it today, replacing the clavier for which Bach wrote.

Of the "Big Three" who ushered in the new age of German

music, none worked more ceaselessly than did Beethoven to push musical forms to their absolute limits—and further. His Ninth, and final symphony, for example (composed around 1818), was nearly four times as long as a typical Haydn symphony, making listening demands on audiences unprecedented at the time. After three movements bursting with one melody after another, complex rhythms, intricate harmony, and shattering dissonance, the composer, perhaps having exhausted the possibilities of the orchestra, added a new dimension of sound—the human voice. Requiring over a hundred singers, as well as an enormous orchestra, the fourth movement of the Ninth Symphony took listeners to places no one had ever visited before (to the very gates of heaven, as one music critic described the experience).

Anyone who hears the Ninth symphony for the first time is likely to be swept away by the incredible momentum, and is likely not to hear human voices, but a dazzling combination of sounds there is no time to identify. Those who have sung in the gigantic chorus needed for the last movement frequently testify that the music is "unsingable." One tenor has admitted:

> *I keep my mouth open and manage to hit about every third or fourth note. The pace is frantic and the notes, the conclusion of the work, are beyond my reach. I think they are really beyond the reach of most voices. Nonetheless, a curious exuberance is created which compensates for the straining of vocal chords. The singers' struggles are concealed by the crashing of the orchestra, and the entire work, perilously close to disaster, miraculously escapes and achieves a glory most people experience only a few times in their lives, if they are lucky to do even that.*

In the same year, Beethoven finished his Sonata no. 29 for piano, usually called the *Hammer-Klavier.* Before Beethoven's time, piano sonatas were pieces of moderate length (averaging perhaps fifteen minutes), divided into three movements, each with its own structure and rhythm. The major purpose of the form was to allow concert pianists to demonstrate their virtuoso skills, so that in this particular instance the performer's abilities were usually paramount—not the composer's emotions.

With the *Hammer-Klavier,* however, Beethoven decided to see just how far he might push the limits, not only of the form, but of the instrument as well. What Beethoven did, in

Bach

was committed to religious music.

•

•

•

•

•

•

Beethoven

composed above all else purely for himself.

point of fact, was to see whether he could replace the entire orchestra with a single instrument. Few pianists in his time were equal to the demands of the work. Throughout most of the nineteenth century only Franz Liszt and Clara Schumann were able to meet the demands of both its technique and feeling. The *Hammer-Klavier* illustrates what was true of most of the work composed during Beethoven's high period (from around 1804 to the end of his life in 1827): namely, that the needs of both audience and performers were always secondary to the composer's own wielding of the music. Frequently baffled by sounds totally unfamiliar to them, Beethoven's listeners had trouble identifying with the music at first hearing. But in the end, Beethoven was exonerated. He created something new, and he made it seem inevitable.

In 1804 Beethoven composed his Third, or E Flat Major, symphony, later nicknamed *Eroica* or *Heroic.* Perhaps no work so completely illustrates how music can become the external anchor of the listener's inner self; for the *Eroica* was Beethoven's first major experiment in pushing the form of the symphony beyond its established limits and finding an almost inexhaustible number of ways for seizing the emotions and projecting them out into space.

The expansion of the art of the symphony can be seen at a glance. Haydn wrote over one hundred symphonies; Mozart, over forty; Beethoven, nine. Prior to the *Eroica,* Mozart's Forty-first, or *Jupiter,* symphony seemed to have reached the very summit of musical art. But now came the *Eroica,* nearly twice as long, staggering in its dimensions— so much so that again some listeners were at first bewildered, even incensed.

A symphony was intended to be an exercise for the orchestra in four movements, or short pieces, each with a definite structural scheme. The first—or sonata—movement is usually a bit longer than the other three; and it consists of the following structure: *exposition* (in which two melodic themes, A and B, are introduced); *development* (in which the composer explores the possibilities of the themes); and *recapitulation* (in which they are played again in their original forms). The tempo of the first movement is normally moderate, lively enough to engage the listener but slow enough to involve him or her in the melodies. It is usually followed by a slow movement, then a brisk one, and finally, a rousing fourth movement which gives the orchestra a

Leonard Bernstein

Nobody has proposed that Beethoven leads all the rest solely because of his rhythm, or his melody, or his harmony. It's the combination—

chance to "show off" and assures an audience ovation.

In Mozart's final symphonies, the four movements seem to fit together in a way not considered necessary before. In the *Eroica,* the four movements seem destined to have been as they were. You should listen to this symphony absolutely alone, and with no distractions, so you are open to all the interior vistas the music is capable of providing.

It is clear that Beethoven did not finish one movement and later tack on another as though the preceding one had not existed. The first movement of the *Eroica* symphony is on a grand scale. (Indeed this movement gives the work its name.) The story is that Beethoven was inspired by the heroic image of Napoleon and created in this opening movement a musical parallel for all noble feelings.

But, so the story goes, Beethoven became disillusioned by his inspiration. While the symphony was in progress, news reached the composer that Napoleon had crowned himself Emperor, and the dedication to Napoleon, already written, was removed. The second movement, called the "Funeral March," is the slowest of slow movements, dirge-like and heart-broken. One can veritably *hear* disillusionment in the sounds. This movement will remain forever an external form representative of everyone's facing up to reality—the shattering of idealism—the passage from heroic youth to tragic maturity.

By contrast, the third movement almost shocks us with its galloping pace and precise horns, all of it sounding like nothing so much as a hunting party. Out of place? Surely not. If you listen carefully to every note of the "Funeral March," you'll find there is only so much emotional "wrenching" you can take. Life must go on. The depressed spirit must pull itself up.

The finale (as opposed to what *had* been the typical symphony's fourth movement) begins with a graceful, dance-like melody, suggestive of polite society: civilization restored, so to speak. This leads through an intricate process of development back into the same heroic mood which opened the symphony. The *Eroica* is Beethoven's epic sound of the soul's passage from romantic illusion to the depths of tragedy and through struggle, upward again to a more mature, sober, and deliberate affirmation. It is not four separate pieces for orchestra. It is a complete unity. After 1804, the symphony—*music*—would never be the same.

> **The more we listen, the more variety we develop in our musical tastes.**

> **The willingness to open one's ears is fundamental to the entire humanizing process.**

Epilogue

One cannot in a single chapter deal with all possible musical experiences. But we have explored the essence of music; that is the important thing. We have learned that while the sounds may be different, *all* music exists as an anchor of our feelings, of our emotional make-up. Thus, the more we listen, the more variety we will develop in our musical tastes, the stronger will become our identity with sound. To limit yourself to only one form of music is to know only one side of your personality.

There are hundreds of composers today, no longer satisfied with what Beethoven did, seeking to expand the limits of musical form and musical sound in ways that are meaningful to *them.* There are composers working with electronic instruments, and composers who say that anything (even a scrubboard) can be a musical instrument. You can hear sounds today that would have scandalized Beethoven himself, who in turn had shocked his own generation with dissonance which some critics said ought never to have been inflicted upon the human ear.

As Beethoven won his case and set the new standards, so will new music eventually have its day and win acceptance. But many of us will not live to know of the success of today's forms. Beethoven did not ever know that his *Hammer-Klavier* sonata would become the standard by which all works for piano would be judged. It's essential to take chances—to seek out the new sounds—to sit back, withholding judgment, letting the music assert itself, seeing what it might be able to do. Even if the experience seems too unfamiliar to permit identification, the willingness to open one's ears is fundamental to the entire humanizing process.

Virgil Thomson

Music in any generation is not what the public thinks of it but what the musicians make of it.

5

THE POWER OF MYTHOLOGY

Overview

There is a widespread misunderstanding of mythology, but almost always among adults who think they have long outgrown the need for it. The adult mind finds it difficult to take myths, fairy tales and fables seriously. Myths are often viewed as ancient, highly improbable stories used by primitive people to explain things before there was science.

Some myths do, of course, offer imaginative explanations of the creation of the world, the appearance of humanity, and the reason for death. For primitive people, myth explained the origin of sunshine and thunder, envy, and pain. The profound significance of myths, however, goes far beyond their utility to early peoples. Myths, like fairy tales, came to be because they helped to make the human endeavor possible. They are still being created, even in this age of super-science; for example, some modern myths, such as those of space travel, have been developed straight out of scientific theories and discoveries.

As used here, mythology is the parent term, and it includes both myths themselves and fairy tales. Mythology is a broad category for a very considerable body of stories, some older than history itself and some quite modern, which help people organize, evaluate, or respond to the experience of living.

Unlike those works of literature which are of known authorship and can be tied to a definite place, time, and audience, mythology is part of the whole human atmosphere, part of the very air we breathe. Mythology sustains life in the psychological sense. The values, ideals, hopes, and fears which underlie mythological stories are fundamental to the human outlook. The average adult gradually loses his consciousness of mythology, whereas literature, as a sophisticated form of human expression, acquires greater stature in the adult years.

We can scarcely utter a sentence, however, without dropping a hint of the current mythology which has influenced today's people;

> "If you're good, Santa will visit you."
>
> "The honeymoon is over."
>
> "My luck is bound to change."
>
> "Well, he's no Prince Charming, but . . ."
>
> "Hold on tightly to every minute, because everything changes after midnight."
>
> "It's all downhill after you reach 30."

> **Salustius**
>
> **Myths are things which never happened but always are.**

> **Carl Jung saw myths as the collective dreams of mankind.**

Mythology can be called the cumulative wisdom of the human race. Some of it is far wiser than words can know. Some of it—especially fairy tales—may stand in the way of accurate perception if used at the wrong stage of our lives. Since mythology is so deep-rooted, we often find it very hard to distinguish the mythology that has ongoing positive value from that which blinds us to the truths we need to face. In saying it is implied that humanity, in adapting its consciousness to the conditions of living, may sometimes discover, sometimes create truth. For this reason it is imperative that the study of the humanities include some consideration of mythology.

Fairy Tales: Our Earliest Mythology

The fairy tale has been a sadly neglected art form. In fact, for a species of mythology that has been around for so long, it has not been taken very seriously until quite recently. Perhaps it has been a source of embarrassment for many of us. We hate to admit how very much our lives were molded and conditioned by these "silly" stories. We dislike, as adults, to admit the degree to which the fairy tale is still in our bloodstream, though its form may have altered somewhat.

It is difficult to imagine just how much more fairy tales need to do for us before critics "allow" them to be an art. If an art can move, arouse, or stir us up; if an art takes us from where we are and changes us irreversibly, then the fairy tale definitely qualifies as art. Unlike sophisticated art —say, opera—the fairy tale cannot be accepted or rejected. It comes along at the earliest possible stage in our lives, when we have no choice but to take it and use it as it was meant to be used. No matter when where somebody is born, whether he or she is rich or poor, or comes from intellectual parents, the fairy tale will leave its mark.

It also seems strange that with all the scientific studies of child development, the fairy tale is conspicuously absent from many standard texts in the field. We read of stimulus and response, positive and negative reinforcement, and adaptation and assimilation—psychologists' labels for processes of early childhood. But the fairy tale is a process too. Children would not listen to a fairy tale if it were meaningless, nor would children insist on hearing old favorites again and again if these were merely passing entertainment.

The big thing to remember is that children do not, in the beginning, choose fairy tales. Fairy tales choose them. Parents read them. Nursery school teachers read them. Older children tell them to younger children. They are there long before the conscious self begins to emerge, and since this is the case, it seems clear that whatever is in a fairy tale, whatever magic it weaves in the child's misty, dawning awareness, will influence what that self will become.

One reason for the neglect of fairy tales may be the negative view adults often have of them. Many a parent has been heard to say the equivalent of, "Well, I was scared stiff by demons and goblins and witches on broomsticks. This did a job on my head that could not have been good for me. I'm sure it made me fearful and dependent. I'll make sure it doesn't happen to *my* child."

Children do, have "it" happen to them, whatever "it" may be. But in our sophisticated, technological society the fairy tale often acquires the status of the Santa Claus story: maybe necessary, but thank heaven, for only a very short time. We need to remove the child from its clutches as soon as possible.

The Fairy Tale
as Artificial Reinforcement

Reinforcements are happenings—whether in real life or in fantasy—which affect what we think, feel, and do in the future. Behavioral psychologists base their entire science on reinforcement as the crucial aspect of human experience. And parents who have never heard of behavioral psychology often use reinforcement as a prominent means of raising their children.

A thunder storm occurs. The little child is terrified. He screams and carries on in his bed. Finally his mother appears and holds him in her arms, rocking him gently until the storm subsides. If this happens every time there is a storm, we can say that the mother's behavior has given *positive* reinforcement to her child. That is to say, the mother's certain appearance every time it thunders has convinced the child that his screams and cries will always be followed by mother's arms and the security of the rocking motion. So why stop crying? What's in it for the child to lie there weathering the storm to show his parents how brave he has become?

On the other hand, suppose another child screams and carries on the first time he is old enough to know what a thunder storm is. Suppose *his* mother decides it would be unwise to encourage such outbursts and thus makes no appearance at the bedside. After repeated attempts the child might well refrain from crying aloud, though his fears would probably take a different form. At any rate, this child experiences *negative* reinforcement; repetition of his behavior has been discouraged.

Scoldings, spankings, being sent to bed without supper, hurt looks on a parent's face are all forms of negative reinforcement in the home. Low grades, being kept after school, not being asked to erase blackboards are forms of negative reinforcement in school. Throughout our lives we face both positive and negative reinforcement for our behavior, and both our actions and our values reflect the kinds of reinforcements we have experienced.

Psychologists disagree over the extent to which negative reinforcement should be avoided. Some say it is impossible, actually undesirable, to raise a child with only positive reinforcement. The so-called "permissive parent" is the compulsively positive reinforcer. Such parents believe punishment stunts creative growth, turns into resentment later on, encourages psychotic behavior: "I've been told how bad I am by your actions, so now I'll get my revenge on the whole world!" They believes positive reinforcement develops the full potential of their children.

Others insist it is unrealistic and dangerous to plan a child's early life so that *only* positive reinforcement is encountered. Life, they contend, has both positive and negative qualities, and the sooner we experience both sides, the sooner we begin to mature.

One way to look at fairy tales is to see them as *artificial reinforcers,* relaying both positive and negative feedback to the child. "Artificial" is used here in the sense of not being authentic, not arising out of the actual context of living. Those who are pessimistic about the value of the fairy tale believe it is always potentially harmful, because the reinforcement it offers is so unpredictable and because little can ever be done *on the spot* to gauge the effect it is having on the child.

Consider, for example, the enduring tale of Little Red Riding Hood. It is hard to imagine a child in Western society who has never been exposed to its simple elements: the innocent little girl setting out to deliver a basket of food to her grandmother; the perilous journey through the dark forest, which, as in all fairy tales, harbors a variety of demonic creatures; the evil craftiness of the wolf in getting to the grandmother's first; and the horror of the wolf's action in swallowing the old lady he later pretends to be. This tale is sometimes cited by those who fear the psychological damage fairy tales may do to children on the grounds that many bizarre and abnormal elements are present.

First, the wolf devours the grandmother. People-eating abounds in fairy tales. Parents and visitors are fond of telling children they are so cute "I could eat you up." Stories like *Red Riding Hood* and *Hansel and Gretel* reinforce the fear of being devoured: that is, they convince the child his terrors are well founded. This *is* a world in which innocent beings are gobbled up.

It is perhaps desirable to expose children at an early age to death, but such a violent death for the old woman? One senior citizen did in fact speak of her lifelong obsession with the fate of the grandmother and her personal fear that one day she too would be alone and defenseless and would meet her death at the hands of a coldblooded murderer prowling the neighborhood.

Red Riding Hood then gets into bed with the wolf. To the adult mind, thinking back at the negative effects of fairy tales, the bed scene is absolutely grotesque. Little Red Riding Hood would have had to be extremely slow-witted not to suspect something at once. Couldn't she see the wolf's face peering at her from under the bonnet? Why would she have climbed into bed but for the undeniable fascination with the evil possibilities of the act? And why the prolonged question and answer period in which the little girl carefully scrutinizes the wolf's eyes, ears, hands, and mouth? Is it that the fear of being devoured is really the secret delight in having forbidden pleasures, which the child does not even understand on the conscious level? Critics of the fairy tale maintain that children should not be exposed to psychological experiences they are unable to comprehend or handle.

Then there is the moral confusion of the story. Most adults have forgotten, but *Red Riding Hood* exists in different versions, some of which seem to offer only negative reinforcement. In one negative version, both the girl and the grandmother are devoured, and the story ends there. Nobody comes to the rescue, and the wolf presumably slinks off into the forest, licking his chops, and waiting for the next unsuspecting victim. The critic asks what the child, whose own value system is mixed up, is likely to make of so bleak, so ghastly an ending?

But the principle objection is raised against the overly

The so-called permissive parent is the compulsively positive reinforcer.

positive nature of most fairy tales. The most popular version of *Red Riding Hood* is, of course, the one in which the hunter, hearing the cries of the heroine as she is being devoured, enters the cabin, captures the wolf, and slits the animal's stomach with a pair of scissors. The girl and the grandmother spring out all in one piece, none the worse for their terrible experience. The wolf must be imagined as dying, though the very vagueness surrounding his fate can be cited as evidence of the unreality fairy tales impart to such depressing truths.

Critics of the fairy tale complain that children, hearing their old favorites over and over, develop the wrong expectations from life. The hunter will come and make everything right. Hansel and Gretel will fool the old witch and push her into the oven. The Prince will kiss Sleeping Beauty and awaken her from her century-long slumber. Prince Charming will discover that the wretchedly dirty girl in the corner has the only foot capable of fitting the glass slipper. And so, they contend, we grow up believing that true love will find a way, fortune smiles upon people, and bad people always get what's coming to them.

Closely related to these tinsel expectations from life are the stereotyped thinking, the class distinctions and the sexism which some critics say run rampant in the fairy tales. Characters are seldom named and, when they are, their names often represent broad characteristics (Charming, Beauty, Beast) instead of suggesting unique individuals. Everything is morally sharp: the good are thoroughly and unalterably good, the bad are rotten through and through.

In addition, physical good looks are always stressed as important. Cinderella's stepsisters are not only horrid, they are ugly, which is made to seem just as bad. Underneath all the grime, Cinderella is breathtakingly beautiful; and well she must be, for would the Prince look twice at someone who was *only* virtuous and a good hard worker? Snow White's stepmother is not only thoroughly evil, but, when she is at her conniving worst, she comes disguised as an ugly old woman. Old age almost never fares well in the fairy tales, and the critics point to the fact that children tend to shy away from any close contact with the elderly. May the roots of society's treatment of the aged lie somewhere in childhood fantasy?

Fairy tales take place in magic kingdoms, dominated by

castles and, naturally, by a rigid class system. Since they originated long ago, they reflect values that are different from those of today's society, but, so say the critics, they have never been brought up-to-date. Therefore, we believe it is always better to be a princess than a working girl, and it would not do for the rightful king to go through life undetected. Quality—not only moral, but social as well—always shines through. Even more unbelievable: goodness is substantially and *materially* rewarded. Jack and his mother never have to go back to their poverty even after Jack's apparently foolish deal, swapping the cow for a handful of beans.

The charge of sexism in fairy tales is easy to justify. Women are clearly expected to be pretty, refined, and docile. The universe is so arranged that the weaker sex is taken care of as a matter of course. Sleeping Beauty has nothing to do but lie there and wait for the kiss of life. Red Riding Hood need only scream, and the big strong hunter will be there in a flash. Women who are dynamic and aggressive are bound to be wicked, like the queen in *Snow White.*

Fairy tales can even be charged with the crime of encouraging many of us into compulsive behavioral patterns that stay with us throughout our lives. There are so many rituals, incantations, magic numbers, and charms in fairy tales that, so the critics contend, it is almost impossible to mature on even terms with reality. Many people spend time searching for a superstitious necessity like a rabbit's foot, refusing to drive a car without it. Others go back a block to step on a missed sidewalk crack or run back down a flight of stairs to touch the one that was inadvertently skipped. Having heard that two neighbors have died in the same week, many a person will gasp, afraid he may be the third victim.

The repetitive element in the fairy tale process may well induce some kinds of compulsive behavior later on. After all, there is the whole going-to-bed ritual, with its "Read me a story" beginning and its "Read it over again" follow-up. The child learns the stories word for word and often cries out the magic number or the name "Rumpelstiltskin!" before the parent can say it. Comfort and security often lie in such repetitions, and who knows but that the compulsive adult—knocking on wood, doing things in units of three or five or seven, throwing salt over his shoulder—does these things to complete an action rather than out of

---

Sexism in Fairy Tales:

Women are either helpless or evil

women never end up in positions of authority

women never discover anything with happy results

women's acts usually involve them in danger

any true belief in magic? In contrast, the so-called normal adjustment to life is supposed to be one in which the adult can be comfortable in open-ended and uncertain situations.

The Fairy Tale as Agent of Maturity

Do Fairy Tales Promote

Racism?

Stereotyped thinking?

Naive expectations?

The establishment?

Social unrest?

•
•
•

•
•
•

Or Do Fairy Tales Promote

solid values?

a moral direction in life?

positive thinking?

If the last sentence of the preceding section has any validity, if the mature adult is one who can accept life on whatever terms are necessary, then, one might ask, how does such an adult come by his maturity? Is it by renouncing the childhood fantasies and saying, "Reality, here I come"? Is it only after he has been bruised and battered by life, his romantic expectations lying about him in a million pieces? Some psychologists believe maturation need not be a dreadful, traumatic experience. They say that each of us is naturally equipped to cope with maturity if allowed to do it. Fairy tales, in this view, are part of the natural process of growing up. They are as they are because human psychology requires their peculiar characteristics.

Psychiatrist Bruno Bettelheim contends that the fairy tale is crucial to normal psychological development not because it represents wish fulfillment, not because everything always works out for the best, and not because it creates within the child fantasy expectations of what reality is like. Rather, the fairy tale is a completely amoral phenomenon which evokes multiple responses and works on many different levels.

Take for example the story of *Snow White.* On one level, there is, to be sure, the stereotyped figure of the beautiful innocent, preyed upon by evil forces, but emerging triumphant in the end. There are the familiar prince, the storybook castle, the magic kingdom, and the "happily ever afterward" motif. There is the reassuring fact that the house of the seven dwarves is reality reduced to the child's size. But there is more than reassurance in the story.

Perhaps no child reacts to this or any other fairy tale according to the script written by adults. A child is small and helpless in a vast world dominated by powerful adults—to this extent, a parallel to the magic kingdom dominated by the evil queen. But, according to some child psychologists, as the child listens to the story—uncritical as he is, with no sophisticated faculties of knowing how such a story is *supposed* to go—he responds on a pre-conscious level, that is, emotionally and without sorting out his feelings.

When the evil queen is in the spotlight, the child may identify with *her;* for she has power, and small children often identify with power figures, like their parents. Children may not readily distinguish good from evil, but they know when power is being wielded, and they know when someone is defenseless against that power. There is, according to this view, no reason for the listening child to wish to identify *exclusively* with the powerless.

After all, if Snow White is all good, the child cannot truly

The fairy tale is a completely amoral phenomenon which works on many different levels.

and honestly identify with such purity. Has not the parent repeatedly pointed out how naughty the child is or can be? There may well be far more of a secret alliance between child and ruthless queen than adults ever dream.

On the other hand, as the queen's powers become increasingly directed toward the beautiful innocent, the child's concern may begin to shift. A familiar structure is recognized: the parent is on the way *with punishment,* namely, the poisoned apple. In the guise of the ugly old woman, the queen probably becomes increasingly remote; she comes to represent the entire adult world bearing down on that of the child.

It is now that the necessity for thwarting the queen's power becomes critical, for the child has learned to value strategies for evading punishment: hiding, blaming a brother or sister, making protestations of love to the angry parent, and so on.

> For Bruno Bettelheim the fairy tale is a completely amoral phenomenon which works on many different levels.

Psychiatrist Bettelheim believes in the therapeutic value of fairy tales to children, tells us it does not matter with whom the child identifies. A child will become involved with any character or action that suits his or her needs at the moment. If the child has recently behaved badly, he or she may go strongly for the evil queen. Snow White may represent the alter ego of the listening child and even the "enemy"—the grown-ups against whom the child's secret "badness" vows retaliation.

Many adults no doubt make the mistake of explaining fairy tales, or at least stabilizing a moral framework within which the child is supposed to experience the story. Bettelheim believes such a course is not only mistaken, but perhaps even dangerous. Children take what they need. They put things together in ways that are meaningful and workable at the particular stage of development they have reached. Since children can scarcely verbalize—cannot be expected to announce, "I am at a stage in which I am ready to deal with the following problems . . ."—adults can only assume that what they tell a child will be suitable. More often than not, explaining adults are merely projecting themselves into the child's place.

One parent, worried about teaching her child a frightening story, was careful to change the popular ending of *Red Riding Hood* so that the grandmother was rescued rather than destroyed. Her young daughter dissolved in tears at the conclusion of the story. The mother was mystified, since she had used only the positive version and thought her child would be relieved to hear of the hunter's fortunate arrival. It turned out the child couldn't bear to think of the wolf's dying such a horrible death. The mother was amazed; clearly the child was identifying with the *wrong* character. Repeated moral instruction, to the effect that wolves deserve exactly what they get, did not appear to console the child. Finally, in desperation, she told her daughter that a mistake had been made in the details of the story: "Actually, the grandmother went to her sewing basket, found a needle and thread, and sewed the wolf up again. The wolf was so grateful that he romped off into the forest and was never wicked again."

In Bettelheim's theory, the alteration of the story, the *manipulation* of the story to bring it within the mother's moral control, was clearly an error. The "corrections" may have been almost as damaging to the daughter as the excessively realistic explanation of death may have been to another child, whose mother died when he was barely five. The father of the suddenly motherless boy is reported to have dragged him to the open grave, required him to look down inside, and insisted that he face the truth: his mother was going to lie in that dark hole forever and ever and would not see him again. The boy grew to manhood, but just barely: he committed suicide at the age of twenty-one. It is not known for certain whether the experience at the grave was a contributing factor.

The "moral" of the above examples is that inner life of a child is something fragile, and not something to trifle with, push, or otherwise upset. As with physical development, which progresses no matter what parents do to speed up or improve the process, inner development has its own methods and pace. A recent play, Peter Shaffer's *Equus,* dramatized this very point. The main character, a psychiatrist with many emotional problems of his own, takes on the strange case of a teenage boy who has blinded a number of horses. As the play unfolds, the psychiatrist with surgical precision uncovers the source of the youth's psychosis: poor sexual adjustment, combined with terrible guilt feelings.

At this point the drama takes a sudden and wholly unexpected turn. Instead of being happy that he has straightened the boy out and "cured" him of the psychosis, the psychiatrist begins to realize that the boy had been far better off than he himself. After all, the boy had dealt with his emotional disturbances in some definite way, although a violent one; whereas the psychiatrist feels a vague sense of incompleteness about his life, a growing sense of alienation from all thought and feeling. He understands psychology so well that he has blocked all of the avenues of emotional release for himself. He comprehends, but he does not cope.

In arguing for the continuation of the child's fantasy life, especially as it is lived through fairy tales, Bettelheim places himself firmly in opposition to those who take an anti-fantasy stand.

> *As to fairy tales, one might say that the child who is not exposed to this literature is as badly off as the girl who is anxious to discharge her inner pressures through horseback riding or taking care of horses, but is deprived of her innocent enjoyment. A child who is made aware of what the figures in fairy tales stand for in his own psychology will be robbed of a much-needed outlet, and devastated by having to realize the desires, anxieties, and vengeful feelings that are ravaging him. Like the horse, fairy tales can and do serve children well, can even make an unbearable life seem worth living, as long as the child doesn't know what they mean to him psychologically.* [1]

There is a story about a scientific father who wanted his son to be armed with the toughness required to face a harsh world. He decided the fantasy of Santa Claus was nonsense, and on his son's fifth Christmas, he forced the boy to stay awake all night to observe the source of his presents. The child, rubbing his eyes, watched as his parents assembled the gifts under the tree. At dawn he pleaded to be allowed to sleep. His father, however, insisted that he have breakfast and then play with his toys. Before he was allowed to eat, the boy was required to finish the sentence "There is no. . . ." When the boy kept meeting the command with silence, the father became angry and threatened to beat the child if he did not comply.

Wearily, the little boy looked up and said: "There is no father."

Myths: The Whole Human Story

Fairy tales, so say some psychologists, contain underlying truths about a child's nature that the child is not yet ready to confront. In "Snow White," for example, the child may alternately identify with the evil queen and the innocent heroine without knowing why she or he does so. Bruno Bettelheim believes children must do whatever they want with fairy tales, that such stories should never be explained or analyzed.

If there is any truth to this view—and evidence seems to indicate there is—myths can be regarded as "fairy tales grown up." That is, myths are far more than naive explanations of existence invented by early people who knew no better. They represent a highly sophisticated psychological process whereby the adult mind projects its underlying hopes and fears, its sense of guilt or of being threatened, its longings, and, in general, its profound awareness of life's tragedies.

Unlike fairy tales, which usually take place in far-away countries—never-never lands in which the supernatural dominates—myths happen in surroundings familiar to the creators and listeners. They are not wish-fulfillment fantasies. Myths are filled with war, violence, suffering, death.

But like fairy tales, they contain heroic elements. They have brave, noble characters, who slay dragons and other dreadful creatures. They show love, sacrifice—every noble attribute of which humanity can conceive. Like fairy tales, they are unpredictable. Ecstatic joy can turn to sorrow without warning. A great and beautiful love can turn to hate. Life is snuffed out. Success turns to failure. But hope can spring up once more. People can be reborn. Out of the ashes of despair often flies the bird of renewed promise.

To say all of these things is indeed to say that myths offer the full spectrum of existence. They do not lie about life. But they *do* offer a symbolic version of life. They face the painful truth, but the fact that myths are stories makes the truth bearable. Myths are among humanity's most ingenious achievements.

The World Myth

The basic myth, one found in just about every culture that exists or has existed, is termed the *world* myth. It was labeled by James Joyce, the Irish novelist, as the *mono-* myth, indicating its universality and its uniform nature as we discover version after version in place after place. There can be little doubt that the world myth seems to tell the human story: *it sums up existence from the human vantage point.*

The world myth usually tells a *complete* story. It has a hero, a central character who represents humanity in some idealized form; it usually describes the hero's birth, mission in life (purpose of being), and his death. It often involves romantic attachments, so that the nature and/or meaning of human love is confronted, if not entirely made clear. Almost with-

Myths are filled with war, violence, suffering, and death.

out fail it projects the hero into a social setting, so that the nature and/or meaning of human relationships and power systems is likewise confronted.

The myths of the Greeks continue to have tremendous influence. One reason may be that in their mythology, as in their plays and philosophy, the Greeks anticipated almost every major concern of the human beings who came after them. To read Greek mythology is to be squeezed through an emotional wringer: there is not a single aspect of human life—particularly a tragic one—which is not explored.

Greek mythology offers a number of world myths, especially those of Perseus, Theseus, Oedipus, and Jason. Some of these are works of a very high tragic order and must be considered among the supreme human achievements.

The central characters of the world myths illustrate one very important fact: a mythic hero need not be a person of outstanding virtue or moral perfection. He must, first of all, represent *the human dilemma.* He must be faced with terrific problems and do battle against gigantic odds. He is not always successful. Our present-day Superman belongs to the world of fairy tale wish-fulfillment, not myth. He is still there in the comics. He is never conquered. He never dies.

Since myths are adult stories, their heroes tend to have many faults. They make blunders. They do not rise above all obstacles, for the myth-making mind knows that to create such a hero is to falsify life. The purpose of myths is to *clarify* life in a way that human beings can understand.

From the very beginning the phenomenon of birth must have preoccupied human curiosity. Of course people knew the causal sequence which led to reproduction, but how they must have marveled over the very *fact* of that sequence! That such a thing should be possible! Long before organized religion, myth-makers must have responded to birth as a wondrous, miraculous thing. So it is not surprising that in the world myth, the hero's birth is often attended by wondrous circumstances. Perseus, who grew up to slay the dread Medusa, was conceived in a shower of gold which fell from the heavens upon his mother. Hercules, the strongest of all the heroes, was conceived when Zeus, the king of the gods, visited Alcmene in the form of her own husband. In most cases the mythic hero is sired by a supernatural being, or chooses to believe he is.

Intrinsic to the humanization process is the idea that the

Superman belongs to the world of fairytale wish-fulfillment, not myth. He is never conquered. He never dies.

person who comes into the world through the miracle of birth is special in some way. The universe does not roll idly by, indifferent to each birth. Each new person is a unique individual, and it will matter that he or she has arrived. Thus it is that the mythic hero is born with a particular, often very strange destiny. For the Greeks especially, it was less important that the destiny should be a glorious one, filled with fame and fortune, than that it should make people sit up and take notice.

An indispensable ingredient of the hero's destiny is that he must be recognized early in his life through some unusual process. The young Arthur is the only one able to draw the sword Excalibur from the stone. Theseus, who would one day destroy the Minotaur of Crete, was recognized as a king's son when he was able to lift a heavy stone and find there a golden sword and sandals. A prophecy was given that Jason, the hero of the Golden Fleece, would arrive in the kingdom as a stranger wearing only one sandal.

Myths identify and magnify milestones in human life. There is always a moment in growing up when one first asks, "Who am I?" An answer like, "You're nobody," would surely not do. As self-consciousness develops, it seems crucial that each of us nurtures the sense of counting for something. Children start out in life feeling definitely inferior. They are so small, their parents are so big, they cannot help making unfavorable comparisons. Then, too, they are constantly being warned not to do this or that, constantly being scolded for lapses in acceptable behavior. They quickly develop an "I'm not OK" obsession that must eventually be countered by a more attractive self-image. Many people later admit that in early childhood they harbored fantasies of being "secret" princes or princesses, stolen from their cradles by gypsies or given away by their true parents, but to eventually be, like the mythic heroes, *recognized.*

Then comes the vital part of every world myth: the hero's performance of some magnificent feat no one else is able to do. King Arthur created the Round Table as well as an absolutely noble state governed by such kindness and good will that all crime ceased. Oedipus performed the most intellectual of all the mythic feats. He was able to answer the riddle of the frightening Sphinx, that huge birdlike lady who ate her victims in one gulp. Theseus not only killed the Minotaur, but later went into Hades with his friend

---

The Mythic Hero

is born miraculously

has a strange destiny

is recognized through the performance of some extraordinary feat

reaches a pinnacle of fame through some youthful success

becomes a powerful ruler for a time.

Then his fortunes go downhill.

Pirithous to abduct Persephone, the wife of Hade's king.

If the world myth magnifies key points in the idealized version of a human life, it also gives that life a structure. Performing great and unusual feats is not enough. The hero must reach a pinnacle of success, a high point at which he can say "I have arrived; I have made something great of my life." But then his life begins to go downhill. Myths never avoid presenting this aspect. In this respect they differ dramatically from those fairy tales in which time seems to stop after the pinnacle is reached and the reader is left with a vague idea of "happily ever afterward." (Such fairy tales almost seem to be saying to a child: "You are not yet old enough to understand that nothing stays the same, there is no such thing as being happy forever and ever. The comprehension of this sad fact will come to you later.")

Oedipus, who does not know that he has murdered his real father and married his mother and who, in a fairy tale, would never *have* to find out, plummets from the height of power to almost total self-destruction. He learns about the horrible crime of patricide and his incestuous marriage to his mother by whom he has sired four children. Blinding himself, he goes forth in exile and shame to wander homelessly for the rest of his life.

Theseus, according to one version of his myth, was gone for so long on his adventure in Hades that when he returned his subjects rejected him, driving him from Athens. He takes refuge with King Lycomedes, asking for the return of lands given to Lycomedes by Theseus's father in trust until the hero would come and claim them. But Lycomedes, wishing to leave the lands to his own son, treacherously pushes Theseus from a high precipice to his doom.

Jason, having won universal fame as the man who took the Golden Fleece away from the horrible serpent guarding it, sees his own life dashed to pieces. His wife Medea, in a fit of jealousy over his infidelity to her, murders his two sons and escapes scot-free, leaving the once-mighty hero childless and broken.

Though the myth of Arthur is lacking in some of the extreme violence and suffering which beset the Greek heroes, the good king is, after all, mortal and must die like everyone else. His wonderful reign in Camelot inevitably comes to an end as he, all alone, is placed on the ship for the one-way voyage to Avalon. There is certainly no indication in Arthurian legend that anyone ever took his place.

The myths of Oedipus and Theseus also demonstrate the fickleness of society, as that of Jason demonstrates the fickleness of the human heart. None of Oedipus's once-loyal subjects try to stop Oedipus from exiling himself. Instead they quickly transfer their loyalty to Creon, the new king. Theseus, as we have seen, was driven out by his own people, who are remorseful after his death, and in a ritual repeated many, many times in the subsequent history of humankind, they erect an enormous tomb to honor his memory. Jason, having brought home the Golden Fleece and thereby having won much power for himself, forgets that it was Medea who helped him accomplish the task. Instead he finds his affection turning toward a young, beautiful, and rich princess.

Some people may think myths are only unimportant stories about superhuman beings. But no one who steeps himself in enough myths ever comes away with romantic illusions about what life holds. Plato no doubt recognized this; in *The Republic* he recommends that education begin with myth, as did Aristotle, who observed: "The friend of wisdom is also a friend of myth."

Myth Themes and Symbols

The range of themes and symbolism found in myths is almost inexhaustible. Scholars devote entire lifetimes to the myths, the accompanying symbols, and the various historical periods and differing cultures found in them. Mountains, rivers, oceans, and monsters of all shapes and sizes are usually involved, together with magic rings, magic weapons, and magic phrases. Disguise is an ongoing motif, as is the separation of identical twins at birth, and potions which make people beautiful or ugly and fall in or out of love. There are also curses, prophecies, skirmishes, major battles, and gigantic wars. The only ingredients notoriously absent from myths are continuing peace, happy lands where change is unknown, and a community of people who only love and wish to help each other.

Bruno Bettelheim maintains that myth is always pessimistic, that people devise or listen to myths when they are mature enough to face reality, but need to have it presented in a fanciful way. Disaster and tragedy are not minimized, but they take on such bizarre forms that they can be faced.

The myths often demonstrate the fickleness of society, which first accepts then rejects the hero, only to glorify him in death.

Joseph Campbell

Dreams are private myths. Myths are public dreams.

The transformation of reality into myth is a little like what happens when someone pointedly tells a close friend, "I know a certain person with a severe drinking problem. This person probably knows he needs help and no doubt would like to ask for help, but I'm afraid he doesn't quite know how to do it." Both the speaker and the friend know what is going on, but the added distance of "a certain person" makes it easier for both of them to handle the situation.

Of course, myth-making seldom happens on so conscious a level. The need for the transformation is generally felt in the unconscious—that mysterious realm in which stored memories, unexpressed ideas, hopes, and fears glide about like so many divers exploring a sunken ship. The transformation process is the same as that which causes our dreams. In fact, a dream is nothing but a personal myth—a way each of us has of facing the truths of his own life. (Sigmund Freud believed that we dream in order to *avoid* facing unpleasant realities, but there is no reason to equate transformation with avoidance in every case.) A review of your own dreams immediately upon waking and a careful notation of recurrent situations, characters, symbols, and events in them may improve the understanding of your own nature.

Joseph Campbell, an expert in interpretation of myth, has said that dreams are private myths, while myths are public dreams. That is, a myth—such as the stories of Oedipus or Theseus—gains popularity and endures because it brings together key symbols and happenings which make sense out of the realities experienced by *many* people.

Freud was convinced that the story of Oedipus was a quintessential myth; that it embodied a universal fear of incest. The hero is doomed from birth by a prophecy which says he will kill his father and later marry his mother. In good mythic tradition he is raised by other than his natural parents, and in manhood encounters his predicted fate without knowing it. According to Freud, children develop erotic desires toward the parent of the opposite sex at a very early age, long before they are conscious of feelings and what they mean. Family and social conditioning eventually take over, and the possibility of incest—actually acting upon those desires—fades away. But the horror of incest remains.

In Bettelheim's terms, the story of Oedipus reinforces that horror. It continues to fascinate because we continually experience the emotions involved. The real possibility of incest may disappear, but the unconscious thought of it does not.

Expanding on Freudian theory, Bettelheim sees myth as an embodiment of the *superego.* Freud maintained that within each adult there occurred an uneasy balance among three forces: the id, or the basic drives (such as sex and hunger); the ego, or the conscious, rational mind; and the superego, or the presence within the mind of the prevailing morality of one's society, a morality transferred through family, religion, school, and peer group. Thus the myth of Oedipus can be interpreted as a stern reminder from the superego: incest brings about disastrous consequences.

But, of course, we need not limit the interpretation of myth to adult concerns about sexual matters. Nor must we so limit the interpretation of the Oedipus story. To do so would be to simplify a rich and complex art form. Another very crucial concern of Oedipus is his *identity.* Perhaps no other story in the history of myth deals so profoundly with the matter of who the hero is and where he comes from. In fact, the tragedy is really a direct result of the hero's ignorance of his own past, and hence of his present, and his mistaken conception of his own, as well as humanity's, real nature.

That Oedipus would one day murder his father and marry his mother was foretold. No one knew why the gods would ordain such a fate. The Greeks knew only that the gods were mighty while humankind was limited in vision and power. When a young man, Oedipus is told the prophecy. Horrified, he leaves the people he believes are his parents and comes to Thebes, where his real parents are. Every action he takes brings him nearer his fate.

Many years later he is again told the prophecy, this time in retrospect. He is told what he *has* done. Still, he refuses to accept the truth. He denounces the prophet, insists the truth is what he says it is. At the same time, he is impelled by a desperate urge to track down the secret of his birth. He will show the world that his situation is not what the prophet has charged. The final discovery, of course, destroys him.

So here we have cross themes. On one hand, Oedipus tells us that human beings are ignorant of their true natures, lacking the full insight on who they are and what they are capable of doing. On the other hand, the myth tells us it is tragic to look *too* carefully.

It is difficult to locate any theme in myth that is not tragic, or that does not conclude with the hero's being overcome by some force beyond his capacity to challenge. The universe itself, fate, a deity, or simply the very process of aging inevitably catches up with the hero, no matter how brave and powerful he may once have been.

The destructive effects of love represent a tragic theme found universally in myths. In one version of the Theseus story, the hero in later life marries a beautiful woman named Phaedra, much younger than he. Unfortunately for both of them, the wife falls in love with Hippolytus, Theseus's son, even though the boy displays no physical interest in her. Her stepson's lack of attention causes Phaedra's love to turn into an obsessive passion, which eventually destroys both her and Hippolytus.

In the Jason myth, the hero marries Medea out of gratitude for the help she has given him in obtaining the Golden Fleece, but, since there is no "happily ever afterward" in myth, Jason finds himself sexually attracted to a beautiful princess. Maddened by jealousy, Medea kills her rival and then her two sons, determined to leave childless her philandering husband.

Even the noble Christian kingdom of Camelot is not free of love's tragedy. The moral strength of Queen Guinevere is sorely tested after her meeting with the handsome Sir Lancelot, a test she ultimately fails. Similarly, Arthur's Christian code of forgiveness is tested when the issue involves his own wife.

The contrariness of human nature is thus central in myth. A number of myths contain the element of faith-testing: that is, the hero is required to be steadfast and *not* contrary; he is asked to have faith and not waiver. Often he fails.

There is, for example, the Greek story of Orpheus and Eurydice, in which the hero goes down into the underworld to request the return of his love from the dead. His plea for her resurrection is granted on one condition: he must not turn his head to make sure she is following him on the perilous journey back to the world of the living. But Orpheus cannot stand the suspense and eventually looks back for the briefest glimpse of his beloved, who is immediately reclaimed by the powers of darkness.

There is also the story of Pandora, the curious lady who was told never to look inside a box sent down from Mount

The myth of Oedipus shows us the tragedy of human beings unaware of their identity, their destiny.

•

•

•

Paradoxically, it also shows us the tragedy of looking too carefully into the truth.

Olympus. Unknown to Pandora, each god had placed inside the chest something harmful to humanity. Perhaps the gods counted on humankind's (it appears to be in this case specifically woman's) instability, and the box was their perverse way of making sure that human life was full of tragedy. Whatever the gods' reasons, Pandora became obsessed with the box and finally disobeyed the gods' command. Out of the box flew every evil (war, plague, pestilence, and so on) known to humankind. Horrified, Pandora slammed the lid shut, not knowing that one thing remained inside: hope. The optimistic interpretation of this myth is that hope is about all humanity has going for it; the opposite interpretation is, of course, that, while the other "gifts" continue to make human life miserable, the one thing that could have helped, hope, is not available. It is still imprisoned in that box.

> **The destructive effects of love represent a tragic theme found universally in myths.**

The biblical story of Lot's wife shows what happens when faith is weak. The woman, warned not to turn around (much like Orpheus), does so anyway, only to be transformed into a pillar of salt. But the supreme biblical story of a failed test has to be that of Adam and Eve, who were instructed not to eat the fruit from the tree of knowledge but did anyway.

In Christian philosophy, however, the fall of man and the loss of Eden are not viewed as tragedies. For one thing, since God is all-powerful and all-knowing, it became clear to theologians that, in warning Adam and Eve against yielding to temptation, God already had the knowledge of their failure. The question, "Why didn't God stop them from failing?" had to be answered, and it was. The option of sin, illustrated by the fall, also represents the basis of human dignity. God has given man free will; the first sin proves it. In John Milton's epic poem *Paradise Lost* (1667) we are given the further assurance that the "fortunate fall" paved the way for the coming of Christ. Had man not sinned, the earth would have been denied Christ's example.

In myths not only themes but symbols are recurrent. Because they apparently are of paramount significance as representatives of the efforts of humanity to become oriented in the universe, certain objects or situations keep appearing.

Swords

Heroes like Theseus, Roland, and Arthur cannot do what they do without the help of a magic weapon. (In contrast, Oedipus saves Thebes by the use of his wits.) One interpretation may be the human need to believe that the resources for coping with life are literally in hand. Another—somewhat less glorious—is that certain people have the delegated responsibility to take on big tasks. In other words, if you don't have the sword, you can't be expected to slay the dragon; it's somebody else's job.

Words

Language is also associated with magic, reflecting an early fascination with the mystery of words and their relationship to events. Saying, "Open, Sesame!" has a direct effect on reality. To name something is to control it (as we also find in the fairy tale "Rumpelstiltskin").

We must not forget that the Gospel according to Saint John begins: "In the beginning was the Word." Before creation, God had language by which to make it happen.

An interesting variation of this motif occurs in a modern short story about a cowardly knight, who proves unequal to the task of slaying dragons, until the local wizard gives him some magic words to utter. The hero kills fifty dragons in rapid succession and wins fame as the bravest of all knights. His benefactor decides he is ready for the truth: the secret lay not in language, but in the hero's own bravery and strength. The words were empty nothings. The story concludes when the hero sets out for his first non-magic encounter with a dragon. Of course he never comes back.

Numbers.

Magic words must often be repeated a specific number of times. Humanity *discovered* numerical units. People did not say to themselves, "Just see what we have invented." It seemed as though numbers, like words, were basic to the design of the universe. Numerical sequences indeed offered clear proof of such a design. Dante Alighieri probably made the most spectacular use of numbers in *The Divine Comedy,* which has:

> three major parts (for the Trinity)
>
> 33 cantos in each part (for the age Christ had attained at death)
>
> plus an extra canto to bring the total to 100 (considered a perfect number)

People still have mystic feelings about numbers and sequences. If two deaths are reported, many anxiously await news of the inevitable third. If a man could do 99 push-ups, it is almost certain he will do one more "to round it out." It is difficult to leave out an element in a series or sequence often in a long flight without often finding it necessary to go back to "rectify" the situation.

Nearly everyone has a "lucky number" that will guarantee winning the door prize or the roulette chips. It is hard to be human and be indifferent to numbers.

Curses

The myths of virtually every culture contain strong powerful threats as one way of accounting for the dreadful things that happen. An elaborate version of the curse myth is found in stories of the disaster that befalls each generation of an aristocratic family because of some sin committed by a distant ancestor.

The Greek myth of the House of Atreus is probably the prototype. Atreus murders his brother's sons in order to insure an inheritance for his own sons, Menelaus and Agamemnon. The curse descends upon Menelaus, whose wife Helen proves to be the direct cause of the Trojan War, and upon Agamemnon, who returns from that war after ten years only to be murdered by his wife Clytemnestra. The curse then becomes the legacy of Orestes, son of Agamemnon, who kills his mother to avenge his father's death.

The American playwright Eugene O'Neill (1888–1953) wrote a contemporary version of the Atreus myth for his marathon tragedy, *Mourning Becomes Electra.* O'Neill changed the original curse into unconscious drives, particularly abnormal sexual attractions, and made the characters' Freudian selves the true basis of all action. Critics of the play tend to regard its simplistic use of Freudian psychology as modern myth, not science. Nonetheless, the work offers an example of a continuing human need: to elude responsibility for life's tragedies.

Special Myths: The Circle and The Journey

There are two symbolic elements in myths so pervasive and universal that they deserve special consideration. One is the circle as an ever-present geometric shape. It is found as a shield, a ring, a pendant, the sun, the moon, and markings on cave walls or stones. Its importance to the myth-makers is paralleled by countless examples of circular structures throughout the world which have survived from early times: temples, stone circles, and, of course, that most intriguing of all round monuments to ancient humanity—Stonehenge.

The universal form of this myth symbol is the *mandala*, found in the art of almost any period. It is an enclosed circle, often with an intricate design representing the organization of the universe and the various deities which control it. The exact nature of the design is perhaps less significant than the implications of the circular shape. It tells us that the universe is an entity—*one* thing, as indeed our very word for it suggests. It tells us that if it could be viewed from an alternate universe, it would be a round object, something like a gigantic crystal ball, self-contained and distinguishable from anything else hovering in space.

Both the Eastern and Western minds apparently came to similar conclusions about the universe. Both decided on the circular, hence perfect, shape, which made the universe seem somehow *manageable,* that is, within the scope of human comprehension, if not control. Contemporary scientific

The circle, or mandala, told the myth-makers that the universe was manageable, within human comprehension.

The circle and the journey are the most widespread myth symbols.

theories, which imply that the universe is misnamed, believe it to be in fact not one thing but an infinite series of galactic systems. Such scientific views push that dreamed-of comprehension of the universe so far into the future that it seems reasonable that we may never be able to understand it. Yet we have Einstein's belief that space is both infinite and *curved;* curved because the principle of gravity is such that an object, attempting to move in a straight line forever, would be pushed by gravity into a circular orbit, making it eventually return to its place of origin.

Einstein's universe is circular: space is at once infinite and curved.

•
•
•

Carl Jung has seen in the mandala a universal symbol not only of cosmic but of psychic organization. Just as humanity from the beginning appeared unwilling to exist within a shapeless, infinite universe, he believed that same humanity resisted disorder in human existence; rejected discontinuous sensations, made up of a hodge-podge of sensory reports, emotions, and thoughts ever bobbing around inside us. The circular shapes in myths, according to Jung, are projections of an inner need to identify a coherent *self,* a shaped self, one that can be thought about and discussed.

Just when human beings began to think self-consciously about themselves is hard to say. We do not find Plato or Aristotle talking about themselves in this way. The notion of an inner ego or self seems absent from their work. One recent study concludes that in Plato's time people still believed their inner thoughts were voices from the gods and that the self did not originate until people stopped believing in such supernatural phenomenon. In any case, if Jung is right, the continual appearance of round objects in myths is an indication that early people were instinctively visualizing the human psyche as a shaped entity.

•
•
•

For Jung, the circles in myths are projections of an inner need to identify a coherent self.

The other pervasive myth symbol is that of the journey or quest. The myth-makers recognized that human existence proceeded through various stages past certain milestones, and so it made sense to them to think of existence in terms of physical traveling from one place to another. In the journey myths, moreover, the hero keeps having to pass one test after another—an objectification of the "rites of passage" approach to human life now taken as a matter of course by anthropologists and social scientists.

A *rite of passage* is an institutionalized milestone in anyone's life: for example, puberty; the rituals insisted upon by one's social group; graduation (with the appropriately named ceremony of commencement); marriage; parenthood; and so on.

The idea of "passage" connotes that if one does not success-fully reach each milestone, one is not entitled to move on to the next stage of the journey. People have incorporated the language of passage into their everyday vocabulary: "He is behaving like an adolescent, not an adult;" "She's still at her same old job, imagine that!" (implying is that she is "stuck," as opposed to progressing). Similarly, the high school drop-out who does not graduate has evaded an essential rite of passage and may be forever branded as misguided or unfor-tunate. In other words, society has taken the journey from early myths and transformed it into a social myth by which the course of anyone's life is defined and measured.

Since the journey is usually a quest—for one's homeland, a buried treasure, a beautiful princess held captive—it must have an object, a goal. The classic example is Homer's *Odys-sey*, which traces the adventures of Odysseus (Ulysses) through an epic ten-year voyage following the Trojan War. The motif of the goal or prize creates within the myths a conflict between two ways of looking at journeys.

Ulysses' prize is supposedly getting back home and getting together again with his faithful wife Penelope, who has not betrayed their marriage in all that time (which happens to be twenty years, when you add the ten years of the war). And in truth, the hero makes it back to Ithaca in the nick of time, clobbering Penelope's would-be suitors and restoring order in the old homestead. Presumably husband and wife live happily ever afterward, making *The Odyssey* virtually a fairy tale. It is one of the few major myths without a tragic ending.

The journey is one of the secret influences of myth. It organizes our lives into goals, destinations, and milestones.

On the other hand, people know that life's journey never comes full circle. You do not get back to your point of origin and put things back where they were when you left. What wife, after twenty years without a husband's companion-ship, can behave as though that much time had not elapsed? The poet Tennyson, in a nineteenth-century version of the myth, has the hero speaking frankly about his aging, unat-tractive wife and the boredom he is experiencing now that he has stopped traveling. He is clearly anxious to set sail once more.

> *How dull it is to pause, to make an end,*
> *To rust unburnish'd, not to shine in use!*
> *As though to breathe were life!*

This being the case, Tennyson's hero decides he must keep traveling and make the most of whatever time he has left.

If Tennyson's version of the journey is accurate, the idea of viewing life as an unending quest for an indefinable, unreachable goal may still have its drawbacks. It is all right to take a drive on a pleasant Sunday afternoon, but few would enjoy driving indefinitely, with no destination. The motif of the treasure or the promised land or the reclaimed princess has always been very strong—the suggestion that, if life is an arduous journey with many pitfalls and dangers, the whole enterprise had better be worth the struggle: "Now that you're back home, tell me what you have accomplished."

In the "rite of passage" approach to living, when milestones are everything, the notion of some final success, some master stroke, some spectacular achievement is almost unavoidable. If one is branded for being a high school dropout, what is the penalty for having no great aspirations or not being able to give evidence of any notable success at all?

People often associate the milestone of age with the milestone of achievement:

"Now that I am twenty-one, what do I have to show for it?"
"Here I am thirty-five, and I am not even into management yet."
"My daughter is pushing thirty, with no sign of a husband."
"He refused to retire until he had become vice-president."

None of these considerations is intended to suggest that existence ought to be one thing or another, or that any myth contains the full truth about living. The important thing to remember is the *secret influences* of myth. Long before humanity organized its thoughts about what being human meant, the myths were organizing experience into certain patterns. These patterns in turn provided, and still provide, a basis for the human interpretation and comprehension of experience.

It is impossible to imagine what our consciousness would be like without stories of journeys, treasures, rings, and wars; without the mythic ways of depicting heroes and heroism; without fairy tales to launch us on the whole enterprise of living.

Mythology is a set of molds. Had these molds never existed, the definition of a human being would be radically different.

Chapter 5 Footnote

[1]Bruno Bettelheim, *The Uses of Enchantment: The Meaning and Importance of Fairy Tales* (New York: Alfred A. Knopf, 1976), p. 57. Copyright 1976 by Alfred A. Knopf, Inc., and reprinted with permission of the publisher.

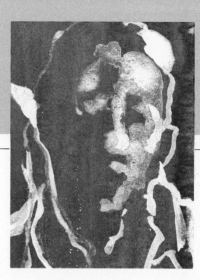

6 APOLLO AND DIONYSUS

Overview

Two Greek gods and a German philosopher have furnished our vocabulary with terms which express important states of mind and which represent the dynamics of social change.

The god of the sun Apollo and the god of wine Dionysus were used by Friedrich Nietzsche to exemplify these major forces in tragedy, and by extension, in human development. Apollo, according to Nietzsche, represented reason, order, clarity, and heightened experience through art; Dionysus represented passion, spontaneity, and the unconscious forces which, he said, were repressed by the leaders of society.

Nietzsche's analysis divided values into two opposing sets whose merits are still being debated today. In general, the Apollonian spirit is scientific; though emphasizing reason, it is based on the faith that the universe can be understood by the human mind. The Apollonian delights in the connections which make sense out of apparently unrelated phenomena. The great rational philosophers from Aristotle to Kant can all be described as Apollonian forces.

The Dionysian state is emotional, trusting that indulgence (even to excess) in life would reveal its true nature, as opposed to the Appolonian's rational approach to understanding life. When Sigmund Freud made his discoveries about the importance of the subconscious, he was exposing the Dionysian self to Apollonian awareness. The dominant contemporary philosophy, existentialism, is Dionysian in its rejection of values imposed by others than the self. This

Apollo and Dionysus

chapter will explore the Apollonian and Dionysian states in human personality, literature, education, drama, and in ways of both experiencing and communicating experience. As part of the relentless movement from one state to another, we will recognize some recent attempts to arrive at Dionysian truth, in disappointed rejection of Apollonian claims to have all the answers. We shall see, too, that an "authentic" experience is difficult to achieve, when words keep interfering with the free expression of the body. This book, like most books, is Apollonian. If it were not, it would stress instinct, intuition, even frenzy and hallucinatory visions, or at least some way of acting upon profound feelings. Being a book, it can only present both sides, sympathetically, using Apollonian tools, in the hope that conscious recognition will lead to the perfect balance long believed to represent the ideal mode of living.

Apollo
reason
order
clarity
moderation
analysis
control
•
•
•

•
•
•
Dionysus
passion
spontaneity
instinct
frenzy
faith
excess

Personal Temperament

Social history emphasizes the main currents of an age, pointing out dominant themes which then become textbook labels: "The Age of Reason," "The Romantic Era," "The Age of Faith," etc. The labels, while useful, give a false picture of uniformity. Even during an age of "reason," people lose their tempers. The majority of Athenian contemporaries of Socrates did not engage in dialogs exploring ultimate principles. And in the years called "romantic," when poets wrote as if all prosaic tasks had been forbidden, houses were swept, bills paid, and medicine swallowed.

These, like any labels, are useful as reminders of common social assumptions and as evidences of styles in the arts or trends in philosophy. Yet individual differences have always existed within each era, differences which may be conveniently termed Apollonian and Dionysian. People do tend to run their lives according to one or the other designation— now sane, moderate, thoughtful, and reflective; at another moment enthusiastic, emotional, and passionately spontaneous. Historical periods, in the eyes of historians, are stable units of time. Real human beings oscillate between extremes.

The act of dividing life into these two patterns is, of course, the act of an Apollonian, who is comfortable with language, lists, and patterns. The Apollonian of any age would enjoy an attempt to find order in this way.

Ways of Walking

Walking in a forest, the Apollonian would derive pleasure from recognition of the kinds of plants growing there, not just naming them but comparing the shapes and textures of their parts. It would be a delight to observe that a tiny fragment of a fern had the structure of a giant plant seemingly unrelated to it. Such recognition reassures the Apollonian of the order in a planned universe. Botanical information would be available to the scientist, who is Apollonian. But even the casual walker, unaware of species or genus, can and does notice, group, and compare, almost automatically. The Apollonian walk is a way of seeing and thinking with care and reflection.

Walking in a forest, the Dionysian would feel the cool air, touch leaves, smell fragrances, sit, run, or climb, without the need to analyze sensations and feelings. The experience would be worthwhile for its own sake. With no need to discover order, real or assumed, the Dionysian accepts what comes. There is no need to debate with the Apollonian (who tends to win debates, as well as succeed in other language-related activities). On a different "wave length," the Dionysian refuses to compete, or destroys the site of competition. The Dionysian becomes part of nature in a way envied by Apollonians (who may rush back to their desks and compose poems about fortunate savages they admire conceptually).

The simple act of walking in the forest may change according to different sensibilities. The two described do not, of course, exhaust the possibilities. We have seen that the Apollonian remains aware, while the Dionysian simply experiences without thinking about it. But the Dionysian moving through the forest derived as much delight from this venture as the more controlled Apollonian gained from keeping an alert mind throughout the walk. Another possibility would have been to move so routinely and unconsciously that there would be no memory of having been in the forest at all. Such might be the experience of someone who had become accustomed to taking a certain path in a daily trip from one point to another. Because the trip was routine, there would be no sense of novelty, no particular

With no need to discover order, the Dionysian accepts what comes.

need to notice or to mentally record the scene, and no desire to open one's senses—to hear unfamiliar sounds, touch unusual surfaces, and look at what the filter of overlapping leaves does to sunlight. The routine walk would leave the individual somewhere between the rich extremes—not maintaining a balance between them, but ignorant of both sensibilities, and unable to enjoy life from either perspective. There are, unfortunately, many such instances:

> *He used to laugh and tell jokes and was the life of the party. After we were married I noticed that he didn't laugh when we had to make decisions. He avoided them. I thought he'd be a happy change from my serious family. But it turned out the fun was all on the surface.*

Saturday Night of Dionysians

Long ago, when the work day for shepherds and farmers began early and ended late, the Sabbath was decreed as a means of making the change from work to rest. One of the Ten Commandments stresses the importance of that change in the rhythm of the week: "Remember the Sabbath and keep it holy." This designation for the end of the week was so important to the Hebrews that nothing, not even a recent death in the family, was allowed to interfere with the keeping of the special day. The Sabbath has been a major contribution to human development. Whether tied to religion or not, it has perpetually sounded warnings against allowing work to completely dominate us.

Today, when the Sabbaths of Jew and Christian combine to form weekends, an end to work offers many choices for a welcome change of pace. In recent years, emphasis has been on the Dionysian weekend. Advertisements attract our need to forget work, get away from it all, give in to hidden desires. With only a hint of the Puritan need to "deserve" fun, advertisements encourage pleasure and weekend abandon, accompanied by a deliberate rejection of thought and control.

Drinking

Though liquor companies do not openly urge the loss of restraint, drinking continues to be a tribute to the old god of wine himself. Drink loosens the tongue, makes us say and enjoy hearing remarks which our more critical selves would find foolish. Drink is a group activity which discourages rank or titles and invites the forgetting of self in revelry.

Music

Dionysian music is loud, rhythmic, hypnotic. Its message has nothing to do with language. Rather, it encourages the letting go of inhibitions, tasks, and meaning. Because Dionysian music has appealed to the unconscious, moralists have decried its effects. For years, jazz was considered a detrimental influence on the young, partly because its origins were outside the mainstream of white-dominated power, and partly because its lure was, like liquor, aimed at passions considered base. Today, jazz has become a studied art form which honors both patterns and improvisation. Rock music, however, continues to sound like a threat to the established order and respect for authority. The disco has become the new temple of Dionysian excess.

Dance

In Nikos Kazantzakis's novel *Zorba the Greek* (1953) two contrasting personalities represent the Apollonian and Dionysian approaches to life: the Englishman, studious, quiet, dispassionately observing the primitive people in the little village on Crete; and the Greek man, Zorba, who attempts to teach fundamentals which the Englishman has not found in books: compassion for the weak and lonely; acceptance of those elements in other people which cannot be changed; recognition of the futility of plans and scientific efforts. Zorba laughs exuberantly, drinks heartily, follows his instincts, and always takes chances. Energy and irreverence eventually demolish the reserve of his inhibited English friend. In a memorable few moments at the end of the book, transferred to an equally memorable film, when a profit-making scheme has failed and left the Englishman bankrupt, the man, who would once have despaired, asks Zorba, "Teach me to dance." The hypnotic repetition of the music fills the theater, inviting viewers to a Dionysian response as

---

E. M. Forster

Reliability isn't a matter of contract . . . it is a matter of the heart, which signs no documents. In other words, reliability is impossible unless there is natural warmth.

the two men give themselves over to movement of increasing abandon.

Food

The Dionysian approach to food has nothing to do with diet, health, or moderation. Those who cook the food may require Apollonian skills painstakingly acquired. But those who eat it can indulge in gastronomical pleasures without concern, permitting no prohibitions of any kind. "Go on, you only live once," says the Dionysian host urging a friend to eat forbidden fat or sugar. In eating to excess, in indulging in pent-up food fantasies, the weekend Dionysian is likely to reject all rules of nutrition. A deliberate lawbreaker, the Dionysian gives in to madness which may bring eventual regret, but which, for now, is believed worthwhile. This breaking of diet represents more than the weakness of someone who would like to obey but lacks the will to do so. It is also a challenging of medical authorities, a desire for the suspension of rules. When we read about a celebration of the 100th birthday of someone who brags about having outlived the doctor who put him on a restricted diet, we have met a worshiper of the god of good luck, another Dionysian diety. There is a Dionysian delight in the deliberate flaunting of medical science, the nutritionists, and the many other kinds of restraints which insist we do only what is good for us.

Sex

Though we have been discussing possible Dionysian activities for a Saturday night, we don't mean to imply that these activities could occur on that one night only. As a fundamental event, sexual excitement is Dionysian. Sex in the natural sense of attraction and fulfillment frequently is uncontrolled and inevitable, without plans, appointments, or vows. Songs and stories celebrate the unaccountable attraction of one person for the other. The words describing passion are strong, natural, without control: thrill, surrender, a heart which stood still, a roller coaster ride, an enchanted evening. (Evenings which are enchanted have more to do with witchcraft than with science or careful, rational marriage counseling.)

Saturday Night of Apollonians

Any of the Saturday night activities discussed above can be enjoyed by Apollonians. They eat, drink, dance, and make love—but with more awareness of consequences. An Apollonian diabetic avoids fudge. An Apollonian drinker is likely to remain quiet and introverted while drunk, not wishing to do things which can be regretted later.

Apollonians out for the evening would know their limits in advance, would probably not enjoy total confusion, and would even think in advance about the possibility of enjoying a sexual encounter, using the rational moments preceding the weekend to help shape the pleasures to come.

At their worst, Apollonians are killjoys. Such Puritanical reminders as, "Well, I've got work to do tomorrow," or, "Are you sure you know what you're doing?" have given the moderate folk a bad name. Culturally, the English and, to a lesser extent, Americans and Scandinavians have international reputations for dampening the spirits of the allegedly free-and-easy and historically Dionysian Mediterraneans.

In literature, a common plot concerns the repressed Apollonian, sometimes an excessively scholarly man, who is tutored in the ways of love by an uninhibited and very experienced Latin woman. In *The Rose Tattoo*, Tennessee Williams's Rosa is among the Italian heroines who give vent to strong feelings. In *Summer and Smoke* (also by Tennessee Williams), a physician's son learns about sexual expression from the Spanish. (Drinking, dancing, and cockfights at an illicit tavern contrast with the pious small-town Victorianism of the Anglo-Saxon world.) In fact, much of Williams's work deals with the decline of the genteel, Apollonian South and the rise of an uncouth, inarticulate, but perhaps healthier Dionysian society.

A good example of the intellectual who learns that there is more to life than books is found in the film *Never on Sunday*. The Apollonian American male tries to teach the Dionysian Greek woman about the great heritage of Athenian culture, her own heritage in fact. But she prefers to greet the sailors at the port of Piraeus, and to flash her dazzling smile as she sings and dances in the Greek taverna. After a dispute with the bookish American, she reverts to her natural self, hurling textbooks and records of classical music to the floor.

William Wordsworth

Thanks to the human
  heart
  By which we live,
Thanks to its tenderness,
  Its joys and fears,
To me the meanest flower
  That blows can give
Thoughts that do often lie
  Too deep for tears.

Since real life is happily less schematic than fiction, Apollo-oriented people need not choose to be strictly so, and *can* enjoy a Dionysian Saturday night in a number of ways. It is sometimes important to relax your inhibitions, to break out of the mold and simply have fun. Dionysian excess can be all the more enjoyable if it is uncharacteristic. The "professional" follower of Dionysus can become bored by having surrendered to abandon so frequently that there is little structured life left to throw away.

Dreams

Because they are beyond our control, the dreams which come to our unconscious in sleep are Dionysian. In dreams we defy gravity and orderly time sequences. We experience (often true) feelings which we do not admit in the conscious life of day. Fear, hatred, helplessness—these and other emotions emerge in dreams. When we awaken and try to recall them, we use an Apollonian analysis in trying to put together an explanation from which we can learn and act.

Sunday Morning

The weekend gives opportunity for Dionysian passion and Apollonian reflection. Though the time for worship varies with different religions, and though many people attend no regular worship service, leisure time *is* available in which to consider our place in the larger scheme of things. Sundays are good times for Apollonian walks, for solitude and silence, for taking stock of things. Too many people sleep through Sunday in order to recover from Dionysian Saturday nights before plunging once more into the routine work week, thus never really looking at themselves.

During a time devoted to neither work nor play, the reflective self may seek the spiritual companionship and inspiration of a church service. Hearing familiar prayers, reciting articles of faith, being stimulated by the insights of a spiritual leader can all be ways of heightening consciousness. They prevent the dull acceptance of unthinking routine. Sunday morning is a reminder that the supposed life-or-death concerns of every day represent neither life nor death. In perspective, anxiety about success can be seen as insignificant.

The rituals of religion, experienced from Sunday to Sunday, have a steadying effect. They reestablish the broken rhythms of our lives. They remind us that the process of being human is more important than the amount of experience (or success) available. To be human is to have limitations, to adjust one's expectations. It is not possible to experience, to *do* everything. The world cannot be embraced. One cannot be totally possessed by an overriding passion. Whether one accepts some or all religious doctrines, the process or religion is valuable in conducting our lives.

In life there are carefully measured ages, and appropriate behavior designated for each. There are rules; good rules to guide the lives of reasonable human beings willing to listen to the laws of God or to the many wise individuals who have shared their insights over the years, leaving humankind with a calm, ageless wisdom.

In submitting to the rules for a reasonable and balanced life, the Apollonian accepts and enjoys each age. The acceptance of one's age is evidenced in the folk wisdom of old women delightedly admiring a new child, congratulating the parents, but agreeing with one another, "I wouldn't go through it all again for anything," or saying, with tart philosophy, "When children are young they don't let you sleep. When they're old they don't let you live." These are the truthful statements of people who have the experience of years and the critical awareness to fit them into a large pattern of significance.

Of course, the Apollonian approach includes morality, the insistence on distinguishing between right and wrong. Nietzsche is among those who insist that morality weakens a society, preventing strong energies from seeking a healthy outlet.

Apollonian religions stress reason, having calm ceremonies with an ordered ritual. They offer rational sermons which may involve the supernatural but also emphasize human social actions. Even the celebration of holidays is a reminder of social order and the benefits of fellowship.

Dionysian religious practices, on the other hand, seek a fellowship which goes beyond words; in lengthy, uninterrupted dance; repeated chants; ritual removal of sin through some animal sacrifice; a literal purification through washing in the sea; in recent times, the taking of hallucinatory drugs. The aim is to attain altered consciousness and community

The Cycle from Apollonian to Dionysian

1. Ruling group: Apollonian. Maintains order, logic, and universal precepts.

2. Powerful become rigid; take privileges for granted.

3. Revolution erupts.

4. Dionysians have control: revolutionary leaders govern, reforms are turned into law; stability wanted after chaos.

5. Dionysian sub-groups hear about liberty, justice for all, but don't personally experience it.

6. Revolution brews again.

Friedrich Nietzsche

. . . his Apollonian consciousness was but a thin veil hiding from him the whole Dionysiac realm.

feeling through touching and staying together for many hours at a time.

The Apollonian and Dionysian may both exist as separate manifestations of the same religion, changing with the dynamics of the religion. From extremes of emotional frenzy the individual may counter desire with calm; then after building up a too-rational response which fails to set religious practice apart from ordinary life, needs once again to introduce less rational, more emotional elements.

There can also be Apollonian/Dionysian factions within a given religion. In other words, there can be both a Dionysian and an Apollonian response to a specific religion. These responses may not always be compatible. One group may accuse the other of being bloodless and pompous. The counter accusation may mention undue liberalism, too much relaxation of rules that threatens to weaken the foundation of the religion. Such factionalism often takes place when people become ashamed of their parents' foreign beliefs and modify their own practices to seem more in accord with the dominant culture. Jazz masses and the singing of folk-rock hymns on once hallowed altars bring the young into the churches, but often alienate many older members of a congregation. In the inevitable attempt to restore lost balances between Apollonian and Dionysian extremes, reactions are bound to occur, and it is likely we shall see the more strictly religious return to more controlled and powerful rituals once more.

Apollonian Morality versus Dionysian Stimulation In Art

Although the Apollonian and Dionysian outlooks may be seen in diverse elements of human life, Nietzsche made his most powerful statements about their impact on art and audiences.

His basic accusation against Apollonianism in tragedy was its emphasis on moral precepts, which, he said, separate audiences from emotional experiences. By concentrating on what there was to be learned from a tragedy, critics, he believed, ignored excitement in favor of schematic patterns which exalted the heroic nature of the protagonist as a means of instructing audiences in the proper way to behave.

Tragedy, then, became a pale replica of basic human passions, as audiences were taught to concentrate on a noble individual with heightened sensitivity and to ignore the unconscious self.

The fall of the hero is described by Aristotle, the critic who was so intrigued by the effect of tragedy on audiences that he formulated a famous theory to account for it. The result was a pattern by which classical tragedy could be measured. In the works of Aeschylus and Sophocles, the moral element is indeed strong. Aristotle encouraged critical inquiry into the nature of the tragic conflict, the flaw or error in the main character, the demands of the gods, and inevitably, what lesson could be learned by the "lesser" mortals viewing the play.

This, according to Nietzsche, represented an interest in morality to an extent which made no allowance for the strong emotions a tragedy unleashes. Empathizing with the suffering of tragic characters, Aristotle said, results in the purgation of emotions, which for him was the true purpose of tragedy. The purgation pacified viewers, calming them by the vicarious experience of watching somebody else's disaster and encouraging them to be law-abiding citizens with no need to give way to passionate outbursts of their own. In this way, art could tame; it could separate audiences from their own unconscious selves, and make them subject to whatever the rules of their society desired of them.

This calming effect can be seen at work in the last part of a formal tragedy, the moment following the climax, sometimes called the *obligatory moment*. Once the hero has been shown suffering the loss of strength, power—all that made him proud—the writer of tragedy shows justice reasserting itself, often in the guise of a new king. Old wrongs have been dispatched, the chorus has commented on what the events mean to other mortals, the fallen protagonist is led away. To end at an earlier moment would be, according to Aristotle, inappropriate. The play could not end, he thought, with the appearance of the blinded Oedipus. It required the new authority of Oedipus's successor, Creon, as well as concern for the fate of Oedipus's children and the former king himself. To end a play without these final moments would be to eliminate the resolution, during which the passions excited earlier could be cooled.

Many centuries later, the French philosopher, Jean-Jacques Rousseau (1712–1778), was to condemn this use of

---

Erich Fromm

The groups with whom one is at war are, often from one day to the next, looked upon as cruel, irrational fiends, whom one must defeat to save the world from evil. But a few years after the mutual slaughter is over, the enemies of yesterday are our friends.

Albert Goldman

. . . the network officials were wary. There were certain vibes that Lenny gave off, a certain uneasy feeling of anything-can-happen. The people in charge didn't want to take another chance."

Ladies and Gentlemen Lenny Bruce!

art as a barrier to revolution. To obtain committed revolutionaries, he believed, it was necessary to inflame them, to show a wrong, and to leave it unresolved, thus allowing audiences to stream out of a theater and into the streets with the determination to do something in real life rather than be tranquilized by this leveling-off of emotions onstage. The ending would be played out in physical action, in the rallies and riots which would put into play the Dionysian elements deliberatedly ignored by scholars and critics such as Aristotle.

For Rousseau the purpose of art was to provoke rather than soothe, to show an injustice, draw the audience to the side of one clear victim and then reach an abrupt, unsatisfying ending. Unless the wrongdoer were brought to justice, audiences would remain indignant. They would not be allowed the calming luxury of sighs and tears in witnessing a victim's death and release from suffering, nor be calmed by a philosophical acceptance of disappointment as a part of living. They would simply be aroused and left at a peak of emotion. Aristotle would not have approved, but leaders of revolution no doubt have done so.

Nietzsche insisted that the Apollonian approach alone was a distortion of tragedy. He found *Oedipus Rex* generally misrepresented. He agreed that Oedipus was "the greatest sufferer of the Greek stage . . . a pattern of nobility, destined to error and misery despite his wisdom, yet exercising a beneficent influence upon his environment in virtue of his boundless grief." But then Nietzsche went on to cite Oedipus as an example of a wise magus who *had* to be incestuously begotten:

> *If we examine Oedipus the solver of riddles and liberator of his mother in the light of this Parsee belief, we may conclude that whatever soothsaying and magical powers have broken the spell of present and future, the rigid law of individuation, the magic circle of nature, extreme unnaturalness—in this case incest—is the necessary antecedent; for how should man force nature to yield up her secrets but by successfully resisting her, that is to say, by unnatural acts?*[1]

It is necessary, contends Nietzsche, that Oedipus break the natural order, "as though the myth whispered to us that wisdom, and especially Dionysiac wisdom, is an unnatural crime."

Nietzsche contrasts the human defiance of gods in Greek

R. D. Laing

We can see other people's behavior; but not their experience.

and Hebrew literature. The Greek Prometheus dared to steal fire from the gods, whom he believed to be unjust in wanting to withhold it from mankind. But the disobedience of Adam and Eve is considered in Hebrew scripture to reflect wrongfully gained knowledge, and therefore punishment (in the form of banishment from Eden) is justified. In the Greek myth, we sympathize with mankind against the tyranny of deity. In contrast, religions based on biblical teachings emphasize the sinfulness of Adam and Eve as opposed to the stern mercy of God.

It was time, said Nietzsche, to give due credit to the importance of the Dionysian side of human life and to decry the unbalanced emphasis on the tame, cerebral, and passive aspects of human nature which he believed was the legacy of Apollo.

Apollo and Dionysus in Education

Almost nowhere in the personal experience of the average person are Apollonian and Dionysian factors likely to be as evident as they are in schools and colleges. For education itself as a process is inevitably doomed to a showdown between the two forces.

On one hand, education aims at the growth and unfolding of the individual, which can be Dionysian matters. If a person were allowed to fully explore his or her creative potential, to develop in any chosen direction, without regard for the requirements of the teacher, the School Board, parents, and society, he or she would be following a purely Dionysian course. But even before the creative potential of the kindergarten pupil or the first-grader is ever perceived—in fact, often *before* the child has entered school—certain Apollonian expectations have been impressed upon the pupil. For example:

The pupil must learn to behave.

The pupil must remain confined for long hours.

The pupil must show the results of certain teaching methods.

The pupil must therefore learn things which he may not want to learn.

Others know better than the pupil what is worth learning.

The Lower Grades

Many problems arising in the early years of education can be attributed to the imbalance between Apollo and Dionysus. Whether the problems were understood in precisely these terms or not, about half a century ago, sweeping changes began to be made. Educators recognized the need to allow pupils more Dionysian freedom to learn who they were and what they wanted to become. Experimental schools sprang up everywhere, many of which developed reputations for over-permissiveness and abandoning the three R's in favor of chaos. Typical of these early Dionysian classrooms would be sessions in which pupils banged objects together in a "rhythm band," got together in little groups to act out plays (which were really unconscious fantasies in disguise), and engaged in finger painting, much to the detriment of their clothes, the other children, and the classroom floor.

Most elementary schools, however, have sought to maintain a balance between excessive order and unbridled freedom. Educational theory, which is basically Apollonian, demands organization, planning, the writing of objectives, and the development of ways to measure a pupil's growth. Some teachers are overly Apollonian, insisting upon the lesson plan to the exclusion of all else, even when a given lesson appears not to be working. Others allow for Dionysian free spirits, with the result that they always seem to be running to catch up with their own objectives.

Schools tend to be top-heavy with administration, which is a very Apollonian entity. The teacher is answerable to the principal, the local school board, the PTA, county overseers —ultimately to the state department of education. The extreme Dionysian has a hard time bringing pupils into line and getting them ready for the battery of tests which come along frequently, not to mention for classroom observers.

Schools are Apollonian in their insistence upon ordered rituals, from flag salutes to the straight-line march along the corridors to the cafeteria or the playground. Even where permissiveness reigns in a particular classroom, the schools themselves are often run like army training camps. Pupils must have a pass if they are found walking through the halls. They may not be many minutes late, if at all. They

---

Empathizing with the suffering of tragic characters, Aristotle believed, results in the purgation of emotions, which for him was the true purpose of tragedy.

•

•

•

•

•

•

Rousseau believed the purpose of art was to provoke rather than soothe, to show an injustice and then reach an abrupt, unsatisfying ending.

usually may not rise from their seats at will or talk to their classmates.

Since children are too young to comprehend the why's behind the subjects they study, they must do a great deal of rote learning, which is Apollonian too. They must memorize the spelling and meaning of words as well as the multiplication tables. They must learn the capitals of every state and country and what crops are grown in the "black earth region."

Critics of excessive Apollonianism in education cite the fact that pupils become memorization machines at too early an age to defend themselves. After a time, pupils become exasperated with meaningless rote learning and start rebelling. The rebellious stage, say the critics, begins in the junior high school. It soon becomes obvious to the student that even though requirements are many, one need not shine in order to get by.

It also becomes obvious that as students "put out" less and less, the Apollonian demands, while still there, do not have to be taken seriously. Tests are made for cheating. The classroom has become so artificial, say the critics, that few teachers are able to convince students to apply themselves. The content of most classes is irrelevant to the student's own life.

The charge is also made that schools in Western society are dominated by a *white-*oriented Apollonian system. The value system of the dominant culture determines what is to be studied, and how. Grammar workbooks may ask the student to analyze sentences like the following:

> Mother and Jeff have gone to the shopping center to buy vinyl upholstery cleaner, and Jeff will polish the station wagon in the afternoon.
>
> After returning from a fourteen-day Caribbean cruise, Grandmother felt completely rejuvenated and no longer required the services of her psychiatrist.
>
> Father came home from the office looking very tired after a full day of business conferences and was in no mood whatever to learn that Eddie had been swimming in the deep end of the pool without permission.

Apollonian critics, on their part, charge that efforts to make the lower grades "relevant" usually end in disaster. They contend that changing grammar workbooks to make them

---

Montaigne

If this pupil happens to be of so wayward a disposition that he would rather listen to a fictitious tale than to the narrative of some fine voyager or a wise conversation . . . I see no other remedy but that his governor should . . . bind him prentice to a pastry-cook in some good town, though he were the son of a duke.

reflect a multi-ethnic social base does not motivate students to learn how to spell, write, and speak any more effectively than they did before. Often, they say, their hands are tied. The pressures are Dionysian rather than Apollonian. Parents are becoming less and less concerned, having already given up themselves. School administrators are afraid of having so many students fail that the newspapers will do an exposé; hence the better part of valor is to pretend that standards are important but let students get away with anything.

High Schools and Colleges

In the secondary schools and in institutions of higher learning, the Apollonian/Dionysian conflict becomes acute. High school teachers often inherit students who are barely literate but don't care, having become alienated from school long ago. The recourses are few:

Remedial programs with long hours of drill and rote learning, which are in their turn immediately rejected as dull and irrelevant.

Acceptance by teachers of the "facts of life," abandoning the classical educational ideals and taking the student "wherever he is."

Attempt to rekindle interest in school through innovative strategies like games and self-paced studies.

Sophocles

The ideal condition would be, I admit, that men should be right by instinct; but since we are all likely to go astray, the reasonable thing is to learn from those who can teach.

Those who cling to the Apollonian hope of raising the literacy of their students often sacrifice real interest in the subject in favor of having a "tight ship" in which the students perform decently on objective tests. Those who want to make education a profound and meaningful experience often sacrifice literacy and the student's ability to perform well on tests in favor of electricity in the classroom.

The degree to which a college leans toward Apollo or toward Dionysus depends upon the prestigiousness of the institution. The pillars of education—Ivy League colleges in the United States and the distinguished institutions of Europe and Latin America—are likely to be strongly Apollonian, requiring long hours of study and the passing of rigorous examinations. Colleges and universities of more recent vintage—especially the community college—are likely to be more experimental and allow for Dionysian exploration. At the same time, some teachers in these institutions, deeply feeling the stigma attached to an "upstart" college with no reputation, can become ruthlessly Apollonian in their damands: "I'll whip you into some kind of academic shape if it *kills* you!"

In schools given over to the free exercise of either Apollonian or Dionysian educational principles, understandable confusion reigns. Students come from a calculus class in which there is no room for personal expression to an experimental English class in which finger painting is an acceptable substitute for a theme and in which strict guidelines are often missing entirely. Some teachers within a given department acquire a reputation for being "tough" (hence Apollonian) while others are known for grading on a generous curve, accepting substitutions for last night's assignment, allowing students to steer a discussion away from the homework so that the teacher never finds out who was prepared and who was not. While a student might want to learn something substantial, the temptation to enroll in the Dionysian class may be irresistible because, since no clear objectives have been stated, most people receive high grades.

No easy solution presents itself. The Apollonian college with its traditions and high standards may be paying little attention to the real needs of the student as human being. The Dionysian teacher with a "like me, like me at all cost!" approach may be paying little attention to the real needs of a human being as student.

*Apollonian Rules
and Dionysian Feelings*

Theory is Apollonian; practice is Dionysian. The rules are Apollonian, whether for calculus, a bridge game, or living in organized society. Every classroom must have its rules of operation. Not even a Dionysian creative unfolding can take place in a totally disorganized atmosphere.

But the flow of life itself is Dionysian, as is the willingness to adapt to new and unfamiliar circumstances. Education must allow time for experimentation, exploration, and the discovery of possibilities that may lie dormant within the student.

A rigid objective test is Apollonian all the way, particularly when answers are either True or False. But a critical essay about a poem, a novel, or a painting is also Apollonian when the teacher insists that the writer actually deal with the work in question and not respond to it on a purely personal level.

Apollonian discussions relate to theme, color, use of language, historical effect, similarity in the works of two artists, growth from one period to another in the work of the same artist, the use of a particular technique of fiction, symbolism, and the influence of certain key events in an author's life on his work. Apollonian analysis is critically detached, objective, maintaining perspective at all times. It is fundamental to the Western tradition, which venerates rationality and clear-sightedness.

A teacher fails to fulfill students' needs when denying them the right to become objective and clear-sighted. If students are invited to express themselves freely at too early a stage in their growth, they are likely to have less and less to say. For expression to be full there must be a command of words and practice in putting one word after another in some kind of meaningful sequence.

Long, long ago humanity discovered the magic of words. Long, long ago humanity realized that the way to control things was to name them first and then to find more and more to say about them, to determine what was *possible* to say. And when children first become aware of the world about them, they are hungry for language; they can never have enough of it. Nor can they ever have their fill of cause and effect. "What makes it do that?" they ask continually, once having learned "its" name. Some say the basic human condition is Dionysian, but child observers will tell you there are mighty Apollonian "instincts" as well.

Feelings of pleasure and pain, joy and sorrow, which accompany human experiences, are just as important; the impulse to change springs as much from emotion as it does from reason. If you are to change and grow, you must stay in touch with your feelings.

In the Dionysian classroom, a picture is shown, music is played, or a story read. A typical Dionysian response from the student might be the creation of an original work of art, unhampered by rules or limitations of any kind. In a balanced classroom Dionysian responses may be invited, but within certain parameters set forth by the teacher.

Helen Keller

I knew then that 'w-a-t-e-r' meant the wonderful cool something that was flowing over my hand. That living word awakened my soul, gave it light, hope, joy, set it free!

> **Robert Browning**
>
> **The truth was felt by instinct here,—Process which saves a world of trouble and time.**

> **Coleb Gattegno**
>
> **Most of the things that are without importance to educators today, are the source of what is going to make us do a much better job in education.**

Out-of-control Dionysianism becomes a subjective free-for-all with tears, laughter, sounds of "ooh," "ah," and "yuck!", protests of discomfort, sneers of derision, shouts of praise and blame, all in answer to the Dionysian question, "How do you *feel?*" So long as the follow-up is on the level of feeling there can be no dispute. Passionately Dionysian teachers cannot then defend the value of an art work which has been admired for centuries, nor can they "pull rank" by announcing their own superior taste and experience. Dionysia is egalitarian. It would not do to ask for feelings and counter with the requirement of substantiated critical thought. One person's opinion is, after all, as good as another's.

No ideal of a human being could be less attractive then that of a coldly rational, unfeeling person, bent on schedules, deadlines, delivery dates, with no compassion or empathy for others. Therefore education which ignores feelings, which discourages any subjectivity on the student's part, may be helping to create an inflexible, one-tracked machine, not a warm-blooded human being who, although capable of making blunders, is also capable of growth because of having been allowed to err and to learn through making mistakes.

At the same time, educators of the Apollonian perspective point out, the Dionysian promise can be misleading and ultimately cruel. If students are granted excessive subjective license, if the statement, "Shakespeare has nothing to offer as far as I'm concerned," is allowed to stand unchallenged, students may be sent into the world unprepared for reality. For society never has been and never will be dominated by Dionysus. What does it profit a student to go through many years of school receiving high grades for undocumented, undefended opinions based on feelings, only to discover that in the Appolonian world such feelings are irrelevant to others?

But the truth of the matter probably is that the purely Dionysian teacher does not exist. Authority is authority when all is said and done, and often those teachers who claim to be facilitating student learning by keeping quiet have developed subtle tricks to bring about certain predetermined results. Not to share these techniques with students—allowing students to imagine that they are developing freely and according to their own true natures—can be fostering a very dangerous delusion.

There seems no genuine alternative but to provide students with both Apollonian and Dionysian approaches in the classroom. Such influences will thus enable and motivate students to take responsibility for what happens to them in higher education. The awareness that disciplined Apollonian approaches to learning are important for success in life should motivate the student to seek out the most demanding and challenging courses and teachers available. Yet as students meet these challenges, they will recognize the value of Dionysian warmth, good humor, and flexibility in their teachers. Students and teachers alike should recognize that the classroom need not imitate the world, but neither is the world going to be a very meaningful place without some principles to take into it.

Chapter 6 Footnote

[1] Frederich Nietzsche, *The Birth of Tragedy,* trans. Francis Golffing (Garden City, NY: Doubleday, 1956), p. 61.

7

THE MORALITY PUZZLE

Try to learn to love her. After all, she's in her last year at law school.
Advice from parent to son

The only security you have in life is the security you create for yourself.
Insurance company advertisement

We had to print the story. We don't make news, we just publish it.
News editor to parents of kidnapped child

I thought you ought to know, Sir. I know she gives the impression of being competent, but actually . . .
A fellow employee to boss

If I can afford it, I deserve it!
Self-made man showing visitor his estate

No, I don't want the promotion. I'll stay where I am.
Mailman

Listen, I've always admired that antique clock of yours. So since you

probably don't have much longer, remember me in your will, O.K.?
Visitor to hospital patient

Listen, we owe you another $2.49. The waitress forgot to write it on the check.
Restaurant patron to cashier

If it feels good, do it!
Popular moral precept

Overview

The statements beginning this chapter reflect moral beliefs. Whether openly stated ("Live and let live, that's all there is to it") or implied ("He didn't even have nerve enough to show up"), morality exists in every remark about the nature of good and evil.

Nor can morality be easily dismissed in a slogan. For instance, the restaurant patron quoted above, feeling virtuous for having paid more than he was charged, may claim that "honesty is the best policy" and yet behave less openly if there were greater amounts of money to tempt him. Like most of us, he has his code but probably his price as well. But also like most of us, he probably has not pinned either down in any consistent way. To do so would be to clarify values and to recognize their source in religion, songs, parental advice, peer pressure, and personal experience. We live surrounded by moral ideas, and it would be as arrogant to imagine that we had invented a code of ethics as to claim credit for having discovered the wheel. In morality, as in other aspects of human behavior, there is (almost) nothing new under the sun.

One of the enduring concerns of the humanities has been the issue of morality: more particularly, an investigation into the meanings of "moral," the justifications for needing to be "moral," and the expectations of "moral" behavior from others. Indeed morality remains one of the strongest items on the humanist's agenda.

The humanist defines moral value as the basis of making free choice between actions.

The humanist defines a moral value as *the basis of making a free choice between actions.* Perhaps not every choice of alternatives involves a moral issue, but it is hard to draw a line. Moral choices tend to be those in which the outcome of an action could bring about a significant change, a change for which the choice is responsible; most important, the chooser must have been able to do something else.

The classic example of moral choice is that of Abraham in the Old Testament. An angel brings the order from God that

Abraham must offer up his son Isaac in sacrifice. The point of the parable is that God wants to see what Abraham will do. It is fundamental that Abraham can choose to obey or disobey the order. Refraining from making the painful choice is the same as disobeying. The alternatives, then, are clear. Either way, a significant change will have taken place. If he obeys, he is without a son. If he disobeys, he is no longer God's faithful servant.

A moral value is therefore *the difference in price tags.* How much do I love God? How much do I love my son? God minus son equals what? Son minus God equals what?

Very probably morality comes down to:

The anguish of Abraham. "If he obeys, he is without a son. If he disobeys, he is no longer God's faithful servant."

recognizing price tags

ignoring price tags

switching price tags

being appalled by prices but paying them anyway

shoplifting

Moral shoplifting is probably more common than most people care to admit, especially when they themselves engage in it. It *may* be the most widespread approach to morality that exists, though few shoplifters are honest enough to identify themselves as such.

There are people who "cheat" on tests. This is a well known fact. The shoplifting issue concerns whether their actions can be called cheating and whether they regard themselves as cheaters. They are shoplifters if they acknowledge to themselves that cheating is what they are doing but are willing to—even delighted to—do it anyway.

Making a free choice between actions, the moral shoplifters in this case have decided to accept the rules of the test while breaking them in secret. They do not make up their own rules. They have acknowledged the rule forbidding cheating; they make no protest against it. They give no passionate speeches in defense of an alternative rule. They are perfectly conventional in outlook. But their actions contradict what their minds accept. To the humanist, they are pitifully absurd.

A moral shoplifter may even despise others for cheating. After all, they may cheat more successfully and receive even higher grades for it. Another moral shoplifter may be sentimental and share with others what has gleaned by deceitful methods. ("I stole a copy of the test, and here it is.") In this case, the shoplifter is operating within a time-honored tradition of thoughtfulness, even charity. But who would expect a thoughtful, charitable person to be deceitful as well? After all, if someone else announced that he had stolen a copy of the test and wished to share it with our first shoplifter and it turned out that the "friend" had willfully changed the questions around, would not our shoplifter be shocked, or incensed? He expects the friend to be "honest" about the accuracy of the questions he stole.

Humanism surveys the scene and is aware of much

confusion, much contrariness, an eminent lack of integrity in moral matters. *Moral integrity is consistency between the value and the action: I value this, and I do this.* Moral integrity does not hypocritically claim, I value *this,* but I do that; or I value this and want *you* to do it, but *I* do not have to.

The Ring of Gyges: The Sources of Values

The value scene is vast and complicated. It is best approached in terms of component parts—the pertinent elements. Moral values have been defined. The next step is to determine where they come from, because it is difficult not to be confused about your own set of values if you are not clear why you do certain things and avoid others.

Glaucon versus Socrates:
Reason as the Source

The Republic of Plato is one of the major works which embodies the belief that moral values are universal and unchanging and the appropriate action to take in any instance is always clear to a rational person. In Plato, "appropriate" means "virtuous," and "virtuous" means "rational." When faced with a choice, one selects the intelligent action, not necessarily the one which promotes one's own interest or is conducive to one's pleasure.

Although Plato does not use ordinary examples, the choice of that which is appropriate exists for all of us in daily, sometimes unnoticed, ways. The overweight person choosing between consuming or not consuming a rich dessert has the opportunity to act in either a rational or irrational way. Passing up the dessert is assuredly an act of virtue, because it is appropriate, intelligent. Reason shouts to the sky that overweight people harm themselves by indulging in fattening foods. True, the painful act of not eating dessert (when others may be doing so) ultimately benefits the sufferer, but in Plato the justification for the rational choice is *not* self-interest. That one profits from the virtuous act is superfluous. One chooses it for the sake of its virtue.

To cite another kind of example: the wealthy businessman

who could afford to drive a large, expensive, gas-burning car but chooses instead a very small, economy car is clearly benefiting society more than himself. In the very long run —when fuel supplies are nearly exhausted—he may be said to benefit; but in this instance the wisdom of conserving energy far supersedes any motives of personal profit.

The Republic is a series of dialogs between Socrates and various young men who enjoy discussing philosophical issues. The major subject of the dialogs is *justice,* by which Plato means the rational order of humanity, society, the universe.

Socrates, of course, was a real person, whom many consider to be the true father of philosophy. He died in 399 B.C., executed for what were considered crimes against the state: specifically, teaching atheism and therefore corrupting the young men of Athens. Plato was one of his ardent admirers and considered Socrates to have been the victim of a conspiracy to silence his clear-headedness and outspoken criticisms of the true corruption, which was the state itself.

After Socrates' death Plato embarked upon a series of writings, using the dialogue form, with the master himself as the principal spokesman. To what extent the dialogues represent Socrates' actual beliefs and how much are Plato's own thoughts will never be known. But it hardly matters. The dialogues, taken as a whole, are a treasury of philosophical analysis, dissecting every profound issue that humankind faces, including the nature of life, death, love, art, and of course, morality, the subject of *The Republic.*

Socrates is always on the side of reason. He believes implicitly that truth is universal, eternal, and accessible to the open mind of the just (or rational) person. When it comes to moral choices, there is never any question about which is the right, proper, and good choice.

Early in *The Republic* a debate arises over the reasons why people behave morally more often than not. Is it indeed for the sake of virtue, or for another reason?

Glaucon, the debater in this case, presents the argument that people are just because the laws require them to be so and because they fear possible punishments for breaking these laws. Doing wrong, he maintains, is far more basic to human nature; he contends it is even very pleasant. But because suffering at the hands of the wrongdoer is so *un-*

pleasant, there are laws which allow a compromise between doing wrong without being punished and suffering wrong without the power to retaliate. The person with the power to do wrong is held in check by these laws. If, however, all restrictions were suddenly removed, if the compromise balance were shattered, justice would disappear.

In the "Ring of Gyges" dialog, Glaucon maintains that people avoid committing wrongs for fear of being caught.

I shall maintain that it is always practised with reluctance, not as good in itself, but as a thing one cannot do without; and thirdly, that this reluctance is reasonable, because the life of injustice is much the better life of the two—so people say.[1]

To illustrate his point Glaucon tells the story of two men who possessed magic rings. Whoever wore them had the power to become invisible at will. One man, Gyges, a shepherd, was totally unjust; the other, totally just. Gyges used his power to take whatever he wanted without fear of being caught. He stole, raped, murdered—all with impunity. Above all, his invisibility protected his reputation, his good name in the community.

Glaucon maintains that the just man who discovered that he had godlike powers would do no better.

No one, it is commonly believed, would have such iron strength of mind as to stand fast in doing right or keep his hands off other men's goods, when he could go to the market-place and fearlessly help himself to anything he wanted, enter houses and sleep with any woman he chose, set prisoners free and kill men at his pleasure. . . . Surely this would be strong proof that men do right only under compulsion; no individual thinks of it as good for him personally, since he does wrong whenever he finds he has the power.[2]

Socrates believes that the good and just person behaves morally whether others know it or not.

To counter Socrates' argument that a just man values the just act for its own sake, Glaucon suggests that the just man is driven by the same motive as the unjust man, namely, his good name in the community. He scorns unjust actions allegedly out of respect for virtue, but if, Glaucon adds, everything were to be taken away from him *except* virtue; if he has a reputation for wrong-doing even though he has done no wrong, would he continue to find satisfaction in the exercise of virtue? Suppose he were thrown into prison for crimes of which he was innocent? Would his innocence comfort him then?

By the same token, Glaucon asks us to imagine the unjust man who nonetheless has the reputation of being just, who can go merrily along, reaping rewards because of his good name.

With his reputation for virtue, he will hold offices of state, ally himself by marriage to any family he many choose, become a partner in any business, and, having no scruples about being dishonest, turn all of these advantages to profit.[3]

Society does not even *expect* virtue to be anything more than an appearance. Society is content so long as the pay-off system, so to speak, is working, and man's fundamentally selfish, deceitful nature is not allowed to assert itself.

The issue is not, Glaucon concludes, whether justice is superior to injustice, or right superior to wrong. Everyone acknowledges the virtue of justice. The issue is whether the human capacity of reason is accountable for, the sanction, the justification, of moral behavior, or whether morality is the result of pressure brought to bear upon each of us by society.

Socrates is unwilling to accept Glaucon's pragmatic view. How could he? He himself was, in Plato's eyes, a martyr, a victim of society's own corruption. Society was simply an extension of the unjust man, but on a bureaucratic level— injustice institutionalized. In the ideal or just state, officiated by the philosopher-king, the supreme man of reason, the exercise of virtue is natural to rational persons as a matter of course. To argue that because society is corrupt, it is better to be corrupt oneself is absurd. The remainder of *The Republic* is devoted to an exhaustive, and for many, still unconvincing, analysis of the just state. Glaucon's view that the ultimate impetus of morality is a person's fear of losing his or her reputation (and we could add losing one's job, right to vote, and so on) remains very powerful and still requires consideration.

William Wordsworth

. . . that best portion of a
  good man's life,
His little, nameless,
  unremembered, acts
Of kindness and of love.

Morality and Self-Interest

Our society is filled with suggestions that we do good— not for the sake of goodness itself—but for practical reward. *Give to medical research,* we are urged; your family may be the next victim of this disease. *Give to charity,* so the helping hand will be there if you need it. *Give to education;* society and your children will benefit.

Even the slogan on a church marquee *Make yourself humble before God, and He will raise you up,* suggests that humility is not encouraged for its own sake but for that of some future gain, however spiritual it may be. Even philanthropy may be based on the premise that society will benefit, and since the philanthropist is a member of society, he is possibly helping himself. Help to "those less fortunate" includes centers for job training and low-cost child-care centers, sponsored not only to help those people in need but to prevent crime which may injure or otherwise inconvenience; hence, the gift is in a sense self-serving. Any fund-raiser knows that the anonymous giver is rare. Hospital wings are named after donors and their relatives. Public buildings of all kinds are bedecked with statues and plaques of visible gratitude to the generosity of the supposedly selfless donors. There may exist no way to avoid the accusation that all giving has its reward, for even the completely *anonymous* donor may give in order to benefit from her or his own sense of satisfaction.

And why not? If we accept the principle that the seeking of pleasure and the avoidance of pain motivate everything we do, then we are also accepting that self-satisfaction is a primary incentive for giving. Our society expects people to seek and claim rewards for generosity. The patron who makes possible an opera performance is rewarded with a full-page photograph in the program. Folklore is filled with models of admirable, heroic givers. From childhood on, we are taught to give and to receive—Robin Hood gave much of his booty to the deserving poor, who reciprocated by turning him into a legend.

Just as Plato's Glaucon argued that people are only interested in their *reputation* for goodness, not in goodness itself, a present-day Glaucon might argue that the generous insist upon *recognition* for all they do. Why do we remove price tags from gifts? Is it not, at least sometimes, in the hope that the recipient will suppose we have spent more than we actually did? Imagine someone's intentionally lowering the value on a price tag and keeping it on a gift to save the recipient from embarrassment! Imagine sending gifts only to people you dislike just to make *sure* no one will

---

Ernest Hemingway

What is moral is what you feel good after.

Our society expects and reinforces actions performed out of self-interest.

say thank you, just to *prove* that giving is its own reward!

The counter argument, that self-interest does not matter so long as others benefit from charitable actions, is surely valid, but when we examine the assumption behind it, what happens to the moral issue? If self-interest is an acceptable motivation for giving, may it not be taken as an acceptable motivation for a less praiseworthy action—say, stealing? At what point do we limit the use of self-interest or the degree to which self-interest may be invested? Socrates would assuredly insist that self-interest, for whatever reason, obscures the rational awareness of what is right and appropriate in a given situation.

If it is argued that, Socrates notwithstanding, people *are* self-centered and do nothing that does not profit them directly or indirectly, then the whole concept of abstract moral values—of rightness, wrongness, goodness, and badness—may have to be reconsidered and approached in a radically different light.

Or, so say some extreme doubters, it may have to be abandoned altogether in favor of a hard-boiled, pragmatic approach that says we need to enforce the rules of the game whether people like it or not.

And then, who does the enforcing? What stops *them* from playing their own game?

Religion

The legend of the Ring of Gyges is people-centered; it focuses on the reputation society grants the person who is able to do what he or she likes without blame. If the wearer of the ring had been a believer in the omniscient God of Jews, Moslems, and Christians, there would have been no invisibility, for all deeds would have been observed and judged by a deity from whom there is no hiding. Not Jonah in the depths of the sea, not the sinners of Sodom and Gomorrah, not even the long-suffering Job, who attempted to question the relationship between wrongdoing and punishment, could escape God's eye. God's knowledge and strength are all-pervasive.

The interpretation of sin was carried a step further in The Sermon on the Mount, with emphasis on thought as well as deeds:

> **Few donors to charitable causes remain anonymous; most seek recognition.**

Ye have heard that it was said by them of old time, Thou shalt not kill; and whosoever shall kill shall be in danger of the judgment. But I say unto you, That whosoever is angry with his brother without a cause shall be in danger of the judgment.
Matt. 5:20–21

The Golden Rule is difficult to practice with people who don't want the same things.

The moral view of life based on the religious belief in personal judgment makes for a profound difference in the way the believer chooses between alternatives. His or her knowledge of right and wrong is based on a written document, usually a holy book and a list of requirements (as in the Ten Commandments) which are partly obligations toward God and partly obligations toward other people. The rules have been interpreted and reinterpreted according to the emphasis of various religious sects; however, regardless of emphasis, it is clear that there are many opportunities to disobey each moral law, with penalties which may include an uneasy conscience, denunciation by fellow church members, prescribed penalties to achieve sanctity, and even possible eternal damnation.

Violation of the Sabbath, coveting the property of another person—these are among the many ways to violate religious laws, which may be quite separate from the criminal code of a community. For some religious observers, working or shopping on the Sabbath is forbidden, no matter what their neighbors may do. And there are, of course, rules for dressing and eating and observing festivals and waiting an appropriate length of time before remarriage.

Most religions have some version of the so-called Golden rule, which is surely a cornerstone moral principle. Whether it is stated, "That which is hateful to you, do not do unto others," or, "Do unto others as you would have them do unto you," the rule is difficult to practice with people who don't want the same things. People who belong to no formal religion may claim that their moral code is also based on some version of the Golden Rule. But that rule, like other rules, requires interpretation. It is easy enough to claim that in general one wants people to be kind. "I'll be kind to them, and they'll be kind to me." But one's notion of kindness may include unwanted offers of help and involvement in the life of a person who prefers privacy and solitude.

To the believer, every moment is tied in with faith. Nature provides constant reminders of God's teachings: the spider

*If at critical times man's inhumanity to man seemed to gain
ascendency, there has always been a Hillel, a Francis of Assisi, a
Pasteur, a Nightingale to remind us that the chief intimation of our
immortality is our unique human power for loving our fellow man.*
Joshua Loth Liebman

spinning a web suggests the lesson that every soul may be ensnared by evil; light coming through the shadows may be interpreted as the mixture of good and evil in which we all live; dawn after darkness may be the promise of redemption after despair. For those imbued with a sense of God's watchful eye, religion permeates every action: choice of food, frequent prayer, choice of vocation, times to travel, names of children, which direction to face, or where to build a house. Adherence to daily prescribed religious practice has been a source of comfort, purpose, and identity for many believers.

For some, however, religious belief has meant a vague, uneasy sense of guilt for possible wrong action or thought. The violation of a belief practiced in childhood but abandoned as an adult may call for visits to a psychotherapist to purge the recurring sense of wrongdoing which remains after the solace of religious faith has vanished.

Religion as remnant can consist of the wearing of a jeweled insignia, the lighting of a candle in memory of an ancestor, or a superstitious saying like, "Don't talk about something you hope will happen until you know it's certain." Even otherwise civilized members of developed societies invoke superstitions in the effort to explain or control events, a continuing tribute to the memory of an earlier time when belief in a supreme power infused every waking moment of the entire populace.

The Public Moral Conscience

Truly devout believers, perceiving a daily struggle with Satan, often take it as their responsibility to assist others along the path of righteousness. Early Puritan church leaders rudely awakened those who slept during long church services. Even the Salem witch trials ostensibly had salvation as the underlying justification for persecuting and then hanging those found guilty of traffic with Satan.

The Puritans lived in tight communities. Everyone knew everyone else's business. Puritan morality instantly became the community morality. In the witch hunts the Puritans were linking themselves to an ancient tradition, stretching back long before the Judeo-Christian era—a tradition in which the community possessed one mind when it came to right and wrong. Evil-doers had to be driven out, or else the entire community would suffer the vengeance of some deity.

In modern communities some of the same tradition survives. Certainly we note lingering reminders of the Puritan public moral conscience in the continual advice people give to others on how to live their lives and how to raise their children. Whether conscious of it or not, the advice-givers serve as guardians of the dominant, mainstream morality, which has had both religious and communal sanctions for so long that no one dreams of questioning it. Instant guilt often accrues to the parent who is told by a neighbor: "Far be it from me to tell you what to do about your own children, but if that were *my* daughter, I'd want to know who she's with until all hours of the night."

If such moral advice is acceptable to those who receive it, if it does indeed create guilt, then the public conscience is not necessarily a bad thing or an invasion of privacy. Some parents probably do *not* know what to do with their children. Often the children themselves sense the confusion of their parents and secretly wish *someone* would exert strong moral authority over them. The public conscience, which exists in every community in the world, acts as a check upon flagrantly antisocial behavior.

On the other hand, the institution of the public conscience is notoriously conservative, updates itself very slowly, and can leave untold damage in its wake. A magazine article printed in the Victorian England of a hundred years ago had this comment: "Poverty and misery, be it remembered, are more generally the results of vice, laziness, and improvidence, than of misfortune." A century later it would not be surprising to find many people staunchly agreeing that welfare recipients are lazy good-for-nothings and that, if the unemployed really wanted to work, there would be no unemployment.

People often believe in what is convenient, and it is often highly convenient to use the public moral conscience as a mask for self-interest, as reinforcement for the way one has chosen to view things.

It is also possible to use that conscience as a smokescreen to divert attention from oneself. Morality is all too frequently what other people do wrong. People form tight communities not always in the name of a true moral tradition, but to gain strength by banding together against the novel, the original, the unorthodox. As long as there is enough questionable behavior around, the finger-pointers need not be accountable for their own.

In such circumstances, public morality is a means whereby an insecure individual may find safety in numbers. During the nineteenth century the great libertarian philosopher John Stuart Mill wrote a famous essay called "The Tyranny of the Majority" in which he said that the:

> *object of this essay is to assert one very simple principle, as entitled to govern absolutely the dealings of society with the individual in the way of compulsion and control, whether the means used be physical force in the form of legal penalties, or the moral coercion of public opinion. That principle is, that the sole end for which mankind are warranted, individually or collectively, in interfering with the liberty of action of any of their number, is self-protection. That the only purpose for which power can be rightfully exercised over any member of a civilized community, against his will, is to prevent harm to others. His own good, either physical or moral, is not a sufficient warrant . . .*

Though Mill's intentions are clear enough, the sensitive question still arises: who decides what constitutes or truly threatens the "self-protection" of the majority? And who decides what methods of this so-called protection are justified? For some, no doubt, such things as cross-burnings and even more outward shows of violence are nothing more than a "decent community's" attempt to preserve its standards.

Childhood

An awareness of right and wrong begins for most of us in childhood, with the acclaim or disapproval of the parents who observe our actions. In the earliest years, comments directed toward the child are almost always moral, are matters of "yes" and "no." There is praise for learning to drink from a cup or climbing stairs without help, and anger for touching hot stoves, having biological accidents, or crossing the street. Originally childhood morality centers on survival. Later on it branches out and becomes the socialization process.

Disgust may greet a child who breaks things, gets dirty, refuses to share a toy. Almost invariably, parental disapproval comes to equal "bad," perhaps for a lifetime. Being required to kiss grandparents, whether one wants to or not, teaches family attitudes toward the elderly and puts a restraint on preoccupation with self.

Among the rules learned are some not directly pointed out to the child. Children observe and listen to adults fighting with and praising each other, and discussing the behavior of other people. From these observations come many of the automatic assumptions of later life, the rules for what are regarded as courtesy, order, or concern for the opinion of others. The child who often hears, "What will the neighbors say?" may for the rest of his or her life find it difficult to get over the feeling that someone is watching and that somehow apologies are always in order.

Transactional Analysis, a popular form of therapy, holds that disturbed, problematic, human relationships are the result of childhood moral conditioning. The proponents of the theory say each of us begins as a "child," but gradually acquires the identity of the "parent" as well. The real parent's constant moral evaluation of everything one does is transferred to the inner self, which acts as the scolding voice of conscience. Finally, a mature "adult" struggles to emerge—the self which is activated by objectivity and reason. A three-way conflict ensues. All too often the "parent" holds the "adult" back, and the essentially amoral "child" tries to manipulate both the "parent" and the "adult."

Difficulties between people arise when the parent in one personality evokes the child in another, or when the adult in a person is countered by either the parent or the child in another. An office worker, for example, is convinced that the boss has organized the place inefficiently and that adhering to the boss's regulations will only waste money and delay production. He decides to do things his way, but in secret. His methods prove to be very successful. Soon his co-workers are following his example.

The boss notices signs of increased productivity. He is at first pleased, then decides to inquire into the reason. When he learns the secret, he is at first defensive with himself. The parent in him scolds the child for having to be shown up in such a way. The child pouts and then throws a tantrum. The efficient worker acquires the character of the goody-goody brother or sister, who is always praised, while he, the child, is always blamed. Instead of warmly appreciating the efficiency, the boss upbraids the rebellious worker in no uncertain manner: that is, he becomes the parent and forces the worker to become his own child in defense.

Transactional Analysis maintains that successful relationships can exist only between two adults, two persons in full command of their mature value systems. But the numbers of people who have visited the TA Institute in California indicate the degree to which childhood training remains dominant in the lives of grown-ups trying desperately to be precisely that.

"Of Course"

Parental moral authority is sharp, direct, and to the point. No one ever doubts where she or he stands with respect to it. Woe to the rebellious child who insists on knowing the source of that authority. Often a sharp blow is the stinging reminder that the authority is over five feet tall and has very large eyes—and hands. If parental morality is seldom to be questioned, it is at the same time unconfused and never obscure.

In school the teacher becomes the authority figure, and sometimes (though not legally in some states) the reminders can be just as stinging. Gradually, however, another form of authoritarianism takes the place of that found in the home. It is more subtle, pervasive, and harder to pin down. It grows in intensity through the school years. Frequently it assumes the guise of statements prefixed by "Of course."

> Of course you heard the assignment.
> Of course you're prepared for the test.
> Of course our country is the best.
> Of course you'll work to earn a living.

Even less obvious than "of course" are such things as classroom design. How about this one? Big leader in front

---

Transactional Analysis shows our values to be molded by the continual battle for supremacy among the Child, Parent, and Adult in all of us.

Make a list of value statements beginning with "of course," and you learn a lot about your basic moral assumptions.

of room watching little people in back? How about being asked to join the group in the corner, only to note that they are doing nothing while the evidently favored group is reading front of teacher's approving smile?

Sex role stereotypes are formed during these years as well. Terms of derision greet unfamiliar or unacceptable behavior, and these are variations of "Of course. . . ." The way one dresses, the companions one keeps, the sports one plays are all influenced by the approved male/female labels. During these years one learns what it means to walk a different, lonely path.

Work

In most capitalist societies that which produces a good, secure income with solid benefits has been traditionally right; that which leads to unearned money or produces income through shady dealings (gambling, escort services, soft-core crime) is technically wrong, though people sometimes experience moral confusion over it, finding themselves inwardly envious of material benefits obtained too easily. On the surface, at any rate, ours is a work-approving, leisure-scorning society.

There was a time, when hard work was a dignified activity for a man, while being industrious around the home was good for a woman. Now the work ethic has been extended to women as well, and the American success story contains both heroes and heroines.

It is still considered a virtue to have started out in life with almost nothing and to have climbed the ladder "rung by rung." Still on the "disapproved" list are:

marrying the boss's son or daughter

hiring an inexperienced college graduate and paying him more than an old hand

getting by on looks rather than ability

being supervised at one's job by somebody hired from "outside"

In noncapitalist societies an effort has been made to impose a collective morality, and for decades the results have been controversial. To be sure, the novels, plays, and films of such societies frequently try to persuade citizens that work per se is a virtue and wallowing in material benefits is bad, especially when these derive from the exploitation of others. Much evidence exists to indicate that the propaganda doesn't always work. Collective farming continues along its unsteady course in the Soviet Union, but it has been an abject failure in satellite nations like Poland. The Polish farmer has declared in no uncertain terms that he will till the soil diligently for himself and his family, but not so diligently if the fruits of his labor are snatched away.

It was one of Karl Marx's main contentions that the exploited worker was losing contact with the products of his hands, but it is not clear that the collective system has done much to improve this situation. In capitalist countries workers have probably grown accustomed to bringing home nothing but their paychecks, but craftsmanship, associated with high-grade carpentry work, and custom furniture making, is still a virtue.

People who are good with their hands tend to be admired: people who improve their homes by building things themselves, who do their own landscaping and cooking, and who make their own clothes. At the same time, since ours is so clearly a money-oriented society as well, no one is offended by those who can afford to have things done *for* them, so long as the money originally came from the sweat of their brow.

As the life span lengthens and retired people are often able to lead vigorous lives for many years after they leave their jobs, the notion of "work" has been broadened to include all sorts of activities: hunting, fishing, shuffleboard, card-playing, traveling, even entertaining. Retired people often hasten to tell you that they "don't just sit around all day watching TV," but are extremely "active." The extension of the work ethic into retirement years has become almost obsessive. Innumerable articles have been written on the "problems of senior citizens," who insist they are still able to work but are often treated as people who shouldn't have to.

It is rare to find someone of working age talking fondly of retirement and "being able to do nothing." The majority think of retirement with terror. That mandatory retirement at 65 is now a thing of the past must be taken as a triumph of persistent political campaigning by the older members of society.

Whether one should be allowed to work beyond 65 is not

> Oscar Wilde
>
> **Work is the refuge of people who have nothing better to do.**

the issue here. We are talking about the assumption that useful employment, with remuneration, carries a highly positive moral value. Long before reaching 65, many people find themselves going to pieces when faced with large blocks of unfilled time. People who have never known what it is to not own a television set sometimes have difficulty imagining a time when the family "just sat there," listening to the radio. And the very idea of sitting perfectly still and becoming friends with oneself would strike many as absurd.

Work and living have become more and more pointless and empty.
. . . Our working days are used up in work that lacks meaning:
making useless or harmful products, or servicing the bureaucratic
structures.

Charles Reich

Nonetheless, the conditions of the future must be faced. We may be approaching a time when values must change. There may not be enough jobs to go around. The number of working days each week may radically diminish. People may live longer and longer. Excessive leisure can become a serious problem, indeed a national moral evil, unless people begin *now* to develop the flexibility to entertain alternatives to work-as-the-highest-good.

One reason for the prestige of work may be that it is preferable to thought. Since many regard thinking as difficult, it is a simple matter to label it as undesirable. When young people are asked about the future, the question invariably takes the form of, "What are you going to do?" Even "What are you going to be?" is asking for information about how the person intends to earn his or her livelihood. An answer of "happy" or "satisfied" to the latter question would be confusing to the questioner.

Loyalty to one's trade or profession is also considered morally good. Two strangers, meeting in a bar or on a plane and discovering that both are in "the same line," will automatically warm to each other. The trade identification can obscure many traits in people which might otherwise incur criticism. During the painful times of labor strikes, when violence often erupts, it is difficult to imagine a union member sharply upbraiding another member for taking part in a riot. Similarly, one who is willing to work on a non-union

Ernest Hemingway

Retirement is the ugliest word in the language.

scale, especially during a strike, can be considered evil incarnate.

Though management and labor are historically on opposite sides of the fence, loyalty to the organization is in some cases a virtue. When there is no strike or other kind of dispute, the average worker often feels as much pride toward the company for which she or he works as, say, the average football fan feels toward "his" team. Posters, memoranda, and company after-dinner speeches stress the team spirit. As in sports, the world of work has its we/they split.

In smaller companies the family model persists. And why shouldn't it? People spend the better part of their lives not in the houses they struggle to pay for, but in the offices or on the assembly lines in which they work. When management and labor remain relatively stable within a given company over a period of years, a parent/children relationship inevitably develops. Christmas bonuses and other testimonies of appreciation are all part of the work morality. And maybe running off to a rival company for only slightly higher pay is high on the list of immoral actions.

On the other hand, when the organization is very large, and the management is comprised merely of names, often not fully known or familiar to the lowly worker, a different value system usually prevails. For one thing, the well-known conspiracy theorists run rampant, claiming "they" are up there, plotting ways of doing workers out of their rightful benefits. "They" only care about themselves.

What's more, "they" are undoubtedly dishonest, otherwise "they" would not have so much power and so much money. Therefore, it is entirely ethical to cheat on "them." Arriving late, taking lengthy coffee breaks and lunch hours, doing as little as possible whenever one can—such behavior is condoned and encouraged. In large department or grocery stores, employee shoplifting is taken for granted. Employees do it, management expects it, and company losses are passed on to the consumer.

What should be said about the federal government as an organization and the ethics of dealing with it? Income-tax time often represents a most enjoyable matching of wits: the taxpayer versus "the system." There is seldom any thought given to the numbers of poor and unemployed who benefit from tax money. Emphasis at this time of year is always on government waste and political corruption, and "whatever you can get away with serves them right!" By the same token, the efforts of the taxpayer to cheat the system are recognized and not unduly frowned upon, unless the fraud amounts to many thousands of dollars. People who are audited by the IRS are always treated cordially, no matter what embarrassing "mistakes" are uncovered.

During the late 1960s, young people tended either to refuse to enter the system at all or to "put up with it" as a necessary evil, a means of earning "bread." Traditional canons of ethical behavior with respect to work proved unacceptable to vast numbers. But many of the leaders of the rebellion have since entered the world of business; some are doing very well and no doubt own large suburban homes. Some have gone into management, still imbued with the humane ideals of the rebellion and are attempting to make labor/management relations as open and honest as possible. Others, one might assume, have been willing to settle for much less.

Morality in Action

The Secular Zealot

Zealots are moralists who feel so comfortably assured of having a strong moral code of their own which can be adhered to with no trouble, that they turn their efforts and direct their energies toward improving the moral scene around them. Religious zealots believe that members of other sects, as well as nonbelievers, will be much happier if they change their own value system and adopt theirs. In Christianity this is often referred to as "missionary zeal," and indeed the conversion of non-Christians is a crucial element of the Christian way of life.

But there exists a kind of human being to whom the label *secular zealot* must be applied. This is a person who sees so clearly what other people must do and the values they must hold that he or she is driven by a similar missionary spirit. To the secular zealot morality is never a private matter. It is always *what needs to prevail if the world is to be saved.* She or he is the crusader *par excellence;* and, while the zealot and his or her fellow zealots can do much good for society, they can

Chinese Proverb

Do not use a hatchet to remove a fly from your friend's forehead.

easily go to extremes and become single-minded and obsessed with particular causes.

The secular zealot sees public issues as manifestations of the need for reform, based on the principles of a nontheological discipline, usually derived from the social sciences. Zealots are a passionate believers, often single-mindedly devoted to a cause deemed vital to the welfare of many people; hence the activities of zealots usually involve laws, attitudes, and behavior outside themselves.

Causes espoused by secular zealots vary from one decade to the next, as current events change. But there is often a belief underlying proposed changes which 1) is formulated without specific examples; 2) always includes the words *should* or *ought;* and 3) is based on a secular authority such as a survey or study of social conditions, or the opinions of a prominent newscaster or journalist.

In recent years, causes have included the following:

vegetarianism

conservation of wild animals, fresh air, water, forest

reduction of military weapons

more equitable distribution of wealth

prison reform

abolition (or reinstatement) of capital punishment

redefinition of mental illness

consumer protection

equality for ethnic and minority groups

changes in attitudes toward sex roles

revision of laws concerning drug use

censorship of books, films, television programs

abolition of (or encouragement of) public prayer

support for pluralism (and universalism)

raising (or lowering) standards for schools, the arts, professions

encouraging (or opposing) the traditional family

allowing euthanasia, variously defined

making abortion easier (or more difficult)

encouraging (discouraging) heterosexuality as the norm

The causes most likely to attract the secular zealot are those which involve a state of affairs which seems to be personally injurious and are presumed injurious to others as well. The zealot is passionately concerned about clashing freedoms—situations in which one right (such as that of the smoker to smoke wherever he or she likes) infringes upon another right (such as that of the nonsmoker to breathe nondangerous air).

The freedom of businesspersons is infringed upon by consumer advocates. The school subject made mandatory in response to one pressure group displaces a subject another group believes to be equally as important. A change in laws affecting the status of women—for instance, offering equal opportunity in sports for girls—affects the amount of money available for the group previously in control. And, of course, the creation of shows for family TV programming is an affront to viewers who want quality entertainment.

The zealot is notorious for taking on powerful opponents, and for this reason is often frustrated. The sign on the bakery window reads THANK YOU FOR NOT SMOKING. The zealot, pleased, waits his turn at the counter and becomes aware that someone is smoking. He raises a loud protest, demands that the smoker leave, and when the latter refuses, urges the other customers to assist him in a citizen's arrest. They decline, embarrassed, and pretend that they do not notice the smoker. Even the manager of the shop wishes the zealot would go. He is bad for business.

Zealots sometimes become bitter and pessimistic. They often take no comfort in their own concern for the environment, endangered species, and boycotting packaged foods with chemical additives. At other times they may take arms and charge ahead, using any method at hand, whether realistic or not, and consequently often overshoot the mark.

If, for example, one is committed to a healthy diet, one chooses groceries carefully, ignoring those items which threaten human health. Yet does that commitment include a march on the school board in an effort to change food selections in the school cafeteria? Even if one argues that poor nutrition leads to illness, which leads to a run on hospitals, including charity wards, which leads to a drain on the taxpayer, can one individual or one group hope to control the long-range effects of everything? The secular zealot readily accepts the charge of being his brother's keeper.

The previous example was based on a cause involving health. Other causes are even less saleable to the majority.

Junius

There is a wholly mistaken zeal in politics as well as in religion. By persuading others we continue ourselves.

In the London *Public Advertiser,* 1769.

Protection of national forests, of wild animals, even of micro-organisms have been espoused by environmentalists, some of whom are motivated by a desire to have available for themselves and future generations places untouched by the building developer. Others may take a more mystical, less pragmatic, view: if a creature exists now as part of nature, humanity should encourage its continued existence rather than destroy it, whether or not it seems to serve any immediate or eventual purpose. The secular zealot has linked hands with like-minded believers to prevent the building of nuclear plants or cutting down of trees which have taken centuries to grow.

Another species of secular zealot is the person with a highly developed esthetic sense who lives in a society which honors popular ratings as a sign of excellence. The elitist (so-called because he or she likes works of art not enjoyed by the majority) may wish to subscribe to a season of concerts which includes musical compositions not often played. To sit in a well designed hall and listen to a major chamber or symphonic group playing brilliantly is high-priority pleasure for that zealot. If in a position to help choose a program for a partially subsidized concert season, the zealot may assume an obligation to provide lesser known works, scorning the familiar program of Tchaikowsky's 1812 Overture, Beethoven's 5th Symphony, or Schubert's "Trout" Quintet as part of a "duty" to the general public. And if a reviewer of music for a metropolitan newspaper, the elitist zealot may use as criteria the ideal performances he or she has witnessed, criticizing local concerts for flaws which would be recognized only by fellow music-lovers who share similar knowledge and taste.

The zealot committed to democracy in every phase of life may well answer that there is no real choice: *Vox populi, vox dei*—the voice of the people is the voice of God. But the elitist zealot may respond that democratic esthetic and intellectual standards have debased the general cultural level without really doing anything for the people (who are largely ignorant of cultural opportunities anyway). The conflict brings charges and counter-charges, and often ends up damaging the self-esteem of people who have the right to believe their lives do not need forced enrichment.

Secular zealots are usually careful with their money, and like the oldest and wisest of the Three Little Pigs, patiently build with bricks while the imprudent are out playing around. Observing that an economically unstable friend has involved himself in a loan he will never be able to repay, the zealot knows his friend is in danger of losing his house, car, or boat unless *someone* helps him to budget his money. The secular zealot will be the one to look out for others and to say, "I told you so." He believes the compulsive spender needs help as much as the alcoholic does, and that the compulsive eater must be constantly watched to prevent the consumption of fudge and eclairs.

An anti-zealot view holds that the remedy is worse than the disease. "Over his own body and mind, the individual is sovereign," said Mill. Dr. Thomas Szasz, a psychiatrist, carries the principle a step further, urging would-be do-gooders to stop interfering with the rights of individuals to do whatever they like. In a society run according to Szasz' beliefs, no one would be prevented from using drugs of any kind or even from committing suicide. No one, according to the psychiatrist, has a right to ascribe labels of "insane" or "undesirable" to behavior which happens to be different.

Secular zealots are sometimes caught in a paradox. The demand for individual freedom is often one of their most sacred causes. At the same time they are very likely to press for legislation which will limit freedom for the good of all. Driving big cars, smoking, the decision to have children— these matters they believe can no longer be left to individual discretion as they obviously do affect others, just as the homeowner who burns a rubber tire on his front lawn cannot expect to confine the resulting odor to "his" air.

"Nonsense!" respond the opponents, invoking "the common experience of mankind" as proof that curing one set of ills through restrictive legislation will only lead to further problems, with tyranny the inevitable result.

The moderate citizen who has no strong opinions may urge zealots to reach some sort of compromise. In the struggle between environmentalists and developers, cut down some trees, he says, and save some. But it is impossible, answers the zealot, to be only a little bit pregnant: some issues do not lend themselves to compromise. The worker contaminated from poisons in products he handles may not know for many years that he has contracted a deadly disease as a result. It is small comfort to know that while the statis-

Saul D. Alinsky

The American radical will fight privilege and power, whether it be inherited or acquired by any small group, whether it be political or financial or organized creed.

tics point to special danger for workers in one industry, many others are spared.

Sometimes a "remedy" may be set forth, but found too extreme for general acceptance. Nonetheless zealots have a way of pressing on. They point to "evidence" that children brought up by enlightened families have higher I.Q.'s than they would have had with their natural but less intelligent parents (or parent). They believe such children should be taken away from unpromising environments.

There is no end of debates. Sterilization of the mentally defective? Protective custody for conspirators? Greater supervision for those with a criminal record? This zealot says the threat to society is greater than the threat to individual freedoms. Other zealots attest to greater faith in the human potential.

The humanist generally prefers not to be a zealot, though occasionally acknowledging a cause which seems to warrant impassioned devotion. Humanists, alarmed at the prospect of upholding all principles at the expense of what appears to be common sense, would prefer causes that need not be approached as though civilization were at stake. They prefer to take life at a less frantic pace so that they need not impose their chosen moral codes upon others.

Two dramas, one old and one new, deal with the zealot's obsession with being honest whatever the price. In the seventeenth century, the French playwright Molière wrote *The Misanthrope,* a play about a man who insisted on telling the truth to everyone. Asked his opinion of a poem written by a friend, he told the truth: it was terrible. Losing the friend was only the beginning of his troubles. By the end of the play, he had also lost the woman he loved. As a result he became a man who found no pleasure in human society, the misanthrope depicted in the play's title. Molière apparently believed that certain human traits will remain unchanged and must be tolerated.

Some years ago, a movie made the same question more current. As an aftermath of a weekend marathon at Esalen Institute, a married couple began telling the truth about everything to friends and to each other. Honest self-expression was to be honored above all other qualities. When the husband returned unexpectedly from a business trip to find his bedroom door closed, the wife appeared and calmly announced (she didn't confess) that she was having an affair with her tennis coach. The husband stifled any traditional feelings of jealousy he might once have had; after all, he was now living according to different rules. He didn't own his wife. "Adultery" was an old-fashioned word. The only modern commandment was "Thou shalt be true to thine own feelings." But the audience suspected that such extreme honesty was not going to work indefinitely. At the end of the film monogamy prevailed. Switching partners with another married couple turned out to be more awkward and embarrassing than honest.

Whether the issue is marital reform, the prevention of government-subsidized abortions, or a ban on television commercials for children, the batting average of the secular zealot varies. Some zealots point with pride to the fact that women may now keep their maiden names after marriage and unmarried couples may jointly buy property or maintain joint checking accounts. They remind us that equal pay for women was once unheard of and might still not exist but for their tireless efforts. Black activists insist—and with good reason—that equal opportunity and housing legislation would not have come about but for their vehement protests, marches, and sit-ins.

The effect of the zealot on the public moral conscience cannot be measured, but it has surely been profound. Many may still secretly oppose the integration of neighborhoods or the busing of children, but more and more people are keeping their opinions to themselves. "Adult" movie houses and book shops may legally remain open in some areas, but the majority—whatever their secret desires may be—would not dream of patronizing them and openly defying the efforts of some zealots to shut such places down. The zealot, though perhaps only a self-appointed moral guardian, does influence the course of morality far more than can the philosopher whose thoughts are confined to professional journals.

The Lifeboat: Morality is Determined by Situation

The coin of morality can be flipped over and looked upon in a different way. The morality of Socrates, summed up in his contention that a basically good person would never abuse the power of Gyges' ring, rests upon the belief that moral values are eternal and unchanging *no matter what situa-*

tion develops. In our time, however, a brand new kind of moralist has come forth, the *situationalist,* who says that moral choice depends upon circumstances, motivation, consequences, and the numbers of people who can benefit or be harmed by a particular choice.

> The situationalist says that moral choice depends upon circumstances, motivations, consequences, and the numbers of people who can benefit or be harmed.

There is a famous legal case involving the aftermath of the sinking of a great ocean liner. A high-ranking ship's officer found himself on a lifeboat, which could accommodate no more than 25 persons. Amid the panic and desperation many more than 25 people attempted to climb on board. The officer instructed several crew members to throw them into the sea to insure the survival of those already on the life boat. In a few instances those who resisted were shot. Later the officer was tried for murder, found guilty, but subsequently pardoned. The case attracted widespread attention. Some observers pointed out that the issue was not whether the murders were justified, but whether the method of selecting those who remained on the lifeboat was fair. The officer, as a matter of fact, had tried to restrict the deaths to men only, but the suggestion was made that straws should have been drawn for the "honor" of leaving the lifeboat.

In another famous case, two men and a young boy were marooned at sea on a life raft. Recognizing that the child was clearly weakened and near death, the men decided to end his life so that he could be eaten and thus insure *their* survival. They too were found guilty, but pardoned.

The situationalist is fond of citing such cases, for they are the stuff of which real life is made. Can one say that murder is always wrong? Or that cannibalism is never justified under any circumstances? Does the need to survive take precedence over any other need?

What of the man whose wife was ill with cancer and in great pain, who had exhausted almost all of his funds and could no longer afford the price of a certain drug the wife needed in order to ease her pain? What of the additional fact that the druggist, knowing her need, decided to take advantage of the situation and charge an exorbitant amount for the medication? Suppose the desperate husband broke into the store and stole the drug. Suppose he were caught in the act, arrested, and brought to trial. Ought the judge to take his motivation into account? The unfairness of the price? Or is stealing, stealing?

The situationalist knows that decisions of this sort are not easy. To say that murder or stealing in one instance is not the same as murder or stealing in another gives to the judge an awesome responsibility. Yet to argue the reverse—that murder and stealing are never justified and are never to be condoned—can lead to miscarriages of justice.

The advantage of situationalism, say its spokespeople, is that each problem is examined on its own merits and not in terms of an abstract moral code devised long ago to fit a very different world. The disadvantages, say its critics, are that situations can be interpreted to someone's private advantage and that unfortunate precedents are always being created. If it was morally permissible for the two men to eat the young boy, what would prevent some future survivors on a raft from taking a life long before it was clear that that life was nearly over?

The Lifeboat:
How the Existentialist Views Morality

During the last century a Danish philosopher named Soren Kierkegaard acquired the rare distinction of being the founder of a new school of thought. Called by him *existentialism,* the new philosophy was really not a philosophy in the traditional sense of the word, for it held that existence could be comprehended only through the concrete realities of living it, not in terms of abstract intellectual concepts. It held that human reason was incapable of discovering, with absolute certainty, a vast cosmic scheme and that consequently reality must always be a subjective matter.

Kierkegaard began as a pious Christian, went through phases of agonizing doubt and feelings of abandonment, and finally reaffirmed his Christianity on radically new grounds. To Kierkegaard religion was a psychological need, not a philosophical truth, and had to be dealt with on that level. It was when one reached the point of absolute despair and felt ready to turn to God, one could take a "leap of faith." One chose the path of faith because one wished to, not because the choice could be intellectually justified.

In that leap, however, lay undeniable anxieties. The leap had to be made over many counter arguments, especially scientific evidence which seriously questioned religious beliefs. On one's knees in the darkness of the church, one might feel one's prayers soaring heavenwards and have an almost mystic sense of union with God; but one could not

> **Existential morality grows out of the concrete realities of living, not abstract concepts.**

know for sure that God was listening—or was even there at all. To have *faith* in the existential (that is, to have faith in the concrete existence of something, even something cosmic, such as God) meant exactly that; it did not mean to know, to be sure; it meant to *believe without knowing.*

To dramatize the existential plight of the believer, Kierkegaard recounted the Biblical tale of Abraham and Isaac. An angel appears to Abraham and tells him God demands the sacrifice of his son Isaac. Abraham is no doubt appalled, but what can he do? If God wants the sacrifice and if he is God's servant, he must obey. But in that leap of faith, in that raising of the knife, must not Abraham experience unutterable anguish? Faith is faith, but Isaac is also Isaac. And suppose the angel was not really from God— what then? This anguish of Abraham represented for Kierkegaard the very heart of the existential dilemma of humankind.

Conversely, a good man—one who does the right thing most of the time—may not be a responsible man, if he is uncritical about his own grounds of action and insensitive to possibilities which surround him. How then does he act rightly, in the complex and subtle affairs of moral life, if he does not know what he is doing?
Stephen David Ross

Contemporary existentialism has developed since World War II. The tradition begun by Kierkegaard is usually referred to as Christian existentialism, and it has its supporters. But the most influential strain of existential thought is undoubtedly that associated with the French philosophers Jean-Paul Sartre, Albert Camus, and Simone de Beauvoir, all of whom represent an atheistic approach. Existence, they say, is absurd in that it cannot be shown to serve any purpose. Species simply are whatever they are, *including* humanity. Species serve no purpose either. Since God cannot be shown to exist, there can be no such thing as a divine master plan for humanity, no such thing as humanity's basic "nature."

If humankind has no mission, has nothing to prove worthy of, has no sins to atone for and no paradise to attain someday, the brutal fact must be faced that each of us is alone in an absurd situation. None of us makes any sense to begin with.

Who can go on living with such an idea? Once one recognizes the fundamental absurdity of one's existence, one also recognizes the basic premise of existentialism: each person is completely free to define himself as he wishes, free to create his own reason for being.

> *If man, as the existentialist conceives him, is indefinable, it is because at first he is nothing. Only afterward will he be something, and he himself will have made what he will be. Thus, there is no human nature, since there is no God to conceive it. Not only is man what he conceives himself to be, but he is also what he wills himself to be after this thrust toward existence.*[4]

A person, says Sartre, has two and only two choices. One may accept the existential challenge, defining one's own nature, creating one's own identity, and *taking responsibility for it;* or else one may decline the challenge, remaining undefined, uncreated, unauthentic, hence irresponsible. One may remain a thing, instead of becoming a fully human being. In other words, to be human is to be authentic, to announce to all the world who and what one is and to be consistent with the identity one has developed. It must be added that as he has grown older, Sartre has become increasingly pessimistic about the willingness of the average person to accept the challenge. It is too difficult. People, he believes, do not want to define their own natures because they do not want responsibility.

If one does attempt to become authentic, however, one runs into the same problem as Kierkegaard's Christian existentialist: that is, one can never be completely sure of choosing rightly, or of choosing *well.* It is one thing to be free and responsible; another, to have one's choices proven wise. But what can one do? One can only act from the full integrity of one's defined being and hope for the best.

For this reason, existential choice is filled with anguish for the chooser. An existential ship's officer, faced with the awful decision of having to kill people or risk sinking the lifeboat (see preceding section), might eventually shoot desperate people in cold blood. But he would not be able to argue later that he had been a victim of circumstances. He would have to admit responsibility for his actions.

Clarifying One's Own Values

"Do as I say, not as I do" is such an ancient slogan that we seldom really hear it any more. Yet, like many an old saying, it contains profound insight into the way people live their lives. Much of what has already been said about moral values pertains to price tags people honor and acknowledge, but *not necessarily to prices they are actually willing to pay*. It bears repeating here that a good many people define morality by noting what others are doing wrong. They often fail to apply a similar situation to themselves. Company loyalty may be a virtue in the work ethic, but this is no guarantee that someone who accepts this ethic will always let

The Existential Lifeboat

company loyalty stand in the way of personal benefit.

The continuing issue involves determining what human nature is basically like. Is it selfish and pleasure-centered? Or is it able to transcend self-interest in favor of the moral principle? Or are some people selfish, while others are truly concerned with principles? How does one find out what is true one's own human nature?

A crucial aspect of being human is to know what your values are, and then to determine whether these have anything much to do with the way you actually behave. In today's society, with its rapidly accelerating rate of change, people often have a hard time remembering what day it is and what they must do in the next ten minutes. It is often difficult to be fully conscious that an action is taking place, much less aware of the values underlying it.

Nonetheless, a periodic inventory of your values is absolutely necessary if you hope to acquire any measure of authenticity as a human being.

> **A periodic inventory of your values is absolutely necessary if you hope to acquire any authenticity as a human being.**

"Should"

In the preceding section it was pointed out that you can learn much about yourself from determining what kinds of statements you would write down after the opening words "of course." One means of clarifying your values is to see what statements you make using the verb "should." You can become enlightened by listing subjects for the verb "should" and then completing the sentence.

Parents should . . .
Children should . . .
Teachers should . . .
Policemen should . . .
Tax examiners should . . .
Major religions should . . .
Politicians should . . .

For variation, add "not" every so often.

It is perhaps not surprising to learn that the most people's "should" lists are strikingly similar. Many, many studies confirm this to be a truth of human nature: namely, that the underlying morality, the set of moral principles, does not differ radically from one person to another or from one nation to another. There is a common moral outlook, whether people are religious, young or old, rich or poor.

In even extreme cases, such as among persons labeled as criminals—people who have been given psychiatric tests and determined to be dangerously antisocial—researchers have discovered a fundamentally conventional morality in *expectation of others' behavior.* That is, a murderer may test out as being flagrantly amoral when it comes to the deeds he himself has committed, but he values words like "decent," "honest," and "honorable" as labels for the actions of others toward him. One convicted murderer, awaiting execution, reported to a social psychologist that the warden and the guards had been "really fine fellows who always treated me with kindness and respect."

Another research study among black teenagers confined to a Youth Hall for alleged delinquency, disclosed unexpected results. Asked to rank order a random list of social types from "least" to "most" admired, they revealed, again, very conventional values. People who contributed to the support of their parents were more admired than people who were skillful in disposing of stolen goods. People who were loyal to their friends were also admired, as were those who went to church regularly.

These and similar studies suggest that the average person entertains a view of the world as a place in which basically decent behavior should and does exist; a world in which people are trustworthy and honest with one another; a world in which mutual respect is the rule, not the exception.

The antisocial behavior of certain elements of the population by no means indicates a conscious flaunting of the public moral conscience. If anything, crimes against society are often justified on moral grounds. Theft is sometimes defended as retaliation for social evils, while countless acts of violence are the result of heartbreak over infidelities. There is no reason for supposing that many of the people who commit these crimes are unaware of what *should* be done, of the rules of society.

If this is the case, then we must confront the sad truth that "should" is obviously not enough. When behavior dramatically contradicts values, there is a misfiring somewhere. Perhaps the problem stems from a human unwillingness to bring the self into contact with unpleasant realities. The

> **The average person views the world as a place in which basically decent behavior should and does exist.**

notion of the self is kept sacred, and for this reason, people are often willing to act in violation of moral principles in order to benefit that self. When survival itself is at stake, morality is frequently abandoned, though not the *idea* of morality.

"Would"

"Should" is theoretical; "would" refers to probable action. Take the statement, "I know people should not steal, but, if I had to steal for my family's survival, I would do it." A list of things people believe they would (or would not) do can bring to light some fascinating insights into the problems of morality.

According to a famous story attributed to George Bernard Shaw (among others) a woman was once asked, "Would you sleep with a stranger if you were paid a million dollars?" "Well, yes," she answered. "And would you sleep with a stranger for two dollars?" Her response to *this* question was: "Certainly not. What do you think I am?" The by now classic reply was: "We've already established that. Now it's a matter of determining the price."

The moral absolutist argues that there is no question about what the woman *is*. The situationalist argues that what the woman does in one instance may have nothing to do with what she does in another; therefore it is unfair to conclude that her entire nature has been established. The existentialist argues that morality does not exist in a vacuum; it is not an immaterial state. One's morality is defined at the moment of choice. Hence "would" is the telling verb.

Assuming for the moment that "would" is significant and may often negate "should," you can gain additional insight into yourself as a moral being by anticipating questions asked by moralists of different persuasions:

1. Does the choice really matter?
2. Does the choice involve survival?
3. Who would be injured or benefited by the choice?
4. Does the choice involve one individual or many?
5. Does the choice involve a seemingly anonymous institution?
6. Will the results of the choice be permanent or temporary? Is the choice something which appears valuable in the long or short run?

7. What does "should" have to say about the choice?
8. What if everyone behaved in the manner recommended by the choice?
9. If the outcome of the choice is morally questionable, will a question of blame arise?
10. Is a compromise possible—a way of avoiding unfortunate consequences?

Another way to clarify your values is to examine specific situations involving moral choice. Project yourself into the situation and determine what you would do.

Situation A.

A television executive has the choice of scheduling a routine, crowd-pleasing game show or a more challenging program which will require work and time, with the distinct possibility of low ratings. How much risk would *you* take?

Situation B.

A surgeon has scheduled two operations at the same time. He has been in the habit of allowing his assistant, a doctor still in training, to perform "ghost surgery." The medical ethics committee has been overlooking this breach thus far. Would *you* continue the lucrative practice?

Situation C.

A divorce agreement allows the ex-husband to pay a small amount toward the expenses of his family. He knows that his ex-wife is seriously interested in another man and is reported to be near marriage. One of the children needs money for braces. The husband is not legally liable, but the child has requested help. What would *you* do?

Situation D.

An office worker has a demanding job, which meets his expenses but allows no extras. The chance to do some "moonlighting" comes along. The additional job brings welcome money, but makes the worker very tired on the regular, main job. The boss objects and tells the worker in no uncertain terms where his loyalty lies, urges him to quit the second job. What would *you* reply?

Clarifying your values—separating the "would" from the "should"—is a necessary first step toward the goal of becoming a fully consistent human being, toward having what is often called moral integrity. Not everyone agrees that the goal is worth the price, which frequently involves sacrificing self-interest in the name of something else: an abstract principle. Some moralists, both religious and secular, take a pessimistic view and say that principles do not really interest people, no matter what they *say*.

In addition, the objection is often raised that moral integrity is hardly worthwhile in a world in which it is not repaid in kind. People are going to deceive you, so why should you be honest? Why live by a code at all if you can't count on others? If no one is watching (to go back to Glaucon's argument in *The Republic*) get away with as much as you can. Socrates was sure the rational person does not think this way, and religious leaders tell us we had better not. Needless to say, neither position offers any guarantee about what people actually do. If moral values are not consistent with practice, one is tempted to wonder who is listening to moral questions besides those who don't need to.

Can anything ever be different?

Cornelia Otis Skinner

Woman's virtue is man's greatest invention.

Chapter 7 Footnotes

[1] *The Republic of Plato,* tr. Francis Macdonald Cornford (London: Oxford University Press, 1971), p. 43.

[2] *Ibid.,* p. 45.

[3] *Ibid.,* p. 47.

[4] Jean-Paul Sartre, *Existentialism and Human Emotions,* tr. Bernard Frechtman (New York: The Philosophical Library, 1947), p. 15.

8

FAITH AND SCIENCE

Overview

The American novelist William Faulkner has written a long short story called "The Bear." The story deals with a hunting trip into a dense Mississippi woodland for the purpose of finding and killing a giant bear which has been around for as long as anyone can remember, a constant threat to life in the area. The hero of the story is a boy, raised in the hunting tradition, bred to the woods and the rifle, taught from earliest childhood that passage to manhood inevitably depended upon some spectacular hunting feat. His burning desire, of course, is to be the one to kill the bear.

Near the end of the story the boy, having strayed from his father and the other hunters, finds himself in a remote area of the woodland, in the midst of a terrifying silence—a silence which houses some awesome presence. It is, of course, the bear. The two finally meet at close contact. The bear simply stands there, looking at the boy, who is neither friend nor enemy to him. The animal is not hostile. The boy could easily shoot the huge animal at such close range. Yet *the boy cannot bring himself to do it.*

Faulkner's meaning has been debated since the story first appeared. Like all great pieces of literature, the story is rich with symbolism and no doubt allows many interpretations. One is that people must have fabulous legends—awesome myths—to give their lives a sense of purpose. Another is that, just as the bear is needed to complete the woodland atmosphere, to give the woodland its sense of poetry and excitement, life itself needs a touch of poetry, a feeling of adventure, *a definite lack of certainty.* Had the bear been disposed of, had the woodland been cleared of its lurking dangers, what then? Why would a hunter venture into a safe forest anyway?

The histories of human ideas refer to a dramatic conflict between faith and science (or between religion and science). It is often held that one must finally make a choice between the two. Indeed there *have* been times when such a choice was forced upon people. Galileo (1564–1642) is a notable example. Coming along at a time when technology was in its infancy and the lure of scientific investigation was romantic and exciting, Galileo ran into opposition from the Catholic establishment, which represented the "certainty" established by religious dogma. Galileo's position was one of *faith* in science, and the Church's one of religious *certainty.* In any case, Galileo, under threat of torture (or possibly even death), came out in favor of religious absolutism, abandoning his intellectual voyages into the unknown.

For the average person, however, no such final and drastic choice need be made. It is not necessary to say one will either kill the bear or never go into the woods again. It is really not even necessary to meet the bear face to face. One can lead a useful, happy, meaningful life by coexisting with even the possibility of the bear. "There is a bear" and "there may not be a bear" are compatible statements.

A fully human person recognizes that choices exist. Many people who swear by science and technology may doubt that a legitimate choice can still be made between faith and science, but intelligent arguments abound on both sides. It is not impossible to go back and forth from one pole to the

> **Faulkner's bear represents a vast number of symbols people seem to need—symbols of higher truths—symbols of possibilities beyond the range of common sense.**

> H. L. Mencken
>
> **Faith—an illogical belief in the occurrence of the improbable**

other, from a certainty that the truths of science are over-whelmingly more impressive than the speculations of faith to a renewed concern for those gray areas which lie beyond the scientist's grasp.

The apologists for science point out that faith has no business venturing beliefs on matters that admit of scientific proof. For example, they rule out the beliefs of religious fundamentalists, who deny the theory of evolution and insist that the creation of the world is accurately described in the first book of the Bible. Yet there are psychologists who do not make light of fervent religious belief, even in matters which appear to contradict the strongest findings of science. The inner experience of religious truth, they contend, exists on a very different plane than the laboratory.

This chapter does not take sides. Its major premise is that faith and certainty coexist in many forms in nearly everyone's life. The important thing is to be able to distinguish between them—and to not close your mind to other versions of truth, or even to the possibility that final, ultimate truth may be the exclusive property of no one.

There Is Either Truth or Falsehood

The struggle between faith and science may have its roots in the ancient idea that truth and falsehood are opposites and that a given belief cannot be both true and false at the same time, or neither true nor false at the same time, or partly true and partly false at the same time.

In very early times the word of the tribal leader was no doubt all the truth considered necessary. As time passed, the beliefs underlying tribal customs were unquestionable. Yet is hard to imagine a time when some version of certainty did not exist.

Carl Sagan

Absence of evidence is not evidence of absence.

The Voices of the Gods

Early people, so goes a prevalent theory, did not talk things over with themselves. They did not go for long walks to think things through and arrive at a solution to a problem. The interior language we know of today as "talking to yourself" was not recognized as such. Such an outlandish thought would hardly have occurred to people who knew nothing about the geography of the mind. The theory is that early people believed they were hearing the voices of gods.

This notion surely helps to explain the many rituals—including that of human sacrifice—which went on for centuries, unsuccessfully if at all challenged. It helps to explain the fact that some people were especially favored: seers, prophets, wizards, oracles, high priests. Since everyone heard inner voices at some time, it was not difficult for them to believe that selected individuals heard especially long, sustained speeches coming from another dimension of reality.

The earliest form of religious certainty may have been faith in these inner voices. The Old Testament is filled with accounts of divine instruction. Abraham was instructed by God to take his son Isaac to a mountain top and there slay him in sacrifice. He was then instructed by God's angel not to kill the boy. Moses was said to have talked to God on Mount Sinai and to have received the Ten Commandments there. Job, writhing in agony over his sufferings, hears the voice of God coming from a whirlwind, assuring him that there are divine reasons for everything that happens.

In Greek religion the oracle was considered to be the human vehicle of divine revelation. People traveled from far and wide and paid great sums of money to have their fortunes told or to receive advice on anything from getting married to preparing for an invasion. Since Greek religion believed that human actions were all determined beforehand by fate, it was important for the Greeks to believe that *someone* could see into the future and dispel human ignorance of it. In other words, if the future were already planned, then some things had, in a manner of speaking, already happened and were absolutely true. Those who could see into the future therefore possessed absolute certainty.

But the hearing of divine voices is not a phenomenon limited to the far distant past. In all times and places there have been people who believed they were being told certain secrets or allowed to perform certain feats by a spiritual being. Joan of Arc was such a person, as was Bernadette of Lourdes, who only a scant century ago claimed to have both seen and heard the Virgin Mary in a rustic grotto; who said she had been instructed to drink the water from a spring that seemed to onlookers to be nonexistent until one actually began to flow up from the ground soon after the bizarre "drinking" incident occurred. Millions of people have come —are still coming—to the spring since this unusual event occurred. There have been claims of sudden and dramatic cures for all manner of ailments, though medical science can discover no curative properties in the water itself.

Thousands of testimonies have come from persons who have in one form or another been "visited" by presences. We read of sudden conversions to religious faith on the part of people who had never shown the slightest inclination in that direction and who deny having been in a "receptive" psychological mood prior to their experience.

We read of incredible premonitions which come to people in their dreams: a mother, for example, who dreamed that her baby was being run over by an automobile and woke to find the crib empty and the child—somehow, no one knows how—crawling in the street, about to be struck by the very same car! Research into occult phenomena of similar and even much stranger kinds will reveal more material than science can explain.

Some people are comfortable in the presence of such data, though they may not personally believe in the occult. Some are able to coexist with phenomena they cannot explain. Others must account for such things in the most plausible, naturalistic way. The theory mentioned previously, that early people had no knowledge that they could talk to themselves, is based on current information about the structure of the brain, and offers a scientific explanation for many sorts of occult experience.

The theory makes reference to *hemispheric asymmetry*—the division of the brain into two halves, a left and a right hemisphere. Apparently research has disclosed the startling fact that one side of the brain quite literally does not know what the other side is doing. One side (the left if you are right-handed and the right if you are left-handed) becomes dominant and takes care of conscious thought and practical decision-making. The other side appears to be the source of intuitions, dream symbols, and *perhaps* occult experiences.

> One theory suggests that these inner voices were the brain's right hemisphere talking to the left hemisphere.

This partitioned or, as it is sometimes called, *bicameral* mind of ours may have been the reason early people thought they were hearing the gods. They really *were* talking to themselves; that is, one hemisphere was communicating with the other, but lacking any knowledge about the brain's structure, they could only assume some higher force was "taking over" for the time being.

The devil is in this . . . the devil is in it! I can feel his terrible presence! He it is who is making her refuse to give up these clothes of immodesty and vice, no doubt of that. [1]
The Prosecutor, about Joan of Arc, in Jean Anouilh's *The Lark*

It is possible that the medieval furor over demonic spirits invading the bodies of the innocent—a mythology which has had a considerable revival in our own time—can be explained in terms of the bicameral theory. Surely everyone

"This partitioned mind of ours may have been the reason early people thought they were hearing the gods."

has had the experience of suddenly "blurting out" something that seemed highly uncharacteristic of him, and of stammering an apologetic, "I don't know why I said that."

The lesser understood hemisphere is gaining prominence in our age. Those who argue for the legitimacy of occult data often do so as an anti-science gesture, shaking their heads at what they regard as the dull positivism of a technological society and repeating Hamlet's famous observation:

There are more things in heaven and earth, Horatio,
Than are dreamt of in your philosophy.

In times past, those who heard the voices of the gods had no need of apology or an anti-science argument. *They* were the guardians of certainty. In the Book of Job there is no question that God speaks from a whirlwind; the assumption is that God's explanations suffice and are not to be questioned. God has his reasons; everything works toward the ends God ordains. It is not for man to know too much.

But this attitude changed. Next was the growth of a new and exciting principle: *human intellectual certainty.*

An Ultimate—and within Human Grasp

The people who listened to divine voices may or may not have had a sense that these voices could speak the ultimate truth of things if they so desired. They may or may not have believed that somewhere there existed an ultimate wisdom, something utterly contrary to pure ignorance. They may or may not have said to each other: "We are humble mortals who know so little, while the gods know everything." Perhaps they did what they thought the gods wanted and let the matter go at that.

At the time of the Egyptian Pharaohs—as far back as 3000 B.C.—certainty meant the word of the Pharaohs, and certainty was not ultimate truth, but ultimate power. The Pharaoh ordered how things should be done and what things should be done and when they should be done, and people obeyed. Instead of wisdom versus ignorance, there was power versus fear.

One Pharaoh, however, named Amenhotep IV (later called Akhenaten), who living during the fourteenth century B.C., is supposed to have shattered tradition by asserting that the Pharaohs were not gods, that only one god existed. There is

Socrates to the jury of his peers, as recorded by Plato

You have often heard me speak of an oracle or sign which comes to me . . . this sign I have had ever since I was a child. The sign is a voice which comes to me . . .

no indication that Akhenaten held interior conversations with this one god, but this may well mark the first historical instance in which the proposition was made that "something else" existed beyond what had always been believed; that there was some other possible "order" in life, the full knowledge of which was beyond human conception. Akhenaten would have preceded even the earliest of Hebrew sacred writings by a number of centuries.

But an enormous revolution occurred with the coming of Greek intellectualism, beginning around the sixth century B.C. Why these people, whose ancestors had been warlike tribes sweeping down from the north, should have been so curious about everything, no one can say. All we know is

Akhenaten: "Some other possibility, the full knowledge of which was beyond human ken.

they must have differed immeasurably from everyone else who had come before. True, they created the Olympian gods and goddesses and had their high priests and oracles, but by the sixth century the Olympian religion (dating back to the ninth or eighth century) was probably on the wane, and by the fifth—the so-called Golden Age of Athens—there seem to have been few intellectuals left who still believed in the literal existence of Zeus and the other deities. Something was replacing the need for supernatural creatures, and that was *humanism*—a transference of awe from both inner voices and remote gods to the flesh-and-blood potential of people themselves.

For the first time there was speculation about how much could be known. There was speculation about how much could not be known. There was speculation about *what does the knowing*—that is, if not the brain and its structure, then surely about the human mind as a phenomenon which could itself be an object of thought. The Greeks seem to have invented the idea of thinking about thinking.

Consider the word *philosophy,* itself a Greek term. It means "the love of wisdom," but it also connotes the joy that comes from knowing. Knowing what? The answer seemed clear: what was *there* to be known. Starting out on the new adventure of using the human mind in a way that, so far as we know, had not been defined before, the earliest of the Greek intellectuals assumed there was a limit to what could be known—*The* Truth, if you will—waiting at the end of the road.

What engaged them at first was the idea of an Ultimate, a first or basic reality they believed would then help to explain everything else. They were scientists as well as philosophers, most of these sixth-century intellectuals who have since become known as the Pre-Socratics. The Ultimate seemed to belong to the world of physical reality. If it were within human grasp, it seemed it must be "out there" rather than "up there."

Yet if it could not be seen, the Pre-Socratics felt it still could be known through a process of understanding which eventually acquired the label "reason." In other words, through the intellectual labors of the Pre-Socratics was born the art of analysis, a mental process most of us use in solving problems:

If this is true . . .

Oh, but *that* may be the case . . .

On the other hand, what if . . . ?

I must therefore rule out that . . .

Since the world at large obviously had so many tangible things in it, the Pre-Socratics, convinced that basic reality was only *one* thing, concluded—amazingly, astonishingly!—that all of the different things they saw about them (hills, rocks, flowers, clouds, people, animals) were reducible to a prior, a parent, substance. Thales, an astronomer who lived in Miletus on the coast of Asia Minor, is given the credit for asking the first pointedly analytical question in the history of philosophy: "What is everything made of?" Noting that water seemed to be the most prevalent substance around, Thales decided that water was indeed the parent substance —the Ultimate.

One after another of those who followed made their contributions to the burning issue of the Ultimate. One said the parent substance—that beyond which nothing else existed —must be air, another that it must be fire. Still another argued that, since the four known substances—earth, air, fire, and water—seemed to be of equal "status" in the world, it seemed more reasonable to conclude that all of them derived from the true parent substance whose nature and identity were as yet undiscovered. This philosopher, with uncanny foresight, the named Ultimate "Boundless Unknown."

Still the Pre-Socratic philosophers pressed on, apparently unsatisfied with vague possibilities, with uncertainties. There seemed to be an especially strong need to locate the Ultimate in physical, or naturalistic terms. Two philosophers of the early fifth century B.C., Democritus and Leucippus, advanced an entirely materialistic theory, concluding that since almost everything in the world was composed of matter, there must exist an ultimate *form* of matter. The material objects we see around us often come and go, to be replaced by other material objects. Some—like the mountains and the stones—appear to be solid and eternal, but perhaps even they are subject to change; perhaps they are undergoing changes undetected by the eye!

With, again, astonishing foresight, these philosophers

produced the first atomic theory. They said that the parent substance was a particle of matter of almost infinitesimal size, unable to be seen by the human eye, but having continual motion as its basic property. They suggested that the physical universe, as we know it, is the result of collisions between such dense masses of atoms that the "clusters" take on an *apparent* solidity. Since atomic motion is perpetual and eternal, nothing in the physical universe is permanently solid or unchanging.

We now know that Democritus and Leucippus were on the path of the truth, but in their effort to find the Ultimate, they stopped at the atom. We know that now the atom is a collection of even smaller particles. We know that all particles can be reduced to energy, but also that energy is continually converting to matter. Einstein, who developed the equation for this conversion—$E = mc^2$—said the secret of which came first, energy or matter, would probably never be known, if indeed such a secret exists. What is important, he said, is the knowledge of the equation. The Ultimate may well be that equation itself!

The exact or true nature of the Ultimate is less important than the fact that human beings have been pursuing it doggedly for several thousand years. It is probably the single most important concept of all time. It has shaped the whole human endeavor since the moment Thales of Miletus sat back, convinced that in choosing water, he had come face to face with the outer limits of truth.

Underlying the continuing counteraction of faith and science, the shuttling back and forth from one pole to the other, is the idea of an Ultimate. Like Democritus and Leucippus, a good many scientists harbor the conviction that a final explanation exists, and *will* be found someday, and will be physical rather than spiritual. But those who hold to faith remind us how elusive the Ultimate has been to science. A current scientific work, for example, attempts to recreate in our minds what actually took place at the beginning of the universe, but admits that the initial "split second" remains in the realm of pure speculation.

The fact is science does not yet know whether the universe ever actually began. For a long time the "steady state" theory of the universe held that "it" (if indeed there is such a thing as *the* universe about which we can speak as though it were a contained entity of some kind) has always been essentially as it is now, never having had a "beginning." This theory was opposed by the "big bang" theory, which said that at some point a primordial particle exploded (for whatever reason) and the universe is the result of continuing explosions that will one day die out as the whole enterprise goes back to what it was before the explosion. The "big bang" theory has also been challenged, and the debate seems likely to last indefinitely.

The very nature of an Ultimate, say the anti-science groups, precludes the possibility of its existing as something physical. They like to point out that even some scientific explanations of the Ultimate come close to or pass into areas of highly abstract metaphysics. One physicist, Dr. Behram Kursunoglu, for example, in arguing against the "big bang" theory, has advanced the belief that at one time no matter existed, but only a pervasive energy field. Then "some supernatural force" manufactured two elementary particles of matter supercharged with energy, setting off massive explosions and chain reactions that are still going on.

Whether the force which lit the fuse is called supernatural or a "Boundless Unknown," the fact remains that the phantom of the Ultimate still haunts us and, while it does, the shuttle bus between faith and science will continue its run.

Werner Heisenberg

It seems to me fascinating to reflect that today . . . men are seeking to wrest solutions from problems posed by the Greek philosophers more than two thousand years ago.

First Reason, Then Faith

With the coming of Socrates and later of his dedicated follower and champion, Plato, the case was made for human intellect as the *sole* resource in the quest of certainty. A split occurred, not between faith and science, but rather between the intellect and science.

Science Is Not The Way

Actually, what Socrates objected to was not science *per se,* for this human endeavor had not yet become institutionalized. The objection was to materialism, the name by which the earliest atomic theory had become known; and the reason for the objection was that materialism was based on the idea of perpetual change. Socrates taught—and Plato then formalized the belief—that whatever was true, *by definition,* must be unchanging and universal. If the materialists were right, if the only true knowledge were the knowledge of matter, and if the material world were in a constant state of change, then what we call knowledge must consist of scattered observations about changing things. Something believed true today would not necessarily be true tomorrow.

The materialistic approach, Socrates was convinced, would result only in mass confusion. When Plato later set down in writing the overwhelming body of thought of which Socrates was the father, he made a momentous distinction between *knowledge* and *belief*. Belief is rooted in personal observations and in sense experience. The term is a huge umbrella which covers both the casual, everyday opinions people develop for both good and bad reasons, *and* the considerable body of scientific thought. What these two categories share, however, is the *transitory nature of belief*.

Soaring over both is the realm of pure knowledge.

While the Pre-Socratics *did* engage in rational analysis, they did not develop a full-bodied theory of knowledge. Parmenides came close, and no doubt his thought exercised some influence on the theory of knowledge Plato was eventually to set forth.

Before Parmenides, a great controversy broke out among the Pre-Socratics concerning the nature of reality. In particular, they asked whether the world was a stable, unchanging phenomenon, subject always to the same laws, or a fluid process of continual becoming. Heraclitus proved to be the champion of becomingness. Nothing ever *is,* he said; everything is continually in a state of transition to something else. "You cannot step twice into the same river."

Parmenides challenged this view. Something either is, he argued, or it is not. It cannot be in a state of becoming something else. Whatever it is, *it is.* Moreover, it is absurd to believe that something can become something other than it is, for that would be saying that the "something else" was nonexistent one moment, and existent, the next. Where did it come from? Nonbeing cannot come from being. There is either being or nonbeing. One entity cannot be in both states.

Well, we might say from where we sit, this argument may *sound* logical, but it is clear that things and people *do* become different from what they were and are. A person of twenty-five is clearly different from a child of six. Parmenides would have agreed most emphatically. He would have said: "The only constant reality in the life progression of a human

---

Plato believed the human intellect capable of comprehending ultimate realities.

•

•

•

•

•

•

St. Augustine reached the position that the human intellect could inquire only so far, but could never grasp the true nature of the Ultimate.

Percy Bysshe Shelley

Spirit of beauty, that
  Dost consecrate
With thine own hues all
  Thou dost shine upon
Of human thought or
  form,
  Where art thou gone?

---

being from childhood to old age is being itself, his existence. All of the other changeable characteristics are therefore not real."

It was Parmenides' momentous separation of matter and truth which deeply impressed Plato. Since the world of matter was in a continual state of change and transition, nothing one said about it could be the truth, since *truth only pertains to what is.* From Parmenides, and certainly from the teachings of Socrates, Plato was able to put together his famous theory of knowledge, which holds that only universal, unchanging ideas are real. Beauty, justice, virtue are realities, because they do not belong to matter, hence cannot change.

Plato held that material things can partake of these unchanging realities or Forms (see Chapter 2). That is, one can say that an object—or a person—is beautiful, which is to say that *for the time being* it partakes of the form of beauty. But, while the object itself can and will pass out of existence eventually, the quality cannot. There will always be beautiful things (and beautiful people) because beauty exists eternally. Even if we happened not to run across beautiful things, we could not say that beauty itself does not exist.

Much of Plato's writing, which takes the form of dialogs between Socrates (as the spokesman for philosophy) and others, is devoted to the analysis of eternal ideas and to the proposition that their definition does not depend upon time, place, and experience. The "others" with whom Socrates discusses these ideas are actual people who may either have been members of Socrates' circle of youthful followers or were known to Plato as having been critical of Socratic ideas, and they tend to set forth the belief that truth is relative and circumstantial—always changing.

For example, at the opening of Plato's most famous work, *The Republic,* there occurs a discussion of the meaning of the word "justice." Thrasymachus expresses the opinion that "justice is whatever serves the interest of the party in power." In other words, there is no such thing as a universal definition.

It takes Socrates nearly the whole of *The Republic* to piece together a vision of what justice truly is, but in the preliminary conversation he succeeds in arguing down Thrasymachus' contention. The following is our summary of the argument, as it might have sounded had Socrates lived at the time of the United States involvement in Vietnam. However updated, the argument illustrates the purely analytical method of reaching certainty.

Soc: *You say, Thrasymachus, that justice is whatever best serves the interest of the party in power.*

Thras: *Yes.*

Soc: *So tell me this. Is it possible that any party in power could pass a law that was clearly a mistake?*

Thras: *Certainly. I would say the law authorizing that troops be sent to Vietnam was a big mistake.*

Soc: *Because it has been an increasing source of embarrassment for the party in power, right?*

Thras: *Indeed!*

Soc: *Would you call it an unjust law?*

Thras: *I would.*

Soc: *You would have to—by your own definition. For it has not served the best interests of the party in power. But are people supposed to obey this law?*

Thras: *Yes, unless they want to be prosecuted for draft evasion.*

Soc: *True, but in any case, the people involved have to obey any law that has been duly passed, do they not?*

Thras: *Yes, otherwise the party in power could not be said to have power.*

Soc: *I could not agree with you more. There could be no justice in a state in which people need obey only such laws as they choose to obey. But here we have an obvious contradiction. In the case of Vietnam, it is right and just that people obey a law that, as we have said, does not serve the interests of the party in power. It is clear, then, that justice is something quite different from what you have said.*

In typical fashion, Plato's Socrates has trapped the opposition. The only way in which Thrasymachus can hold to his original definition of justice is to say that, if an unjust law were passed, the people would have to disobey it since it did not serve the interests of the ruling party. But then the party's power would vanish, and then how could it have the clout necessary to make people fear and respect it so that the relativistic definition of justice could make sense?

Throughout the dialogs Plato performs similar feats of rational analysis with ideas like love, the soul, and immortality. The technique is basically the same. A subject is

> **Socrates maintained that "justice" is the same everywhere regardless of place and circumstances.**
>
> •
> •
> •
>
> •
> •
> •
>
> **Thrasymachus maintained that "justice" is whatever best serves the interest of the party in power.**

presented for discussion. One or more views are stated, and then Socrates comes forth to trap the debaters in their own illogic.

In the Platonic dialogs knowledge and wisdom are the same. The wise person knows *what is true.* Moreover, such wisdom is not attained. Rather, it is discovered within each person wise enough to recognize it. Essential to Plato's philosophy is the concept that truth, not being a quality resident in the world of matter, cannot be "learned" through experience, through what *we* know as trial-and-error. Proper understanding is in the mind from the beginning. In one of the most famous of all the dialogs, *Meno,* Socrates demonstrates that an illiterate, untutored slave boy can perform feats of higher mathematics through the painstaking guidance of someone who, like Socrates, knows that reason is the birthright of all human beings.

As further refined and developed by the most brilliant student at Plato's Academy, Aristotle, the Greek model of clear, precise rational analysis remained for a long time the standard by which certainty was measured.

A Political Ultimate: The Roman State

Vergil (translated by John Dryden)

But, Rome, 'tis thine
  alone,
  With awful sway,
To rule mankind and
  make
  The world obey,
Disposing peace and war
  by
  Thy own majestic way.

Aeneid

The Romans may have considered themselves militarily superior to the Greeks, to *any* nation. But they greatly admired Greek culture, especially the model of rationalism, the achievement of certainty through an impeccable sequence of logical connections. The children of the wealthy and powerful were almost always educated by Greek slaves, who transmitted the model. Whatever excesses took place during the extreme decadence of the Empire, whatever rampant hedonism we may still identify with the very word "Rome," the fact remains that the Roman ideal was the man of calm and controlled reason, one who allowed his intellect, not his emotions, to guide his behavior. The philosophy of Stoicism (see Chapter 13), fully developed by the Romans, had as its underlying premise that one could endure pain and suffering by allowing reason to carry one to a state of cool detachment.

Stoicism was based on the principle of a rational order, not only within the human mind, but within the universe as well. It was an order comprehensible to the members of humanity who had no need of supernatural aid. The Roman

empire was receptive to such a philosophy. This rational
order was not part of the same universe in which Job lived
—Job, who was told by God's voice in the whirlwind that
it was neither appropriate nor possible for a human being to
question matters eternally beyond human ken.

With Rome so successful in empire building, with its military genius for plotting invasions, with a state machine that,
in its heyday (the period of Augustus Caesar, who ruled
from 27 B.C. to 14 A.D.) probably worked with incredibly
smooth efficiency, the rational model must have proved itself time and time again. Rome's legal system, intricate network of highways and viaducts, open forum for discussion
and debate . . . all must have seemed awesome. The rational
order seemed to lead up to such achievements—and to further greatness. Small wonder that, as Rome's power and
wealth increased, the emperors became more and more in-
toxicated with the myth of Rome's (and their) unprecedented magnificence, came to see themselves as gods, very
much as the Pharaohs had done many centuries earlier.

Christianity: A New Kind of Ultimate

It seems clear that Christianity would have had broad
appeal for people who either had known oppression at the
hands of Roman justice or were world-weary and tired of
Roman philosophical materialism. Whatever the reasons for
conversion, the new Christians must have felt that something was missing—for them—in the lifestyle and the philosophy around them. Christianity, as interpreted by Saint
Paul, promised a new kind of order, one in which the meek
and the humble, not the powerful rulers of the earth, were
supreme.

The new religion thus offered its own kind of certainties.
Vain, materialistic, godless tyrants would come to grief. The
poor would inherit the earth, *if* the moral precepts were
carefully observed. Paul helped to turn Christianity into a
solid framework of absolute moral values within which to
live. In particular Paul urged a turning away from the pleasures of the flesh in favor of the joys of spiritual union with
God. From Paul's record of many of Christ's teachings
(found in the four gospels), there emerge definite, not-to-
be-questioned separations: body and soul; flesh and spirit;
materialism and spirituality. There also emerge definite connections (equations): wealth and nonspirituality; frivolous

pleasure and sin; worldly power and a deficiency in the important values, such as faith, hope and charity.

Rational Problems with Christian Belief

On the philosophical level, early Christianity had its problems. The rational model of logical analysis had been dominant for so long that many Christian thinkers naturally began to apply it to their own religion. Often they came up with more questions than answers. Three examples are:

Can this world really be the extent of God's creation?

If the ability to create matter *ex nihilo* (from nothing) is intrinsic to God, then why must one believe that He stopped with this one achievement? At the same time, the thought that God might go on endlessly creating worlds staggers the imagination.

Could God have had any purpose in creating the world?

While the Old Testament (which Christianity viewed as containing accurate prophecies of Christ's coming) had suggested that God created the world for man, and the New Testament had given Christ a reason for coming down to earth, early Christian philosophers often had difficulty determining God's purposes. Can an all-powerful, all-knowing God be so limited as to have a purpose? To have "something in mind" before doing something is, they argued, to have a need. If God were in *need* of anything, could He then be all-powerful?

Does God think?

If, as the New Testament stated, Jesus had come to earth to redeem a sinful mankind, then there is the suggested image of a God the Father who had developed a "plan" for salvation. But, philosophers sometimes asked, can an all-powerful, all-knowing God be said to have a plan? To them, the very definition of "all-knowing" implied a static condition, a transcendent understanding that never moved from Point A to Point B, never used logic or any of the intellectual techniques people had invented to try to increase their paltry comprehension of things.

Voltaire

To believe in God is impossible—not to believe in Him—absurd

Faith is the Answer

The major philosopher of the first phase of Christianity— that is, before the Middle Ages, when Christianity became a worldly as well as spiritual empire—was Saint Augustine (354–430 A.D.). Like Paul, who preceded him by several centuries, Augustine became a convert during his mature lifetime. In his case the catalyst was a Christian mother, who had despaired over his wanton ways and kept urging him to reform, to acknowledge and confess his sins in prayer to a loving and forgiving God, and to devote the rest of his life to God's work. Though Augustine eventually renounced his life of sin and entered the Christian fold, he brought with him many of the problems that had troubled his mind earlier.

The writings of Augustine—especially his remarkably candid *Confessions*—represent a synthesis of Christian beliefs and the analytical methods of both the classical (that is, Greek and Roman) and early Christian philosophers. Augustine, who must have pondered many of the rational "difficulties" in Christianity before making his choice, brings into focus his own doubts and then deals with them one by one. We will next consider Augustine's ideas, drawing upon his *Confessions*.

> Pope Gregory I
>
> **If the work of God could be comprehended by reason, it would be no longer wonderful.**

I was taught sacred history, the Gospel, and the Catechism without being given the means for believing. The result was a disorder which became my particular order.
Jean-Paul Sartre, About his Catholic upbringing

One of Augustine's first concerns is his own rationality, the intellect by which he is able to ask questions which in turn seem to require rational answers. He asks, why are some people given the gift of intellectual reasoning when it is inadequate to comprehend the divine scheme?

And what did it profit me, that all the books I could procure of the so-called liberal arts, I, the vile slave of vile affections, read by myself, and understood? And I delighted in them, but knew not whence came all, that therein was true or certain.

To demonstrate that certainty cannot be achieved through the analytical method of human reason, Augustine shows how fundamental Christian doctrines baffle the intellect: for example, the concept of the Creation itself. In Christian belief, God is divine substance (as opposed to the material substances which some of the Pre-Socratics had identified as the Ultimate). Yet the world is material substance (matter) and cannot be of the same substance as God. God's divine substance cannot be the "parent" of matter, as, for example, the atom was thought to be the "parent" of the visible world. Yet where had material substance come from? The only possible answer is that the divine substance brought material substance into being out of nothing; the two constitute an everlasting dualism—that is, they will always coexist although they are incompatible. Augustine's intellect wrestles mightily with the idea of creation from nothing. Where in all the physical world is there evidence? What does the world offer to help one comprehend such a thing?

> *. . . nor in the whole world didst Thou make the whole world; because there was no place where to make it before it was made, that it might be. Nor didst Thou hold anything in Thy hand, whereof to make heaven and earth. For whence shouldest Thou have this, which Thou hadst not made, thereof to make anything? For what is, but because Thou art? Therefore Thou spakest, and they were made, and in Thy Word Thou madest them. But how didst Thou speak?*

Augustine considered the existence of evil—or the *apparent* existence of evil—both physical and moral, to be an even graver problem. If God created the world, it follows that the world must be an ideal, a perfect order. How might a perfect God make a mistake and bring into being something less than perfect? Yet it is clear that things are far from ideal. From physical disasters to moral depravity, the human race is continually plagued by monstrous deviations from perfection. How does one reconcile the existence of evil with the belief that God, being perfect, is all-good?

Evil, Augustine concludes, cannot be a "thing," cannot exist in the way that material substance exists. For if it were a material substance would evil not be—as is all matter—the creation of God?

> *That evil then which I sought, whence it is, is not any substance: for were it a substance, it should be good. . . . I perceived therefore . . . that Thou madest all things good, nor is there any substance at all, which Thou madest not.*

The problem posed by Augustine stipulated that nothing made by God can be evil, but yet evil exists.

Or does it? Augustine answered the problem by defining evil as *the absence of good,* comparing it to a disease which temporarily attacks the body:

> *In the bodies of animals, disease and wounds mean nothing but the absence of health; for when a cure is effected, that does not mean that the evils which were present . . . go away from the body and dwell elsewhere: they altogether cease to exist; for the wound or disease is not a substance, but a defect in the fleshy substance—the flesh itself being a substance, and therefore something good.*

Reason, however, is not completely satisfied with such an answer. If all substances are good but are subject to the defect of the temporary absence of goodness, where does the good *go?* To use a homely example, one might argue that a tear in a cloth is a defect but that this defect does not exist in the material itself; the tear can be sewn and the cloth will be whole once more. While the tear is present, the wholeness of the cloth is absent. Yet if the wholeness can come and go, even as the defect can come and go, then can it be said that the cloth is always whole no matter what seems to happen to it?

Augustine considered still another problem, this one concerning God's omniscience and human freedom of will. The church insisted that human beings were sinful creatures, responsible to God for their actions. Such responsibility assumed the ability to choose between right and wrong. But if God is all-knowing, human choices should not surprise Him; He would know in advance what every person is going to do. Does this mean, then, that human destiny is already mapped out?

In a sense, it does; and Augustine readily accepted the idea of *predestination.* Anything less, he believed, detracted from God's perfection. On the other hand, the fact of predestination in no way altered the fact of human responsibility. But how may both conditions prevail?

It seemed clear—finally—to Augustine that human reason was a material substance and could in no way partake of the divine substance. It would therefore always be limited. He concluded that the human mind cannot see things as God does; what seems paradoxical to human reason must not be so for God. An Ultimate *does* exist—God—but there is no Ultimate for human understanding. At the outer circle of the mystery, reason pauses and retreats. Only faith—the acceptance of that which cannot be rationally known or analyzed—dares venture beyond this circle.

And for centuries faith, not human reason, represented the only certainty.

Faith Is Not Enough

The certainty which transcended human analytical thinking began to lose its hold on Christian intellectuals just about the time that the great universities of Europe were being founded. Oxford, the University of Paris, Bologna, to name a few, opened their doors to young men studying for holy orders. But the growing need for disciplined training of the mind as well as the spirit set in motion an inevitable intellectual movement. A university by its very nature brings together students and teachers engaged in the common purpose of learning and teaching a body of doctrine, and exchanges of ideas and debates surely must take place. Little by little the university movement, also called scholasticism, created a new approach to religion, one which attempted to reconcile faith and reason.

An important personality in the very early history of the new movement was not a university person, but rather the Archbishop of Canterbury: Saint Anselm (1033–1109). Anselm's work in philosophy clearly paved the way for later developments in Christian thought, which were to result in a new approach to religion aimed at agnostics and atheists, one still used to convince those who cannot accept Christian belief on faith alone.

Anselm did not see himself as a rationalist, but rather as a mystic. His mission, as far as he was concerned, was to protect the faith against those who assailed it. He lived at a time when, in the inevitable course of things, established truth was questioned. The questioners used reason as their weapon and scoffed at religion on the grounds that it would not dare—would not know how—to counter the attacks with the same weapon. Anselm's reply was that Christians had the same right to use reason as anyone else and, though rational proof of God's

> **The swing toward mysticism no doubt has its roots in the failure of science to produce a happier world.**
>
> The New York Times

> **According to St. Anselm, rational proof is not nesserary for the devout believer, but such proof is possible.**

existence was not necessary for the devout believer, such proof was possible.

Anselm's most famous contribution to early scholasticism was the so-called *ontological argument.* Ontology is that branch of philosophy which deals with the phenomenon of being. An ontological argument for God's existence seeks to prove that it is illogical and absurd to suppose God has no being.

Though Anselm's argument is complicated in its wording, the outline of it is as follows:

> We must assume that nothing greater than God can be conceived (for if there were something greater than God, that something would have to be called God). In other words, God by definition, is the Ultimate.
>
> There are two ways to conceive of something. It can be an idea that exists only in one's mind, or it can be an objective reality of which the mind can become aware.
>
> Whatever exists in objective reality is necessarily greater than an idea that exists in the mind alone.
>
> Since nothing greater than God can be conceived, it follows that God necessarily exists, independent of the mind.

Others who were to follow in the Scholastic movement would argue that it would be impossible to conceive of God at all if God did not actually exist, for from what other source should the idea of God have come? Much later, in the seventeenth century, the French rationalist Rene Descartes (1596–1650) would offer the following logical sequence to prove God's existence:

> God is a perfect being.
>
> Non-existence is not an attribute of a perfect being.
>
> God necessarily exists.

No doubt the most ambitious effort to prove God's existence through analytical means came from Saint Thomas Aquinas (1225–1274), who many believe sums up the scholastic movement. Educated originally by Benedictine monks, he then entered the University of Naples, became a Dominican, and later moved to Paris, which was already a major intellectual center. Here Aquinas came into contact with the analytical method of Aristotle

and achieved his major fame as a philosopher by applying logic to every phase of Christian doctrine. More than
any other person, Aquinas was responsible for making
the philosophical approach to religion both fashionable
and acceptable after many centuries dominated by mysticism and faith.

Even today, students in Catholic seminaries are
thoroughly trained in Thomism, the name given to St.
Thomas Aquinas's logical method of teaching Christian doctrine.

Aquinas developed the famous Five Proofs of God's existence, which are briefly summarized below.

Argument from Motion:

Some things in the universe are in motion. It is clear that what
is in motion must be set in motion by something else. But it is
impossible to trace motion back infinitely. There has to be a first
mover, which is itself unmoved. Only God can be the first
mover.

Argument from Causation:

There is no known case of something's having been the cause
of itself. Everything is caused by something before it. But as
with motion, it is impossible to trace causation back infinitely.
There has to be a First Cause, which is itself uncaused, and this
can only be God.

Argument from Being (Ontological Argument):

Though we have only to look around to see that things *are,* it
is indeed possible to imagine that they should not be. That is,
the possibility of there never having been existence can and
does occur to reason. On the other hand, though it is possible
for nothing to be, it is clear that there *is* existence. Hence there
must be a necessary being from which all other being derives,
and this can only be God. *This third proof is generally regarded as the
strongest.*

Argument from Gradation:

Wherever we look we see greater or lesser amounts. We do not
conceive of "better" unless it is also possible to imagine "best."
Everything we know of points to the existence of an Ultimate
—a Best in everything—and this can only be God.

Argument from Design

Since there is evidence of order and design in the universe, there must exist a designer, a super intelligence responsible for this order; and this can only be God.

In this "enlightened" age, it is easy to scoff at some or all of these proofs, to say—as indeed many have said—that Aquinas always begs the question. But whether one is prepared to accept logical arguments for God's existence or not, due respect should be given to the ingenuity of Aquinas. If, for example, you counter with "Why should the super intelligence be God?" the Thomist can come right back with, "Call it by any name you wish, as long as you grant there *is* a super intelligence." If you persist, saying, "How can we know there is order?" the Thomist can come back with, "Show me how your life is founded on the assumption that there is chaos in the universe."

Alternatives Today

From the time of Aquinas right up to the present, the debate over whether (or to what degree) the tenets of religion are acceptable has continued. The need to choose between faith and science is only one issue, and it is crucial only to those who elect to make it so. A hundred years ago the forced choice was more intellectually imperative. Church leaders feared that acceptance of scientific theories, such as that of evolution, would mean the death of faith, and so they often urged their flocks to turn their backs on science. Today many leading religious figures seem to have no difficulty coexisting with science.

People who have no interest in religion often argue that there is no point in even looking into the matter, since science has made religion outmoded and unnecessary. Indifference or simply a vague agnosticism is one alternative many choose to adopt, but this decision is hardly demanded by science.

The old pattern which has repeated itself for centuries is also still with us. For many, the certainties of science and technology, while in some respects beneficial to human life, have proved dehumanizing as well. Many people look with alarm at predictions that biological science will soon be able

John Stuart Mill
___

Religion may be morally useful without being intellectually suitable.

to create live cells in laboratories and behavioral science will soon be able to produce the most ideally "conditioned" beings who ever lived. The possibilities offered to humanity by the "uncertain" disciplines, including religion, seem more and more attractive in comparison.

At the same time, there are still people who are raised within the absolute confines of *religious* certainties, of unquestionable doctrines, fundamentalist interpretations of existence, whose parents cite the Bible as the only source of truth. There are many who are content with these beliefs, and there are many who break away from the fold at the earliest possible moment. For the latter, *science* may represent the unknown, the adventurous, the daring alternative.

A genuine commitment to a religious sect and its practices, or to one's private beliefs and methods of communicating with God, remains, of course, not so much an alternative, but an inalienable right. Thousands of devout believers have no trouble separating religion from science, aware that religious faith and the acceptance of scientific laws exist on different levels of human consciousness.

S ome turn to religion as a way of finding certainty. Having been accustomed to looking at all sides of every issue, having kept an open mind for a long, long time and having become confused by the number of possibilities, they have found in religion an anchor for both their intellectual and emotional life. They have taken what Kierkegaard (see Chapter 7) called the "leap to faith," crossing over the boundaries of purely rational thought, claiming the right to accept that which reason cannot comprehend.

The following alternatives are specific approaches to the faith/science question which have attracted a considerable popularity in our time.

The Pragmatic Approach to God

Pragmatism is a broad term covering those philosophies which are rooted neither in rational analysis nor in faith (or mysticism). They are based on workability, feasability, function. A pragmatic approach to religion would say that the existence of God cannot be proved by reason alone or by the scientific method. To insist God does not exist on this ground is to deny the possibility of other outlooks.

Often considered an ancestor of the American pragmatic

Albert Einstein

Science without religion is lame, religion without science is blind.

philosophers, the German thinker Immanuel Kant (1724–1804) was also a rationalist when it came to what can be *known* of the things of this world. He believed each person was born with certain innate "categories" of knowledge, such as the knowledge of time, space, causation, and so on. As sensory experience was absorbed, the raw material from the senses came in contact with these inborn categories, and the result was understanding. How could the senses alone tell you of time, Kant argued, unless you already had some knowledge of it?

Kant even included the moral sense as one of the categories. He called it the "categorical imperative" or the inborn "sense of ought." Otherwise it was impossible to explain how young children could learn morality so readily. True, parents imposed rewards and punishments, but without the categorical imperative, how could young children comprehend right and wrong as quickly as they do?

Yet when it came to the issue of God, Kant found himself at a loss. He could identify no God category, for all of the other categories were ways of comprehending experience. Since there could be no direct experience of God, human beings lacked direct or intellectual comprehension of God. Did this mean there *was no* God?

Not necessarily, Kant answered, though he found himself highly critical of the rational arguments of philosophers like Aquinas and Descartes. All logical proofs of God's existence, he said, assumed that existence to begin with. All of them assumed God to be that which must exist. Those which begin "God must be a perfect being" assume His existence. Kant believed all such rational explanations really amounted only to this: God exists because God could do nothing else. Or: God exists because, being God, He must exist.

On the other hand, God's existence satisfies many intellectual needs that human beings have. Kant's recognition of the *need* for belief as being just as essential as the *grounds* of belief is what makes him an ancestor of pragmatism.

> **Kant said all logical proofs of God's existence assume His existence to begin with.**

Sophistication consists in the attempt to deduce the knowledge of God (which is the basic principle of religion) by rational necessity. There is no need for this. In religion the knowledge of God is properly based on faith alone. [2]

Without the certain knowledge of God's existence, for example, we should not be able to account for the order in nature. We know that the moral law seems to be universal among people, but must they not "feel" God's existence as a way of justifying that law?

Thus did Kant make a crucial separation between *critical* (or rational) philosophy and *practical* philosophy, without which we could not function as human beings but which we cannot precisely document or analyze. In other words, if we cannot prove something (such as God's existence) the fact that we feel compelled to believe in it indicates another kind of certainty.

Kant's contribution is far more profound than might appear on the surface. Whenever the burden of proof is placed on the side of religion, one can counter by saying that "proof" need not necessarily be limited to rational analysis *or* to the method of science. An inner conviction of God, as a way of accounting for the uniformity science has discovered in nature—or just an inner conviction that God is there—cannot be lightly thrown aside, especially if it is profound and honest. Practical philosophy can be valuable—even crucial. The urgency of sincere belief is not to be easily dismissed.

The Psychological Approach

The American philosopher William James (1842–1910) was also one of the pioneers in psychology, and his interest in both fields was no coincidence. James's concern is less with the ultimate mysteries of the universe than with the phenomenon of belief itself: the need people have for belief, the harm that can befall them when belief is shattered, and the fact that two people can hold contradictory beliefs and both be right.

James is identified with the mainstream of American pragmatism, a philosophical approach which says that nothing is true that cannot be tested out in experience. But pragmatism is a broad concept, covering a wide range of possibilities. The crucial term is "experience." To James's predecessor Charles Sanders Peirce (1839–1914) experience meant the testimony of the senses. You have to be able to see something or touch it to know it is there. To James, however, psychological, or inner, experience can be just as important.

As a philosopher James sought to illuminate problems which were psychologically meaningful. As a psychologist

L. A. Reid

Here am I, here are we, *existing* . . . most of the time, like half-wits, we do not realise this. When we do, we are having an experience which I should call essentially religious.

he sought to help people plagued by doubt, afraid to believe what they thought others would attack, by providing for them a solid philosophical basis for what they believed.

James taught at Harvard, which like most intellectual communities of the late nineteenth century, was permeated with scientific fervor. The new century was beckoning with shining promises of intellectual certainty reachable through the sophistication of scientific methodology. The wide acceptance by the academic world of Darwin's theory of evolution (first presented in 1859) marked, in some minds, a point of no return, an irreversible trend, especially when it came to matters of faith. For had not religious belief arisen in an earlier time when humanity's understanding of the world was quite limited? How, for example, could one continue to believe in the six days of creation as recorded in Genesis, when it now seemed certain that the earth had evolved over a very long period indeed?

Yet it was precisely on behalf of the intellectual community of Cambridge that James gave one of his most famous and ringing defenses of an intelligent person's right to hold onto his faith:

> *In the midst of our Harvard freethinking and indifference I have brought with me tonight something like a sermon on justification by faith to read to you—I mean an essay in justification of faith, a defense of our right to adopt a believing attitude in religious matters . . .*[2]

William James said two people can hold contradictory beliefs and both be right.

James is too meticulous a philosopher to advise people to believe what they want and let the matter go at that. Nor does he say (as some *do*), "As long as they can't disprove it yet, go ahead and believe it." Such tactics can prove ruinous as new scientific reports keep coming out of laboratories. No, James's idea is to clarify the whole nature of belief. He asks what belief is *for:* what function does it serve? What matters to him is the vitality—the *liveliness*—of a belief.

Beginning on science's own ground, he calls the belief that God exists a hypothesis; and like any other hypothesis, it must meet certain criteria before one may accept it in good conscience. Moreover, there are two, and only two, kinds of hypotheses: living or dead. It is important to grasp this fundamental distinction.

A dead hypothesis is one *which would make no difference if it were true or not.* By "difference" James means "causing an action or a certain kind of behavior." It would be like the experience of rushing up to a friend with a prediction, "It looks as if our team will finally win a pennant," and of being greeted with a bland look, followed by a bored, "So what?"

By contrast, a live hypothesis would indeed make a difference if it were true. To someone who has just lost a loved one and who cannot accept death as final, the hypothesis that there is an afterlife in which reunions take place would, if true, make all the difference in the world. To someone whose intellectual grasp of existence requires God as a first cause, the hypothesis that there is a God would, if true, make a difference.

A dead hypothesis is one that would make no difference to anyone whether it were true or not. For James, God was a live hypothesis.

Assuming that the hypothesis is a live one and is valid as an hypothesis, the next step is to find a basis for choosing between the hypothesis and its opposite. For example, the hypothesis "God exists" has a negative counterpart: "God does not exist." Both options, James says, are live possibilities. Nor is it possible to decide the issue on either scientific or purely intellectual grounds. What can science offer to back up the proposition that there definitely is no God? What self-respecting scientist can do more than say the matter of God is neither here nor there as far as he or she is concerned or that it lies totally outside his or her jurisdiction. On the other hand, what persuasive argument in *favor* of God's existence can be offered? Proof does not exist on either side. What does one do then? James says:

> Our passional nature not only lawfully may, but must, decide an option between propositions, whenever it is a genuine option that cannot by its nature be decided on intellectual grounds; for to say, under such circumstances, "Do not decide, but leave the question open," is itself a passional decision—just like deciding yes or no—and is attended with the same risk of losing the truth. [3]

By "passional" James means that aspect of ourselves which fully and totally makes a commitment to action. If we waited for proof positive on every option for belief, how would we ever *do* anything in this world at all?

To sum up, James is in favor of examining belief carefully in terms of the difference it really makes and the integrity that we bring to it. He is not against faith; he is against indifference and also against the closed-mindedness of people who scorn the beliefs of others on the vaguest grounds, without carefully scrutinizing their own.

Reconciling Science and Religion

It must not be thought that science and faith can maintain, at best, only an uneasy truce, that each must stay on its side of the intellectual fence, any more than that science must inevitably discover the Ultimate and have no further need for faith. What must be grasped is the historical pattern: too much certainty leads to a renewed interest in faith; too much dependence on faith causes some people to begin looking around for certainty. Viewed in this light, science and religion continually feed each other, continually motivate the other.

There was the famous lady astronomer at the Harvard Observatory who said that astronomy was "the most poetic of the sciences, taking us further and further into the unknown." One suspects that behind such a statement may be an ambivalent wish: to accept the challenge of the unknown and probe its farthest recesses; yet hoping there will *always be* an unknown. More than one scientist is motivated by the lure and fascination of the "Boundless Unknown," is moved by a sense of awe that is not devoid of religious feeling.

No less a scientist than Albert Einstein has said:

> *Although it is true that it is the goal of science to discover rules which permit the association and foretelling of facts, this is not its only aim. It also seeks to reduce the connections discovered to the smallest possible number of mutually independent conceptual elements . . . whoever has undergone the intense experience of successful advances made in this domain is moved by profound reverence for the rationality made manifest in existence.*[4]

The university movement called scholasticism created a new approach to religion that attempted to reconcile faith and reason.

Einstein's position, which became strongly reinforced during his later years, was that the more profoundly science was able to see into the workings of the universe, the more convinced would science become that an Ultimate did in fact exist. Coming closer to the Ultimate could not fail to inspire a sense of awe, a feeling that "appears . . . to be religious in the highest sense of the word."

During the last century, in the heat of the first major

confrontation between religion and science, when forces on both sides were shouting, "All or nothing!" some tried to effect a union of the two. One author, explaining the new science called geology, said that the new discoveries were only retracing the "footsteps of the Lord." That signs of uniformity in nature testify to God's presence was a possibility often rejected by intellectuals who declared themselves "unafraid" to look their conscience in the eye and deny God's existence. Yet for Einstein there is no question of fear or courage—merely of true understanding.

The theory of evolution has historically proved a major obstacle to those who would reconcile science and faith in the Bible's explanations of the world's mysteries. But the burning issue which produced the 1925 Scopes Trial in Dayton, Tennessee—whether to deny a teacher the right to inform students of something unacceptable to fundamentalist religious belief—has cooled down considerably. Some biblical literalists have ventured the opinion that the six days of Creation, as recorded in Genesis, really meant six *ages,* thus explaining how the Bible and Darwin are *not* in conflict. Others, somewhat more conservatively, have refused to accept as fact what they say is still theory (for example, Darwin's theory of evolution), pointing out that the "missing link" between man and the primates has yet to be discovered, and never will be. As such, the truths of the Bible are not threatened.

Those who do not rely on the factual authenticity of the Bible, who view the Bible as a collection of symbolic tales not as actual history, have explained evolution as "God's method of creation." What matters, they say, is not human *origins,* but the present *results.* How could so rational and spiritual a creature as man have emerged from anything but a divine source, regardless of what stages it may have passed through?

Perhaps the most ambitious effort to reconcile religion and science is that of Pierre Teilhard de Chardin (1881–1955), who begins with the premise that faith alone is weak support in a scientific era such as ours. Scientific methodology has demonstrated its powers too often to be either ignored or negated. It is better to work *through* science rather than around or above it.

Looking squarely at what science has brought to light, one cannot but be amazed at the ingenuity of existence, the

---

Robert C. Wood

Scientific *and* humanistic approaches are not competitive but supportive, and both are ultimately necessary.

apparently unlimited creative energy of earth, which has brought into being more and more complex systems of life, culminating in the human brain. Whatever humankind has been in the past, who can deny our present capabilities and the promise of our future? In the name of a narrow religious faith, why need we cut ourselves off from the joyous contemplation of marvels that are yet to be?

Teilhard sees the soul as evolving, sees God as evolving—sees both as astonishing products of natural development. Is the old doctrine of a deliberate creation out of nothing more wondrous to imagine than the innate capacity of matter to give birth to spirit? If some have stated God is dead, why not reply that God is in the process of being born?

Central to Teilhard's philosophy is *Omega Point,* the end result toward which nature is striving. Omega Point is a humanity of infinite complexity, nobility, genius, and capacity for love. It will be epitomized in the Super Christ, the return of that perfected being who showed himself two thousand years ago, long before the earth was prepared for His coming. But this time Christ will reveal "Himself to us in a form and in dimensions, with an urgency and area of contact, that are enlarged and given new force."

Reading words that glow with the fervor of a Teilhard reminds us of the final, awesome moments of Stanley Kubrick's film *2001: A Space Odyssey* (1968). Traveling toward Jupiter, carrying a lone astronaut, a space ship suddenly reaches the speed of light. The astronaut finds himself in fields of anti-matter unfolding endlessly before his eyes. He has crossed the barrier which limits human understanding and now is hurled wildly into the heart of the universal mystery. The space ship comes to rest in a strange room where, sitting at a table is the astronaut himself, now a very, very old man. Time is no longer a human dimension, so that the astronaut sees the future taking form. The old man lies down on a bed and, lifting himself toward the infinite, he is transformed into the embryo of a super child held in the womb of the universe, waiting to be born.

Kubrick's film is no less religious than Teilhard's philosophy or Einstein's "profound reverence" for existence. In the opinion of many, science has now passed beyond its own earlier and narrow positivism, lighting up wonders little suspected by religions of old. It is, they say, no longer a question of holding fast to the faith of our ancestors, but coming at last to terms with a faith that is only beginning to come close to what faith *can* envision.

Chapter 8 Footnotes

[1]Immanuel Kant, "Errors of Religion," *Lectures on Ethics,* trans. Louis Infield (New York: Harper & Row, 1963), p. 87.

[2]William James, "The Will to Believe," *The Will to Believe and Other Essays in Popular Philosophy* (New York: Dover, 1956), p. 1.

"The visible world is no longer a reality and the unseen world is no longer a dream.

W. B. Yeats

[3]*Ibid.,* p. 11.

[4]Albert Einstein, "Science and Religion," in *Patterns for Living,* Oscar James Campbell, Justine van Gundy, and Caroline Shrodes, eds. (New York: Macmillan, 1955), p. 276.

9

WESTERN TERRITORY, EASTERN SPACE

Overview

The fascination with Eastern beliefs, practices, and life styles, which appears to be gaining momentum in this country, is not new. In one respect the very discovery of the Western hemisphere was made possible by an interest in the East. Even before Columbus, Europeans had been intrigued by Eastern lore, had invented the myth of the exotic Orient, where life was much more dazzling than it could ever be at home.

In our time the mass media—particularly Hollywood movies—have kept the mythology alive in varying guises. Before World War II, audiences could think of the Orient in the exciting terms of Charlie Chan thrillers—of silent knife thrusts in dark alleys, beaded curtains through which mysterious faces smiled sinisterly, and of teeming ghettoes where people disappeared, never to be heard from again. Or they could project themselves into stories like *The Good Earth,* in which family ties and traditions *really* counted and in which the elder citizen held an honored position in the community.

During World War II, Japanese characters in much fiction and *all* movies were portrayed with sneers and quiet sadism. After the war, the actors who had made fortunes playing cruel Japanese kept their incomes healthy by playing Chinese communists. But as the East became gradually less threatening, interest in the Orient took the form of poetic, lotus-blossom romances in which lovers from the two hemispheres almost, but not quite, got together. Nonetheless, after they parted, the boy or girl from the West would always cherish the memory of wind chimes, jasmine tea, and flower boats.

But the world's dimensions are truly dwindling. People in the West can watch an American presidential party seated at a state banquet in Peking *live and in color,* with a newscaster vividly describing each dish as it is served. Travel between the hemispheres has become commonplace. American business has invested heavily in the industries of Hong Kong, Japan, and Taiwan. A criss-crossing of life styles is beginning to take place. Tokyo is beginning to look more like New York than it does the cherry-blossomed stage set from *Madame Butterfly.* Conversely, if you have the money, you can find an architect who will build you a house with teakwood furniture, rice-paper sliding doors, and a lily pond. In many areas of the United States serious interest in Oriental religions and value systems is growing. That is, *serious*—as in life-time commitment.

This interest first developed along the West Coast. For over a century now there has been a steady stream of emigration from the Orient to California. In the beginning the emigrants were mainly from China, lured or brought here as cheap labor for the railroad companies. But over the course of time, as Chinese roots deepened and a true alternate culture made its presence felt, the way was opened for other Eastern strains. California universities—notably U. C. Berkeley—have distinguished programs in Eastern studies, which have attracted many scholars and philosophers from Eastern countries. These in turn have brought with them more and more genuine flavors of the Orient, so that a profound understanding of the Eastern mind is now available to the Westerner who seeks to broaden his perspective.

The impact has been greatest from two particular Eastern schools of thought: Tibetan Buddhism and Zen Buddhism. For a number of reasons, which shall presently be investigated, these traditions offer many Americans *genuine alternatives* to a way of life and a value system they no longer find entirely satisfactory.

What Is Buddhism?

There is not one school of Eastern thought or religion to which the label *Buddhism* is applied. There are different *kinds* of Buddhism. But there is a common basis, a foundation shared by the various kinds.

In its most pervasive use, the term Buddhism connotes a religion practiced by millions of people, principally in Asia, including Japan and the Republic of Formosa but not those countries currently under communist rule. It is a religion in the sense that it involves certain rituals practiced in places appropriately designated and held sacred and has an ancient tradition of belief which unifies those people born into it or choosing to follow its teachings.

It differs from both Islamic and Judeo-Christian religions in that it does not have a principle of godhead. Its dominant ritual—the act of sitting quietly without any particular project—appears to resemble prayer, but it is not prayer. Buddhist meditation is a technique for tuning in to the subtleties of the present moment, for understanding the patterns of sensations, thoughts, and emotions that make up human experience, and for cultivating a wakeful state of mind. Buddhists make no attempt to communicate with a transcendent god figure because they believe that before wondering about the godhead they must first come to understand themselves and the operation of their own perceptions.

Buddists believe all unethical behavior is motivated by self-interest.

According to Buddhist belief, the sense that people have of themselves as solid, separate, independent beings in a world of indifferent objects is an illusion—an illusion which is not imposed from outside but rather grows out of faulty perception and overhasty interpretations. Buddhism says this illusion is the source of most of our suffering and the source of all our immoral actions toward others.

Thus while Buddhists do not talk about a god figure, Buddhism is nonetheless profoundly ethical. All unethical behavior is motivated by self-interest. Whether acts of violence are physical or more subtle and psychological, they always spring from intense desire or intense fear, and underlying is always a sense of the self as isolated, vulnerable, and needy. Buddhists claim that as people see more clearly, and realize that the sense of separation is illusory, they uncover a tremendous warmth and resourcefulness within themselves which allows actions to be spontaneously appropriate to situations as they arise. Buddhist morality is not dependent on a transcendent god who lays down rules and punishes people for breaking them. It is instead dependent on freeing oneself from the idea of existing as a separate being, on discovering one's own *egolessness*. The recognition of egolessness as the natural state and of ego as an illusion is often in dramatic conflict with Western value systems which take the reality of the self for granted.

> **The recognition of the ego as an illusion is in dramatic conflict with Western value systems.**

Hinduism and Buddhism: An Historical Perspective

Hinduism came before Buddhism, and both religions share certain views. Buddhism is founded on the teachings of the Buddha, who, according to belief, was an actual person, an Indian prince named Siddhartha Gautama.[1] Siddhartha lived around 500 B.C., roughly a hundred years before the death of Socrates, and over a century before the great period of Greek philosophy dominated by Plato and Aristotle. His historic life span preceded that of Jesus by half a millenium.

The Buddha (a Sanskrit term meaning "He who is awake") was no doubt raised on Hindu scripture and must surely have been aware of the Hindu world view. What the Buddha was seeking is clearly implicit in Hindu belief. Hence it is impossible to understand Buddhism without some reference to the earlier religion of Hinduism.

In Hinduism there are deities with specific names like Brahman, the Creator; Shiva, the Destroyer; and Vishnu, the Preserver. Buddhism dispenses with deities, though many devout Buddhists have regarded and no doubt continue to regard the Buddha with as much awe as Jews and Christians regard God or Moslems regard Allah. The Buddha was very much flesh and blood, however; he was not the incarnation of godhead in any sense. To be a practicing Buddhist one need believe only that the Buddha was a perfectly actualized human being and that the enlightenment he attained represents a model, a *goal,* to which all may aspire.

The gods of Hinduism are really personifications of cosmic forces, much as the Egyptian Ra was the personification of the sun. These forces are said to have existed from the beginning and to be imperishable. They represent the workings of the universe. Brahman is the principle by which the endless variety of things comes into being. It is the inexhaustible creativity of existence. Shiva—familiar to Westerners in the famous guise of the multi-handed dancer—is the principle by which created forms pass out of existence and disappear. If Brahman is viewed as birth, then Shiva is assuredly death. If Brahman is youth, Shiva is age. If Brahman is the excitement of a new society in development, Shiva is the excitement of revolution and the shattering of old orders. Between the rising and falling actions of the universe, a balance is somehow achieved. For every birth, there must be a death. Hence the third member of the Hindu trinity: Vishnu, or the principle of balance.

In actuality, the three gods are all different facets of the same force: *existence itself.* They represent its modes of being. Underlying the diversity of things we experience there is fundamentally only *one* thing. For example, a person who is being born and a person who is dying share the common fact of being alive. Existence either is, or is not. In Western terms, we would say that the baby coming into the world and the person leaving it both have existence. But if we change the wording and say that they both *are* existence, then the *oneness* of everything according to Hindu belief becomes clearer. Differences—in age, sex, degree of intelligence, even species—are regarded as the *properties* of existence. Absolute separateness is an illusion, and is called *maya* in Sanskrit, the ancient language of India. It is not a negative term. The Hindu is not asked to believe differences are not real, only that they are ultimately not important.

The American poet Walt Whitman, who was very much influenced by Hindu thought, has captured the principle of unity-in-diversity in these lines:

> *I believe a leaf of grass is no less perfect*
> *than the journeywork of the stars,*

> *And the pismire is equally perfect, and a grain of sand,*
>   *and the egg of the wren,*
> *And the tree-toad is a chef-d'oeuvre for the highest,*
> *And the running blackberry would adorn the parlors of heaven,*
> *And the narrowest hinge in my hand puts to scorn all machinery,*
> *And the cow crunching with depress'd head surpasses any statue,*
> *And a mouse is miracle enough to stagger sextillions of infidels.*

The continual equation Whitman makes between the gigantic and the tiny is characteristically Hindu. He refers to himself, in the humblest of terms, as a "kosmos."

Consider also the very title of Whitman's major work *Leaves of Grass.* Why this title? Why single out grass unless one mode of nature's being is just as important as any other?

"So long as one drop of water exists, there is water."

And is not one *leaf* of grass—one spear—just as important as all the grass there is? So long as one leaf of grass exists, there is grass. So long as one drop of water exists, there is water. Who needs oceans? Similarly, if the humblest human being that ever walked the earth survives a devastating nuclear blast, has not humanity itself survived?

In Hinduism Brahman is also identified as the world soul —the ongoing *isness* behind everything. It is without beginning or end. It manifests itself, however, not in its pure wholeness, but rather in its individual forms. Hence the term *atman,* which means the individual soul. Atman is to Brahman what the leaf of grass is to grass as a whole, what the drop of water is to all the water on earth. (Hence Whitman's line "I believe a leaf of grass is no less perfect than the journeywork of the stars. . . .")

When human beings regard themselves as separate entities, unrelated to the whole, they perpetuate an ancient human mistake—the source of all human misery. Separateness creates desire, for the individual self seeks to possess all that is not itself. It acts out of self-interest. But needs born of such a misunderstanding of existence can never be satisfied. If one sets out with the idea that the purpose of living is the gratification of desire, how can there *ever* be fulfillment? What, in the long run, is "enough"? Thus life, from the perspective of the individual, amounts to continual frustration.

Not only that, but life from the perspective of the individual is limited, while existence itself in reality is limitless. But the individual knows only that, having been born at a particular time, he or she is stranded—"stuck"—in one tiny historical moment, which will never recur and which will soon be gone. Hence, having been born, one may anticipate, in addition to the frustration of all desire, only the pains of aging and the agonies of death.

Hinduism thus views the human lot as one of suffering. Like many other religions, Hinduism has a vision of how such suffering is to be overcome—or more precisely, what it is that constitutes *relief* from suffering. In Hinduism this relief is *nirvana.*

Nirvana is not a place—not heaven, not the abode of the blessed—but a state of being free from all desire, frustration, and pain. It is the total *absence* of all the things that generally plague human life. It is therefore obliviousness, much closer to unending sleep than it is to heaven, though through the ages in *popular* Hinduism nirvana has probably been conceived in poetic terms—conceived as an active experience of bliss, if not indeed a place in which bliss happens.

In the strictest sense of the word, however, nirvana represents the reunion of atman and Brahman. It is the end of separateness. One's awareness of being a personal, discreet entity disappears. One is free of desire, confusion, and the frustration borne of continual striving for achievements and possessions.

Nirvana is unbroken sleep—deathlike, but in a special way. Central to the Hindu view of life is the doctrine of *rebirth.* Unlike the religions which believe the soul lives on after death in a realm far different from earth's, Hinduism believes that the soul keeps returning in a new body, beginning once more the cycle of striving and suffering until, at some distant point in time, it attains nirvana and is liberated from the pain of rebirth. Nirvana is the end of the road. It terminates the cycle.

What keeps the cycle going? That is: why is nirvana unattainable in one lifetime? The answer should not be illogical to those who practice any of the other major world religions (such as Judaism, Christianity, or Islam). All of these maintain that the knowledge of how to achieve the final goal is given to each person; that the requirement is purity of soul. The requirement is not, however, easily satisfied. There are too many temptations. The apparent pleasures of this world deceive us and lure us away from the practices that will keep the soul pure. In Hindu scripture these practices are clearly stated:

> The requirements of duty are three. The first is sacrifice, study, almsgiving; the second is austerity; the third is life as a student in the home of a teacher and the practice of continence. Together, these three lead one to the realm of the blest. [2]

Hinduism puts rebirth into an economic and sociological context. The idea is that in each lifetime the soul is supposed to have attained a somewhat more elevated state, and if this comes to pass, rebirth will take place in more comfortable surroundings than in the previous incarnation.

India has been for centuries dominated by a system of castes, social ranks or plateaus which once permitted absolutely no social mobility. Those born into the lowest caste—the so-called untouchables—could expect to remain there a lifetime. The highest caste, that of the Brahmins, was not only the wealthiest and most aristocratic, but traditionally was assumed inhabited by the purest and most virtuous. The Hindu caste system is somewhat similar to the class system of the European Middle Ages, in which the nobility were supposed to be quite literally nobler in virtue than the lower classes, who were supposed weaker and more readily ensnared by Satan's temptations.

The apparent pleasures of this world deceive us.

But even for a Brahmin the path of life was never simple. It could take eons of time for one soul to pass through all of the cycles before attaining nirvana. Also, *downward* mobility in reincarnation was always a strong possibility: that is, you might be reborn into a lower caste. Even the virtuous Brahmin might require many lifetimes before experiencing reunion with Brahman, before release from suffering could be attained.

Buddhism is founded, as has been stated, on the teachings of Siddhartha Gautama, who, according to legend, achieved nirvana after his coming had been prepared for some 25,000 years earlier. Buddhist scripture records that in all of his rebirths the eventual Buddha had intuitive knowledge that he was destined to find enlightenment and to lead others in the true path. His own "terminal" lifetime, however, was filled with doubt and suffering, and after his enlightenment, he was to alter the Hindu world view to such an extent that a new religion arose, as pervasive and powerful as the one it sought to replace.

John A. Hutchison

Misery is rooted in ignorant craving, or the delusory, itching will to exist, to get, and to possess.

on Buddha's teaching

What distinguished the Buddha from the many sages who had attained nirvana was that he renounced the privilege of remaining in nirvana and instead elected to dedicate his life to sharing his wisdom with others. In fact, the Buddha claimed that the attainment of nirvana is only a partial experience of enlightenment. He said clinging to nonexistence, cessation, and detachment as goals meant still being caught up in the delusion of a separate self. Although a major cause of suffering may be the belief in the self's separateness, thinking of the self as totally nonexistent is also a delusion and still a cause of suffering. It is not, the Buddha said, a matter of ending everything but rather a matter of waking up completely to see things as they are.

In his teachings, the Buddha came forth with a radical

reinterpretation of the old Hindu scriptures and put matters in a far less mystical, far more psychological perspective. In fact, the story of Siddhartha Gautama's enlightenment reads a good deal like a contemporary novel of an alienated human being's struggle to save himself from being dashed to pieces on the rocks of despair.

According to legend, Siddhartha was born into the highest, or Brahmin, caste of India, had every possible advantage, every luxury, the opportunity to indulge himself in every imaginable sensory delight. And indeed he did indulge himself as a young man. He met and married a beautiful, sensual woman, showered her with jewels and other magnificence, had children by her and surrounded them also with the trappings of wealth. Gradually, however, his hedonistic, materialistic life style began to grow stale. The more Siddhartha possessed, the more he wanted and the less satisfied he felt. His life was somehow empty; his spirit seemed dead. At length he communicated his misery to his wife and family and told them that he must now leave them and undertake the long quest of purification. Somewhere an answer had to found—the way to live a holy and spiritual life.

In Buddhist terminology the prince was, like everyone else, caught up in *samsara,* a Sanskrit term Buddhists use to define the general futility of a life lived for the satisfaction of momentary desires, a life guaranteed to be hollow and frustrating. He was also trapped in *karma,* another Sanskrit term taken over by the Buddhists from Hinduism. In Hinduism karma is the debts accrued over a given lifetime—the unfinished business which prevents a person from attaining purity of soul, thus necessitating yet another rebirth. In Buddhism, karma is defined as the "law of sowing and reaping"—that is, the endless round of cause and effect, of one thing leading to another, that perpetuates the confused idea of a separate self which underlies samsara.

Siddhartha spent many years wandering, questioning people, going to holy places. At one point he decided that his problem had been too much wealth, too much self-indulgence; to make up for it, he began to live as an ascetic and hermit. Some stories say that in this period of his life he lived on as little as one sesame seed each day. He grew thin, emaciated and weak, but he seemed as far away from purity of soul as he was when he was self-indulgent. He began to realize that trying to purify his

---

Chuang Tzu

To pursue infinite knowledge in this finite life is indeed hopeless!

'self' reinforced his separateness just as much as his earlier attempts to gratify it.

At length he resolved to seek a *middle way* between the two extremes of total asceticism and total materialism. After restoring himself to health, he continued his wanderings, still sick at heart, still confused, still seeking a fulfillment for which he had no name.

Stories of the enlightenment—of Siddhartha's elevation to the status of the Buddha—are varied, but all agree that the transformation took place underneath a tree. Supposedly the former prince—weary in body after walking for days and sick at heart because of the confusion inside him—decided to rest for a bit, selecting a large tree with enormous shade. Many reports say that it was a rose-apple tree, but it has become known ever after in Buddhist legend as the Bodhi-tree, or Tree of Enlightenment. From some accounts one can imagine the coming of a great light, or the opening of the heavens and the revelation of all truth. Here is one such account:

> The earth swayed like a woman drunken with wine, the sky shone bright with the Siddhas who appeared in crowds in all directions, and the mighty drums of thunder resounded through the air. Pleasant breezes blew softly, rain fell from a cloudless sky, flowers and fruits dropped from the trees out of season. . . . Mandarava flowers and lotus blossoms, and also water lilies made of gold and beryl, fell from the sky on to the ground near the Shakya sage, so that it looked like a place in the world of the gods. At that moment no one anywhere was angry, ill, or sad; no one did evil, none was proud; the world became quite quiet, as though it had reached full perfection. [3]

Other stories indicate that evil demons attempted to distract the Buddha during his long trance, to prevent the enlightenment from taking place. But in any event, it *did* happen: the prince saw that all notions of self were beside the point. He opened completely to things as they are, and discovered boundless wisdom and compassion.

By the miraculous signs in the atmosphere it became known that the Enlightened One had indeed arrived. The Bodhisattva (he who is destined through all his previous lifetimes for enlightenment) had indeed been Prince Siddhartha (whose own given name had meant "he who reaches his goal").

When at length the Buddha again rose, it was not to

Hee-Jin Kim

Man is still to live with his native frailty, ambiguity, and sinfulness, i.e., his karma-boundness—but no longer bound by them.

remain in nirvana, but to teach his followers the Dharma, or the Way, the Path of Enlightenment.

Buddha-Dharma Updated

Buddhism broke radically with Hinduism on the crucial matter of the identity of Brahman and atman. In doing so, it established itself as a completely different philosophical road with far different implications for the individual traveling on it.

The basis of the Hindu religion is the longing of atman for reunion with Brahman—a goal that is reached only after innumerable cycles of birth and rebirth. This belief presup-

poses that only one soul, one self, exists. The Buddha, however, denied the idea of an absolute self. For him, the Hindu concept of an atman—an entity that inhabited the body and gave to each one of us an absolute "personhood"—was an illusion.

Central to Buddhist thought is egolessness. This is not a doctrine of self-sacrifice, or of loving your neighbor as yourself. It is the basic, true condition of human life. Nobody is a "me" or a "you" as something distinct and separate from all other beings, enduring through time as an unchanging central core.

> *A man does not have a core or a soul which he can consider to be his true self. A man exists, but he cannot grasp his real being—he cannot discover his own core, because the existence of a man is nothing but an 'existence depending on a series of causations.' Everything that exists is there because of causations; it will disappear when the effects of the causations cease.*
>
> *The waves on the water's surface certainly exist, but can it be said that a wave has its own self? Waves exist only while there is wind or current. Each wave has its own characteristics according to the combination of causations—the intensity of the winds and currents and their directions, etc. But when the effects of the causations cease, the waves are no more. Similarly, there cannot be a self which exists independent of causations.*
>
> *As long as a man is an existent depending on a series of causations, it is unreasonable for him to try to hold on to himself and to regard all things around him from the self-centered point of view. All men ought to deny their own selves and endeavor to help each other and to look for co-existence, because no man can ever be truly independent.*[4]

Though the enlightenment took place 25 centuries ago, contemporary exponents of Buddhism still transmit the Buddha's experience from teacher to disciple.

Many psychologists are especially interested in the nature of this experience, for the doctrine of egolessness has profound implications for mental health. According to some modern theories, *it was the act of sitting* that constituted the central experience of the enlightenment. The longer the Buddha remained there under the tree, the more he came to see and understand his own mind. Whatever thoughts, whatever emotions, whatever bodily sensations arose, he allowed them simply to be. He did not use them to fortify his own sense of self, but allowed them to rise and fall. For

Buddhism rejected a belief in one soul, one self.

Buddhism advocated the doctrine of egolessness.

just as important, he became aware of the impermanent nature of the flow of his thoughts. No thought lasts forever, and one is always replaced by another. All of us know how the agonizing problems of one day may not seem so bad the next day, even though they are not resolved. The reason? We have responded to other causes and so become distracted. Who has not been angry over the way someone has behaved, only to forget the provocation altogether within a few hours? Who has not known an all-consuming love to fizzle down to indifference after a few months, even weeks?

The Buddha recognized that what is usually called the "inner self" is solely made up of thoughts and feelings that come and go. As the commentator pointed out: take away the causation, and the self disappears. By extending this logic, we see that, if one is not chained to causations, one will not be chained to an idea of self. What is then taking place within? Where is that "self"? The self can be known only when these thought processes—these reactions to causations—are happening. But if the thoughts themselves become transparent, so does the self.

One of our thoughts concerns this very impermanence. Fundamentally we recognize how fleeting and how unstable the self can be. It is discontinuous, and in the gaps "we" disappear. To resist such discontinuousness, the illusion known as ego is created. It too is a thought, an idea; it is a reaction to a causation, namely, the fear of nonexistence. To sustain the illusion, thoughts keep generating themselves. Buddhists call this "mind chatter." We are afraid to let it stop, for then the sense of self fades.

In this interpretation of the Buddha's enlightenment, one can imagine the Buddha experiencing the liberation that comes with the simple acceptance of discontinuousness. He does not struggle either for or against his thoughts. Whatever thought arises is simply acknowledged as thought. Its nature is "nowness," and the Buddha makes this discovery of wakefulness continuously.

Nirvana is therefore not some eternal haven of rest. Enlightenment is not some final security. It is not the union of atman with Brahman of the Hindu tradition, or the dwelling in some transcendent truth. Enlightenment is a continual process of waking up to things just as they are. In this sense, one is free of the struggle of ego, because one is no longer caught up in the tension of thought and emotion, making mountains out of molehills.

But the Buddha carefully observed the sources of pain and clearly saw the path that people should follow to achieve such composure, such equanimity. This is another point which signals a major break between Hinduism and Buddhism.

If one human being, through the gentle discipline of meditation, could come to understand and tame his or her own mind, then why was it impossible for others? And why should the process take eons of time? Thus did the Buddha teach that *enlightenment is attainable in the course of a single lifetime* and that *the attainment of it is not the exclusive right of the aristocratic class.* The Buddha taught that every human being possesses the potential of wakefulness. And so he taught the Four Noble Truths:

"To resist such discontinuousness, the illusion known as ego is created."

Life is filled with pain.

Pain is caused by the need to possess.

There is a way out of pain.

The way to nirvana is the Eightfold Path.

The Eightfold Path is the Middle Way the Buddha had sought for so long a time. It is divided into the fundamental phases of anyone's life, which need to be approached without ego. These phases are:

Right Views	Right Livelihood
Right Intentions	Right Effort
Right Speech	Right Mindfulness
Right Conduct	Right Concentration

One cannot, the Buddha reasoned, sit through one's entire lifetime, though it is through sitting that one becomes aware of the "series of causations." It is always necessary to acknowledge the flow of cause and effect, but it is not necessary to be swept along by it like a fragile leaf picked up by the wind.

The act of sitting (called *meditation* by Buddhists) allows one to be entirely awake, to become master of one's thoughts in the sense of being able to see them for what they are: fleeting responses to temporary stimuli. Such mastery is the gateway to pure intelligence. The "right" way in all things, so says the Buddha, is instantly clear to intelligence, not to ego.

Thus Buddhism stresses that the Eightfold Path is really the intelligent approach to all human activities, and it is climaxed by Right Concentration—or sitting meditation—to which one must always return. Buddhism is a religion built around the disciplined practice of sitting perfectly still, with legs folded and back erect but not rigid—a position receptive to Right Concentration, the maximum degree of wakefulness. Right Concentration sees through ego strategies and continually allows for the operations of intelligence.

In some contemporary interpretations of the Eightfold Path, "right" is often made synonymous with common sense. Exponents of Buddhism argue that what is appropriate for anyone to do in a given situation will be clear if one allows oneself to be completely present without preconceptions. Unfortunately, however, most people cannot see beyond the needs of their egos, and react in a way most guaranteed to protect and preserve them.

To me the tragedy and comedy of life lie in the consequences,
sometimes terrible, sometimes ludicrous, of our persistent attempts to
found our institutions on the ideals suggested to our imaginations by
our half-satisfied passions . . .
George Bernard Shaw

To appreciate the difference between ego and mind (intelligence), consider the experience of watching a movie. There are two ways to view a film. You may identify with the main character, believing all of his motives are good, despising those who threaten him, rejoicing when the good things he richly "deserves" come his way. Or you may intelligently survey what happens in the light of common sense, recognizing that the film is manipulating events so that they turn out as the audience wishes, not as they probably would in real life.

Popular entertainment is often geared to the ego desires of its audience. It presents a picture of a world in which absolute selves do indeed exist, and these are categorized as good and bad and they never really change. Good people stay good; the bad stay bad and are punished.

Because of the illusion of ego, so say the Buddhists, we face the world with illusory expectations. We think there is an indestructible core, "me," to which things happen. Often—in fact, most of the time—the events we experience are not what our egos would like to see happen. Hence, instead of observing what is actually the case and acting appropriately, we attempt to change things around, to manipulate events: from a simple refusal to believe that something *is* the case ("I am not alone"; "We did not break up last night", "The phone will ring any second"; Everything will work out for the best") to irrational actions aimed at stemming the onrushing tide of events—striking someone, committing murder, setting fire to an entire block of buildings.

Intelligence sees that ego always acts out of self-interest. It decries such actions, for, since the self is an illusion, there can be no such thing as self-interest. It is insane to behave out of illusory motives. No sane result can take place. This, the Buddhists tell us, explains why the world is always in a state of chaos. *There are simply too many conflicting illusions serving as the basis for what people do.*

According to Buddha-Dharma (or the Way of the Awakened), seeing through the illusions of ego will reveal compassion as a fundamental fact of existence. This does not mean feeling sorry for others. Pity is very often a subtle action of ego; it bolsters one's illusion of a positive self to believe that others are going to pieces. The nature of Buddhist compassion is described in this interview with David Rome, executive secretary of Vajradhatu, the central administration of the most prominent Buddhist meditation center in the United States:

Compassion

It's not really a question of the need for compassion, but in fact when there's no demand, only then can real compassion take place. Actual compassion is based on a person's ability first of all to be clear about what's going on in a situation: what's going on with his own energy, his own desires, his own uncertainties as well as those of other people. When he sees those things clearly, then spontaneously he does what is appropriate to the situation. This is the real meaning of compassion.[5]

As one meditates, and understands the patterns of the mind, one becomes more and more even-handed, not only about one's own processes, but those of other people as well. One recognizes with ever-deepening insight what drives others to say or do certain things. It is not a matter of forgiving and forgetting, not of turning the other cheek. One merely withholds judgment and responds intelligently —as one does with oneself. The friendliness one feels for oneself gradually begins to extend to other people.

An overly doting parent who loves a child to distraction, "understanding" every action and overlooking every action, however indiscreet or even illegal, is hardly being compassionate. There are times when a very hard line of action may be the only compassion which makes sense in the situation. Nor in the Buddhist sense is hard line action a matter of doing something for someone's good or "because I love you so very much." These are motives which stem from self-interest. (To do something for someone's good, if this is the sole reason, can be a projection of self-interest, acting out a wish fulfillment in which one identifies with the child for whose well-being events have been manipulated.) In the Buddhist sense, one acts directly, without indulging in the ego game. Hence true compassion in the Buddhist sense may not always be recognized or appreciated by society.

One may well ask: what do I "get" for following the Eightfold Path? At first glance it sounds as though Right Actions and Right Views do not always make people happier or richer, either materially or spiritually. The Path does not appear to have happiness or personal satisfaction as its goal, and in truth, it does not. The Buddhists see no reason why it should, no reason to believe that life is supposed to yield happiness or dividends of any kind. Life is simply what it is; it must be taken as it unfolds.

At the same time, one *is* spared the suffering caused by an exaggerated concern with self—a far different thing than tingling with excitement over prizes won, possessions secured, fame and glory reaped. We must remember that in Buddhism, enlightenment is a return to humanity's fundamental condition: egolessness. In such a state, there is no self to crave happiness or to fear sadness. This is not, however, a dry retreat from the world, as non-Buddhists often believe. On the contrary, the Buddhist believes a sense of delight accompanies the experience of life as it is, and a sense of appreciation for whatever arises.

In Buddism a sense of delight accompanies the experience of life.

The Tibetan Tradition in America

Like any other religion, Buddhism has split into many sects since its founding 25 centuries ago. They share a fundamental acceptance of the Eightfold Path, but they differ with respect to ritual and practice.

The Buddhist tradition which developed in Tibet has emphasized the Buddha's decision not to enter nirvana but remain in the world to guide others. It is based on the concept of the living, ongoing Buddha-mind as opposed to centralizing an homage to the historical Buddha. It places great importance on the *lineage* of enlightened beings and on the vitality of transmitted teachings. It is, in short, highly oriented to the Everlasting Now aspect of Buddhism. The Enlightenment is not something that took place long, long ago under a tree. *It is continually taking place.*

Features of the Tradition

You will recall that Buddhist scriptures conveyed the belief that a Buddha appeared at the end of each eon and that an eon could last as long as 25,000 years. Almost from the outset a Bodhisattva (one who is destined for Enlightenment) possessed an intuitive comprehension of his eventual destiny and role in life. Eventually he would be born, as Prince Siddhartha was born, to a final lifetime when the long-awaited goal would be reached.

Buddism is not a dry retreat from the world.

In Tibetan Buddhism there have been and will continue to be more than one Buddha and many Bodhisattvas. (Mainstream Buddhism, on the other hand, prophesies the coming of the new Buddha in a very far-off century.) Each generation, as a matter of fact, produces a recognized Bodhisattva, who is known to the world as the Dalai Lama. The term Dalai means "the sea—measureless and profound."

The Dalai Lama does not inherit his position. It is not passed down from generation to generation in the same family. The incarnation of the Bodhisattva for each age must be discovered by means of an elaborate ritual:

> *The first step is to find out from the State Oracle the locality in which the Dalai Lama has reincarnated. As soon as this important fact is known, search parties, which have been selected by lot or by the State Oracle, are sent out. On the basis of their reports the government draws up a list of possible candidates. In the meantime, the Regent of Tibet visits the sacred lake believed to be the abode of the Goddess Kali—for she appeared to the first Dalai Lama and solemnly vowed to watch over all his successors—and there he sees in the depths of the lake a vision indicating the location of the Dalai Lama's new birthplace.*[6]

But the Dalai Lama is not the only Bodhisattva in each age. In Tibetan belief there can be a number of others, some totally unrecognized, living in humble circumstances, dedicating their lives, as the Buddha did his own, to guiding others along the spiritual path to Enlightenment.

The Bodhisattvas are regarded as potential Buddhas at the middle stage of the way to Enlightenment. But even having reached a middle stage in the progress towards spiritual perfection is awe-inspiring; thus the Bodhisattvas earn the highest possible praise and respect from their followers.

Implicit in Tibetan Buddhism is a hierarchy of persons, arranged according to their proximity to the ultimate goal, which is the full incarnation of Buddha-hood. A lama is a Bodhisattva, and he is also a *guru* or holy teacher. There are many gurus, not all of whom become lamas. But even so, the guru is a very special, very fundamental unit in Tibetan Buddhism.

The Buddha Shakyamuni walked the path essentially alone. His enlightenment was a lonely experience. Sitting meditation, which is the very soul of Buddhism, intensifies each meditator's sense of aloneness. As the distance increases between one's wakeful intelligence and the flow of one's thoughts and feelings, the awareness of space grows. The longer one sits, the more spacious is the experience. (Thinking—staying close to one's thoughts—is, by contrast, a crowded, closed-in sensation.) But spaciousness can be unsettling if one is not a Buddha. That is why Tibetan Buddhism places so much importance on the role of the guru.

It is a requirement in this tradition for one who proposes to begin sitting practice to ally oneself with a teacher. A teacher can provide a link with the tradition, can give advice on the discipline of sitting, and can share the many doubts which occur to one when on the long path toward the distant goal, which can sometimes seem totally unrealistic and unattainable.

Finally, the Tibetan tradition stresses the *sangha,* or community (though all Buddhist strains recognize the importance of the fellowship of meditators). Again, without a home base, so to speak, without the community, the meditator runs the risk of being overwhelmed by space long before coming close to his or her goal.

Sitting meditation intensifies each meditator's sense of aloneness.

The Growth of the Tradition in America

In 1959 the Chinese communists embarked upon a massive campaign to rid Tibet of the Buddhist religion. The Dalai Lama went into exile, along with a number of other major lamas. Among these was Chögyam Trungpa, called Rinpoche ("The Precious One"), who while still in his teens, was recognized as occupying a very high place in the Tibetan spiritual hierarchy. He fled to the West, attended Oxford University, where he became familiar with Western thought and the Western value system, and has since emerged as a major philosopher, the primary spokesman for Tibetan Buddhism in the United States.

As the Buddha's approach to the practice of meditation evolved, he realized that gimmicks are merely neurotic affections. He decided to look for what is simple, what is actually there.
Chögyam Trungpa

Rinpoche, as he is known to his many followers, has established a substantial Buddhist *sangha* in Boulder, Colorado, surrounded by the towering Rocky Mountains, an area which somewhat resembles Tibet. At present there are over eight hundred members of the community known as Karma Dzong. Its affairs are presided over by an administrative body known as Vajradhatu, which in turn serves as the

———————
Buddha
———————
**The no-mind not-thinks
no-thoughts about
no-things.**
———————

unifying force behind all of the smaller Buddhist communities that have sprung up throughout the country. These communities, called Dharmadhatus, are found in major metropolitan centers like New York, Boston, and San Francisco, but are being organized in smaller locales as well. Under Rinpoche's guidance, Vajradhatu has also created a number of retreats, such as the Rocky Mountain Dharma Center in Livermore, Colorado and Karme-Choling in Barnet, Vermont, where Americans dedicated to Buddhist practice may go for periods of intensive discipline, ranging from a week to a year.

A number of important American educators, writers, philosophers, and psychologists, recognizing the implications Buddhism holds for a society they believe is rapidly disintegrating, have migrated to Boulder and become part of the American Buddhist movement. Many have joined with Rinpoche in establishing the Naropa Institute (1974), a liberal arts college which attempts to prepare its students for a useful, productive life in science, the fine arts, or social services while also including in that preparation the insights of Buddhist philosophy and practice. Naropa Institute is the only institution of higher learning on American soil that is inspired by the meditative approach. Especially in summer it attracts thousands of Americans of all ages and backgrounds. There the student enrolls in courses with provocative labels, such as "The Tao of Physics" and "Introductory Space Awareness Training." Famous names like Allen Ginsberg, William S. Burroughs, and Gregory Bateson can be found on the faculty roster.

Zen Buddhism in America

Zen Buddhism is that strain of the parent religion which has come to be most closely associated with Japan. It originated in India at the same time as Buddhism itself. In the beginning it was that aspect of Buddhism intensively concerned with the meditation practice and the techniques one must acquire to master it. Its name stems from the Chinese word for meditation: *Ch'an.*

The founding of the Zen tradition as a specific school of Buddhism with its own rituals, methods of sitting, and folklore is attributed to an Indian monk named Bodhidharma. A thousand years after the enlightenment, Bodhidharma traveled to China with the missionary zeal to win converts to the Buddha's teachings. Zen legend sometimes adds the awesome story of how Bodhidharma sat so still for the full nine years that his legs fell off, thus demonstrating in somewhat hyperbolic terms the tremendous importance of the sitting practice in the Zen tradition.

Obeying the instruction of Prajnatara, his teacher, Bodhidharma started for the East and arrived in China in 520 A.D. The Emperor Wu-ti invited him to Nanking for an audience. The Emperor said: "Since my enthronement, I have built many monasteries, copied many holy writings and invested many priests and nuns. How great is the merit due to me?" "No merit at all," was the answer. "What is the Noble Truth in its highest sense?" "It is empty, no nobility whatever." "Who is it then that is facing me?" "I do not know, Sire." The Emperor could not understand him. Bodhidharma went away, crossed the Yangtze River and reached the capital, Loyang, of Northern Wei. After a sojourn there he went to Mount Wu-t'ai and resided in the Shao-lin Temple where he remained and for nine years, facing a cliff behind the edifice, meditated in silence.[7]

The anecdote recounted above also demonstrates the traditional Zen delight in indirection, whimsy, and cryptic utterances. Of all the schools in Buddhism, Zen has become the most systematically devoted to the transcendence of not only ego but the rational process as well. It views pure intelligence as something greater than rational knowledge. It is arrived at through the intuition that comes only after years and years of steadfast, disciplined sitting meditation. In a very real sense Zen intelligence begins in the buttocks and works its way slowly upwards.

Zen Flavors

Complex historical currents carried the Zen school from China to Japan, where it eventually found a lasting home. To explain how and why this happened would require a detailed analysis of the Japanese character and way of life, both of which have found in Zen a most congenial practice.

Everyone knows, however, that the Japanese have traditionally exhibited a strong feeling for the beautiful, especially the delicately, exquisitely beautiful. Graceful movement and hand gestures in drama, dance, and puppetry are prime examples of the Japanese esthetic bent. The Japanese delight in taking that which can be clumsy and graceless and making it fluid and rhythmic. They delight in fine craftmanship—in the tiny brushstrokes of the painter's art or the intricacies of the carver's art. In short, the Japanese prize all artistic expression which can be achieved only after long years of often painful discipline. Discipline and form are quintessential to the Japanese, and of all the schools of Buddhism, Zen is probably the most formal and the most disciplined.

Of course, this is not the modern Japan of auto assembly lines, the lucrative electronics industries, and the fastest moving, most crowded mass transportation system the world has ever known. We are not talking of a Tokyo or an Osaka with teeming populations and a frenetic pace that can make downtown New York seem comparatively quiet. It is well known that, amid these hectic surroundings, all of the Japanese religions sometimes gasp for air.

> **The heart of the Zen experience is the sitting itself, which is not exhilarating or relaxing. The point of sitting is not to transcend pain and boredom but to confront them directly . . . to discover the void.**

On the battle against ego:

A monk said to Seppo, "I have shaved my head, put on black clothes, received the vows—why am I not to be considered a Buddha?"
Seppo said, "There is nothing better than an absence of goodness."

R. H. Blyth, Games Zen Masters Play

True, tourists find tea ceremonies and exhibitions of martial arts that have Zen roots and implications. Visitors sit cross-legged in restaurants with sliding paper doors, sipping on warm cups of saki, listening to softly tinkling wind chimes. They can watch and snap pictures as a Japanese girl in a bright kimono demonstrates the art of flower arranging. They can buy a Zen painting to be hung on a livingroom wall, all the while decrying the vulgarization of beautiful things in our society. But these activities are a long, long way from the Zen spirit.

The full and devoted practice of Zen is virtually monastic in nature. It requires daily sittings of many hours in duration and untold years of meditation before one can presume to claim even a remote understanding of enlightenment. It is said that Zen practitioners often hold themselves somewhat aloof from other Buddhists, perhaps because they consider that the battle against ego is hard won, if at all, and that too many persons deceive themselves into supposing they are well on the way to nirvana when in fact they are proud as peacocks over their accomplishments (which is an egocentric emotion), thus having come, in reality, not one step along the way.

Of the growing Buddhist movement in the United States, Jakushō Kwong, Sensei, a Zen master living in Northern California, said this during an interview:

> . . . the growth of Buddhism in America means in some way that many people are being taken care of. This is a very positive feeling. And at the same time this growth is dependent on our own understanding, and . . . my feeling is that the point, the foundation or the heart of the meditation is not understood so well. The growth or the expansion of growth itself is dependent on the inside, the heart of the practice. [8]

The "heart" is found in the sitting itself, which is not intended to be exhilarating or relaxing or a positively spiritual experience of any kind, though doubtless many beginners hope it will be just that. The point of sitting for hours at a time is not to transcend the pain and the boredom until a state of euphoria is reached, but to confront that pain and boredom directly—to discover the Void which underlies all existence, the Void which ego insists on covering up. Zen masters know that the beginners entertain themselves with mind chatter, and so they must keep sitting until they grow weary of entertaining themselves and are able to see the Void for what it is. Only then have they begun to understand and free themselves from ego.

> The Zen tradition in Japan creates a definite style of boredom in its monasteries. Sit, cook, eat. Sit zazen and do your walking meditation and so on. . . . The black cushion is supposed to suggest no color, complete boredom. [9]

One of the strengths of the Zen tradition, and one of its appeals to some Americans is, of course, the attainment of a passive willingness to accomplish any required task. It becomes all the same whether one must sweep a floor or carve a statue. Without ego, there can be no protests of, "But that's not my job," or "I'll never get anywhere if I do work like this." Fame, fortune, and glory are playthings of the ego. The oft-repeated Zen maxim is, "Wash your rice bowl."

This is many times given as an answer to the most profound and searching questions.

Zen masters can be rough. There is always an overseer to the zazen, or sitting period; and if he catches someone beginning to doze, he will take a long stick and strike him soundly on the shoulders.

Zen masters can be biting and satiric, seizing every opportunity to knock somebody's ego off its pins. On the occasion of the interview with Jakusho Kwong, Sensei, a portion of which was quoted above, tea and cakes were served. One of those present tasted a little cake and commented: "My, it doesn't have any sugar in it." The person then asked someone else if *his* cake had sugar. The other replied that it had

". . . do your walking meditation, and so on."

not. Kwong, Sensei with a twinkle in his eye bit into his own cake and said that it too was free of sugar, whereupon he added: "Now let's go around the room and find out if anybody's cake has sugar in it." The observation called attention to the absurdity of the conversation. Zen masters are acutely conscious of the confusion of thought and purpose in which they believe most people wander.

Zen teachings are full of seeming paradoxes and riddles, all of which emphasize the fact that the real truth—the stark reality—is always staring people in the face but that they are too caught up in words and ideas to see it.

Kassan had a monk who went round all the Zen temples but found nothing to suit him anywhere. The name of Kassan, however, was often mentioned to him from far and near as a great master, so he came back and interviewed Kassan, and said, "You have an especial understanding of Zen. How is it you didn't reveal this to me?" Kassan said, "When you boiled rice, didn't I light the fire? When you passed around the food, didn't I offer my bowl to you? When did I betray your expectations?" The monk was enlightened. [10]

But what *is* that truth, that stark reality, one is tempted to ask? The Zen answer, typically cryptic, is: *if you have to ask, you will never understand it.* And yet the "truth which has no name" is also absurdly simple, perhaps best summed up in this simple line by the old Chinese sage, Lao-Tzu: "Everything is what it is." There is just what happens—the flow of things—nothing more. It is to be observed with neither joy nor sorrow—without judgment, without analysis. The myth that the rational mind is capable of not only comprehending but *altering* reality to suit its own purposes is, to Zen, the biggest joke of all, but perhaps too tragic to laugh at.

Living, Working, Practicing Zen

San Francisco's Zen Center is an unpretentious building which contains 22 tiny apartments where people live, singly, in couples, and in families. They are all Americans. Some work at the Center for little remuneration; most work at almost any conceivable kind of job. All of them rise early in the morning, go to the *zendo* (meditation hall), sit, and repeat the process at night.

Practitioners who want more intensive opportunities for

meditation may go to work at Green Gulch Farm north of the city, for working with one's hands rather than with one's head is important in Zen. Those who want to go even further and lead a purely monastic existence may apply for admission to the Zen Mountain Center in Tassajara Springs, hidden away in the Santa Lucia Mountains of Carmel, California.

Like Tibetan Buddhism, Zen is developing centers all around the country. The tradition one chooses to follow probably depends upon which one is encountered first. They differ in degrees of emphasis and in their "flavors," but both lead to profound and dramatic changes in the typical American life style and value system.

Why Buddhism Appeals to Some Americans

To the average American the East probably still seems remote and mysterious, a place unlikely to be visited, populated by beings difficult to comprehend. It is nevertheless true that genuine interest in the East is growing more rapidly now than at any previous time in the history of the United States. Interest is no longer confined to a few university scholars and a small coterie of students. The East—especially the Buddhist East—is beginning to effect a radical and profound change not only in the way some Americans live, but in the way they think and perceive.

Buddhism is opposed to the evaluation of events, people, achievements.

A meditation hut used for solitary retreats by American Buddists.

The Success/Failure Syndrome

The American Buddhist believes he or she has succeeded in becoming detached from a vicious circle in which, always intent on "getting ahead," the individual must move from one plateau to another, never really believing he or she has "arrived." Even if one is lucky enough to earn in the millions or to hold the record for the most runs batted in, or achieve seven Olympic gold medals or three Academy Awards, and even if one finally moves to Beverly Hills or Palm Beach— there are still such constant threats as:

the Dow Jones average plunging to the lowest figure ever

someone else eclipsing the old record

spending as though there were no tomorrow and finding out there isn't

putting on weight and losing the leading roles

falling out of favor with the powers that be

waking up dead one morning

The Buddhist philosophy is predicated on the continual, unending flow of existence, in which the only constant, the only *peak,* is change itself. It is opposed to the evaluation of events, people, achievements. It recognizes everything which occurs, to be sure, but it is always willing to let go, to move on.

American Buddhists view success and failure as illusions —arbitrary opposites, which distort the perception of events as they really happen. For example, a man loses his job after twenty years. He and his wife start bickering over finances until at length she leaves him. Unable to stand the thought of living in the same house without her, he moves to New York. He cannot find a job. He is too old or overqualified, and the good-paying jobs are held by people of his own age who have moved steadily "up" the ranks. In a short time he has all but exhausted his funds. It is late autumn. As he walks along the cold and windy streets, he begins to see the city as a cruel, heartless place and himself as a total failure.

There is a song from a famous musical comedy that describes how the leading character feels in the early morning: the sun is brightly shining, the corn is high and ripe for harvest, and "everything's goin' my way." An inward feeling of success seems to integrate the world for us, while a sense of failure makes the environment seem bleak and callous. Most Americans, so believe the Buddhists, find themselves somewhere between the extremes and judge everything that happens to them solely according to this one scale.

In Buddhist philosophy, the feelings you have about your-self are *only* feelings. You may harbor them, or you may disown them. It is entirely up to you. It is unnecessary to let society call the plays. It is unnecessary to compare your own situation with someone else's. "Successful" people have no objective existence. They are *perceived* as successes, and fail-ures are of their own making.

Territory

Man, says Robert Ardrey in *The Territorial Imperative,* is property-oriented, sharing this characteristic with all the other animals. The instinct to find, protect, and preserve a nesting place, a point of continual return, or a "good sound investment" is basic animal nature and is informative about almost everything human beings do. The behaviorists, how-ever, say human beings do *not* have instincts, that their tendencies and actions are the results of conditioning.

The Buddhists no doubt would agree in this instance with the behaviorists. That is, the urge—the obsession—to ac-cumulate property (including objects and other people) may be bred into us by the society in which we live. But we have the option of rejecting this urge. Living for the sake of one's territories means imprisoning oneself, making it harder and harder to remain wide open to the flow of change.

There is also *inner territory.* The "size" of the world within each of us cannot be measured as we might measure acreage, but anyone who has allowed her or his thoughts to wander where they will, who has caught glimpses of the further-most reaches, the hidden corners of the mind, knows the distances one can travel in this way. In contrast to the im-mensity of inner space is the familiar geography of the con-scious, disciplined locales of our rational thought process. The ego, too, which is responsible for the inward sense of identity, of "meness," tries to occupy a small piece of ground.

In Buddhist terms, both intellect and ego seek continuity of existence. Without such continuity, each of us seems to lose the sense of individual being. Buddhist sitting meditation discourages clinging to thoughts and the sense of self, and encourages the individual to be open to what Chögyam Trungpa, Rinpoche, has called the "fluid intelligent quality of space."

The fear of the absence of self, of the egoless state, is a constant threat to us. "Suppose it is true, what then? I am afraid to look." We want to maintain some solidity but the only material available with which to work is space, the absence of ego, so we try to solidify or freeze that experience of space. [11]

Buddhists are respectful toward, but at the same time critical of, the Western intellectual tradition which began with Plato and Aristotle and which, reinforced by the philosophy of Descartes in the seventeenth century, built the "myth" of the separation between the mind within and the universe without. It was Descartes who uttered the famous words: "I think; therefore I am." He concluded the only certainty was that of the inner intellectual process, and he was then forced to accept on faith alone the objective existence of a world outside himself.

Buddhists do not disclaim the achievements of the Western intellectual tradition, particularly those of science and technology. But then, Buddhists do not deny the objective existence of reality, which is the domain of science. What Buddhists decry is the dualistic approach, which separates "me" from "that"—and which encourages the nonscientific, absurd delusions that "meness" can inspire. (One might consider the Nazi era in Germany as a terrifying extension of "meness" into "usness." The belief that one particular group was superior to another led to the most shameless, inhuman acts of the twentieth century.)

Buddhists rely on universal intelligence—on wisdom—which they believe is the same no matter which particular mind serves as its vehicle at a particular moment. In other words, the accurate perception of what is taking place at any given time and the appropriate action that ought to be taken will occur to the mind which is not narrowly preoccupied with the preservation of ego. Moreover, the exercise of universal intelligence does not entitle one to any special credit.

But the spaciousness of existing in the egoless state *does* alarm and terrify, say critics of Buddhism. They claim that it is *natural* for the human organism to develop a mental

Garma C. C. Chang

If you want to grasp it, it runs away from you; but if you cast it away, it continues to exist there all the time.

sense of separateness, just as the biological system develops a biological integrity and seeks to preserve its existence whatever the cost. They point to the philosophical, artistic, social, political, and technological achievements of human beings as evidences of the human need not only to be whole and continuous but to be projected into space—to cut down the size of outer as well as inner space. Why do sculptors wish to cut and shape a block of stone, eventually producing a three-dimensional reproduction of an image that occurred to them? Why do muralists insist upon placing their lasting imprint on a blank wall? What made Beethoven curse the heavens when he realized that he, of all people, would be denied the chance to hear his own music coming back to him?

> **If something is worth doing at all it must be worth doing for its own sake.**

The Buddhist reply is that the Western stress on individuality instills in us the following:

the importance of being a separate entity
the need for praise
the need to possess and be known to possess
the need to keep confirming our identity

This last—*the need to keep confirming our identity*—is probably the crucial element, for it relates directly to our fears of extinction, our rejection of the thought of ever dying.

Some would ask the Buddhists: what can you offer us if we disown ego and forego the continual confirmation of identity? What can compensate for the sudden disappearance of the self? The Buddhist answer is: since the self is an illusion to begin with, it is not only unnecessary but absurd to perpetuate a myth. Scientific discoveries, brilliant thoughts, and creative products will not diminish. All that will be given up is the involvement of the ego. In other words, if something is worth doing at all, it must be worth doing for its own sake, not as a gratification for the ego.

Still, the majority of those raised in the Western tradition would probably find the Buddhist view difficult to accept. Self-interest—the fundamental territory—is very deeply rooted in our culture. It is hard to imagine our culture's being the same without the drive for recognition which seems to underlie all forms of human endeavor. For example, it is hard to imagine capitalism without self-interest, especially if one accepts capitalism as a workable economic system, responsible for the standard of living that people in the West enjoy and/or believe they deserve. Critics of communism often point to the failure of collective farming as being caused by an unrealistic expectation; that is, can people be expected to till the soil if it does not belong to them or if they cannot anticipate some degree of personal gain from it?

In any event, many of the Americans who espouse Buddhism and the practice of sitting meditation have given up lucrative jobs and the promise of financial security in order to join a *sangha* and devote the necessary amount of time to sitting. They believe it is possible to do so without "wasting time," without surrendering the chance to "make a name for themselves." For many, involvement with meditation allows for a fresher and livelier approach to a career, which becomes part of their path. But all American Buddhists have gladly renounced what they regard as a whirlpool, a vicious circle of challenge and response which leaves one confused, exhausted, and ultimately, unsatisfied—a way of life founded on a myth, they say, *cannot* satisfy.

Critics of American Buddhism sometimes charge that the giving up of territory in exchange for the spaciousness of living without ego is an outgrowth of the many cults of the 1960s which spoke of "alternate consciousness" and often experimented with drugs in order to achieve it. They regard it as another passing fad, ill suited to the pace and goals of American life. They believe many who attempt to adapt Buddhist elements to their lives are the survivors of the rebellious '60s, still trying to escape, still unrealistically critical of the Establishment to which they must inevitably return. The American standard of living, they maintain, is too high for anyone to remain detached from it, to scorn the desire for better homes, faster cars, and, above all, entertainment.

Buddhism, in their opinion, is most effective in less-developed countries, where the individual counts for less than he or she does in the United States. It works best for people whose lives tend to be without hope and so monotonous that the boredom of continual meditation goes unnoticed. The Americans, on the other hand, are raised to be competitive, aggressive, and continually mobile. The passiveness of sitting is totally foreign to their nature, and anything which goes against its own nature is doomed to fail.

Buddhism in America

Pro:

brings a new and much-needed spirituality to American life.

Con:

most effective in less-developed countries, where the individual counts for less.

American Buddhists reply that they are bringing a new and much needed spirituality to American life. They believe the egolessness and nonaggression of their practice will offer a legitimate alternative to all those who are weary of futile striving and the unending frustration of trying to keep one step ahead of their neighbors. If they have given up the narrow confines of territory, they say, it has been for a transcendent cause: the openness of space, the delight of finding every situation in life completely workable, without the burden of either hope or fear.

Chapter 9 Footnotes

[1]The Buddha was born into the Shakyas, a warrior tribe living hear the foothills of the Himalayas. He is often referred to as the Buddha Shakyamuni (or Sage of the Shakyas)

[2]*The Upanishads,* The Chandogya Upanishad.

[3]Edward Conze, trans., *Buddhist Scriptures* (London: Penguin, 1959), p. 51. © Edward Conze, 1959. Reprinted by permission of Penguin Books Ltd.

[4]Junjiro Takakusu, *The Essentials of Buddhist Philosophy* (Delhi: Motilal Banarsidass, 1975), p. 17.

[5]Interview conducted July 21, 1977, Boulder, Colorado.

[6]Lobsang Phuntsok Lhalungpa, "Buddhism in Tibet," in *The Path of the Buddha,* ed. Kennth W. Morgan (New York: The Ronald Press Company, 1956). Reprinted by permission of John Wiley and Sons, Inc.

[7]Takakusu, *op. cit.,* p. 167.

[8]From an interview with Jakushō Kwong, Sensei, conducted July 21, 1977 in Boulder, Colorado.

[9]Chögyam Trungpa Rinpoche, *The Myth of Freedom* (Boulder, Colorado: Shambhala Publications, 1976), p. 25.

[10]R. H. Blyth, *Zen and Zen Classics* Vols. 1–5 (Tokyo: Hokuseido Press, 1960–1970). Reprinted by permission.

[11]Trungpa Rinpoche, *op.cit.*, p. 21

THE SAD CLOWN
The Tragic and Comic Sense of Life

Overview

Life is neither wholly tragic nor wholly comic; instead, it is made up of events which are interpreted as being successes or failures to the extent that they conform to individual human hopes. "Pure" tragedy and comedy are found in the arts, which remain under the control of the artist, who can emphasize through careful selection and structure the approach he or she chooses.

Within a few hours, a tragic drama can present a view of life which convinces an audience that humankind, like the hero, is noble in its aspirations yet doomed to suffer.

Or a classical comedy can present a view of life which makes light of every potential danger faced by the hero, which reassures audiences that, when needed, outrageous coincidences can occur, whether probable or not. This chapter is concerned with the tragic and the comic elements found in human experience, and will draw upon the arts in which these two opposing views are presented.

The Basic Differences

Aims

It is not necessary to choose a view of life which is *consistently* comic or tragic, but it is useful to compare the assumptions of both views.

Tragedy encourages feeling, strong empathy toward a character palpably human and worth caring about, so that

his or her suffering, whether partially "deserved" or not, is shared by those observing it.

Comedy discourages feeling, so that those who laugh are not enjoying the misery of a real human being. It is thus not cruel to laugh at the comic mishap of a character desperately hanging by his fingernails to the upper story of a skyscraper, or to laugh at foolishness, vanity, and pretentiousness. Caring too much would elicit tears, which are the enemy of laughter.

Tragedy	Comedy
I feel.	I suspend feeling.
Man is free to choose.	Man is foolish and mechanical.
Life may not have a purpose, but I can face that.	Life may not have a purpose, but I can laugh at that.

Tragedy aims high, urging a view of humankind which is special and heroic, having great aspirations and the ability to endure major disappointment. Even at the moment of recognizing the failure of his plans, the tragic hero is noble, eliciting admiration for his courage.

Comedy recognizes and makes allowances for human frailty. At the same time, the comic writer may be urging a saner view of life through exposure of people who are vain or corrupt. In this way, comedy can work to improve society as well as reassuring those who laugh that they are clear-headed after all.

Unlike tragedy, comedy is frequently tied to a particular society. Nonetheless, there are universals in comedy—violations of the norms of rational behavior which take place in *all* societies and historical periods which deserve our laughter. Tragedy is meant to be free of a particular territory, and concentrates on the universal rather than the topical. In keeping with its generally lofty aims, tragedy emphasizes free choice, so that the tragic hero's plunge into despair is at least partly of his or her own making. Except in modern deterministic tragedies showing suffering caused by forces beyond individual control, the freedom to choose is intrinsic to tragedy.

Comedy amuses by deliberately showing people as sometimes mechanical—who unthinkingly repeat a phrase, blindly pursue a foolish goal, act automatically in response to some outside stimulus. We laugh because we like to imagine that we know better, that we would not be manipulated in the same way. Thus, comedy reassures us by showing the foolishly mechanical character in contrast to the rational, freely choosing character each of us imagines him- or herself as having. It is a delight to watch comic characters so dominated by some overwhelming passion that they respond in predictable ways. Watching them behave as puppets we seem doubly certain of our own human flexibility.

Both comedy and tragedy recognize the possibility that life may not have purpose. This possibility is treated soberly in tragedy, humorously in comedy. In tragedy it matters that only humanity has purpose and is continually thwarted by a cosmos which either laughs at our frustrations or, worse, makes no response at all to our heart-break. In comedy it is we who laugh, and we do so at the expense of the fundamental smallness of humanity.

Tragedy is never small. It is always conceived on the grand scale. If it ends in failure, it is always a grand, important failure, at least from the human viewpoint. Comedy sees the meaner aspect of human nature. It is, as Aristotle observed, "life perceived from a distance."

Pride, up to a point, is
  wonderful and heroic.
Pride, overstepping its
  bounds, is disastrous.
Foolish pride is funny.

But in the long run, comedy may save us from the despair which tragedy could force us into adopting. Comedy says, "hold on; keep calm; make the best of how things are." Both the tragic and the comic sense of life reflect the wisdom of the broadest possible outlook—a magnanimous view of existence without illusion.

(Captions for all color section art are found on page xi.)

PLATE I

PLATE II

PLATE III

PLATE IV

PLATE V

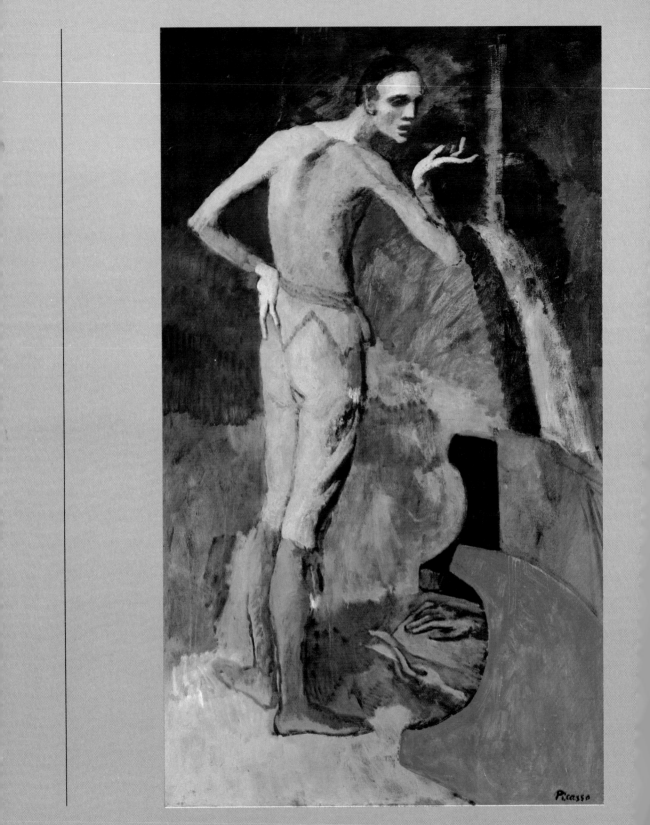

PLATE VI

PLATE VII

PLATE VIII

Sympathies

There is a basic distinction between tragedy and comedy. It is the degree of audience or reader belief in the main character as real and therefore capable of genuine feelings. At its most basic level, the circus clown who is whacked by the paddle of another clown or whose baggy pants are burned by an exploding firecracker cannot be funny if audiences believe he is actually injured. Nimble comic characters take pratfalls, they are shot at and they crash into buildings in accidents which would require hospital treatment if they were "real." Similarly, cartoon cats explode and are flattened by steamrollers only to reappear, intact, in the next scene. Though there has been some outcry against this sort of violence, most observers agree that the damage is so clearly temporary, the actions so stylized, and the characters so unreal that no one is being encouraged to applaud the "cruelty" of these exaggerated antics.

When comedy looks more real than it does in the world of circus, marionette, or animated cartoon, the characters are identifiably human, but the attempt to make the cruelty temporary and less painful continues, sometimes by encouraging an unsentimental view from the start. Even before they speak, certain characters are presented as types, the grotesque shoes of the clown supplanted by clothing plausible but still outlandish, given names which deny realism. Restoration comedy abounds in such examples: Lady Sneerwell (can we believe she was ever young, or was she born to typify the gossip and the snob?) Sir Jasper Fidget; Margery Pinchwife; Waitwell (the ideal servant); Fop (idle gentleman, excessively preoccupied with fashionable clothing); Quack (a physician with minimal integrity); and Lady Wishfort (it's been a long time since any man lavished affection—sincere or otherwise—on her). The names alone prepare audiences for laughter; and the behavior of the characters does the rest. Comic behavior exhibits a lack of proportion and a blind lack of awareness about how it is going to appear to others. When we laugh at comics we do not really injure them. They are so preoccupied with their own simple goals they remain unaware of their effect on others.

Of course, characters in serious plays may be types, and they may have names unlike those found in telephone directories. But the goal of a serious, not to say tragic, character takes on larger dimensions, and at some point there is either awareness of self or a determined effort on the part of the author to let us know that true awareness is impossible for human beings to attain. Human blindness in some tragedies is the whole tragic point.

In comedy the audience sees the characters as small, as through the wrong end of a telescope. This distance can be maintained through the previously mentioned use of type characters, through their exaggerated concern for petty goals, and through their continued unawareness that they have gone beyond limits acceptable to ordinary society.

Comedy is therefore social, impossible to think of in isolation. As Bergson has pointed out, animals are funny only as they do things we think of as human. A man alone is not funny—on the desert, in the forest, or in solitary confinement. No matter what he does with his clothes, no matter how oddly he walks, and no matter what words he mispronounces, to appear comical he needs an audience whose social context he is clearly violating and whose sympathies he is, for this reason, alienating.

Who is "Worth" Our Pity?

In watching the antics of a comic figure on stage or screen, we may sometimes be tempted to use the word "pitiful." But we do so in a condescending way. Because of the distance that has been created between us and the object of our laughter—distance absolutely essential if we are to use laughter as a means of retaining our sanity—we cannot "pity" him as we would someone who was actually in dire straits. As soon as the banana peel becomes a real threat, as soon as the fall is a real one, as soon as the cries of the wounded are no longer pretended pain, we begin to move into the realm of tragedy.

At the same time, can everyone who suffers engage our sincere pity? Surely we would all be wrung out emotionally if we allowed ourselves to empathize with all possible suffering! (Comedy's distance, of course, helps to keep the balance.) The reason for having tragic art is to offer us the chance to channel our emotions—to release our profound feelings—in a selective, intense way that leaves us in a state of psychological equilibrium, able to cope better with the uncertainties of life. But this means the central figure of a tragedy—the character who is able to affect us so intensely

—must have some special traits. At the time Aristotle wrote his famous definition of the tragic hero, the only people thought worthy of serious treatment were the highborn. This restriction was not necessarily as arrogant as it sounds in these more democratic times. People of stature—of noble birth or power (usually the two went together)—were in a position to make serious choices which involved other people, decisions which might invoke the wrath of the gods against an entire kingdom.

A comparable tragic hero of today would be able to order nuclear destruction. The classical idea of the tragic hero was that only powerful people can experience a fall of significant dimensions. Presumably, the loss of a child in the home of

a farmer would have been of less consequence than the loss of a prince.

If Thou didst ever
  Hold me in thy heart,
Absent Thee from felicity
  A while
And in this harsh world
  Draw Thy breath in pain
To tell my story.
                  Shakespeare, Hamlet

Eugene O'Neill

Can't help it. I hate myself. Got to take revenge on everyone else. Especially you.[1]

Long Day's Journey into Night

For years this rule was followed, even in the seventeenth century, in Shakespearean plays, where kings and princes suffer tragically, full stage center, and those of lower birth are allowed to be pathetic but of no lasting concern. In Shakespeare, language is of overwhelming importance in engaging audience sympathies. The Macbeth who kills emerges as more than a common murderer because he is able to communicate so effectively his inner doubts. Noble characters in Shakespeare speak in high poetry, lower class characters, usually in prose.

In our time dramatists have sought ways of making ordinary people the focus of tragedy. Arthur Miller, whose *Death of a Salesman* (written just after World War II) is a milestone in common-man tragedy, has insisted that the fate of any person can engage our sympathies provided that the character has a potential for becoming significant. If so, the disastrous mistakes he or she commits should be just as pitiable as the downfall of a Macbeth or an Othello. On the other hand, many critics point out, powerful as *Death of a Salesman* may be as a play, its protagonist Willy Loman does not have a potential for greatness nor does he make free choices. The play, so say these critics, offers a pathetic glimpse of the unimportant man overwhelmed by a value system which controls his mind and inevitably destroys him.

Some dramatists, like Maxwell Anderson, have tried to solve the problem of creating modern tragic heroes by writing period plays, using aristocratic figures from the past like Mary of Scotland or Queen Elizabeth I. Yet some critics complain that these figures lack any real contemporary relevance. Anderson's most popular modern tragedy has been

Winterset, a product of the Great Depression of the 1930s, in which the author attempts to give stature to his characters —poor people living in the shadow of the Brooklyn Bridge —by having them speak in a Shakespearean blank verse. But, again, critics point out that the poetic characters in *Winterset* do not really belong to contemporary reality.

Goals

The goal of the tragic hero in any age cannot be mean or base; it must be sufficiently great to warrant the admiration of viewers who might not dare for themselves but who admire the daring in others. The sights of the tragic hero are high, and so his or her opposition is formidable. Joan of Arc qualifies as a tragic hero because she willingly set aside personal comfort in favor of a mission she regarded as divine. Opposed to her were the major institutions of the time —the clergy, the military, the throne itself. Tragedy calls for our admiration of people, like Joan, who dare. Comedy looks out for the rest of us. Mel Brooks as the Two-Thousand-Year-Old Man said of Joan, "Sure I knew her. I took her out a couple of times, but she had a mission—to save France. I had to wash up." The Two-Thousand-Year-Old Man, deliberately irreverent, acknowledged the superior qualities of a major heroine, but in taking the safe route, in concentrating on familiar necessities, he spoke for the rest of us. Our history books are filled with the accomplishments of outstanding people, the discoverers, leaders, and zealots who, by their willingness to dare, earn their place in the books. A martyr's death is one way to be remembered, and those with strong convictions are held up as models to the rest of us.

Comedy celebrates both the cowardice and common sense of society at large. So the Two-Thousand-Year-Old Man acknowledges the importance of the discovery of the wheel and of electricity, but he reserves his greatest enthusiasm for Saran Wrap and nectarines. Comedy either begins with a character who is humble, or pulls down to a humble level those who would otherwise seem too grand. Impossible to imagine Socrates or Galileo with indigestion based on excessive acidity? Not for the humorist, who delights in juxtaposing the grand and the domestic.

Comedy thus performs an important function in relieving our anxiety that we must be perfect. Even the tragic hero is less interesting when he seems to have no flaws. An example is Sir Thomas More in Robert Bolt's *A Man for All Seasons,* who seems able to maintain his integrity and purity against all odds. Who can be so perfect? Who can be expected to try? The avowed purpose of presenting heroes is said to be for the edification of even those who fall short of the ideal. But in order for us to believe that a character is human, even the tragic hero dare not be perfect. In fact, it is the falling short of perfection which *makes* a hero tragic.

Comedy and Common Sense

Some years ago, law schools throughout the country made an inflationary adjustment in the degrees won by their graduates. The degree of Bachelor of Laws was upgraded to Doctor of Jurisprudence, so that holders of the degree could receive increased income in civil service and other jobs with a rigid pay schedule based on degree earned—column A for the bachelor's degree, column B for a master's, and column C for the doctorate.

The adjustment was greeted with amused indifference by most practitioners, whose income depended on the volume and value of law cases brought into their office. Those whose government salary was increased were gratified to be granted entry to the higher-paying column. A few jovially met for lunch and referred to each other as "doctor." But at least one of the newly elevated lawyers had a party of tribute given by his wife, who had engraved invitations and other formalities for guests from all over the country, to celebrate the new, grand status of her husband. And her husband seriously accepted the congratulations of the invited guests.

That couple, taking seriously a bureaucratic designation of convenience not tied to real merit, could have become characters in a comedy; both were blind to the beliefs of other members of society. By suffering—in a minor way—from false pride, they qualify as targets of comic ridicule.

Audiences for the perennially successful television series *M*A*S*H* have delighted in the foolish pride of the comic characters: the rank-conscious Margaret Hoolihan, blindly loyal to army regulations; the snobbish Charles Winchester, insisting on the amenities of the "gentleman" in relatively primitive surroundings; and the pompous Frank Burns, who,

---

Comedy restores the balance. It is the great leveler. Comedy delights in deflating the grandiose and pretentious.

Significant comedies like the TV series *M*A*S*H* always have a norm of common sense against which the comic elements are measured.

like the others, lacks the qualities needed for survival in this makeshift medical society: ease, informality, and a willingness to bend army rules in favor of humanness. Hawkeye, the hero, is *not* a comic target. He is the rational norm against which the comic figures are measured, for he has a solid grasp of the main point: healing the sick, regardless of rank or nationality.

Throughout the history of comic literature we find central characters who represent a standard of measurement and in contrast to whose values others become laughable. In 1750, British novelist Henry Fielding published *Tom Jones,* whose hero is morally purer than those around him who boast of their own morality. His tutors—one a clergyman, the other a philosopher—possess the language but not the actions of the truly moral person.

In what may well be *the* great American novel, *Huckleberry Finn* (1884), Mark Twain's fourteen-year-old hero is full of natural goodness and intuitive wisdom, in sharp contrast to the hypocrites, rogues, and charlatans he encounters on and off the Mississippi River.

Foolish pride is the underlying trait of the pompous Ted Baxter in the long-running Mary Tyler Moore series. Never does the vain newscaster recognize the significance of a newsroom. Rather, the televised news is a medium for his own vanity. Intellectuals like Murray can make fun of him —and he is sometimes aware that he is the butt of the joke. But his pride remains unaffected, and though we in the audience, along with the other characters, laugh at him, we are aware of the higher salary earned by this foolish, unknowing, stingy, conceited man. The values of our society may provide rewards in inverse ratio to knowledge. The knowing viewer can laugh even at *that.*

The world of the comic is full of drunks with the gift of survival; of uneducated farmers outwitting smooth-talking traveling salesmen; of fortune hunters outwitting tycoons; and children proving wiser than their teachers. The ability of the weak to sometimes triumph over the strong becomes part of a comic fantasy, which makes us laugh even as it delivers a strong—and cynical—lesson in the harsh realities of life. But perhaps the lesson is easier to take when couched in laughter.

The Euripidean Sense of Life

Tragedy, both as a way of looking at life and as an art form, is sensitive to the quick twist of the knife—to the often seemingly deliberate perversity of events. Understanding the tragic sense of life helps to soften the impact, *can* even prepare us for the worst. It is not that we should have only a negative attitude toward existence, but unbridled optimism is not the answer either. The comic view of existence knows this too.

In the tragic view of life, things turn out badly. Hopes for success are dashed to pieces. Young, romantic love turns sour, or else the lovers, like Romeo and Juliet, are fated to die. Promises are not kept; the letter that might have made all the difference fails to arrive on time. The condemned man awaits word from the governor that his sentence has been commuted. But the phone remains silent; the execution is carried out. Just as the man in the electric chair is pronounced dead, the phone rings with news of what was meant to be an eleventh-hour reprieve.

Shakespeare compared the strivings of humankind to the activities of insects observed by larger creatures: "As flies to wanton boys are we to the gods/ They kill us for their sport." Anyone can become godlike in that sense merely by frustrating at the last moment the efforts of an insect pulling a straw or tiny morsel of food. One can idly watch from the comparatively giant human size as the ant "thinks" it will successfully maneuver its way across a narrow trickle of water and up to its destination, carrying a burden larger than itself. Then, at the last moment, one can send it back by turning on water full force, covering the ant with a cigar box, or stepping on it. As ants are, for most of us, totally insignificant, we may get some mild amusement in either aiding or thwarting the progress of insects. If the insect were truly special, however, it would be another matter.

According to one ironic tale, a prisoner in solitary confinement for many years was able to maintain his sanity by patiently training an insect. Day after day, year after year, he carefully taught his (long-living) ant companion to dance, whistle (!), and tell jokes. Finally, at the end of a long sentence, he was released from prison with his only asset, the talented ant. The ex-convict hoped to make a good living

---

Shakespeare

As flies to wanton boys
  are we to the gods;
They kill us for their
  sport.

King Lear

with the One and Only Most Entertaining Ant in the World. Confidently, he carried his prized creature, lovingly encased in a covered paper cup, into a bar where he ordered a drink. In hope of being led to the nearest booking agent, he asked the bartender for information. "I've got a wonderful act," he confided, as he took the lid off the paper cup and allowed the ant to crawl out. "Sure," said the bartender, crushing the ant with his hand, "how can I help you?"

Alas! In this case the ant was irreplaceable, and the man's hopes were as crushed as the tiny body of his talented protegé. Though the little story is hardly hilarious, it would have to be classified as comic rather than tragic because the subject is (literally) small; the details are exaggeratedly comic (the vision of an insect trained for a vaudeville act lacks the grandeur necessary for serious treatment); and "a prisoner" is a general enough term for us to be able to laugh at his plight rather than identify with the man as we might had he been presented with a fully developed character.

Nonetheless, the irony of the story is exactly the same kind of irony one finds in many of the world's great tragedies. A wholesale use of this particular method of creating tragedy was made by the Greek dramatist Euripides (circa 480–406 B.C.), who seemed to delight in structuring many of his plays in such a way that the audience is led to expect a happy turn of events, only to have its hopes cruelly shattered.

The Trojan Women, for example, focuses on a single situation. It is just after the fall of Troy. The heirs to the throne of Troy are all dead save for one young boy. The women of the title gather around to mourn the dead and to protect the boy. A Greek soldier arrives, anguished because he is to carry out the boy's sentence: death by being hurled from the mountain.

The simplest possible treatment of this situation would, of course, be tragic enough. There would be the soldier's sorrow, the mother's vain pleadings, the charm and innocence of the boy, and the inevitable moment of unbearable pathos, when the boy's body is carried onstage by the wretched soldier. But Euripides deepens the character of the soldier. He also introduces a short scene in which the boy is shown playing with stones on the ground (a grim reminder that the stones will prove to be his own agent of destruction!) The soldier kneels down and helps the boy in his play. This

---

John Webster

O this gloomy world!
In what a shadow, or
  deep pit of darkness
Doth, womanish and
  fearful, mankind live!

The Duchess of Malfi

humanizes the whole event so much that the viewer cannot believe the soldier would actually complete the horrible mission on which he has been sent. *Yet he does.*

In Shakespeare's *King Lear* there occurs a most appalling moment, which also illustrates Euripidean irony. The old monarch is in his eighties and has been on the throne for so long that he cannot imagine what it is like not to be in power. His vanity knows no bounds. Having decided to retire, he summons his three daughters around him and promises to leave the largest share of the kingdom to the one who loves him the most. Goneril and Regan, the two evil schemers, outdo each other in protesting hypocritical affection for the old man. But Cordelia—young, innocent, and truthful—quietly observes that the kind of love promised by her sisters to their father is suitable only for a wife to give to her husband. Since she herself is to be married, she intends to love her father as much as is appropriate, but certainly no more and not as intensely as her sisters proclaim. King Lear is furious, denouncing Cordelia and dividing the kingdom equally between Goneril and Regan.

Euripidean irony in Shakespeare:

Juliet is given a potion to make her sleep so soundly it will appear that she is dead. When Romeo sees her lying in the tomb he believes she is dead and stabs himself. Juliet awakens too late.

Soon he realizes his mistake, but the recognition comes far too late. Goneril and Regan are engaged in a vicious struggle against each other, one which sees Lear reduced to the status of a prisoner without money or power. Cordelia's husband, the King of France, raises an invading army to save the old king, but during the battle, Cordelia is captured and sentenced to death along with her father. As soon as the tide of battle is turned, the King of France sends a messenger to stop the executions.

King Lear then enters, carrying the body of Cordelia. The stay of execution has arrived soon enough for him, too late for her. He cries,

> *. . . No, no, no life!*
> *Why should a dog, a horse, a rat, have life,*
> *And thou no breath at all? Thou'lt come*
> *No more, never, never, never, never,*
> *Never!*

Whenever there is a premature loss—the death of a child, a young wife, an artist just beginning what promises to be a great career—one feels a hollowness not unlike what Lear felt at the recognition of the apparent injustice at the heart of things. One contemporary author has referred to it as the "rotten streak in life's nature."

Whatever reservations critics may have about Willy Loman as a tragic hero, there is no doubt that Miller's *Death of a Salesman* is a powerful play; what is more, its impact owes much to the author's Euripidean instincts.

The crucial scene is the one in which Willy's son Biff goes to visit his father at the latter's hotel room. While father and son are talking, the woman sharing the room makes an untimely appearance wearing a slip. Biff loses respect for his father's values to such an extent that he deliberately fails to graduate from high school, thus becoming ineligible for the football scholarship of which Willy has dreamed.

The timing of Biff's visit plays a vital role in the boy's sense of failure in life. And Biff's failure is the prime motive behind Willy Loman's eventual suicide in an automobile wreck—a sacrifice of his own life so that his son will have the insurance money and get the decent start he needs to be at last a success in life.

But even in death, life mocks Willy. We have no reason to think Biff will turn out well, that he will not squander the insurance money on foolish schemes. As she is laying flowers on her husband's grave, Linda Loman is fully cognizant of life's tragic ironies, the very same ironies to which Euripides was keenly sensitive.

> *Why did you do it? I search and search and I search, and I can't understand it, Willy. I made the last payment on the house today. Today, dear. And there'll be nobody home.* [2]

Euripidean irony suggests the watchful eye of the playful, even malevolent, gods. Everyone remembers the O. Henry story, "Gift of the Magi," in which the wife sells her hair to buy her husband a watch fob, while he is selling his watch to buy combs for her beautiful long hair. Then there is Stephen Crane's story, "The Open Boat," about four men adrift at sea in a frail craft, three of whom survive the fury of the waves, one of whom, the physically strongest, perishes.

Dorothy Canfield Fisher

The skull of life suddenly showed through its smile.

No doubt life itself has its happy coincidences—every so often someone comes along and slips the "next quarter" into the slot machine and wins the whole jackpot. But, in the perverse way of human nature, it is the tragic coincidences which stand out, which convince us of life's ornery way of frustrating our efforts.

Euripidean irony probably helps. It is no doubt better to face the worst life can offer, especially when it happens in a play. After all, one can face almost anything as long as there is a curtain to fall. But watching a tragedy in the Euripidean style strengthens us anyway. We are that much less surprised when we feel those real knife-twists in the back.

Euripidean irony exists in comedy also, as one might expect. We cannot *always* cry over life's seemingly heartless cruelty.

A man rushes into a hospital, demanding surgery. "My doctor says I need a castration," he says. No attempt at dissuasion has any effect. "Castration is what I want," he insists. "And I want it now."

With the speed that hospital procedures exhibit in funny stories, the surgery is performed.

As he awakens from the operation, the man asks the patient in the next bed: "What are you here for?"

"I had a circumcision," says his roommate.

"Oh," says the man, "that was the word!"

The Blind Spots

As art forms, expressing deeply rooted human concerns, both tragedy and comedy are anti-pride. As fundamental approaches to living, the tragic and the comic outlooks understand that human pride is both pitiable and laughable, that pride undercuts all noble or humane endeavors and brings them to chaos and confusion. If it were only to teach us over and over again the lesson—the almost mathematical lesson—that pride is always followed by a fall, the time spent watching tragedies and comedies would be well worth our trouble. And if you view life in the tragic and comic spirits, you will keep a continual check on your own inclination toward pride. Tragedy and comedy make us forever watchful and sensitive to the pretensions, the foolish posturing, and the opaque wall of ego which can blind us to the needs of others, isolating us from the human family.

The Perennial Tragic Flaw

The Greeks called it *hubris,* and they were ambivalent about pride. They recognized its shortcomings, but at the same time, they were humanists and more than a little jealous of their own gods. To compensate for what they may have thought was an unequal distribution of power, length of life (the gods were immortal), and intelligence (the gods knew what was going to happen), they created myths in which gods are often quite human and humans are sometimes godlike.

Zeus and his wife Hera fight all the time and even support opposite sides in the Trojan War. Zeus backs Troy and thus loses, something we would not ordinarily expect from the king of the gods. Aphrodite, goddess of love, becomes infatuated with a mortal and has an affair which ends tragically for both.

Many of the myth heroes are half human and half god. No more appropriate symbol could be imagined, and it is one which has endured. For humankind, after all, *knows* itself to be intelligent, creative, and powerful. Some people are able to build dynasties and to change the course of history by a mere signature. On more than one occasion the fate of the world has been literally in the hands of a few crucial people —a state of affairs never more dramatically underscored than in the spring of 1945, when Harry S. Truman was faced with the choice of continuing the war with Japan or bringing it to an almost certain end by using the A-bomb—with the inevitable and tragic loss of life which the bomb would bring.

Whether Truman's decision was wise or disastrous can still be debated. But the channeling of so much power into one person, or very few persons, has throughout history created blind spots. There is never a way for a human being to know the full consequences of everything he or she does. The balance must lie in caution—and in a dose of humility. Oftentimes, however, the attainment of power proves so intoxicating to the human ego that the need for humility becomes less and less apparent. At such times the writers of tragedy and comedy must come to the rescue and help save humanity from its own excesses.

The *hubris* of the Greek tragic hero is at once the thing that makes him godlike and the thing that makes him blind. In Sophocles' *Antigone* there is the King of Thebes, Creon, who, as far as we know, has always tried to be a good and just ruler. But his fairness is tested after the two sons of Oedipus, the previous king, slay each other in battle. One son has been the rebellious leader of an enemy force, bent on capturing the kingdom. As a punishment to the young man's soul, Creon orders his body left unburied, thus preventing the soul from finding peace in the next world.

Antigone, daughter of Oedipus, defies Creon's order and performs the burial rites for her brother. She too has her pride—family honor versus the law of the land. Her breaking the law sets a dangerous precedent. In Creon's mind there is no choice but to sentence her to death. At the same time, Sophocles asks, may we justify a mortal's decision to defy the law of the gods? In this singular work of art, there is a double tragedy. Perhaps Creon's flaw is the greater of the two, however, for, as ruler, he affects the lives of thousands by his decisions. If they prove wrong, then the entire state suffers for it.

Someday the tragedy of Richard Nixon and Watergate will be written. One cannot imagine more potent material or a story that more precisely fits the model of what tragedy should be. As president of the most powerful nation in the world, Nixon had as much stature as any of the tragic heroes from the past. He had far more power than a Creon, who ruled a city-state with the population of perhaps only a modest-sized American city. Everywhere he went, including Peking, he, as representative of this country, was treated with the reverence and pomp once accorded only to royalty. The blind spot—or *hubris*, if you will—came from the belief that such power was appropriate for someone charged with vital decisions, someone with an assured place in history. It came from the conviction that the retention of such power was imperative, whatever the means, and that it probably would be in the worst possible interest of the United States to lose the election of 1972 to a political radical. Above all, it came from the *unquestioned assumption* that powers can be separated as far as accountability is concerned. The President may do what others are forbidden by law to do. After the exposure of the Watergate conspiracy, the blind spot was still there, and it gave itself a label: *executive privilege.*

"Executive privilege" as an unquestioned assumption is a supreme example of *hubris*.

As in the case of the great tragic heroes of the past, the fall of Nixon was inevitable—and necessary if the state were to survive. It was a fall from a height not enjoyed by Creon; and it was followed—not by death, as often happens in tragedy—but by something infinitely crueller: that final TV appearance in which the decision to resign was communicated to perhaps a hundred million people (again no precedent in tragic history!). Though the words attempted to gloss over the enormity of the humiliation, the recognition which comes to all major tragic figures seemed to be there.

And so was the lesson.

Single-Mindedness: The Comic Flaw

Comedy enjoys nothing so much as poking fun at pretentiousness. It too knows about human blind spots, and when they are not potentially disastrous or when a person remains unaware of his shortcomings, but plunges absurdly through life without ever seeing himself in action, then laughter, not tears, is the antidote.

The tragic hero always has a final moment of painful self-awareness. The comic hero remains blind.

The ruin of a state or the destiny of the human race is not involved in the great comedies. The scope is narrower, and the consequences of foolish pride are less sweeping. At the same time, comedy, like tragedy, teaches a lesson. Beware, it says to the potentially proud; Don't make a fool of yourself as this man or this woman has done.

Ever since the art of comedy was first polished by Aristophanes in the fourth century B.C., the form has been steadily adding to its eternally significant collection of comic types, most of them representing some form of pride, or—if one prefers the comic version of the world—single-mindedness. Among them there are:

the mercenary father who insists on selling his daughter to the highest bidder

the foolish old man who pursues a young lass

the fat and aging lady who believes the young fortune-hunter's protestations of love

the clumsy oaf who sees himself in high society

the semi-literate who uses long words incorrectly

Comedy does not require perfection, either intellectual or moral. But it does require self-knowledge, if the possibility of self-knowledge exists. In Tennessee Williams' (1947) tragedy, *A Streetcar Named Desire,* the heroine Blanche DuBois is self-deluded, viewing herself as a fragile Southern belle, the bulwark of gentility and respectability in an increasingly crass and unfeeling world. She does *not* see herself as a fading beauty or as the prostitute she has become. But as the play unfolds and we learn more and more of the circumstances which have led Blanche to her present pitiable state, the possibility of laughing at her vanishes. Both her background and her psychological imbalance conspire to prevent self-knowledge. Her mind is poised delicately on the brink of schizophrenia, and one can only watch in horror and intense compassion as the final and inevitable breakdown takes place.

By contrast, the character of Mrs. Robinson, who achieved fame in the 1968 film *The Graduate* and as the subject of a Paul Simon popular song about upper middle-class America and its hypocrisies and neuroses, remains, except for in one scene, comfortably within the range of the comic. The woman is single-mindedly concerned with the seduction of Benjamin, a recent college graduate and the son of her dearest friends. She is looking not for love, not for understanding, but for sex alone.

In the now classic scene just mentioned she and Benjamin are in bed together, though he always addresses her formally as "Mrs. Robinson." An idealistic young man of the 60s, with dreams of a better world of true understanding between people, Benjamin attempts to relate to the woman on more than a physical level. "Why can't we talk?" he asks. "What about?" is her bored reply. "Well, how about art?"

he suggests. After she has told him flatly that she has no interest in art, he then tries to involve her in another subject. "Tell me what you majored in when you were in college," he asks cheerfully. There is a pause. We see Mrs. Robinson's face; he does not. It has a grim sort of smile, as she replies, softly: "Art."

In this one moment Mrs. Robinson comes close to self-awareness and thus comes close to warranting our pity. But in later scenes, when Benjamin courts and desperately wants to marry her daughter, Mrs. Robinson becomes a snarling, vicious, totally single-minded character, always laughable as the comic symbol of decadent, affluent America, too rigid in her values and pattern of behavior ever to see herself clearly.

The Graduate, while often very funny, is ultimately serious. Good comedy almost always *is.* The single-mindedness not only of Mrs. Robinson but of her husband and even Benjamin's own parents, who have no true understanding of their son and no way to communicate with him, was (and is) very real. The film, like all serious comedy, has a highly moral purpose.

| All serious comedy has a highly moral purpose |

Of all the comic figures in recent times, Charlie Chaplin's Little Tramp probably comes closest to maintaining the balance between the tragic and the comic. The poor fellow in once elegant but now ragged clothes, in the bowler hat, carrying and forever twirling his cane in the manner of the uptown dandies, is always overwhelmed by the Big City's buildings, police force, wealth, and confusion. In *Modern Times,* considered by many critics to be Chaplin's masterpiece, he is the universal "little man" dehumanized by technology.

Oblivious to the hopelessness of his situation, the Little Tramp is forever asserting his dignity. Hence the comic single-mindedness. He has just enough deviousness in him to survive. Therefore we can afford to laugh, not to weep at his plight.

| "Aside from that, Mrs. Lincoln, how did you enjoy the play?" |

But the Little Tramp is always the underdog as well. The odds are against him. There is no way to watch Chaplin—especially his later films—and ignore the reality of the human predicament. The bullies who pick on the Tramp are comic bullies, but the oppression itself is real enough. The other side of Chaplin, if not great tragedy, is pathos. There is no tragic recognition. There is no tragic flaw. There is only the futile attempt to salvage some dignity from life, and this touches the heart.

As a matter of fact, those who say great tragedy cannot be written anymore often cite the loss of the full possibilities of self-awareness in our society, especially for the ordinary citizen, who never has been and never can be in an important decision-making position. Modern tragedy, they say, can only show the process by which the "little man" is manipulated and eventually destroyed by forces he can never hope to comprehend.

If this view is close to being accurate, Chaplin's work may well emerge as not only the comic highlight of the whole

Chaplin's Tramp is a unique comic figure. We laugh because he is unaware of his plight, but he is also very real and very human.

"Charlie's Tramp—a futile attempt to salvage some dignity from life."

century, but as often having come very near the borders of legitimate tragedy, redefined for an age in which personal choice has become more and more limited.

Tragedy and Comedy as Resources for Living

Whether we want to or not, we are forced to develop a sense of the tragic and a sense of the comic. "It comes with the territory," as Arthur Miller's salesman might say. We cannot be human beings without recognizing that life shows itself to us in both tragic and comic guises, though we can ultimately choose the ways in which we will respond. We *can* laugh at the plight of someone who has fallen on the ice and may possibly have broken an arm or leg. We *can* weep at the thought of corruption in high places. A perspective is possible, however, and this final section suggests how the fully actualized human being may utilize both the tragic and the comic views to maintain his or her balance during the often perilous adventure of living.

The Awareness of Mortality

Life is probably neutral—neither tragic nor comic—until we reach an age at which *the fact of death* strikes home with its first awesome impact. Death counselors and psychologists often disagree about the age. Some have suggested that death awareness happens when a child is able to comprehend the abstraction of time.

The poet Gerard Manley Hopkins (1844–1889) has captured this first poignant opening up to the dreadful truth of mortality in the poem "Spring and Fall."

Margaret, are you grieving?
Over Goldengrove, unleaving?
Leaves, like the things of man, you
With your fresh thoughts care for, can you?
Ah! As the heart grows older
It will come to such sights colder
By and by, nor spare a sigh
Though worlds of wanwood leafmeal lie;
And yet you will weep and know *why.*
Now no matter, child, the name:

Sorrow's springs are the same.
Nor mouth had, no nor mind, expressed
What heart heard of, ghost guessed:
It is the blight man was born for,
It is Margaret you mourn for. [3]

Unless, however, the Margarets of this world come face to face with the very early loss of one or both parents, or are unfortunate enough to be themselves victims of death's seemingly indiscriminate lottery system, this first awareness of mortality takes a while to ripen and mature. The very young, though they may have discovered death, have a hard time applying the notion to themselves. Death may take away grandparents and pets, and then the scary prospect of eventually losing mother and father presents itself (but that, of course, is a long way off). Little by little the personalizing of death takes place.

The fundamental approach to living is tragic, in that the first understanding that an "approach" is needed at all no doubt comes when one *knows* neither oneself nor anyone will live forever. An initial response is, "But how unfair!" One asks, "Why go to all the trouble, being born, growing up, deciding upon a career, hoping, planning, saving, striving— when the whole enterprise comes to nothing in the end?" Or, "Why must I grow old, know pain, lose my faculties? Why is life one loss after another?"

Once the fact of mortality is grasped, one begins to perceive the tragic pattern in all aspects of living. Romances grow stale, die; marriages end; people lose their jobs, sometimes suffering humiliating demotions and a shrinking of revenue; the country goes from prosperity to recession, even depression; the comfort of peace is shattered by another outbreak of war.

Since we are human beings, we have options. One, which will need no further discussion, can be mentioned here. We can keep putting off a confrontation with tragedy. Like Scarlett O'Hara, we can think about it tomorrow. We can refuse to be touched by a mining disaster in West Virginia, an earthquake in South America, a war in Southeast Asia, the death of a neighbor. We can hold out until tragedy strikes *us.*

Psychology tells us the wisdom of such an option is questionable. We may think we will have the capacity to deal

---

Ah, make the most of what we yet may spend, Before we too into the dust descend.

The Rubaiyat of Omar Khayyam

with tragedy when it hits home, only to discover that we are inexperienced at facing appalling truths. The temptation may be strong to seek more escape routes and never look reality in the face. That's why fantasies—*and* drugs *and* liquor—exist.

The Killer Instinct

Another strategy, which some might call "coping," is probably more universal than any of us would like to admit. Yet each of us has almost certainly relied upon it more than once.

The difficulty with the "Scarlett O'Hara Approach," which puts confrontations off—sometimes indefinitely—lies in the sheer volume of tragic events people have to witness. As these accumulate and *if* one persists in looking cheerfully in the other direction each time, emotional tension builds up. One goes about with vaguely apprehensive feelings which lie just below the surface but are not named, discussed, dealt with. Henry David Thoreau made a generalization in *Walden* (1854), which still seems valid:

"The mass of men lead lives of quiet desperation."

The Irish writer James Joyce (1882–1941) wrote a short story called "Counterparts," in which the main character, a lowly clerk in the employ of a tyrannical boss, suffers indignities all day long on the job. He goes to a pub for escape and loses an arm-wrestling match. Frustrated, he gets drunk, returns home, and beats up his young son.

The strategy is clear. The "killer instinct" manifests itself in the urge, if not to do actual harm like the father in Joyce's story, then to delight in the misfortunes which befall others. It is not uncommon to find someone rushing across a room to hear the news of Joe's losing his job, Jennifer's leaving her husband, and Sam's (suspected, but probably certain) terminal illness. There is always someone who will fan the flame of tragic notoriety by calling up everyone of his or her acquaintance in order to report a disaster.

As the identity of the victims becomes more and more impersonal, the intensity of the killer instinct grows. A traffic accident attracts a throng of onlookers, the size of the crowd proportionate to the violence of the event. Psychologists have conducted research into such behavior and report that many people admitted to realizing, after a fashion, that they secretly enjoyed themselves while witnessing disasters. There is always the possibility of a car's suddenly bursting into flames at Indianapolis, whether the untold thousands of spectators are consciously thinking about it or not.

The existence of a killer instinct does not mean that people would either enjoy or be able to cope with the reality of a disaster. It is probable that the forbidden *expectation* is the true source of the secret pleasure, which the unconscious mind allow us to experience.

It is also probable that there are more mature ways of existing in this world.

Laughing at the "Unfortunate"

Viewed from the perspective of the need to cope in some way with the basic awareness of mortality, the comic side of life takes on additional meaning. The assorted disasters—especially the less serious ones—which befall us daily leave some people in an almost continual state of vague uneasiness and insecurity, and laughter is the natural outlet for this tension.

"The only thing dumber than a dumb _____,
[name of ethnic group]

is a smart _____**."**
[name of other ethnic group]

Parallel to the killer instinct is the urge to relieve one's feelings of insecurity at the expense of others'. So we often laugh at overweight people, underweight people, drunken people. We laugh at Poles, Italians, Jews, Indians, Chicanos, and stuffy Englishmen; at liberated women, unliberated men, homosexuals, prostitutes, and mothers-in-law. We laugh at people who do not speak our language accurately, at the handicapped, and at the mentally slow.

There is not so great a need to laugh at unfortunate people as, in truth, to persuade ourselves that these people *are* unfortunate—that is, relative to those who are laughing. As has been said many times, there are two ways to win a race. One is to be faster than anyone else. The other is to hold out your arm and keep people from passing you.

The perpetuation of "anti" or "ethnic" jokes, which may seem to be a harmless, sociable pastime, can do irreparable damage, not only in offending the targets of such "humor," but in further retarding our own ability to face reality. Laughing at minorities, for example, is a form of discrimination which will not aid us at all when *we* suddenly become a victim of inequitable social patterns.

Tragedy as Catharsis

The first critic of the drama, Aristotle, was also the first to point out that watching tragedy on the stage was an invaluable experience. He defined the new art form in this way:

Tragedy is the imitation of an action that is serious, complete, and of a certain magnitude; in language embellished with every kind of artistic ornament; in the form of drama, not narrative; through pity and terror, bringing about the purgation of those emotions.

The last part of the definition is what concerns us here.

The Greeks were a curious people. In their philosophy they venerated reason over emotion. Many of their urban arts—such as that of open discussion and debate—were highly intellectual. Yet in their life styles the Greeks could be unashamedly hedonistic, given to sensual pleasures of the most subtle, as well, no doubt, as the most abandoned kind. The Greeks knew the importance of achieving a balance between emotional outburst and rational control.

Aristotle saw tragedy as a means whereby the spectator could get caught up in a virtual orgy of emotions, utterly moved by the elements of the plot, which always represented the dire extremes of human experience: murder, suicide, agonizing jealousy, incest, and so on. As the tragedy played on, emotions—especially those of pity and terror—were wrenched from the spectators, eventually leaving them calm. After all, you can only experience emotion until it is gone.

In other words, Aristotle believed the whole point of tragedy was the purgation—or *catharsis*—of feeling. Leaving the theater, the spectator would be in a state of restored emotional equilibrium. Though Aristotle does not say so,

> **Aristotle believed the whole point of tragedy was the purgation of feeling.**

modern interpreters of this theory point out that the spectator's *personal* tensions will dissipate along with the emotions
evoked by the tragedy itself. Hence Aristotle's is actually a
psychological approach—a recommendation that tragedy be
used, in a sense, as therapy.

Extending the theory to everyday life, we can say that the
willingness to face tragic, or very unhappy, events openly
and honestly will also lead to the restoration of inner balance.

We can add that such willingness allows one to enter
compassionately into the tragic experiences of others and
that this benefits both the sufferer and the consoler. The
sufferer will have been given sympathetic support, while the
consoler will be building up strength against the inevitable
time when he or she becomes the sufferer.

A sense of humor is to the comic side of life what compassion is to the tragic.

A Sense of Humor

A sense of humor is to the comic side of life what compassion is to the tragic. Real humor is the ability to strike a
balance when events around us become too incongruous or
illogical to bear. If they are not disastrous enough to warrant
a tragic response, we can always laugh or smile.

And what is incongruous or illogical? Being overweight?
Being a member of an ethnic minority? Being handicapped?
Obviously not. Some incongruities which trigger the comic
response of a human being are:

corruption in high places
hypocrisy in human relationships
incompetence in the performance of needed services
misplaced affection
the triumph of the undeserving
knavery and skullduggery
the foolishness of those who should know better

A sense of humor is basic to the rational and moral foundation of our civilization. It is doubtful that any group anywhere in the world can long survive without it, and an
almost absolute certainty that human beings in our fast-
moving society do much better at *being* human if they cherish this gift.

Chapter 10 Footnotes

[1]Eugene O'Neill, *Long Day's Journey into Night* (New Haven: Yale University Press, 1964), p. 166. Copyright © 1955 by Carlotta Monterey O'Neill.

[2]Arthur Miller, *The Death of a Salesman* (New York: The Viking Press, 1949). Reprinted by permission of the publisher. All rights reserved.

11

THE POWER OF
THE MEDIUM

Overview

A street sign is one of the simplest forms of communication in the world. It *must* be. "Stop," "Go," and "No left turn" must be without ambiguity, unmistakably clear to passengers and motorists, no matter what their language or temperament.

The meaning of other forms of communication may be less certain while easy enough to "read": cars with headlights on, coming from the opposite direction, are saying for the city-dweller what dark clouds tell the hunter or farmer: "Rain."

The ability to interpret meaning becomes more difficult when there has been an effort to conceal. Detectives arriving at a murder scene must outwit the criminal who has used gloves to hide fingerprints or has rifled the cash box in an effort to make it appear that the motive was robbery rather than revenge.

Job-seekers are wary of spoken promises which may be polite efforts to avoid outright rejection of the applicant: "We'll call you when there's an opening," "We'll keep your resumé on file," and "We'll probably be in touch with you next week" are not necessarily the signals to discontinue job-hunting.

Even as short and sweet a statement as "I love you" may require further thought. The meaning is, after all, affected by the speaker's tone of voice, the number of people present, the length of time the participants have known each other, and so on. It may mean anything from a proposal of marriage to thanks for having brought the pizza.

To an extent, people have always known that communication was complex. Even in the days before electronic transmission of messages, there was a difference between the terse announcements of tom-tom or signal fire on the one

Marshall McLuhan

Societies have always been shaped more by the media by which men communicate than by the content of the communication.

hand and the playful conceits of an elaborate sonnet on the other.

In recent years there has been increasing attention to the *communication process* itself, as a means of not merely delivering a message but becoming *part* of the message. Prophets like Marshall McLuhan and others have made us realize that the media which deliver messages do not simply provide us with communication: *they help to shape our consciousness.* It is now believed that people who read continually, think and experience things far differently from those who read scarcely at all but are affected by visual and audio media.

It was once thought that the humanist preferred the written word to all other media. Bookishness and humanism are not, however, necessarily so closely associated anymore. This chapter contends that humanists need to be aware of which media are most congenial to them, which media shape *their* consciousness.

> **People who read continually, think and experience things far differently from those who are affected by visual and audio media.**

The Print or Linear Medium

For centuries, communication was limited to speeches, conversation, and handwritten records and accounts on clay or parchment.

The first change occurred with the invention of the printing press in the late 1400s, which created the medium of print and a revolution in the way people receive communication. Ideas were henceforth not restricted to priests and other scholars; they became available to the general public. The impact of the print medium was dramatic. The Gutenberg Bible was the first book to be mass-produced, and from that time on, every family could have access to the word of God. Printing was a democratic force. The individual, at home, could read on his own; there was less dependence on authorities.

Print Perspectives

At first literacy remained a special skill. Reading required a process now called "decoding." That is, the circles and lines on a printed page made no sense until the reader transformed them back into words known aurally. Those who have been reading for a long time forget their own early years of inability to decode. It is a lot like the nonmusician's inability to translate a page of an orchestral score, or like trying to read something printed in a foreign language—particularly if the letters are formed so differently that even they cannot be understood. (Someone once said that the neon signs on Times Square would be a dazzling display for a nonreader. Without the ability to decode all those multicolored advertisements, the nonreader could revel in sensations, as the rest of us do at an Independence Day celebration.)

Most of Shakespeare's contemporaries could not read. They found places they were looking for through the pictures announcing shop names outside each establishment. A painted boar's head or cat's paw signified tavern, appropriate objects signified pharmacy or pawn shop. Yet Shakespeare and other seventeenth-century writers used some of the most eloquent language ever written. For nonreaders, the ear had to decode the elaborately spoken language of the stage. Comic puns, declarations of love, and ringing calls to battle were *heard* by audiences whose eyes were simultaneously seeing the visible action.

From the invention of the printing press until the invention of the camera in the mid-nineteenth century, verbal communication remained unaffected by technology. But within the space of a very few years, the advent of telephone, radio, telegraphy, the phonograph, and television made permanent changes in the way people could reach each other. The new media brought people closer together, people once separated by great distances. At one time, the news of an election had to wait until riders on horseback could deliver the news. Today, it is possible to predict the result of a national election within a short time after the polls close in the East, even before voters in California have cast a ballot.

Even those farmers who still use the most primitive methods of planting crops have access to transistor radios which play music popular around the world and which alert them to people and events in countries their grandparents never heard of. Families who once would have written long letters, delivered after long intervals, now speak to each other by means of long-distance telephone or airmailed tape cassettes. Even in countries with repressive laws, citizens hear, via international radio news programs, what is really going

Marshall McLuhan

Survival is not possible if one approaches the environment, the social drama, with a fixed, unchangeable point of view.

on in matters which their own government attempts to conceal.

Technology has thus made it possible to reach out over great distances. At the same time it has also allowed a closing down of communication. It is possible to say, for example, that a family physically together in the same room and staring at a television screen are actually separated, not by distances but by the medium itself.

A family physically together, staring at a television screen, are actually separated by the medium itself.

Impact of McLuhan

It was a Canadian professor, Marshall McLuhan (b. 1911) who noted that each medium was not only a means of sending out a message, but that the medium itself was an important part of the message sent. He went beyond that. No longer was the medium a subordinate carrier, a kind of conveyor belt on which little packages of words were sent. The medium became supreme, replacing, if not equaling the message itself. "The medium is the message," proclaimed McLuhan, as he noted the different effects each medium had on those who heard, saw, and responded to it.

McLuhan was not the first to be aware of the importance of media. The American educator and philosopher John Dewey (1859–1952) had noted the importance of language, not only as a carrier of ideas but as a necessary prerequisite for the formulation of ideas. Without words, it would be impossible to have the idea in the first place, he said.

But McLuhan focused attention on media in an unprecedented way. He was hailed, denounced, and misunderstood. McLuhan's pronouncement was thought to mark the end of print, as if, television and film so widely available, there would be no further need for print literacy. Academicians pointed out that, if McLuhan thought so little of print, he should not have used such an antiquated medium for his own ideas. And he as an English teacher was called traitor to his own group!

Soon after McLuhan, "books" began to be published containing a minimum of words; many were collections of photographs, showing and reinforcing the many "messages" which surround us, without the print once thought so necessary for every message. Some of the picture books seemed designed to be looked at, idly, with no particular sequence, as "eyewash" counterparts of television.

By the 1960s *medium* had became a fad word, often used indiscriminately: "My medium is glossy lipstick" (meaning, one supposes, "I think I look good in it.") The plural form *media* was used as the singular, or more hideously "made plural" by the addition of an *s:* "The medias are in the Learning Center." Television newscasters were (and are) referred to as "media types." (As opposed to what? Reporters?) "Media" itself is often used to mean television only.

Traditionalists were often denounced by McLuhan's followers for persisting in the belief that books still did what no other medium could do. In particular, teachers were singled out for the campaign. In one professional conference after another, speakers maintained that students are not so much readers as they were watchers of television, and that teachers should take advantage of this fact—to use the new visual medium, making the classroom a "surrounding" experience at times, rather than the linear, sequential lecture/assignment/recall of information which classrooms had been at one time.

At times the McLuhanites overstated, as when they called inveterate readers "a bunch of P.O.B.'s," or "Print-Oriented Bastards," in order to force attention on the importance of changing media, saying in effect, "Those who insist on requiring a medium of the previous century are old-fashioned, if not elitist."

The furor has died down, but the interest remains, particularly now that people are becoming aware of the messages sent forth by environments, as individuals attempt to find the media most appropriate to their own temperaments, and as we continue to be affected by the overwhelming influence of the mass media.

What Print Does

The sending of a message through letters intended for an audience of one or many is possible in a number of ways. For example:

handwriting

typing

telegram

skywriting

"Media" often means television, and the word in this context tends to have negative connotations, especially for politicians and other newsworthy personalities.

billboard signs

magazine print

book print

Pictures may accompany some of the print media mentioned above.

Regardless of message, consider the medium itself. We associate handwriting with intimacy—personal letters and notes. For a time, etiquette books demanded that all letters be handwritten rather than typed. The effort to form the letters by pen and ink on carefully chosen stationery was regarded as a sign of thoughtfulness. (For many years, it was bad form to begin a letter with the personal pronoun *I,* as the first word must show regard for the person addressed rather than self.)

Nowadays, personal letters may be typed, but business letters are more apt to be. The importance of a business letter is designated through the kind of stamp on the envelope and the extent to which the address appears to be individually typed or mass-produced. "Junk mail" is announced by the metered code of the sending organization and the gummed labels or pre-set type of the address, purchased from a subscription list.

Typing is, of course, a major medium for the production of writing. Good typing lends a professional look to the words carried, as witness the improved appearance of an essay written as a class assignment, once the margins are lined up and a strong ink carries the words on good bond paper. When the essay is encased in a folder, it seems to look even more important, especially when the title page includes the professor's name!

In *Alice in Wonderland,* Alice complained that she disliked books without pictures. Books in those days had few. Textbooks, no matter what else they said, sent the message:

Read this and learn. This is a no-nonsense textbook which needs no decoration to appeal to the right sort of student. People in previous generations were able to read straight text, and so should you. Books are meant to be respected, along with parents and teachers. Perhaps a return to a nation of traditional readers is what we've needed all along. And for those with difficulties in language or motivation, so much the worse for you. There are jobs waiting to be done. We don't intend to entertain you as you learn.

By contrast, consider a child's book. No matter what the story is about, the print is large. There are abundant white spaces, and colorful pictures on every page. Children's stories cry out to be read aloud by an adult adapting his or her voice to the sound of giants and different sized billy goats or the "teeniest" pig. The child's book is not just a page containing a story. It is a means of cuddling as a youngster is introduced to a new delight—pleasure from a kind of magic: ink on a page.

Print versus Visual

It would be possible to live without reading; in fact, it has been predicted that the grandchildren of people in their

twenties today will be unable to read. (This may also be a self-fulfilling prophecy. An educator once announced that "it will some day seem as foolish to expect every child to be able to read as to expect every boy to play a violin and every girl to bake a cherry pie." The educator, a high school principal (who, by the way, betrayed sexism in his examples) apparently derives some pleasure in the prospect of fewer readers.

Television is "done" at the pace of those who control.

For most of those who function in a modern society, the ability to watch television requires only eyesight and some slight knowledge of the language. A newcomer, arriving from a foreign country, would understand at least *some* of the narratives shown on television, without being able to understand a word in the newspaper. Television is, therefore, an accessible medium, available to a wide range of educational, class, and ethnic backgrounds while reading requires a kind of decoding, plus the ability to visualize, before sense can be made of the print.

Reading is done at one's own pace, and the order in which pages are read is under the control of the reader, who can if he or she wishes, turn back a few pages to check information, the identity of a character, or to savor the passage read at a different pace.

Television is done at the pace of those in control, a pace which is designed to be understood (it is hoped) by the majority of viewers. Except for the variation in type sizes, the printed page looks neutral. Television becomes personal the moment we see the face of the speaker. In recent years, this personal approach has affected news "shows," in which pleasant-appearing people smilingly announce events of the day. The phenomenon of "happy news" began some years ago. To counter the sober face of one announcer, a group of newscasters at a desk exchange light-hearted comments with one another as the news is announced, commented on, and amended with homey details about the effect the weather will have on the plans of the newscasters themselves. Such news announcements say two things beyond what is written in the script: (1) people aren't really interested in what goes on outside their own immediate lives; and (2) no matter what the event, the face on the screen will be remembered more than the words spoken. It is therefore possible to smile while announcing a tidal wave in a far-off land, even while the casualty figures are recited. The medium is the pictured face, smiling cheerfully, allowing the voice to be modified for a moment, in a few seconds of what passes for sorrow, and then back to the cheerful-sounding business at hand.

Because sight is the most important sense for most of us, we remember the smile rather than the tidal wave. This concentration on the visual has led to a lessened dependence on understanding what is heard. People at a concert—except for the most sophisticated listeners—are sensitive to the movements of the conductor and the appearance of the players, a change in seating, women's new gowns, the way someone bows, as opposed to the music itself.

The Visual Mass Media: Television and Films

The "mass" media—especially television and films—are so-called because they appeal to many people; there is therefore no point in attacking them for not living up to the tastes of the "non-mass," or people with very special preferences (intellectuals, advocates of an unpopular cause, players of little-known sports, and so on). It might be argued that alternative television channels should be available, or that some way should be found to encourage artistic film makers to pursue their art, but these are other matters. More important than further repetitious comment on the appalling state of the visual arts (it's been done!) would be a calm appraisal of what the visual media actually do to the watchers. This section will therefore be a description of that impact, in hope that, whatever they are watching, viewers will be able to see more clearly.

We are more concerned here with understanding visual impact than tearing down the visual media.

TV Commercials: The Subliminal Message

When television stories do not pretend to be real, there is no confusion. Perhaps a small child may be over-stimulated by an animated cartoon, but for most of us the panthers, ducks, and bears are clearly unreal when they wear clothes, talk in funny accents, and chase each other in vehicles loaded with explosives.

Even romantic historical fiction on television is obviously not meant to be believed in any literal sense. It is often pure escapism, offering viewers the opportunity to observe su-per-adventurous men and super-lovely females saying mag-nificently fake things to each other, and providing us with a clearly marked express to Never-Never Land.

The problem lies in two areas: real-looking fictionalized stories and documentaries, and news stories which purport to be accurate.

Among the most pervasive of fictionalized "real-looking" stories are the less-than-a-minute commercials, with their typical-looking families. Commercials may not appear to be stories, but they are. They have quick beginnings in which a problem is presented, some sort of conflict, and a resolu-tion in which the problem is solved. They have characters looking and sounding like the rest of us. But whereas in Saturday morning cartoons the rescue is provided by a flying mouse wearing tights and a cape, in the commercials the rescue is accomplished by the heroic product.

Typically, the stories can be summarized in variations of the following:

A. Husband dislikes something (leaves house without drinking coffee, perhaps); wife worries; grocer or older woman suggests a different product; husband likes it; wife is happy.

B. Newlywed wife sets table for important occasion—visit of in-laws or husband's boss coming to dinner; woman friend notes signs of inadequate housekeeping (spots on glasses, fishy smell); new product is tried; compliments, smiles, recognition, a happy future.

C. Someone tries to kiss someone, is told to use something on breath; doesn't believe recommendation; is convinced; recom-mender is proud, says I Told You So.

D. Child happily runs to mother, tells her about picture he has painted or imaginary giant he has seen. Mother tells him his shirt is dirty. Mother washes shirt with super-product. Child can now "make all the dirt" he wants.

E. Someone "knows" he won't like a certain product but is tricked into using it (as opposed to A, where he is persuaded by com-petitor's product); at end of story, either he is told (and loves having been fooled) or he remains fooled while the clever one conspiratorially tells the rest of us beyond the studio lights.

There are, of course, variations on the anxiety motifs sug-gested above, but even in comic commercials, in which both

> **It is the apparent reality of the TV commercial that constitutes its effectiveness.**

problem and product are spoofed, there remains the commitment to a pretense of reality. Apart from the extravagant claims for product benefits, which most viewers dismiss to some extent, what are these commercials offering as typical of real families?

We have tyrannical husbands with wives who dread their displeasure; women who live for the applause of their families in the endless task of keeping things clean; critical busybodies; guests who judge harshly; lovers who interrupt a romantic moment to offer suggestions for improved odors; the sounds of smugness and retaliation by those who were right about their "contender" over the opposition; the rejection of pleasure and intimacy in favor of nonstop housekeeping; and benevolent dictators certain that men are children or wives are worth keeping.

These are power plays in the guise of domestic dramas. In *Fancies and Goodnights* the short story writer John Collier has a scene set in the hell to which housewives are sent. It is a place where everything is always going wrong.

The fictional world of most commercials is such a hell, demeaning to all who inhabit it and dangerous to the viewer only to the extent that this appearance of reality gives domestic life a name worse than it deserves.

If the bland families on television become even minimal role models, the appeal of living together in a civilized way becomes remote. To flee this concern, some young people have adopted a contrary extreme: a decidedly undomestic mobile world, in which people hitchhike or wander in vans and on motorcycles, listen to rock music, wear clothing free of laundry products of any kind, don't care what any outsider—much less a neighbor—will think, and believe themselves to be the only members of society capable of true love. Rock is as rebellious as television is conformist. Neither embraces the whole of reality.

The Impact of Television on Storytelling

Story-telling was once a leisurely medium of communication. Folk tales were spoken and sung to audiences who were in no particular hurry to leave. Audiences responded with repetition of phrases, nods, claps, and a chorus of praise or blame for the characters in the narrative. Long epics of Africa and Europe were told in this way.

Printing allowed any reader to possess a mass-produced book. Eventually it was common for novels to be in several volumes, and for continuing stories in magazines to run for months—a leisurely process indeed.

In his eighteenth-century novel *Tom Jones,* Henry Fielding is so leisurely he even takes time out of his story to address the reader with philosophical essays. He labels each chapter with a hint of what is to come, as if to say that his main purpose is not suspense. He and the reader will instead share in discovery: "Containing as much of the birth of the foundling as is necessary or proper to acquaint the reader with in the beginning of this history" begins Book I.

Twentieth century fiction tends to be shorter than early fiction to keep pace with the speed of modern living.

Typical of modern fiction:

Lying in bed, Farragut felt his anxiety beginning to mount. He would be denied his fix in the morning. He would die.

John Cheever

Atypical of modern fiction

He shared enough of his contemporaries' prejudices to suspect sensuality in any form; but whereas they would, by one of those terrible equations that take place at the behest of the superego, have made Sarah vaguely responsible for being born as she was, he did not.

John Fowles

Fielding never forgets that he is telling a story, rather than pretending that the events are real. By the manner of his telling, he deliberately "distances" the reader from the experiences recounted. His introductory comment to an early chapter includes himself: "Containing such grave matter that the reader cannot laugh once throughout the whole chapter, unless peradventure he should laugh at the author."

Twentieth-century fiction has been generally shorter than fiction of the past. To keep pace, we are told, with the speed of modern living. Modern fiction experiments with the form of telling, as if readers would be impatient with a straightforward story. There are experiments with space, phrasing and coined words, paralleling the close-ups and jump shots of the film medium. Stories are told quickly, in quick strokes with much white space, as opposed to Fielding's pages of solid prose. James Joyce has been an outstanding innovator, a predecessor of films, but also a prophet in his verbal montages and subliminal flashes into the unconscious.

The French writer Alain Robbe-Grillet writes stories which sound almost like directions for a cameraman. They are told in the present tense, like a film script (*He opens the door and sees on the floor a dead dog, its throat cut* is the style). Objects are concrete, and there is absolutely no editorializing, no talk from writer to reader. The objective form is like the camera which tries not to moralize, but the style is not the Let's-interview-both-sides manner of television documentaries and news shows. Rather, it is numb, without sensation, the presentation of sights and sounds through the objective perception of the narrator.

Story-telling on television frequently includes a "teaser," a glimpse of the climactic moment to come later. If the viewer has been sufficiently intrigued, he or she may wait through the opening commercial and expository scenes. There will not be sustained narrative of any length, for television depends on the break every few minutes for a commercial or public service announcement. Even when time has not been sold, the breaks come anyway, to make it convenient for announcements should there be eventual reruns.

The viewer thus accepts a rhythm of narration broken by these interruptions, often at a suspenseful moment. Long years of such viewing condition viewers to brief attention spans, so that when longer attention is needed (to a sermon or class lesson, for instance) one must make a real effort to keep from squirming. It is said that children in kindergarten and first grade have grown so accustomed to television, even the "good" educational content of Sesame Street, that they find it difficult to visualize stories read aloud by the teacher —or to concentrate on any one activity for longer than the interval between commercials.

The Picture Show

Movies have made their own rules. Movies were surely not recognized as a new medium of art or communication back in the days when for a nickel people could turn a crank and marvel at the illusion of live action. But there were some visionaries who, almost from the beginning, found their minds whirling with possibilities. It was they who made the rules, they who discovered through experimentation what this phenomenon was capable of doing to the viewer.

Even the nickelodeon must have mesmerized its audiences, for by resting their eyes against a black shade, they were able to escape immediately into another world. In 1895 the first image was projected onto a white sheet, thus enlarging the illusion and making it possible for the audience to sit passively, no longer having to do so much as turn a crank. Experiments followed in which movie cameras photographed an unbroken action as in a stage play, and for a time it looked as though movies would be mass-produced theater.

But then in 1903 Edwin S. Porter tried a new technique. In *The Great Train Robbery* he introduced the "cut," whereby one image is suddenly replaced by another—perhaps a close-up of one of the characters, or another action taking place at the same time, but in a different location. In other words, Porter discovered it was possible for the film director to *control* what the audience sees. Not the action, but the camera (and the mind behind the camera) calls the turn. From 1903 to the present, the art of the cinema has been one of increasingly subtle optical effects and complex illusions, and also of continuing audience passivity. We shall not know for a long time—may never in fact *really* know—what profound effects the movies have had on human consciousness; for there is no way to measure accurately the difference between consciousness today and that of a century ago, when people spent more time reading and conversing. Certainly the aspect of passivity has to be considered, as well as film's continual bombardment of senses and emotions and its often minimal appeal to the logical faculty.

We may never know what profound effects the movies have had on human consciousness.

Movies like to mystify, horrify, confuse. Movies can blur the image, turn it upside down. Increasingly sensitive sound equipment can fill the darkened theater with eerie music. Sense experiences undreamed of a hundred years ago are now commonplace.

Unlike the print medium, which became the official medium of learning, movies were the people's medium from the beginning. They have had to *appeal,* and so film makers have had to keep in close touch with what excites audiences and what does not. Movies have no grand past of religious ritual, royal favor, or academic elitism. Even in totalitarian societies, in which mass communication is strictly censored, movies cannot convey "official" attitudes unless they possess immediate appeal to the senses and the emotions. Who is to say that "official" messages ever mean more to such audiences than the medium relaying them?

The print medium is linear. That is, the eye reads, at least in Western society, from left to right in a straight line. Such linearity parallels the point-by-point sequence of the rational thought process. Movies are nonlinear. The viewer can be made to look at any part of the screen the director desires. There is probably no parallel in the mind for the way movies work. Not only are movies not print, but they use a minimum number of words by comparison with print. Some of the most memorable sequences in films are totally wordless. Films can imply and can have ideas underlying their actions, but no one has yet proved that films represent a foolproof method of transferring an idea intact from one mind to another.

Movie messages are there, however, and they inevitably have an impact over a period of time. The messages are not so much straightforward ideas as they are hidden assumptions about people and life in general. Because movies have aimed at general audiences, they have celebrated the little man as well as the mighty hero.

In *Modern Times,* as in other Chaplin films, the little man is shown to understand more and to have more compassion than those who live by rule books. The end of the film shows the Tramp and the Waif fleeing organized society, as the music swells around them, inviting audience sympathy.

In recent years, movies have shown the triumph of illogic over the pompous sanity of Establishment figures such as generals, nurses, and social workers. In *King of Hearts,* the leading character, played by Alan Bates, chooses to remain with a group of asylum inmates rather than go back to a society which is in the midst of World War I; in *One Flew Over the Cuckoo's Nest,* McMurphy, played by Jack Nicholson, successfully rallies—for a time—the victims of a tyrannical and sadistic professional nurse. He and the inmates are shown to be more sensible than the coldly logical people in charge, much to the delight of popular audiences long-encouraged by the cinema medium to abandon their linear thought

> **Film is not a verbal medium. Some of the most memorable sequences in movies are totally wordless.**

sequences and surrender to the magic of the screen's illusions.

The "art" film supposedly transcends the vulgar commercialism of popular films. It plays in small houses to a faithful clientele, who often suppose themselves immune to what the medium does on the popular level. Yet the fact remains that art films belong to the same medium. In their subtler transitions from scene to scene, in their often highly sophisticated camera work, they represent refinements in cinematic technique, but they too play on the senses and the emotions and lure the viewer into an experience which rarely parallels the consciousness of familiar reality.

Whatever kind of film suits your individual taste, an advantage of film-going is that interruptions in the linear thought process are probably helpful. Print, after all, delivers a one-sided version of reality. Print raises expectations that events in the real world will follow one another in a meaningful sequence like the sentences on this page. The film medium explodes that myth and leaves us open to new possibilities; film can blast our fixed notions and make us preceive things in a new way.

The Environment as a Medium

Any place, object, or surrounding atmosphere, is part of the environment which sends out "messages" to those who know how to "read" them. Like other messages, they may be open to more than one interpretation, but they are nevertheless worthy of patient scrutiny, for in ignoring them we overlook an important influence on ourselves.

McLuhan views the human environment as a gigantic medium created by humanity to define its own nature and purpose.

Personal Surroundings

Some environments are straightforward, promising what they deliver. White linen, silver candlesticks, and bone china make a simple announcement: This is a formal dinner, for a special occasion or ritual. Observe traditional manners and clothing. Talk quietly to your neighbor, and do pass the gravy dish.

Paper plates and a carton of fried chicken ask for and receive a different-sounding meal to accompany their atmosphere. In a picnic atmosphere, people may leave the table and return without causing attention. The glasses used don't have to be the same size and shape.

Informal dinners proclaim a relaxed, spontaneous view of life, proclaiming, "Love me for myself. We don't need to fuss in order to enjoy ourselves."

Among roommates at college, informality may include unbreakable plates and chipped mugs or glasses which once contained shrimp cocktail or jelly. The crockery is itself part of being young and on a limited budget. Dishes are washed when the clean ones have been exhausted. Someone's sleeping bag is rolled up in the corner, waiting for a previous visitor to come and claim it. In some cases, the refrigerator exhibits signs of the varying life styles of the inhabitants: the soy bean flakes and carrot juice of one; on the shelf above, the leftover corn flakes and beer cans of another.

When former roommates meet some years later, after one of them has "settled down," the new arrangements—matching furniture, neat shelves, and extra towels—may make the former best friend appear an alien from another planet, until, perhaps, both are domesticated in the same way.

Environments change, and people adapt behavior to the messages, spoken and unspoken.

Libraries usually suggest respect and dignity for the purpose of the building. Though the rooms may be crowded, noise is controlled. People walk slowly. The ceiling is usually high—higher than necessary for strictly utilitarian purposes. (High ceilings are also found in banks, churches, and schools—to announce the sort of behavior expected in them.) The steps leading up to the large doors of the entrance way are also designed to make the building represent the institution.

Messages are coming at you from libraries movie lobbies the inside of a bus airplane seating junk food places expensive restaurants even parking lots

The arrangement of books within the library is part of the environment: either open shelves with books easily available for all to touch or a system requiring that a card be filled out for the desired book, which is then sought out by a library worker. The library, like other environments, makes a statement about intimacy, remoteness, authority, and trust of its clients.

Automobiles are a special, private environment offering flexibility and control (except in the search for parking spaces). They are, of course, more than transportation. The small car with slogans painted on it shows a concern for dwindling energy, youthful exuberance, and perhaps (but not necessarily) little money. Station wagons usually announce sizable families who go many places together. A lavishly appointed luxury automobile can mean a number of things: money enough to buy fuel regardless of cost, insecurity requiring a power symbol, disbelief that an energy crisis exists.

At one time, cars were chosen for their strength and virile appearance. It was said that male drivers made the cars extensions of the masterful men they wished to be. In recent years, machismo is becoming less important than cleverness in finding a car which is relatively trouble-free and inexpensive to drive. In addition, the products favored by youth are imitated by the older generations.

Shopping malls are designed not just for purchases but for family outings. Young parents push children in strollers. It is possible for the different older members of the family to split up and reassemble at an appointed time, hours having been spent in contemplation of goods and consumption of food and drinks. Shopping malls cry out for window-gazing and encourage a yearning for a variety of possessions. Shopping malls say to people: "There is no point in saving for tomorrow."

In most stores, music is nonstop, the louder and faster the better. It is music to stimulate rather than soothe. There is a festive atmosphere. Clerks chat casually among themselves, as they count the hours until closing. They are young, and the store manager is old and not near enough to urge them to find stock for prospective customers. So the sales must depend on abundance and variety of stock, handsome advertisements, and appealing display rather than the personal owner-to-customer dialogue once found in small-town America.

Public Environments: Open and Closed

Closed environments include high surrounding walls, warning signs, closed-circuit TV, a guard at the door, an intercom through which one speaks to an unseen monitor, closed doors inside, a prescribed route allowing no deviation, locked cabinets, and signs informing the visitor of penalties for violations.

Closed environments may belong to hospitals, schools,

Signs of a Closed Environment:

Wait/Walk

Thank you for not smoking

No U-turn

No one under 17 admitted

Keep out

No solicitors

Authorized personnel only

libraries, and apartment complexes as well as prisons. To qualify as "closed," the environment must emit an atmosphere of off-limits and distrust. The restrictive rules are often with the consent of those who live or regularly work there, in order to assure safety, privacy, and exclusivity.

Theme of a Selectively Closed Environment:

People were those who lived on my side of town . . . Those others, the strange pale creatures that lived in their alien unlife, weren't considered folks. They were whitefolks.
Maya Angelou

For example, a high school corridor may be patrolled by an official demanding to see a pass stating purpose of errand. The doors on both sides are locked, as are the lockers which line the halls. The purpose is to assure quiet in the halls, to encourage learning, and protection from intrusions by non-students. In making the rules, the administrators are assuming responsibility for the students, a function which colleges once had, too. Schools exist *in loco parentis* (in place of the parents), the assumption being that minors need the same care in school that they receive at home; hence rules about appropriate clothing, check-in times, lights out, and in some cases, required chapel attendance.

Selectively closed environments may be country clubs and island residences which are shielded from outsiders but which—inside the policed gate—have open spaces for members and residents. Even private homes with high walls around them are protecting the privacy of residents and friends and informing the passers-by of their status relative to the mysterious persons inside.

Examples of open environments are public parks, ball parks, beaches, and streets. Nonetheless, they have limitations. Public parks have signs indicating where to sit or walk. Ball parks have reserved and nonreserved sections, usually with big differences in seat location, comfort, and price. Beaches have markers which tell you how far out you may swim and signs which tell you what is prohibited on the sand. Our free passage on the streets is limited by the plans of a traffic control board.

The extent to which an environment may be considered

closed or open depends in large part on the ability of people to leave or stay. The hospital patient who has agreed to have elective surgeyr for a minor ailment can voluntarily call for discharge as well as admission. But one of the marks of the hospital's closed environment is its short hospital gown ill-adapted for wear in public. But if provided with street clothes, the patient may, theoretically, dress and leave at will.

A major distinction is that of authority: who imposes the rules, who controls the right to leave. People who have participated in the making of the rules are said to endorse their implementation. Members of a condominium associa-tion, in which there is joint ownership of apartments, are restricted to the premises by the large investment each has made. Unlike tenants, they cannot always move on, having lost only a small amount of money; a forced sale of the apartment may bring thousands of dollars less than market value. Condominium rules may concern possession of dogs, number of residents, age of children visiting, time for use of various public facilities such as swimming pool, clothes lines, or car-washing facilities. But these restrictions, though the cause of fierce disputes, are minor when compared to "closed" or "open" environments on a national scale.

Customs agents, passport requirements, and narrow corri-dors at international airports create the environment which plainly separate legal and illegal entry, the welcomed tourist and the jobless foreigner from a country whose immigration quota has been exhausted.

Some countries may feel "closed" in having out-of-bounds shops restricted to visitors with foreign currency. A "closed" country may have guards checking identity papers which must be shown on such occasions as renting a room or traveling on a train; one may even sense oneself being watched by people other than guards, whether one is or not. In Iron Curtain countries the sense of a closed environment is especially acute. "Were you able to go where you wanted to?" is the question most frequently asked of those return-ing from a visit to one of these countries. In some cases, the answer is, "Our guides were afraid we might get into trouble because we didn't speak the language, so we were advised to stay with the prescribed tour." External signs of the closed country are long lines, official permissions required, even the drab clothing of people with obviously few choices or awareness of fashion. Invisible signs must be inferred: theaters whose only offerings are obviously state-approved propaganda or inoffensively "wholesome;" the refusal to talk over telephones which could be wiretapped; polite small talk by natives who avoid political topics.

One of the best known writers about closed environments is, of course, Nobel Prize winner Aleksandr Solzhenitsyn, with his accounts of Soviet prison camps. In *The Gulag Archipelago,* slave laborers come upon a rare fossil of a fish, preserved where it was buried thousands of years ago. It would be a prize for archeologists, studied by zoologists, and displayed by museums. The hungry prisoners eat it. Their environment is so closed that science must take second place to survival.

In many parables, Polish writer Slawomir Mrozek writes of people who are aware that they are constantly watched for signs of incorrect behavior. In a story collection called *The Elephant,* a group of students decide to lay a wreath on the monument of one of their country's leaders. They do so impulsively, even though it is not a day set aside to honor the great leader. When they are questioned by police, they cannot make clear their lack of sinister motivation. It is assumed that they must be part of a dangerous demonstration; officials could imagine no other motive. Such is the nature of a closed environment.

Whether free societies are "closed" or "open" often depends on attitude. The young person who seems to be free nevertheless lives according to rules which restrict choice. Some of these "rules" are, however, self-imposed. In the short story "Death in Jerusalem" by William Trevor, a bachelor lives with his mother in Ireland. He works in the small family-owned hardware store, and refuses to leave the apartment except to go to work. At night, he and his mother sit in the small dark parlor with its unchanging furniture and cluttered shelves. His brother, a priest who has moved to the United States, keeps urging him to go on vacation. The priest suggests that the two of them should visit Jerusalem, which is of religious importance to both. Year after year, the Irish brother refuses, until finally persuaded to go.

Modern Jerusalem is a disappointment to the Irish brother, because it looks so unlike the pictures he has seen in church. The priest tries in vain to help him relax and see the sights.

Philip Freneau, 1791

The world at last will join
To aid thy grand design.
Dear Liberty!
To Russia's frozen lands
The generous flame
 expands:
On Africa's burning sands
Shall man be free!

The priest learns from a telegram on the first day of their vacation that their mother has died suddenly. He wires orders to delay the funeral, and does not share the news with his brother. The next day's touring is filled with disapproval and distaste, as the crowds and remarks still fail to conform to the vision the younger brother had dreamed of in his store-to-home routine back in Ireland. On the second night, when he is finally told the truth, he is outraged and in despair, certain that the mother's death is his responsibility. He is appalled that his brother could have considered continuing the visit. They make immediate arrangements to return. As the priest sits sorrowfully in the hotel lounge, he doubts that he will return for his yearly visits with the brother he has tried to free. Other tourists, looking at him with his whiskey and soda, remark what a shame it is to see a priest drink—and in Jerusalem of all places.

Names as Medium

Names are not just words. Names in print are not simply a part of a linear medium. They constitute a medium of their own. When one is first introduced to somebody, that person's name makes many statements, whether justifiable or not. One's name makes a statement to others and to oneself. The old fairy tale "Rumpelstiltskin" dramatizes the mighty significance of a name. Some names suggest power and prestige; others—alas!—mediocrity, lack of status. People who believe themselves to have come anonymously into the world usually have one burning ambition in life: *to make a name for themselves!*

Personal Names

One of the easiest, most common changes people make in their identities is the change of their own names, either by modifying spelling or by adding to the existing name.

For many Americans, the name change occurred at point of entry, beginning assimilation into the dominant culture of American life. Hard-to-pronounce European names were shortened and adapted to the understanding of the guards who processed immigrants at Ellis Island in New York. In some cases, a last name was added on the spot. People from small villages had not needed last names, but could be identified as the son of someone well known to the small community or by the family trade. These became marks of identification, along with the place of origin, sometimes translated into English as Johnson, Anderson, (son of John or Andrew); Barber, Tailor, Carver (translated from the foreign-sounding Schnitzer, meaning one who cuts), Greenberg (a green mountain).

When immigrant children attended school, they were sensitive to the difference between their own appearance and names and those of their classmates from the "preferred" countries (that is, countries whose immigrants had arrived earlier). They changed their appearances as much as possible, cutting their hair to the length then fashionable, and rejecting outward signs of differences in clothing. The symbolic change was in the name. Often with the consent of the family, sometimes without, names betraying religious and ethnic origin were transformed: Sarah and Abraham, the Biblical couple honored in the naming of Jewish children, were changed into equivalent "American" names beginning with the same letters: the names of film stars, fellow students, or socialite families. Thus, Shirley and Arthur, or, later, Shelley and Alan. The generations often reveal themselves in family names.

Parents have continued to reveal aspirations for their children in the names they select for them. One family named a son James Lowell Smith so that the son could put J. Lowell Smith on the door of the professional office it was assumed he would one day have. Lowell, the old New England prestige name, was appropriated for its traditional sound and its potential for success.

> It has been observed that one has a better shot at the Presidency with a name like Jack, Ike, or Jimmy than a name like Adlai or Hubert.

Children, unhappy with the plain sound of only two names, have added a third, recognizing that what they perceived as "class" included three names. There have been many authors with three names, including James Whitcomb Riley, Dorothy Canfield Fisher, Harriet Beecher Stowe, and James Russell Lowell (who was the inspiration for the Smith family mentioned above).

When T. S. Eliot wanted the sound of a timid name for his inhibited protagonist he devised J. Alfred Prufrock. By the time the poem was written, the envied WASPs, or Anglo population, had begun to represent an inability to act with the ease and spontaneity of the more recent immigrants who were taking their names. Thus, "The Love Song of J. Alfred Prufrock" has an ironic sound. Someone with a first initial used in that way may have an impressive-looking office door, but he isn't a prime candidate for a love song!

Church ritual has recognized the human aspiration to change identity with a name. When a person is confirmed in the Catholic church, he or she selects the name of a saint to take as a middle name. Thus, adults can have names selected by their parents and another by themselves. Since people are first introduced by their names (followed usually by occupation), names do seem important to identity; some name changes are made in hope of assuring higher status and popularity.

In recent years, ethnic pride has resulted in a return to traditional names of the country of origin. The previously rejected Abraham and Sarah are back, along with other names deliberately proclaiming tradition. Black families have selected names of African origin for children and for themselves as a sign of pride and separation from the white culture of repression.

Public Names

The New World remained new, and aware of its past. Names of regions, states, and towns retained European names, with "new" attached: thus, New England, New York, New Bedford, New London, and so on.

Some place names are indigenous, honoring national heroes, from Washington to Eisenhower and Kennedy. Throughout America there are place names honoring local people who have made contributions, perhaps early settlers or recent donors of private property for public use.

Some names cannot be ascribed to place of origin or the contribution of an inhabitant. They are, rather, names specially chosen for their connotations of remote glamor, in a kind of hope that the association of fame and wealth will be mysteriously transferred to the new premises. Such names are often English or French, and most popular are the names of stately homes, ancient families, and royal palaces. Thus, Kenilworth, Fontainebleau, and Eden Roc became the names of hotels on Miami Beach, conveying the sound of luxury and stability associated with the prestigious originals.

Place names chosen for their glamor become models for

the individuals living there. Residents name their children and decorate their homes "in the manner of" the values suggested by their environment. Thus, French provincial furniture, English-looking tweeds, collections of Spode china, and a variety of silver patterns are tributes to the European past and seem to be required by the name given to the environment.

When the names are not themselves based on an actual people and places, the spelling may suggest prestige anyway, as in "Harbour" with the *u*, which usually does not appear in the plain American version.

Recent place names have attempted to sound young and with-it rather than stately and rich, the latter association often rejected as bourgeois. Carnaby Street and Soho have the sound of novelty, excitement, and youth, as opposed to the stately magnificence of older places. Thus an "in" crowd is attracted to the Soho Apartments instead of a place name suggesting conservative wealth.

Through the selection of names people and governments reveal their desire to be associated with strength, tradition, nationalism, ethnicity, current chic, or the past magnificence of other cultures. They reveal the willingness to be original or to conform. Sometimes they show a misunderstanding of the name they are allegedly imitating (as with the misspelling or mispronunciation of the name they attempt to honor). Thus Fontainebleau (Fon-ten-blow in French) becomes "Fountain Blue" to the uninformed on Miami Beach.

The Medium of the Sub-Text

When actors study a part, they learn the sub-text, or what the character may really be saying between the lines which the audience hears. This preparation gives interesting complexity to the role and protects it from the heavy hand of melodrama.

Offstage, we all recognize the sub-text. "What did he say?" asks for the words. "What did he mean?" asks for an interpretation of what else is going on. We all know that it is possible to say one thing and mean another—or to retain hidden reservations. "The whole truth and nothing but the truth" is reserved for courtroom oaths. It is profitable to watch for signs of something less or something more.

First-time visitor to singles bar:

"How do they expect people to read in here? It's too dark to see."

Old-timer:

"Read the dark. It says more than the menu does."

Body Language

Body language tells of hidden emotion, at odds with the spoken words. "I'm delighted to see you. So glad you could make it," someone says, barely concealing the apprehensive glance toward the kitchen. The alert guests, noting the glance, suggest that they eat out—or that it might be more convenient if they were to return in an hour.

Glancing at your watch is a common signal of impatience. But there need be no actual timepiece. The careful straightening of papers and rearrangement of books already in place would also indicate divided attention: time to go—to change the subject—to pursue the cause of this need for distraction.

"Am I boring you?" is blunt and to the point, begging for assurances of interest. "You seem preoccupied" is not quite so direct, but may be construed as an accusation. The more indirect suggestion, "We can do this tomorrow if I caught you at a bad time," alerts the paper-fumbler that there is truly a choice—end the visit, pay visible attention, or explain what is actually going on.

Observers of body language know that it is possible to sound cool and look warm, even when this is not really the case. Silent film stars sent out similar signals to alert audiences. When the heroine pretended to be sophisticated by gazing into the eyes of the hero and asking him to light her cigarette, her fluttering feet sent forth the message that she was really a young innocent. Audiences learned not to trust what was written on the dialogue cards, but to watch for body language. The advent of the talkies made for greater dependence on speech and for the voice which accompanied it.

Exaggerated Body Language: The Soaps

Possibly the closest modern equivalent to the kind of body language messages relayed by silent films is found in modern soap operas. As an experiment it is interesting to look at a soap which is totally unfamiliar to you but which has been followed by a friend. Without previous information about any of the characters, it should be possible to tell very quickly which characters the audience is expected to admire

The message:

"You are invited."

- •
- •
- •

- •
- •
- •

The Medium:

engraved invitation on card

─────────────

penciled note on lined paper

─────────────

a call by phone

─────────────

a shout across the street

─────────────

a silent gesture

or dislike. It was easier in the old days, when a drink in the hand of a divorced woman was the surefire sign that she was stalking the husband of one of the innocents who stayed home taking care of the house, as all nice ladies did then. The game is a little harder today, but no real challenge to the aficionado of body talk. As the camera picks out the man entering the hospital room, he will quickly show signs of his downright goodness or innate evil. If he adjusts the pillows where the helpless accident victim lies, he is signaling tenderness. If, on the other hand, he curls his lip he is following the tradition of the sneering villain. The curled lip in close-up is a dead giveaway. Further coldness is shown by the brevity of his visit and by his formal stance, almost certain to indicate vanity and excessive satisfaction with his wealth and social position.

The heroine lying in the bed will bite her lip to hold back the screams that would be emitted by less heroic patients in similar pain. But she will look good, every hair in place. Wherever her injuries may be, they are not the kind to disturb her makeup.

Sinister people on soaps tend to maintain their glances a long time, as if they are smiling and plotting at the same time. The quizzical wouldn't-you-like-to-know-look is rarely on the face of the truly good woman or man, but on the face of the schemer. So is the frown. And adulterous women smile at men, then stop smiling when there is nothing more to be gained. They're fun to hate, in the modern equivalent of the hiss and boo.

Watching the soaps is good practice for becoming sensitive to sociological sub-texts. For example, one may note an equal number of men and women in a daytime serial, but women are almost sure to be doing subordinate tasks. Most of them will be nurses rather than doctors, or working at some job in which they take orders from men.

For their part, soap-opera men assume women have little serious work to do. They tease the women they visit, asking about lunch and little errands. Women adjust men's collars and remind them to be sure to carry an umbrella. The main function of women on the soaps continues to be gynecological. Their problems continue to center on the love they need from men and the security they need from marriage.

So there is a message transmitted which has to do with

power and function, regardless of what is ostensibly the substance of the plot. These matters have been noted by the advocates of change, with resulting efforts to show previously ignored minorities and women in some daytime soap operas and nighttime situation dramas. It is progress of a sort to have girl detectives actually in pursuit of the criminal, though the girls are still sex objects. In the old days, Della Street took Perry Mason's shorthand, poured the coffee, and sometimes provided a hiding place for a female client afraid to be questioned by the police. And in the still older days, in The Thin Man series, Nick Charles took the risks while wife Nora stayed home. She wanted to go, but she was not allowed; masculine chivalry and feminine cuteness required that she protest but be tricked into a car or closet which could be locked for her protection.

As models for female acquiescence, the Dellas and Noras succeeded admirably. The end of each episode found them enjoying drinks and a meal with their more adventurous partners. Criminals had been shot or arrested, and order was restored as men and women assumed their rightful places in the world.

A message is transmitted in

open stacks in a library

---

blue jeans

---

an open-book exam

---

a self-develop camera

---

radio drama

---

a bare desk in a large office

---

the sound of a disc-jockey

the game of monopoly

Epilogue

This chapter has made no attempt to be complete or definitive on the subject of media and what they do both to and for us. No one chapter *could* be. Our intention has been to alert your sensitivity to messages, the many ways in which they can be conveyed, and to the manner in which different media both create and appeal to different forms of consciousness.

We learn to read at a very early age, and thus become linear in our outlooks. But then television and movies take over, breaking down linear expectations and rational thought sequences.

With reason struggling for its share of our conscious life —often in vain—we can thus be susceptible—really, wide open—to the sub-texts of mass media: the hidden assumptions and the secret persuaders. We find ourselves buying Brand X without quite knowing why. Or we find ourselves expecting to meet people who exist only on the small screen at the far end of the living room or on the large screen in the dark movie house.

The media are so pervasive in our environment that one chapter cannot explore all of them in detail. It is at least a start to notice that the media are there at all, that reality is in one real sense a combination of media.

12

AND BE MY LOVE

Overview

The existence of love, or its absence, is a compelling, sometimes overwhelmingly important part of life. The word itself stands for feelings on several levels. It may be used frivolously as an overly enthusiastic preference for a particular ice cream flavor; reverently to express kinship with all living creatures; anxiously, in the frenzied pursuit of fantasy; smugly, in the two-against-the-world stance affected by some couples; or serenely, in the recognition of what love can be at its realistic best.

This chapter is about love in all its guises and disguises and about the impact of love both as an historical phenomenon and as fantasy.

This chapter also examines the love of self from which perhaps all other love derives; love in the family, where the degree of closeness provides opportunity for both support and injury; love of friends through shared pleasures; the love which reaches beyond immediate family and friends to help the wider world community and is sometimes known as altruism; love in marriage, including new versions in some contemporary life styles; and the barriers to love in the form of prejudices and stereotyped thinking.

It can be assumed that everyone is familiar with theories which dismiss love as being a mere trade of services and needs or an unnecessary addition to sexuality. These theories achieved considerable popularity during the 1920s, when bitter cynicism about once cherished ideals was a "must" among would-be sophisticates. But far more recently there has been a renewed effort to view love in both humanistic and sensible terms. In the psychological theories of Erich Fromm and Eric Berne the reader may discover the basis for a belief that true love still exists, however different it may be from definitions provided by old movies.

Self-Love

It is impossible to love another person or group honestly without beginning with love for oneself. This self-love includes enjoying solitude and silence. If we are whole, we don't need outside distractions—drinks, drugs, music, books, movement or other people—in order to be comfortable. We can not only endure but actually appreciate the opportunity to be alone with our own thoughts, thoughts which are free of self-blame, embarrassing memories, fear of inadequacy, anger, and frustration.

Self-Centered Love: A Different Matter

If being alone means concentrating on what will probably not work out well on the following day, no wonder mind-blurring distractions seem necessary. We automatically reach for television and telephone in order to escape from ourselves. Escape to other people frequently means the effort to get reassurance. No matter what the surface talk, the need cries out: Tell me I'm not those awful things I imagine when I'm alone.

Morton M. Hunt

Love: Any and every form of relationship between human beings which makes sense when used in conjunction with the phrases 'falling in love' or 'being in love'.[1]

Chögyam Trungpa

And this energy is always on-going, whether or not it is seen through the confused filter of ego. It cannot be destroyed or interrupted at all. It is like the ever-burning sun.[2]

Tell me instead that I'm good looking, strong, clever, and right. Tell me that the mistakes I made were not really mistakes at all. Love me.

The self-hating person in love is a potential nuisance who will require constant propping up by the lover. Insecurity leads to jealousy, demands to know where the lover has been and "which of us is more appealing?" It leads to extravagant purchases of products which must substitute for inadequacy of spirit. (A new shirt can momentarily brighten the day by making you feel as good as you look. A new dress with attending compliments can help for a while.) But soon the void within has to be faced again. Neither a closet full of clothes nor the memory of a recent testimonial dinner can satisfy the person who needs daily assurances of worth.

Self-love has nothing to do with self-centeredness, self-indulgence, and selfishness. These absorptions in one's ego are handicaps which probably spring from poor self-concepts to begin with. *I* is the word which dominates the talk of these people: frequent announcements of temperature change ("I'm too cold now. Somebody shut that window. I need a sweater. For a while I was too warm, but now I'm cold") and food preferences and random thoughts, without regard for the possible interest they may have for others. Such babbling has the spontaneous sound of an infant letting the world know he is developing diaper rash.

The Need to Dominate or Use Others

Selfishness is weak. Self-love is strong. Self-love is rooted in a realistic and proper regard for one's own capabilities, as well as limitations. It is rooted in integrity: not "If you don't like me, that's your problem" but "I know what I'm about; I do the best I can without intentional deceit or manipulating others." It is rooted in honesty and a sense of fair play.

People caught up in their own ego needs (their imagined beliefs about what they do or do not mean to the world) often seek what they call "support" from others. The person with a weak self-concept may find him- or herself bolstered by another person and may mistakenly regard the relationship as one of love: "So-and-so really understands me; so-and-so knows precisely what to say or do to make me feel better; I am therefore in love with so-and-so."

"So-and-so," on the other hand, may be less than a

> **Shakespeare**
>
> **Men have died from time to time and worms have eaten them, but not for love.**

selfless, altruistic support service. "So-and-so" may also have a weak self-regard and absolutely demand a feeling of being necessary to the survival of another. He or she is not necessarily deriving pure pleasure from the "joy" of giving. In fact, when excessive devotion goes to extremes, it can become a fanatic insistence upon being used: "You need me." But the person being relied upon can be a subtle, undetected user, manipulating a weak subject into being the passive receiver of continual favors, because the aggressive "giver" needs to be needed.

> Ovid
>
> **Love—a delicious game of seduction.**

Psychologist Erich Fromm speaks of *symbiotic* unions based on either a master/slave or slave/master relationship. It hardly matters which person plays which role. The needs are strikingly similar: a desire to master or to be mastered to compensate for a weak self-image. In Fromm's view, love exists properly between two strong individuals who know themselves, feel comfortable with themselves, and are in a position to share mutual strength.

In an introduction to the *Log from the Sea of Cortez,* a nonfictional account of a marine biology expedition through the Gulf of California, John Steinbeck (1902–1969) creates an unforgettable portrait of Ed Ricketts, the marine scientist who invited Steinbeck to go along. To Steinbeck, Ricketts was *the* model of an actualized human being; Ricketts had a strong, healthy appreciation of himself.

It gave him a great advantage. Most people do not like themselves at all. They distrust themselves, put on masks and pomposities. They quarrel and boast and pretend and are jealous because they do not like themselves. But mostly they do not know themselves well enough to form a true liking. [3]

> Samuel Johnson
>
> **Love is of no great influence upon the sum of life.**

It is the *willingness* to know oneself that matters most. Too many of us are afraid to look too carefully, afraid that our advance expectation of poor results will be matched by a hideous reality. Instead, we look to others to do for us what we *can* do initially for ourselves.

Love of Family: Where We Begin

Basic to human beings is that unique combination of feelings pleasant and otherwise known as family love. The unit of parents and children existed before romantic courtship, before today's "liberated" views of love and loving, and will no doubt be around for a *very long time.* Psychologists, sociologists, and other observers of human behavior would have to revamp almost all of their ideas, were the family unit to be removed from our society.

Recent Attacks

Though mother love has been celebrated since the beginning of recorded history, mother has been accused, in these post-Freudian times, of assorted crimes—usually based on possessiveness—which have blighted the lives of her children, who can never rid themselves of her presence. Mother has also been accused of being cold, manipulative and joyless, with the result that her sons and daughters cannot enjoy adult life. Father has been accused, in recent years, of being insufficiently assertive as a male role model, or of being so preoccupied with making money that he has no time for his children. The accusations have been so severe that parents of both sexes have often been forced to read manuals explaining how to talk to children, how to get chores done, explain sex, have privacy, without scarring the children at the time or in later life.

One young man aged 24 was so much impressed by the recent fad of heaping blame on parents that he brought a law suit against his own father and mother for damages resulting from the decidedly ineffective "parenting" he called malpractice. The parents had tried everything to deal with his drug habits, school truancy, and refusal to work. One damaging effort, he claims, was withholding food until he cleared weeds out of the yard. Another was psychological counseling. After assorted attempts, the parents threw him out of the house, to live away from them while still financially supported by them. He believes now that, after such a beginning, he will never be able to cope with the challenges of the adult world.

Columnist Ellen Goodman points out that while most people do not take their complaints to court, they do file "mental legal briefs against mom and dad," and "wrap themselves in difficult memories like comfortable excuses. They declare themselves as 'innocent as children' of their own actions, free of responsibilities for adulthood. They confess, saying: 'My parents did it.'"

Voltaire

The family—a group of people who cannot stand each other . . . forced to live under the same roof.

Other Fashions

Living in such close quarters these days is accompanied by a belief that togetherness is an inevitable family ideal. Such closeness was not always the case. The Greeks maintained separate doors and quarters within the house for men and women. Many cultures have had separate eating times and places for the different ages and sexes sharing a roof—usually with men eating first and women matter-of-factly accepting the left-overs from meals they cooked.

Upper-class European families have also taken for granted the short time allowed for childhood in the home. Children of nine and ten are sent off to boarding schools where they spend most of the year. Even in their younger years, almost every aspect of nurturing and care, including discipline, is assigned to tutors and governesses. So the current importance given to family play and general togetherness has not always existed, nor is it world wide. Day-care centers provide surrogate parental care for children in many parts of the world, including the United States. The difference is that working American parents tend to feel guilty over spending limited amounts of time in a "tight" family circle.

Nevertheless, despite the assortment of family practices, parents themselves continue to exert the greatest influence on children, and somehow something which passes for family love has managed to survive all customs and pressures and become a universal institution. Though under attack, the family, with modifications, somehow continues.

> **The need for family closeness is not universal, nor has it always existed in Western society.**

Making the Family Work

Unlike other kinds of love relationships, the family is not of one's own choosing. It is not necessary to be as cynical as Voltaire, who defined the family as "a group of people who cannot stand each other but who are forced to live under the same roof." At the same time, the inherent problems of living in close quarters, with various lifestyles and drives, need to be honestly faced. No doubt the intelligent approach is to *assume* the family is an institution and, instead of dreaming of liberation or looking enviously at other families (which always seem to be happier than one's own), for each member of the family to work diligently toward the inevitable compromises that must be made.

• *Maintaining individuality* • Despite family pressures there has to be part of each person which is separate from the family, and all members need to agree that such autonomy rightly exists and must be respected. It should be possible to be "excused" from family expectations whether one's parent has won a Nobel Prize, has always voted Republican, never appeared in public wearing shorts, or "never made it myself, so I'm going to see that you do!" Family counselors frequently report that much unhappiness stems from "gang tackling," as other members band together against the loner or the holdout.

• *Recognizing family differences* • Children know that family habits differ. They talk about the rules: scheduled full-course meals versus impromptu stand-up sandwiches; thorough cleaning of room versus throwing things in the closet when someone gets angry enough; careful return of deposit bottles and recycling of paper versus feast-or-famine cycles of spending.

Children know, but grown-ups forget, hence the surprise when the newlywed answering the telephone awakens a sleeping mate: "It's for you, dear." This, to someone who grew up in a family where only fire or flood could interfere with sleep.

• *Avoiding symbolic trivia* • The small habits—napkins of paper or cloth—remain small until they are the subject of an argument, until they become the scapegoats of some larger sins. When anger arises out of *real* neglect, the differences are magnified: "Of course, I might have known. Nobody turns off the lights when I'm not home. At this rate we'll never have a dime." The light left on has triggered other fears. Families share so much, know so much about each other's habits, all become vulnerable to attack. The extravagance of one affects all, just as the illness or depression of one is impossible for others to ignore. Members of a family have the ability to generalize ("You're always . . .) from a specific instance. It's not only faulty logic, it's the opposite of love.

Shakespeare

How sharper than a serpent's tooth it is to have a thankless child!

King Lear

• *Going for the Achilles' heel* • Achilles as an infant was dipped into the waters of the River Styx so that he would be immortal. But his mother forgot that she had held the child by his heel. He grew up, believing himself indestructible, only to have the dread secret come out at last, the secret which proved his undoing. The term "Achilles' heel" has come to mean everyone's most vulnerable spot. It is the one thing someone can say to you that is guaranteed to offend or reignite the spark of hidden guilt. Or it is that aspect of you about which you are most sensitive (face, eyes, height, weight, teeth?), that aspect which insiders know should never be discussed. Yet family members will at one time or another strike at each other's vulnerability. Not only that, but individual weaknesses are continually brought up in conversation as defense strategies. "You should talk about extravagance when you were the one who . . ." is not always thoughtful or tactful when Uncle Ned is trying to live down the bad stock tip he gave Father 23 years ago.

It's merciful to forget the terrible things family members can say to one another.

• *Looking out for the Soft Spots* • As well as we know and harp on the weaknesses of family members, we know their pleasures, too. We therefore show love by commenting on how well the dieter looks—rather than tempting lapses with a box of chocolates. Knowing that a worried housekeeper is concerned about a special dinner on the following day, we suggest dinner in the backyard to keep the kitchen clean. And we find words of praise for the wall hanging someone finally managed to finish. Too many compliments sound false, but an occasional aim at the soft spot is the sign of good intentions.

All of those deaths! The long parade to the graveyard! Father, Mother! Margaret, that dreadful way! So big with it, it couldn't be put in a coffin! But had to be burned like rubbish! You came home in time for the funerals, Stella.[4]
Tennessee Williams, A Streetcar Named Desire

• *Welcome Amnesia* • The soap operas have used amnesia as a convenient script device for years. Real families need it, too, not in the sense of complete loss of memory but as a means of forgetting hurtful language from the past. Every family has its fill of exaggerated words spoken in anger, words which should be taken as a temporary outburst not as a curse from on high. The child who is told "I wish you had never been born!" is hearing an expression of deep frustration which should have been phrased in another way.

But remembering it and bringing it forth with counter accusations is distortion of truth. People say terrible things to each other in real life. In a melodramatic movie, terrible words are always accompanied by loud music and the slamming of a door—signs that the words will be remembered forever. In our less dramatic lives they don't need to be, and it is damaging to dig them up "when needed."

• *Liability Insurance* • Most automobile owners carry liability insurance as protection against damages they may cause in an accident. Families also need insurance of some sort—or at least a statute of limitations—against guilt. Parents cause guilt when they act martyred ("You run along, I'm used to working") or mention past sacrifices or how much better the young "have it now." Young people for their part can invoke guilt when they mention the advantages their friends' families seem able to afford (camps, braces, special tutors) or remind a parent of a heated word. If home is the place where "when you have to go there," they "have to take you in," it is also the place with the greatest opportunities for both loving and hurting.

The Tribe: Family Substitute

The natural or "nuclear" family was once made up of large groups of people, living together or near each other and available to help, celebrate, or mourn. Today, when families are widely separated and in many cases have been divided through divorce and remarriage, the nurture which went with the traditional family has been lost. Some members wander off on their own and disappear over the horizon. Often the most passionate critic of the traditional family admits to the feeling that something important has been lost. We know that the traditional families had their share of squabbling and even hatred, but there was also the tacit knowledge that a unit bound by blood ties stood together to some degree against a hostile world.

Social observer Jane Howard suggests the formation of new families by choice, of tribes to give members the qualities inherent in the best of the idyllic traditional families of the past. Having collected the best traits of family love, she recommends the following for artificially designed families of the future:

1. Someone to praise achievements so there is pleasure in recounting what was done and what one looks forward to doing
2. Someone to keep track of the other members
3. Signs of activity and interests outside the family
4. Open hospitality and willingness to share and comfort where needed
5. The frank ability to accept disappointment or distress, since terrible things occur along with joys
6. New, made-up rituals along with the prescribed holidays, so there is always an anniversary to look forward to
7. Affectionate hugging
8. A sense of place, or if the family homestead keeps changing, the careful preservation of familiar objects
9. Children as an access to posterity—other people's children who will remember you, if you have none of your own
10. Honor for elders—the importance of grandparents or substitute grandparents from whom new generations can learn.

Friendship: Choices in People and Intensity

Friendship can be the strongest form of love, unrestricted by the requirements of inherent obligation, guilt, sex, age, or social views. Friends are free to choose each other, to be close or casual, and to stay or leave as they like. Friendship ranges from a lifetime alliance in which one would literally die for the other to the short-term coming together of people bound by a common desire to thwart a zoning change and whose acquaintance subsides with the end of the project.

The Ideal

The importance of friendship runs through our culture. The Golden Rule expresses the ideal: "Do unto others as ye would have them do unto you." Following that principle would mean always being aware of the sensibilities of "others," presumably everyone. It would mean constant avoidance of the possibility of hurt, as well as availing oneself of every opportunity to be kind and thoughtful.

The philosopher Immanuel Kant expressed a similar ideal when he wrote, "Use each man as an end in himself rather than as the means to an end." To care for each person as an important individual rather than as conspirator, sales prospect, sex object, or other one-dimensional label would be difficult but not impossible. To try to carry out the ideal would mean not even being able to ask for and receive the directions to an address without first taking time to note that you were dealing with a human being rather than just the source of information. Whether or not we want to take the time to see people as ends in themselves, we can recognize that using them is a barrier to friendship.

Platonic Love

A more personal ideal of friendship is that found in Plato: the closeness of two people who know each other so well

they feel that their spirits have merged, that it is not possible to tell where one personality stops and the other begins. This joining together may be the result of deepfelt exchanges of feelings and ideas, in which each has listened intently and sympathetically to the other. It can go beyond words, to shared silences, perfectly comfortable to both. Separations of many years make no difference. Good friends, true friends quickly regain their old bonds, with no need for a painstaking filling in of all the details of their lives during the intervening time.

The beauties of the body are as nothing to the beauties of the soul, so that wherever one meets with spiritual loveliness, even in the husk of an unlovely body, he will find it beautiful enough to fall in love with and to cherish.
Plato

Because Plato described it, this kind of love is called "Platonic," a word which some have debased to mean any relationship without sexual connections: thus, a couple who hardly know one another are said to be in a stage which is "still Platonic," as if this "high" form of friendship were only a preliminary to the main course, full sexual knowledge. It is possible for a couple to know each other in the Platonic sense, to be close spiritual friends, and also to engage in a sexual relationship.

It is also possible for a couple to consider themselves friends, without sexual experience between them, and still have no spiritual bonds of the kind Plato described.

There is nothing we learned about each other in bed that we could not have learned—had not already begun to learn—in conversation; for that matter, by going to basketball games together. Sex is just a metaphor, isn't it, a way of focusing, intensifying, otherwise inchoate feelings.
Richard Schickel

In *Games People Play* (1964), psychiatrist Eric Berne describes a variety of artificial transactions indulged in by people who see each other frequently. The famous game "Yes, but . . ." is played by the person who prefers making any excuse to avoid changing a situation. The "games" are roles assumed by people accustomed to manipulating through tears, threats, coy promises, and a host of other barriers to love. But the last chapter of Berne's book is called "Intimacy," a state beyond games. True intimacy is the heavenly domain of friendship, a state of trust, understanding, and playfulness. Difficult for inveterate games-players to achieve, it is nevertheless worth the effort.

Loyalty

Dante's "Inferno" showed gradations of punishment in hell. The worst, personally supervised by Satan himself, was applied to those who had used the pretense of friendship to assist in the betrayal of those who trusted them.

Embezzlers have historically been considered worse sinners than armed robbers because the former betrayed a trust. Today, we would be more alarmed by the potential violence of the criminal with a gun. We are less willing to expect so much from a friend, perhaps because profound friendship is increasingly hard to find in a society moving as rapidly as ours.

There are times when friendship is in conflict with some other value—patriotic duty, for instance, or the love of a man or woman. The fictional spy novel shows the agent ruefully turning in a personal friend with the wrong political allegiance in wartime. E. M. Forster, in "Two Cheers for Democracy," said he hoped that if it ever became necessary to choose between friendship and his country he would choose his friend. With all due respects to patriotic fervor, he simply did not trust the political abstraction which is a state, over the known quality of a friendship.

This view is at odds with the one expressed by China's former Chairman Mao, who urged that the good of the state or of the smaller community must come before all else. The worker who observes wrong deeds such as careless waste, even if involuntary, must denounce the wrongdoer no matter how close a friend. And the denunciation must not be done quietly or in private but rather in the presence of a large general meeting. Repeatedly, Mao and other revolutionary leaders have urged that friendship be subordinated to the state if not relegated to an individualism no longer suitable for the realities of the current class struggle.

A free society rejects such values. Indeed, its judicial system even recognizes the tendency of a friend to supply a false alibi for one accused of a crime. "He was with me when the bank was robbed; we played poker all night" is a statement of friendship which prosecutors and juries tend to disregard, not thinking of it as a criminal act of perjury. As to civil violations, the person who turns informer and reports a friend's inaccurate tax returns to the Internal Revenue Service is considered, even by the benefiting agency, to have betrayed a trust more important than loyalty to the government agency.

On a Smaller Scale: The Affinity Group

To love one's neighbor as oneself, to seek intimacy, to embrace all of humankind as part of one's community—these are ideals not part of daily routine. We become loving members of the society of humankind when stirred by a religious service or by a large natural catastrophe. (Hurricanes and earthquakes make us think in large regional terms, and the threat of invasion from outer space might even make us think in the planetary terms popular at the end of World War II.)

On the small scale of ordinary life, the affinity group of friendship for those with common concerns is more prevalent. The natural liking or attraction to a person is an affinity. We tend to (but do not necessarily) like those who are "like-minded," members of the same neighborhood, religion or political group, car pool, or job. We are drawn to those who enjoy the same sports and hobbies. In resort areas there are affinity groups based on city of origin. Bulletin boards at community centers for senior citizens announce a meeting of "The Detroit Club." We have all experienced the special perception we have of a someone from our home town whom we happen to meet on a visit to another city. For the moment that we meet on the street of the "foreign" place, we share the affinity of geography, if nothing else. Signet jewelry and bumper strips on cars are signs of affinity which seek to make smaller groups possible in an increasingly anonymous world.

Because there are so many affinities, we will single out only a few, recognizing that each will suggest many more.

• *Active Sports* • The passionate tennis player can form instant friendship in a game with someone as skilled or just a little better. Tennis is a competitive game in which it is considered bad form to suggest "lobbing a few back and forth without keeping score." The affinity group for the aficionado is made up of those equally devoted to improving their game. It is helpful to have some other topics for the post-game drink. But it is definitely not necessary, nor must tennis players like each other's mates. Pleasant, but not necessary. The friendship can easily be restricted to the court.

• *Passive Worship* • Whether they come together to admire an idol, discuss a controversial play, exchange statistics or photos, fans enjoy the chance to talk about the talents of the actor, athlete, or musician they all admire. Being with each other allows them to share the communion of souls equally reverential and escapist.

• *Connoisseurs* • People who collect the same things like to talk to each other about their hobby. Whether the hobby involves boat models or porcelain milk jugs, there are hours to be spent comparing notes, admiring acquisitions, seeking the rare object together. As in the case of the fan club (connoisseurs are usually older) people can convince each other that there is great merit in their pastime. Some of the connoisseurs are married to people who think money is better spent on house repairs and cross-country vacations. It is therefore reassuring for people with a singular passion to stay with the like-minded and to do their best to avoid hearing condescending statements at the breakfast table, like this: "You mean you actually paid that much?"

Closer Affinities

The affinity groups mentioned above have in common a preference for the same activity, evidenced by some visible sign of preference. The friendships formed of that pleasure in sport or collecting may not reach beyond the objects or activities involved. Those who like automobiles may spend time exchanging information about style, price, and the performance of engines, just as joggers enjoy comparing warm-up methods, routes, and the performance of their own bodies. Such external information may be enough to form the basis for something, but most people want more. Not everyone in the home-town club or the diet group is worthy of the name "friend."

• *A Sense of Mission* • Co-workers, co-religionists, and civic activists may form an affinity which lasts so long as there is mutual need or benefit. People with the same mission often overlook many aspects of each other's personality which may prove to be irritating after a relationship has continued for a time. During the 1960s, for example, many who protested the war in Vietnam or the illegality of marijuana smoking lived together in communes—an arrangement of considerable intimacy which did not always work. "Missionary zeal" can quickly be replaced by boredom when relationships are lacking too many vital factors, such as compatibility of temperaments, mutual intellectual interests, or real physical attraction.

• *Temperaments* • The closer affinity based on similar temperament has a better chance of working. Something strikes two people as funny, when everyone else nods soberly. In a mutual reaction to, say, a speaker's pomposity—two people may instantly recognize an affinity which is unlike all others, strong enough even to lead to a marriage partnership. Classrooms provide the opportunity for people to discover mutual temperaments, particularly in the chance to pursue an acquaintance with someone whose remarks in a discussion cause an instantaneous echo response. Unfortunately, ours is a society in which the individual holds fast to his or her personal territory and resists a sudden intrusion. People who could become fast friends through an affinity of temperaments often miss the chance because one or the other is too shy to take the first step.

• *A Talent for Losing* • Being incompetent about the same things is as much the basis for affinity as is the hobbyist's collection. The gardener whose plants die is relieved to find someone with a thumb equally as un-green as his own. In the recognition that someone else was cheated by paying for a complete tune-up at an unbelievable price (truly unbelievable!) the naive motorist finds solace. In the midst of a general unraveling of things, when a chain reaction has started and nothing wants to come out right, a person often shuns

---

Alvin Toffler

Both sides understand, consciously or otherwise, the limitations and laws. Difficulties arise only when one or another party oversteps the tacitly understood limits

. . .

the company of breezy, complacent (former) friends on whom providence seems to be smiling radiantly. While it may be rewarding on the surface to enjoy charter membership in a losers' club, too great a reliance on the commiseration of fellow members can weaken the will and cause us to believe in Bad Luck as a real, live, malevolent entity. Taking active steps to remedy a bad situation may be a more intelligent course.

Friendships founded on long-range affinities or a true sense of humor may come closer to the Platonic ideal.

• *A Sense of Humor* • There is no infallible test for the close affinity, but a sense of humor comes close. "I happen to be among those who adore jokes," acknowledges one writer. "In saying this I do not mean to say that I am a fine fellow, of that caste of special and superior beings: the good-humored. I used to think that a sense of humor was an absolute requisite for friendship; and while it is true that most of the people I count as friends enjoy laughter, so, alas, do many people who are frivolous, or cynical, or even vicious." It may not be enough, but it is surely a beginning—particularly if the "sense of humor" includes more than the mechanical exchange beginning "Did ya hear the one about——."

The friend with a sense of humor would recognize shifts in mood without having them announced. Friends don't have to be told, "But seriously—" because they know. They know how long to dwell on a matter of grave concern ("What'll I do if my loan doesn't get approved?") before moving on. It may be the sensibility, more than the humor, which proves to be the "affinity factor."

Outward Signs of Friendship

In some societies friends are permitted to make—and actually enjoy making—external shows of friendship. Latins are particularly fond of touching each other. Touch is an integral part of the friendship ritual. Men can grasp each other's arms, hug, or hold each other around the shoulder without incurring immediate suspicion from onlookers. Women not only hug but kiss each other publicly with much greater frequency than happens in the United States.

In the United States, as was indicated earlier, the personal territory of each person seems to be of paramount importance. Only married people and lovers are allowed free passage beyond the invisible but acknowledged borders of the territory. To stand too close to someone you have just met, or to place your hands upon him/her in any fashion is to violate a profound social rule. If you enter a room in which a stranger or casual acquaintance is the sole occupant of the sofa, you will automatically look for a chair across the room.

The at times almost neurotic unwillingness of Americans to touch or be touched is the subject of a very moving play, Edward Albee's *The Zoo Story* (1960). The hero, Jerry, comes upon a properly dressed, obviously well-ordered gentleman named Peter sitting on a bench, reading a book. Jerry behaves in a deliberately eccentric fashion in order to draw Peter into a conversation, and at length into a deep involvement which Peter neither encourages nor wants. So desperate is Jerry for real contact with another human being, however, that he goads Peter into anger by calling his manliness into question. At this point Jerry throws the confused Peter a knife, daring him to defend his manliness. Before Peter realizes what is happening, Jerry throws himself upon the knife, thus accomplishing the suicide he has contemplated all along. To force another human being to touch him has required the literal giving up of Jerry's life.

Not only touching but making eye contact is difficult for many Americans. If the person with whom you are trying to communicate is not prepared for eye contact, he or she will surely resist your direct glance.

In vivid and significant contrast are the external displays of sexual intimacy which are not only permitted in the United States but have the complete approval of almost all of society. Boys and girls walk along the street arm-in-arm almost as soon as they reach their teens. It is nothing to observe men and women kissing each other, even nibbling at each other's ears, on public conveyances, in restaurants, or theaters. Some psychologists have observed that the fear of latent homosexuality is so great in our society that public signs of heterosexual intimacy are eminently preferred to indications that a man and a woman are merely "friends." The fear of being considered anything but "normal" in sexual orientation may help explain the reluctance of many American males to touch each other.

In the world of sports, however, the picture changes. Football and basketball players, in particular, are constantly patting each other as part of the team ritual. Presumably the athlete has already established his credentials of masculinity and need fear no questioning from society.

Prejudice and Friendship

> In Europe it is socially acceptable for close friends of both sexes to make a public display of affection.

The word prejudice is related to pre-judging, forming an opinion without actually meeting/knowing the person or thing being judged. In recent years prejudice has been so often associated with racism that we forget its other forms. Prejudice renders mechanical both the judge and the person who is judged. Since prejudice is not a fashionable trait it is unlikely that anyone would claim to have it. Nevertheless, the following is a list of categories into which we may place certain people we meet and which make it difficult or impossible for a friendship to blossom.

• *The Rich* • The advice to marriageable youth has been "It's just as easy to fall in love with someone rich as it is with someone poor." But the rich often have problems meeting people because they are constant reminders of money. Conversations with the very rich reveal the embarrassed concerns of people trying to avoid the subject in an unnatural way, as though an invisible censor prevented any reference to economics. Or else money is mentioned too much ("I guess this wouldn't make any difference to you, but on my budget——"). The rich have been victims of a reverse snobbishness that prevents their being invited to the homes of those with lower incomes. Though there are sufficient invitations from "their own kind," this restriction places a barrier between the haves and have-nots which prevents friendship or love.

• *Power* • Though ours is not a titled society, rank exists. Any large corporation has its organizational chart with clear demarcations of power indicated by size of an office, its location, decor, and the respect with which people stifle yawns when talking to the possessor of it. As a result, people of equal status tend to have lunch together with the rare exceptions of parties for the whole staff. Colleges, with their allegedly liberated, open-minded faculty, are not free of the power syndrome. A college president or dean may be pointedly avoided by faculty not wishing to appear too ingratiating, with the result that the person with power talks to the same people all the time. The nonadministrative faculty readily accepts its inferior status. A typical opening remark by a faculty member to an administrative official is: "You probably don't remember me, but I was wondering if you've had a chance to look at the requests for leave——."

The awkwardness extends in both directions, as the person with higher rank tries to be natural: "I really enjoyed your presentation. It's so rare to find that kind of understanding in someone of your——." Oops. Robots talking. Computers would be more imaginative.

• *The Humorist* • Once someone has achieved the reputation of being funny, his or her friends expect comedy routines rather than an interchange of ideas and feelings. On a night when the humorist prefers to listen rather than do an act there is concern at this sign of something wrong. Funny people deserve the right to have moods. They need not buy their way into gatherings with their ability to provoke laughter. Humorists, with their irreverence, have found a comfortable place with both the rich and the powerful. They can say outrageous things to them because their conversation has a shock value denied their more conventional friends. But it is artificial just the same to be accepted solely on the basis of one's wit.

• *Calling Cards* • Meeting people for the first time can produce a minefield of questions and answers. In circling around new acquaintances, we can resemble personnel directors interviewing applicants: name, address, school attended, what year, SAT scores, marital status, jobs held and so on. None of these questions is without its prejudice potential. In our search for possible affinities ("You went to _____ High School, did you know _____ ?"), we try to classify as quickly as possible. Even the innocuous first question —name?—has connotations of ethnic background, lineage, and the taste of the parents who chose it. And "How long have you lived there?" can be more than a friendly request for information.

The list above is not complete. It leaves out the common prejudices of race, language accent, father's occupation, and the range of academic achievement from professional school graduate to junior high school drop-out.

The gates of friendship can be opened by restraining the desire for answers to these probing questions and talking about other things, or at least by keeping to a minimum the interrogation which invites the prejudice which prevents human contact.

Such an experiment would still leave room for other affinities: a liking for spring irises, Victorian furniture, ice hockey goalies' masks, early Woody Allen films, and mail addressed to "Occupant." Affinities based on application-blank information take less time but lead more certainly to a mechanical treatment of human beings.

Philosophers and clergymen have preached that the highest order of human response is the full, nonjudgmental acceptance of people who appear to be different from oneself. In this acceptance lies a recognition of the affinity of all humankind while allowing for such human frailties as envy or boredom. The human way is to rid ourselves of prejudice before we decide on the guest list for our next party.

> The highest order of human response is the full, nonjudgmental acceptance of people different from oneself.

Love of Others: Altruism and Its Limits

Both religious and secular societies have encouraged caring for others as a basic precept, encouraged through parables, fables, and laws. The philosophic term for this awareness of the needs of others is *altruism,* a concept which is both complex and controversial.

In Myth and Parable

In its simplest form, altruism is encouraged by stories told almost from the beginning of time. One such story is the Greek myth of Baucis and Philemon, a poor couple barely managing to find food for themselves. One day, the couple were greeted by travelers, coming to the door of their hut, and needing a place to stay.

"We are poor folk," they told the two men, "but you are welcome to share with us." They then offered the strangers their own food and gave up their own bed.

The next morning, the strangers revealed themselves as gods in disguise. As a reward for their generosity, Baucis and Philemon received two gifts: a constantly replenished

> Plato
>
> Nothing but love will make a man offer his life for another's.

pitcher, so that they would never again want for drink, and the granting of one wish. The couple requested the right to live together for the rest of their lives and to die at the same time, so that one devoted partner never need mourn for the other. The wish was granted. Before leaving, the gods pointed out devastation in the valley below. "There are the flooded homes of the people who turned us away. All have been destroyed. Only you were willing to care for us."

The moral of the story seems clear: Help others, with no thought for yourself and be rewarded. Simple enough in the days of the Olympian gods, and simple enough when the act of charity consists of lodging and food for one night.

The destruction of the neighbors introduces a sour note: a most severe penalty for lack of hospitality. Nevertheless, the myth has a pleasant distribution of reward and punishment, suitable for far-away events of long ago, even though it may strike the cynical as one more bit of evidence that in the myths which conditioned humanity, altruism brings a material reward.

The Christian parable of the Good Samaritan, however, encourages caring for others as a means of showing love for God. To inherit eternal life, it is necessary to show oneself a good neighbor, not in talk but in deed, by actually helping a needy person without looking for praise.

The medieval Jewish physician Maimonides cast a different light on the selfless helping of others by envisaging a caring society which would provide so well for people that there would be no need for charity, no matter how generously or anonymously given.

In Secular Life

These early stories are among many which throughout history have urged love for one's fellow man. Altruism has not been confined to mythology or religion but has been tied to national causes as well. Patriotic observances pay tribute to leaders—some of them martyrs—who are said to have acted out of interest not for themselves but for others. Each group has its own list of those who demonstrated this highest form of love, this willingness to sacrifice. Union organizers, missionaries, the Peace Corps, Vista, Civil Rights activists, and protesters against tyranny appear to be among those willing to serve out of more than personal motives.

Altruism can also be caring for the children of a sick relative, providing a place to stay for friends temporarily without jobs, and so on.

Excessive Love

Altruism has seemed both unrealistically demanding and unworkable. The caring for others at the expense of one's own welfare is best illustrated in the story of the man who gave into every demand of his sweetheart. After he had given her many gifts, he asked what else he might do to please her. "Bring me the heart of your mother," was the demand.

Obediently, the lovestruck young man went home, killed his mother, and carved out her heart. Then, carrying it in his hands, he ran to present the gift. On the way, he tripped and fell, the heart falling out of his hands. From the heart came the voice of his mother: "Did you hurt yourself, my son?"

This story of altruism at its possibly foolish extreme was given a slightly different treatment in the popular children's story by Shel Silverstein, "The Giving Tree." Year after year, the tree keeps giving, her shade, her branches, her trunk, everything, as year after year the boy grows into a man who returns and demands more and more. The old man who had once been the little boy, returns for a final visit. Everything is gone now, except a stump. The tired old man sits on the stump. The story ends: "And the tree was happy."

The tree has been used by clergymen as an example of truly selfless giving, but others may decide even a tree can be foolishly masochistic.

It is no nonviolence if we love merely those that love us. It is nonviolence only when we love those that hate us. I know how difficult it is to follow this grand law of love. But are not all great and good things difficult to do?
Gandhi

Some reject altruism as unworkable in any profound way. Bertolt Brecht in *The Good Woman of Setzuan* presents a heroine who is pleasant and cheerful, never turning away anyone in need. Like the couple in the Greek myth, she provides food and shelter, not just for a short time but for as long as help is needed by the poor vagrants who come to her little shop.

In providing the help, lovingly given, she herself loses money. She gives away more than she takes in. The only way her shop can prosper is through the assistance of a tough-minded cousin who cleans out the beggars and demands cash on the line, no freeloading. The playwright observes that the cousin is actually the altruistic heroine in disguise, that no shop and no society based on profit can be expected to prosper by giving.

An even sterner view of altruism has been taken by Ayn Rand, who rejects as outright foolishness the notion that any of us are obliged to help any one else. In her tribute to individualism, Rand claims that society is weakened by the religious requirement of altruism. In putting others before

ourselves, we help neither the needy *nor* ourselves. Rand recommends the opposite of altruism, concentration on the needs of oneself, or egoism.

Someone lying on the side of the road is entitled to no help at all, according to this view. If we feel like helping, we may, but we should recognize that there are no rewards in heaven or on earth for so doing. The person who helps is no more to be praised than the person who, like the first two men in the parable of the Good Samaritan, continued on their way, ignoring the victim of robbers.

According to the philosophy of egoism, those who want protection from fire should pay those trained to put out fires, or should take personal risk and responsibility for their own property.

The Practical Choices

When Abraham Lincoln spoke of "charity for all, malice toward none," he looked forward to the end of a war which had divided a country. With massive tasks of rebuilding ahead of them, Americans from both North and South were urged to put hatred aside and come together to build a loving, peaceful future. As Lincoln used the term, "charity" is selfless giving, the agape of the Greeks.

The rhetoric of wartime encourages such words; they were also used by Allied leaders at the end of World War II. But day-by-day giving does not lend itself to stirring speeches. It is difficult today to practice the love which goes beyond self, family, and close friends to reach the world beyond. Altruism is affected by the motivation of the giver, effective benefit to those in need, and the suspicions of ideological foes.

According to Kenneth Clark, people of means can afford to behave well toward others, while the poor cannot.

These concerns cloud the issue and make pure giving in the Good Samaritan sense difficult to achieve. After all, the Good Samaritan gave personal assistance to someone who clearly needed help. The man in need was cared for on the spot, face to face and at the time of his accident. What help the Good Samaritan did not offer himself he paid an inn-keeper to give. And he was able to know immediately the value of his actions.

By contrast, consider the complexity of the modern giver. Kenneth Clark, in his autobiography *The Other Half,* tells of a drive he took in India, near Delhi, where he and a friend encountered a group of local children. The friend, who spoke the native dialect, told them of love and forgiveness, and had a receptive audience. As they left, Clark put a coin in the hand of one of the children. As a visitor, he did not know the danger of that sort of personal giving. His friend's warning came too late. The children brutally attacked the child who had been given the coin, as the two visitors "drove away, leaving behind a scene of carnage. This taught me the lesson," writes Clark, "that good behaviour is the outcome of latent wealth, however small, and that the Indians are unbelievably poor."

The love and forgiveness in the speech by Clark's friend were empty words in contrast to a tangible coin, and the depth of poverty was apparently too great to be helped by one fortunate man's attempt to give.

Our national attitudes are a blend of individualism and social consciousness. The belief that a person or enterprise is entitled to the maximum rewards achievable by . . . competitive striving is powerful. But it is tempered by a concern for the underprivileged."
Rockefeller Panel Reports, 1959

Nonetheless, for many people "altruism" takes the form of donations to any agency entrusted to select the recipients and the manner by which they receive charity. Cynics could observe that the inducement of a tax write-off argues against the purity of the motive.

On a large scale, altruism can be even more suspect. Before he died, the King of Sweden made a large donation to a national association for the handicapped. The donation was rejected by those it was designed to help—because of the source. Private donors, even kings, were not allowed to perform acts of generosity reserved for "the government." Leftist camps tend to reject private bequests, calling them elitist because they encourage an acceptance of the good deeds of wealthy individuals, as opposed to socialist governments from which they feel all benefits should come.

Leftist camps tend to reject private bequests, calling them elitist because they encourage an acceptance of the good deeds of wealthy individuals.

Some bequests have been rejected because they were designed to help those no longer considered needy. A Swedish government official, Lars Bersstig, is quoted in a *New York Times* article: "There are five to ten small trusts in Stockholm alone that specify that their money should be spent for the moral improvement of wayward women. Can you really imagine giving away money for that in Sweden today?"

So the rich would-be altruist may stir up trouble and criticism with his or her gift. He or she can be called political, decadent, over-privileged. The recipients themselves may refuse the money or protest the manner in which it was given.

Medical missionaries, accused of being colonials, have been banished from the lands they attempted to serve. Indeed they have even been executed for their intrusions. It would appear that nothing could be a better expression of selfless love than their efforts to ease pain, but an opposing ideology can call any motive into question. Even where motivation is *not* questioned, grim statistics intrude: the people cured today will become the parents of tomorrow in countries already overcrowded and undernourished.

What form can altruism can disinterested (selfless) love take (if any at all)?

It can continue to give help to those who obviously need it, in the belief that, even if one cannot help all of humanity, a modest gesture in the right direction is still significant. ("Better to light a candle than to curse the darkness.")

It can make private sacrifices and boycotts, as a gesture toward "the others" of the world. (Thoreau, for example, refused to buy cotton shirts made in New England mills which exploited the workers.)

It can encourage a personal activism, urging others to change their way of living, so that limited resources will be available for all. (Many modern prophets urge reduction in consumption of meat, electricity, and fuel, no matter how many others seem indifferent to the crisis.)

In Dickens's *A Christmas Carol,* the old miser's heart melted after he had his visions. All Scrooge needed to do was practice a personal benevolence to the Cratchit family and earn a hearty "God bless us every one."

Perhaps the modern world makes altruism a much more complicated affair.

Two Dominant Models from the Past

It would be tempting to accept the total pleasure of making up a life without regard to history. "I just do what suits me" sounds as though it is possible to begin each day with an absolutely free choice. One could, for instance, decide to be in love or not, without influence or pressure from any other source.

But one cannot escape yesterday so easily. The choices available to the would-be lover are at least strongly influenced by ideas formed and acted upon by people in the past. Though the past entertained, and was made miserable by, many versions of love, two concepts and practices have shown remarkable endurance and continue to prey on our minds.

Romantic—or "True"—Love

The Middle Ages introduced romance, an elevation of the lady fair as unattainable but utterly desirable, worthy of a life dedicated to her worship. Romantic love is a peculiarly Western exercise, unknown in many parts of the world. It began with playful tributes to women; as the flattery increased, both men and women began to enjoy the game.

He: *I love you, Jennifer.*

She: *I know, Philip. But do you really love me?*

He: *Of course, I really love you.*

She: *I know you love me, like* that. *But do you* really *love me?*
Lines from any number of old, and not so old, movies.

Knights and noblemen prided themselves on the extent of their devotion and the number of sacrifices possible in the name of the lady they made the center of their lives. Though the worshipper might be married, he tended to regard his wife as the "useful" woman in his life, not to be thought of in the same terms as the lady fair, who might also be married to someone else. Separation, denial, unfulfilled desire—all were thought to improve the character of the sufferer.

The fulfillment of desire, if it ever occurred, came only at the end of a long courtship and only if both parties were unencumbered. Lovers otherwise indulged in sex play, which included not only extravagant verbal tributes but many tender caresses stopping short of intercourse.

These romantic ideas have affected modern attitudes in

many ways. Because they have been accepted for centuries, they still underlie the motives of parents who protect their children from premature sexual experience; they help generate the disappointment which marriage often brings to couples who preferred the excitement of courtship; and they may also create the heightened desirability of a "lover", real or fantasized, with whom an ordinary mortal can never expect to compare favorably.

Literature is filled with the romantic ideal, in some of the most beautiful poetry ever written. Shakespeare puts romantic words in a note written by Hamlet to Ophelia:

> *Doubt that the stars are fire*
> *Doubt that the earth doth move*
> *Doubt truth to be a liar*
> *But never doubt I love.*

Such passionate declarations make love truer than any scientific fact. Neither logic nor astronomy nor nuclear physics can compete with the romantic ideal of love. Older generations, decrying the alleged sexual "looseness" of today's society, may not recognize the degree to which, sexual liberation notwithstanding, people still seek the romantic ideal in which the physical and the spiritual are joined in permanent and faithful union.

It is easy to recognize romance. It exists in profusion—in the countless, still popular tales of lovers who will live through eternity because one or both of them died in a cruel, envious world; in advertisements offering endless pleasures in the company of the beloved (with the product assisting in the attainment of bliss.) Even rock ballads, with their earthy words and rhythms, are in the romantic tradition. Romeo and Juliet, Hero and Leander, Tristan and Isolde, and Bonnie and Clyde are romantic. They love, they die. Blondie and Dagwood are not romantic. They have to cope with animals, postmen, and the preference for a poker game with the fellows rather than chores around the house. Archie and Edith Bunker are not romantic and this fact makes their marriage both amusing and sad.

The legacy of romance, which began in the Middle Ages, is present today in the deliberate rejection of the advice of cynics. Romance is the pursuit of an ideal, the more difficult

---

Shakespeare

Being your slave, what
  should I do but tend
Upon the hours and time
  of your desire?
I have no precious time at
  all to spend,
Nor services to do, till
  you require.

Older generations may not recognize the degree to which people still seek the romantic ideal.

the better, to the horror of those whose feet are planted firmly on the ground. Romance hates clinical accounts of love-making (frank references to the sex organs and their function).

Those who decry the loss of spirituality in our society do not perhaps realize how idealistic are the thoughts of love, even among those who do not hesitate to engage in physical contact almost at once. There is a certain pride among many who do not hesitate to enjoy sexual union, a pride in achieving a total oneness of body and soul. Seldom do we hear of frank admissions that sex is all there is; that sex is unrelated to deeper feelings; few in this age believe sex devoid of spiritual value.

The Victorian Model

The Victorian Age, which continued until the end of the 19th century, is still within the conscience of many older people today. The ideal Victorian marriage took place between a successful man, a "good provider," and his wife, who was expected to be competent in the running of the house, assisted by servants and an unmarried female relative. At the same time that the husband was decisive in running his business or profession, he was usually quite boyish at home, where he could lose his temper, become concerned about minor illnesses, and be demanding about his food. The wife's competence in the home would be demonstrated by her meeting his demands, carefully avoiding direct confrontations, meticulously preparing of his favorite foods, and soothing ministrations of cold compresses and headache powders as necessary. But she would not have liked to be reminded of her "competence," for the term sounded masculine. In quite public ways she was clearly to seem incompetent. She needed clear directions for finding addresses, for example, she was not expected to deal in any but the most trivial ways with tradespeople, or to make important decisions about vacations, the education of the children, or any other matter requiring long-range plans and organization. Such things required the sure, guiding hand of a husband.

Because the Victorian Age was clearly so limiting and repressive, because sexual prudishness and male dominance are associated with it, and because its influences are still being felt, it has been widely criticized by the feminist movement. Feminists point out that Victorian marriage did not work for independent women or for families without money or for nonconformists even then. It is not likely to be a successful model for most couples today.

Nonetheless the Victorian model remains, especially in middle-class families, where resistance to change is notable and generational conflicts about the proper definition of love continue to occur. The "well-run household" is one version of the Victorian model which persists. Even as one ascends the social scale, one finds that men expect to come home to a clean house, a well-cooked meal, and an attentive wife. Servants can take care of the first two wishes, but not the third. The role of the woman in the household, whether liberation allows her to work or not, is still likely to be given a Victorian slant, regardless of the social class.

Some people—men and women alike—look with a certain nostalgia to the role certainty that exists in the Victorian model. In the days of our grandparents or great-grandparents, a woman might be told, "Ladies don't wear such things in public." Or "Grown men don't cry." In today's liberation movements proper behavior for men and women is not always clear, though roles begin to assert themselves anyway. In the Victorian model the guidelines are ever present.

Love in the Modern World

Morton M. Hunt

The central problem of modern women . . . is known as 'role conflict' or 'role confusion'. The modern woman does not really know what she wants to be . . . for she still lives in a man's society.[5]

Some people cannot see the forest for the trees, a saying which must surely be true for historians too involved in the minutiae of their own times to know what will be significant for future generations. To a frustrated parent of today, perhaps raised to seek the Victorian model of love and marriage, struggling with a teenager's "premature" concern for sexual experience and need to "go with someone," the modern version of love might seem bleak, devoid of spirituality, and focused on sensation alone.

But in 1968, just at the height of the so-called youth rebellion, when so many young people were leaving home, taking to the road, or moving from one commune to another, and when thousands of parents were convinced that the younger generation was on a speedy course to hell, there appeared *The Graduate,* a film about a young man who could not communicate with his parents but sought and found romantic love with an eminently decent young lady. The movie became the most popular screen entertainment of the decade and seemed a clear indication that young America could be as idealistic as Romeo and Juliet about love.

The Victorian model is still here as well. Popular songs throughout the century have stressed the importance still placed on staunch fidelity to one special person, from "A Bicycle Built for Two" at the turn of the century to the heart-broken lament of the forsaken girl in the rock musical *Hair:* "Easy to be Cold." In 1977 a musical opened on Broadway about "swinging" couples, indulging in wife-swapping

"As it turned out, the 'swingers' were really quite Victorian at heart."

and other playtime activities that would have rendered a Victorian audience speechless. But the show was called *I Love My Wife,* and as it turned out, the "swingers" were really quite Victorian at heart, preferring their own mates all the time

Recent years have nonetheless heard new voices, some deliberately rejecting the romantic notion of love; some denouncing the Victorian ideals of the stable household, the dominant male, and the submissive female; and some insisting that the very idea of love is an illusion.

Lee and I are rejecting marriage. . . . As a woman, I have been through every bit of the denigrating vicious circle, while working toward personhood. I choose to keep my own unique way because I must.

Theodora Wells

Show and Tell

Schoolteacher, early 30s, loves younger men, bored with S/M, wants Mr. Right."
Advertisement in the personal section of a newspaper

We made it five times over the weekend, but Karen still has trouble getting an orgasm every time.
Couple to their friends.

Love is an appetite, like eating or drinking. . . . I love it when Alan is jealous. . . . I haven't heard from him since Thursday. What's wrong?
College girl to dormitory suitemates.

Some people are dominated by an impulse to discuss feelings. Young people tell each other when or whether they have lost their virginity. Derision is reserved for the reticent. Though pre-marital sexual activity is common, those who choose to wait are still able to do so—provided they are certified by their friends to be "free from hang-ups." This is the age of Show and Tell.

The teacher who wrote the advertisement quoted above was, however, telling more than she realized. She has apparently had wide sexual experience, but she maintains a belief in the one true love, the "Mr. Right" of a century ago. Once she has found him she'll never let him go, and apparently the search has taken her to a widely read newspaper in a metropolitan area. While she waits for answers to her ad, she has probably taken the search to singles bars as well, where, even on first meeting she and her dates will discuss past relationships, complete with sexual preferences. The revelations are part of the mating game. But the less modern part of it is a continuing belief in the romance of the one-and-only without whom happiness is impossible. Some see in the singles bar scene not analogies with decadent Rome but the end of the road in the age-old quest of fulfillment the Victorians (perhaps wisely) never demanded.

The couple of the second quotation are concerned with performance. They keep score. The number of sexual encounters is important to the man, who would also be pleased if his girlfriend announced pleasure in his technique. "He's a good lover" has replaced "He's a good dancer" in descriptions to friends. Quality performance includes the ability on the part of the woman to have orgasms—multiple, if possible. By doing so, she can show her own modern freedom from inhibitions, her inventiveness, and praise for the aforementioned lover. This willingness to talk matter-of-factly about sex is possibly without precedent in the past. The closest parallel might in this case be found in the later years of the Roman Empire, when highborn ladies took and discarded lovers as they chose. The difference nowadays continues to be the matter of fidelity, even when temporary. In her search for the super-lover, the young woman is likely to cling to one relationship for as long as it lasts before beginning another.

The college girl who thinks love is just an appetite has also been influenced by the past. If she were as free as she believes, she would be less anxious about seeing "him" and less interested in having proof of love through jealousy. She too is experiencing a mixture, this time the cool of the eighteenth century with the tearful passions of a romantic poet.

All show the truth of the Biblical wisdom "There is nothing new under the sun." But still, there has never been an age like ours for open discussion of love.

In the Name of Love

Whether love will ever be defined to the satisfaction of all, whether love is admittedly romantic or physical and erotic, it continues to be the main topic of thought and conversation in many quarters. If love were to disappear from the vocabulary and the mind of humanity, psychiatrists would be lined up at unemployment offices.

Even without a good working definition, people continue to believe they have been cheated, that is, denied love. Married people who accept the Victorian model and believe they can live with more modest returns for their emotional investments sometimes change their minds and hunger for "the real thing."

Often people become so desperate for "the real thing" they accept poor imitations, thereby finding themselves no better off than if they had given up the search long ago.

Even though statistics show a wider acceptance of premarital sexual activity than in the past, there still exists concern for willful injury to a human being. It has been pointed out by Susan Brownmiller that rape is an act of violence as much as one of overpowering lust. The invasion of a body is an abuse which has no relationship to love.

Less violent is seduction through lies, when one person uses another "only as a body," but pretends to feel affection.

"There are girls you sleep with and other girls you marry" is still a popular remark, as is the cynical observation that "those girls (referring to some particular group or another) are for practice; you marry your own kind." In both instances, human beings are treated as objects rather than people.

More socially acceptable are the various compromises which nonetheless suggest manipulation: for example, marriage for money, marriage to advance a career, or to get through graduate school. A widespread instance of this latter abuse is the familiar story of the young wife working to support her husband during the many years of professional education in medical or law school, only to be dismissed through divorce once the goal has been attained.

Machismo is the deliberate assertion of masculinity or what is culturally believed to be masculine behavior through aggressive attentions toward women and a resistance to feelings of tenderness. Though the term is Latin, machismo exists north of the border as well. The young man who submits to the pressure of street corner companions by going out to rid himself of his virginity is living according to mechanical rather than genuine feelings.

Joan Mellen

These vigilantes of male supremacy still rule the screen, their violence a threat to all our liberties in their . . . attempt to purge our society of those who even articulate the need for change.

Status of a different sort is sought by an older woman who accepts marriage to someone she hardly likes in order to avoid the epithet *old maid.* Though the term is rarely used these days, the fear of being alone can affect even liberated women as they approach their thirties. The partner who is taken in order to avoid censure, real or imagined, is being used.

Though a frankly sexual relationship is no longer as problematic as in previous centuries, using another person in this way with solely one's own satisfaction in mind continues to be low on an absolute moral scale, particularly when the abuse of love results in enduring injury.

It is one of life's pleasant ironies, however, that those who begin as users are sometimes transformed into genuine lovers, and that even those who marry for the "wrong" reasons may joyously celebrate a golden anniversary, a circumstance which confounds those who are so afraid of being used they refuse to risk their feelings and thus can only observe love from the sidelines.

Sex Roles and Love

The assumptions about male and female behavior in male-female relationships continue to obscure the search for love's meaning, as they have done since the very notion of love was first conceived. Many modern people say they want sincerity, honesty, openness—the chance to explore and develop a "meaningful relationship" between two human beings. But whether even the most ostensibly liberated pair can fully escape the deep-rooted prescriptions for behavior is open to serious question.

The *machismo factor,* mentioned earlier, may not be as strong among liberated persons, but the fear of homosexuality is pervasive in our society and controls some aspects of male behavior, particularly expectations about the male's style and endurance in love-making. There have been many studies of such expectations as they relate to the male sense of self-worth and female satisfaction in a relationship. A great many males, liberated and otherwise, have testified to poor self-images on the basis of doubts about their ability to "perform" to idealized specifications.

The masculine sense of unworth is sometimes externalized in a highly machismo appearance or in locker room bragging

Joan Mellen

Compulsive and exhibitionist heterosexuality finally appears to be a mask for the distaste for women.

Theodora Wells and Lee S. Christie

The female sex role defines woman by her sexual function of child-bearing and nurturing 'instincts' . . . the male sex-role prescribes the man's obligation to be achieving and responsible.

about sexual conquest. Appearances can be deceiving, of course, so one must not assume that every bearded, moustached, highly masculine-looking person is quaking inwardly about his true nature. Nor must one assume that in every relationship the male is the only victim of predetermined expectations.

Females can also be subject to sex-role determinants. One must never believe that ours is a wildly permissive society in which all of the old do's and don't's have been swept aside. Young girls who are starting to date still experience many of their mothers' front-door concerns: How far shall I go? Will he think I'm "easy"? If I say no too soon, will he ever call me again? Shall I pretend to have had experience?

When marriage occurs, the sex roles become even more codified. True, many more wives work than was the case in earlier generations, but the "working wife" remains a social role as opposed to "human being who happens to be a woman, who happens to work." The male's role as breadwinner still predominates. On talk shows one often hears from working wives such comments as: "We decided that, since Ed's salary couldn't provide us with everything we needed, there'd be no harm in my getting a job." In other words, the old assumption is still with us to an extent: the man's function in marriage is very much as it used to be. Impressive divorce statistics face us; and divorce testimonials: "When I realized how much I could earn on my own and when I saw Jerry was just not going to push himself to find work, I decided there was nothing to do but leave him."

Rare is the couple who exhibit no concern whatever for traditionally defined sex roles: the man as fundamental breadwinner, except in emergencies; the woman as primary homemaker. Successful marriages take place between *two* breadwinners with enough money for a servant. Successful marriages are reported between a female breadwinner with high earning capacity and a hard-working male who tries but is honestly unable to keep up. Conflicting reports come to us about the degree of success in marriages where traditional sex roles are totally reversed: wife as breadwinner, man as homemaker and child-raiser.

There are marriages between *yoked laborers,* with both husband and wife working away at unrewarding, dull jobs, both bringing in just enough to get the bills paid more or less regularly. Such relationships at least are relatively free of the inequality in some of the others mentioned; but the husband in these relationships is likely to wish he could earn enough to take care of them both.

There are marriages between *playmates,* in which work becomes less important than leisure, either because of inherited money or the decision not to spend a whole lot of time making it. Playmates pride themselves on being in control of their lives. They take classes, do volunteer work, or part-time work for pay. But the focus is always on the enjoyment of pleasure time together. Food is easy, bought at restaurants or take-out chains or casually thrown together whenever hunger sets in. The cocktail hour is likely to extend well into the evening. Since this kind of relationship is unique to our time, there is no telling how long such marriages last or whether there is an eventual tendency to revert to more traditional roles.

The *armed camp* is another kind of contemporary household. In this, the pair may have originally agreed to a certain marriage style only to have one partner become dissatisfied. For example, the man may have expected a traditional marriage and may have experienced one for a time. Then his wife took a job outside the home. She may have run into women who told her how foolish she was to continue accepting responsibility for meals and house cleaning. Such couples tend to argue continually or to maintain a very uneasy truce. Overt discussions invariably center on money, how it is dispensed, who makes the decision, and who is to do what. In other words, the armed camp marriage is one in which sex roles are not being observed, but there has been no easy adjustment to this situation either.

Then we have the *liberated-chic* marriage in which the couples observe the current fashion of disclaiming sex roles. This is to be clearly distinguished from a really liberated marriage. Both partners are likely to proclaim their freedom very loudly and often unconvincingly. Their non-roles become new roles, determined by the circles in which they travel. Liberated-chic couples tend to keep their doubts about their marriage success to themselves, believing that their liberated friends are probably making out much better. There are no statistics available to tell us how many games are being played on the liberated circuit.

Lastly mention must be made of those marriages which

There's an intuition deep inside each of us . . . . no matter what the cynics may say, there *is* such a thing as love.

are said to be truly and completely liberated. Sometimes they can be called "experimental." With traditional sex roles cast aside, participants feel free to try different arrangements.

Sometimes, for example, several couples move in together to share the rent, maintaining exclusive love relationships. Sometimes there is free and open sexual sharing. The Personals section of metropolitan newspapers is filled with "couples wanted" ads.

In sharing households, whether of the "swapping" variety or not, some form of organization eventually takes place. Traditional sex roles often show up. The kitchen activities tend to be women's work, while men chop firewood, light the charcoal broilers, and spend much time talking together while the women prepare the bulk of the meal.

But perhaps more important, in experimental marriages—including the "Until It's Time for You to Go" ideology of living together, which still acquires some kind of marriage structure, however flexible—the old expectations about sexual capacities and skills are usually present and are indeed likely to assume major importance. With the door supposedly always open, the criteria for staying together frequently stress performance level; and when this happens, both partners inevitably begin to have doubts about themselves and each other.

Epilogue

The final answer about love is, of course, that there is no final answer. One can, if one chooses, solve all problems in human love relationships with the question "What did you expect?" But few persons are ever going to enter a relationship expecting nothing and therefore avoid disappointments and frustrations.

There are not only the perpetual echoes of ancient thoughts about love, especially romantic love, but there's an intuition deep inside each of us that no matter what the cynics may say, there *is* such a thing as love; love *does* exist somewhere in an ideal form, and it will *always* be worth seeking.

Signature

If I sing because I must
being made of singing dust,

and I cry because of need
being born of watered seed,

and I grow like twisted
tree having neither symmetry

nor the structure to avert
the falling axe, the minor hurt,

yet of one thing I am sure
that this bears my signature,

that I knew love when it came

and I called it by its name.[6]
                              Hannah Kahn

Chapter 12 Footnotes

[1]Morton M. Hunt, *The Natural History of Love* (New York: Minerva Press, 1959), p. 7. Reprinted by permission of the author. © 1959 Morton M. Hunt.

[2]From *The Myth of Freedom* by Chögyam Trungpa, pp. 86–87. Reprinted by special arrangement with Shambhala Publications, Inc., 1123 Spruce Street, Boulder, Colorado 80302. Copyright © 1976 Shambhala Publications, Inc.

[3]John Steinbeck, *The Log from the Sea of Cortez* (New York: The Viking Press, 1962), pp. xv–xvi.

[4]Tennessee Williams, A STREETCAR NAMED DESIRE. Copyright 1947 by Tennessee Williams. Reprinted by permission of New Directions.

[5]Hunt, *The Natural History of Love, op. cit.,* p. 381. © 1959 Morton M. Hunt.

[6]Copyright by Hannah Kahn. Reprinted by permission of the author.

13 HAPPINESS: ILLUSION AND REALITY

Overview

Since nearly all languages have a word, or several words, which appear to correspond to our "happiness," one might well suspect "happiness" to be of universal concern. It is a good bet that, if you traveled around the globe with an interpreter, interviewing people of different cultures or varying economic strata, engaged in every sort of life pursuit imaginable, you would soon discover that everybody wants to be happy. Indeed happiness would probably claim high priorities on "Most Desired" lists.

At the same time, if you asked those being interviewed what exactly they *meant* by happiness or being happy, you would no doubt receive a very wide range of answers.

One difficulty is that people often become acutely aware of the subject only when they are in a state they call *un*happiness. There is a sense of something missing, of something lost, and then comes the desperate search for the correct definition, at least one that will *work.* People go to psychiatrists, religious counselors, encounter groups, institutes like Esalen; they try primal scream therapy, Freudian psychoanalysis, Transcendental Meditation, Rolfing (a profound kind of massage which ostensibly penetrates the entire nervous system); they read and write any number of books on the subject of being happy. The more desperate the search, the greater the likelihood of winding up confused and frustrated.

The humanities, so often a source of insight into profound problems, raise intriguing questions about happiness without supplying definitive answers. (On the other hand, the humanities *do* teach us how to cope with ambiguities, with tentative answers, with no answers at all; they teach us that the ability to question is sometimes more important than the discernment of an answer!) The issue of happiness is never far removed from the humanist's field of vision, even if the object of his or her gaze—the "thing" he or she is trying to identify—is more than a trifle blurred.

This chapter will "solve" the problem no more completely than it has solved or will solve any other. What it does is to pull together some of the major viewpoints and subject each to fair analysis.

Although the final answer will probably elude people for as long as the human adventure continues on this planet, it is still significant that *some* answers are available. One person has at least as much claim to having found the truth about happiness as another, and it may well be possible to select from among possible choices the one that best fits the unique circumstances of one's own life.

Hedonism: Happiness as Pleasure

Crucial to the issue is whether happiness is considered a "thing" that is found, lost, bought, sold, or stolen; a state of mind (whatever *that* might turn out to be); a condition (like a cold, a pregnancy, or amnesia); a quality or characteristic (in the same sense that intelligence, tallness, or enthusiasm can be called qualities); a feeling or emotion; or a special kind of knowledge. Does one say "I feel happy" or "I am

---

Erich Fromm

Since we are living beings, we must be sadly aware of the necessary gap between our aspirations and what can be achieved in our short and troubled life.

Henrik Ibsen

What right have we human beings to happiness?

happy" or "I know that I'm happy" or "Mine is a happy life"?

A Greek philosopher named Aristippus thought he had the whole problem solved long ago when he declared happiness to be the *sum total of pleasures experienced during one's lifetime.* Pleasure he defined in purely physical terms: taste, sexual excitement, touch, and so on. Man, he said, is a selfish animal, concerned solely with his own comforts. The idea behind living is to seek out the most gratifying comforts, avoiding situations which yield few or none at all. Thus, if Aristippus is right, people prefer not to work but do so only because what they earn will provide them with pleasures. There is no satisfaction in work for its own sake. As a matter of fact, Aristippus believed there was no true satisfaction in the memory or anticipation of pleasure. Nothing counted except what could be experienced at the moment. *Hedonism* is the name given to this philosophy of pleasure.

When confronted with the original definition of a hedonist, many people resist applying the term to themselves. While a good many admit that they seek comforts and avoid discomforts, they do not accept selfishness as their primary motive. High on their list of pleasures are love (in more than a physical sense), the raising of a family, finding a useful and satisfying occupation, having the chance to get ahead in the world, having security, the pursuit of intellectual stimulation, and the opportunity to express themselves creatively.

Aristippus would contend that such persons are secret hedonists, but are afraid to admit that they are and that they *ought* to be selfish. They seek pleasure, but deny themselves too much. They save their money for a rainy day, and there is a drought. They sacrifice everything for their children, only to be confronted later with a thankless "What did you ever do for me?" They live frugally so that their retirement years will be truly golden, and of course they die at sixty-four. They force themselves to think, to keep up with the latest ideas, when all the while what they really want is to eat, drink, and be merry. The pure hedonist advises people to be selfish without shame or guilt.

Friedrich Nietzsche

He that prefers the beautiful to the useful in life will, undoubtedly, like children who prefer sweet meats to bread, destroy his digestion and acquire a very fretful outlook on the world.

Hedonist Assumptions

Hedonists generally feel cheated. There never seem to be enough pleasurable moments in life. There seems to be so much undeserved pain. "Why me?" is a frequent question silently asked. "Did I deserve to be the sole support of my parents when my brothers and sisters flatly refused to help? When am I going to get *my* chance to be happy?"

So assumption number one of the hedonist is that *everyone deserves as much pleasure as possible.* A variant form of this assumption is that *nobody ever really gets as much pleasure as he or she deserves.* Other people always appear to have more. Given this assumption one reason other hedonists seem to have more fun is because they tend to communicate (even exaggerate) their pleasures, especially unexpected bonuses, which point out how truly deserving they really are. To share unpleasant experiences is to advertise unworthiness, and nobody wants to do this. Hence the perpetuation of the myth that other people are "getting more from life."

A second assumption, vitally related to the first, is that *pleasure is automatically good.* During the Great Depression of the 1930s, when so many Americans were barely eating enough to get by, those who were able to eat anything they wanted were undoubtedly objects of envy. Who thought to feel sorry for the affluent people who might overeat, perhaps developing diabetes from too much French pastry?

The hedonist recognizes that no one can possibly have pleasure every moment of his or her life, but this does not stop us from thinking we should. A third assumption, therefore, is that *no amount of pleasure is ever too much.* There may be a submerged feeling of guilt about gorging oneself in an "All U Can Eat" restaurant or downing one drink after another at somebody else's open house, but the typical hedonist response is "There will be time enough to cut down; don't bother me now." Besides, overindulgence in moments of plenty supposedly means "making up" for past disappointments.

Another assumption is that *the absence of pleasure is a misfortune for which compensation is due.* The son or daughter who sits with baby four nights during the week is bound to claim the weekend as a long lost right. Many who have been arrested while attempting robbery have argued in court that they were only getting even with society. If you carry the hedonist viewpoint through life, you find yourself plotting continually: "Just wait until *I* have the upper hand!" Since moments without definite feelings of pleasure

---

Hedonism in Oscar Wilde:

I can resist everything except temptation.

Lady Windemere's Fan

How are you, my dear Ernest? What brings you up to town?"

Oh, pleasure, pleasure. What else should bring one anywhere?

The Importance of Being Earnest

are an abomination, it is entertaining to think how wonderful it is going to be when the rightful pleasures are finally gained.

This particular mindset can be termed the *big earnings theory*. An earning is considered the pleasure owed to a deserving person. The oldest child in a large family, for example, may have gone to work to help out and to assure younger brothers and sisters of proper clothes, education, and so on. In the ledger many hedonists carry inside themselves, there is a strict accounting of pleasures owed them; eventually a vast number may accumulate. Unless something happens to change his or her philosophy of happiness, the hedonist may become obsessed with thinking about pleasures due. If they are paid off, life is good; if not, life is bad. Life is evaluated strictly in terms of payments received, and a supergood life is one in which big earnings are recognized as having come due, the hedonist rushing off to make the big payoff.

The big earnings theory rests upon the assumption that *the gratification of the self is central*. Since each of us possesses the sense of an inner being—an actual person with whom we sometimes talk and who appears to direct many of our actions—it is only natural that this being should seem closer to us than anyone else. If this being desires pleasures, we reason, they must be obtained, for how could the self ever make a mistake?

Is Ours A Hedonist Society?

"You deserve a break today . . ."

"If I have one life to live, let me live it as a blonde . . ."

"You only live once!"

The importance of the self, at least in our society, has led many philosophers and cultural anthropologists to agree that we live in a fundamentally hedonist environment, no matter what fancy terms we may use to cover up the fact. They point out that our value system revolves around selfishness and pleasure, that the payoff is always the main issue, and that it is hopeless to think any of us can ever rise above such conditioning.

While hedonists like Aristippus admitted to being selfish and pleasure-loving, our society does not. It has been deeply influenced by the Judeo-Christian religious tradition and its written expression, the Bible; by the ethics and sin-consciousness of the early Puritans, as well as their emphasis on hard work as being good for the soul; and by a whole host of contemporary anti-materialist philosophies which protest the study of man as simply another form of animal life.

Those who object to the hedonist view of human nature argue that hedonism is a constant *temptation* rather than a true description of what we are fundamentally like. Hedonism, they contend, can and must be resisted. Love, charity, and kindness, and the higher spiritual concerns of humanity show that as well as although we possess an "animal self," we have the power to transcend it. The hedonist argues back that the vehemence with which hedonism is rejected is proof that hedonists are right. It is folly, says the hedonist, for human beings to fantasize what a human being ought to be like, when there is no way on earth to change human nature.

Anti-hedonists often blame advertising, motion pictures, and television for exerting a bad influence and encouraging young people to pursue a hedonist life style. They sometimes cite the changing of the times, pointing out that things were very different years ago. They speak of "decadence," and find ready examples in X-rated films, adult book stores, and a generally permissive attitude toward sexual promiscuity. On the other hand, the hedonist responds by asking where such "decadence" comes from if it is not fundamental to human nature. Campaigns to restore decency, marital fidelity, and sobriety would, if successful, merely create another hypocritical state of affairs, such as existed in Victorian England or during Prohibition in the United States.

A different argument is that there is no such thing as human nature and no generalization about people can possibly have validity. People become what they want to become. If this is so, then one *could* take the position that the predominance of apparently hedonistic tendencies in our society indicates that a majority of people are satisfied with a pleasure orientation, no matter how loudly they protest to the contrary. This does not preclude, however, that it is legitimate to find alternate values for oneself—to pursue a very different approach to happiness.

A Famous Critique of Pure Hedonism

Another Greek philosopher, Epicurus (342?–270? B.C.), made a careful study of the teachings of Aristippus and

---

Tolstoi

The only significance of life consists in helping to establish the kingdom of God.

Strato

Drink now and love my friend,
  For mirth and wine
Cannot be always yours,
  Nor always mine.
With every garland let us crown
  Our head,
Nor leave them to be scattered
  O'er the dead

concluded that they were wrong. Epicurus did not deny that man was a self-centered animal or that pleasure was desirable, but he rejected a philosophy of happiness which was *solely* based on pleasure. His basic contention was that pure hedonism would be fine if it were possible to achieve, but since Epicurus found it was not, he believed Aristippus had been chasing after rainbows. Epicurus preferred to find a more rational, workable philosophy.

To say that happiness consists of the sum total of physical pleasures struck Epicurus as madness. This line of reasoning claimed that perfect happiness consisted of the sum total of every possible pleasure. But what was "enough"? Stopping to catch a few hours' sleep would mean losing some chances for pleasure. Counting such losses one by one would make it impossible to ever catch up. Even if, by some unlikely chance, you succeeded in experiencing nothing but pleasure, you would eventually have to die. In pure hedonism, no life could ever be long enough.

Why, asked Epicurus, burden oneself with a philosophy doomed never to work? Was it not more sensible to change the requirements for happiness? For him life had no meaning, hence no purpose—not even the acquisition of pleasures. If life were without a goal, no life could ever be too short or too long. Death comes when it comes, and only human fancy made death seem to end something significant.

Therefore nobody was *entitled* to a long life filled with pleasures. It was a hit-or-miss world, governed by no rational laws. Everything happened by chance. Hence one had to be extremely fortunate to have things work out in one's favor. To plan for pleasure was to plan for disappointments, except for occasional and quite coincidential strokes of luck.

Living in a hit-or-miss world, said Epicurus, made pain more likely than pleasure, for pain would more often result from the collision between human expectations and chance happenings. If one falls in love and decides to marry, for example, it would be unwise to hope for clear sailing, an untroubled relationship. The pain of disillusionment comes in proportion to the intensity of hope. Intelligent people, according to Epicurus, do not refuse to marry; rather, they count on a certain amount of friction and plan accordingly.

Epicureanism is thus a modified form of hedonism in which the emphasis is on the avoidance of pain, rather than the active pursuit of pleasure. The Epicurean believes it is

If life were without a goal, no life could ever be too short or too long.

easier to expect unpleasantness and to plan strategies to ward it off than to march forward in the blind hope that things are going to be fine. The worst that can happen when you anticipate pain is that you will not be disappointed. But clearly, you have a good chance of doing something about much of life's pain before it occurs *if* you apply yourself conscientiously to the task.

The taste of exquisite food is high on the list of hedonists' priorities. So it is for the Epicureans. The difference is that the latter, anticipating the pain of overindulgence, stop themselves before reaching their limit. They will drink, but never to the point of drunkenness, and not at all if one is certain his or her health cannot stand it.

There is a character in one of Hemingway's short stories who marries a beautiful but flirtatious woman considerably younger than himself. He goes off to war, is injured, and during his stay at a rehabilitation center, learns that his wife has run off with another man. His response is typically Epicurean. Instead of being angry or feeling sorry for himself, he admits to having made a mistake. A man, he comments, should never place himself in a position to lose so much. The Epicureans pursue physical pleasures in moderation, realizing that any excess is likely to lead to pain. But they also seeks out nonphysical pleasures. They are generally lovers of the arts, the theater, books, and music. Intellectual and esthetic pleasures can be experienced in abundance without the fear of pain. But Epicureans are also wary of becoming overly dependent upon such stimuli, for then they run the risk of being unable to compromise. You cannot spend all of your time reading or thinking; there are other boring—but necessary—tasks that need to be done.

Epicureans tend to be highly disciplined. They tend to be lean and trim, exercising their bodies to keep in the best possible shape. They are mentally agile and "up" on the latest developments in many fields. They are good workers, and one who finds a marital partner with a similar outlook is very likely to build a reasonably happy home.

Pure hedonists, however, warn Epicureans that they sell themselves too short and may often settle for much less than they have a right to expect from life. The hedonist maintains that unless you work aggressively at being happy, you will give up too easily, spending entirely too much time in a void.

Stoicism: Strategies for Surviving

There is a famous poster showing a cat holding tightly to a knotted end of a rope and just hanging there in empty black space. The caption reads, *When You Come to the End of Your Rope, Tie a Knot and Hang On.* This, in capsule form, is the philosophy of Stoicism. It operates under even fewer illusions about life than does Epicureanism. It tells us not to plan ahead for a lifetime of unlimited pleasure nor to expect to avoid pain through discipline and moderation. Stoicism asserts pain is intrinsic to living. Even the most dedicated Epicureans will feel a certain amount of frustration when their disciplined approach to living goes awry and the ceiling caves in on them. The best possible course is to be prepared for the worst and to develop a technique for coping with it.

Working On The Mind

Stoicism is still a popular philosophy of happiness, for many still a viable approach to the business of living, despite the fact that it was born over two thousand years ago. Like hedonism and its modified offspring, Epicureanism, it is the product of Greek intellect, but unlike the others, it lays heavy stress on human reason, on the belief that humankind is a superior form of animal life. Zeno, its first major spokesman (?–264? B.C.), is therefore closer in spirit to Plato and Aristotle than to either Aristippus or Epicurus.

The philosophy's name derives from the odd fact that the school founded by Zeno for the purpose of teaching was located in a columned portico area called a *stoa*. Central to Stoicism is that true happiness is not a matter of circumstance, of good fortune, nor a matter of what happens to us, but rather of *how we respond to what happens*. Happiness, like sorrow, is a feeling, not an object, not an event. If no people exist to welcome the first day of spring, how can it be said that spring is a time of hope and joy? If, in some remote civilization with peculiar customs and mores, the birth of a child were considered a dreadful curse, it is possible that the inability to produce offspring would be regarded as a happy stroke of luck.

In other words, Stoicism teaches that to find the roots of

The Epicurean

Moderate eating and drinking, the pursuit of intellectual pleasures

and

•

•

•

•

•

•

An awareness of the impossibility of permanent pleasure.

unhappiness, one must look inward. Nothing is under our control except the way we *feel* about things. Natural disasters, social upheavals, war, revolution, the outbreak of disease, rising crime rates—all happen as a result of either accidental or highly complicated causes. One's happiness should not depend upon their *not* taking place. One cannot alter external circumstances, but one *can* decide not to feel negatively toward them.

"How do you expect me to feel?" is a common response when someone is asked why he is so glum about a certain outcome—say, the fact that he was not promoted to a higher position. Stoics cite habit formations as the guilty culprits. That is, they contend people are conditioned by the values their society puts on what happens to or around them: this is acceptable; that is not. This is cause for joy; that is cause for tears. Reactions become automatic after awhile. People come to *think* they are unhappy; hence they *are* unhappy. But typical responses can be altered. One can refuse to be affected in customary ways, or as others tend to be affected.

One of the best known Stoic teachers was a Greek named Epictetus (60?–120? A.D.), who became a Roman slave. His genius was finally recognized and he was allowed to conduct classes. But prior to that, Epictetus was tortured and oppressed in his captivity. On one occasion his leg was broken on one of his master's sudden whims. During this period of extreme trial and suffering, Epictetus was faced with the choice of surrendering to despair or finding some means of endurance. He chose the latter course, recognizing that nothing, not even torture, was unbearable unless one wished to find it so. After his "liberation," he dedicated his life to spreading the Stoic creed which had preserved his spirit intact for so many years.

Stoicism found ready acceptance among the Romans and eventually became a sort of "official" state philosophy. Its emphasis on reason and the control of negative emotions accorded well with the Roman ideal of humanity. Besides, Rome was an empire-building civilization, requiring a superbly disciplined military machine to carry out its conquests. It therefore found a meaningful application of Stoic teachings. The rigors of military training as well as the hardships of war itself must never depress the human spirit. A good soldier must have feelings so well under his command that he becomes indifferent to suffering.

> **Montaigne**
>
> **Apollo said that everyone's true worship was that which he found in use in the place where he chanced to be.**

> **Marcus Aurelius**
>
> **Live rationally, and part with life cheerfully.**

Matt. 5:38

But I say to you, do not resist one who is evil. But if any one strikes you on the right cheek, turn to him the other also.

When Christianity began to spread throughout the Roman Empire, many of the converts had, naturally enough, already been exposed to Stoic beliefs. The by-now ancient and honorable philosophy accorded well with the outlook and needs of the Christians; for after all, did they not have to face untold sufferings—continual persecution, torture, flight, starvation, separation from loved ones? The Stoic doctrine of inner control blended perfectly with the Christian belief that only the soul, not the body, mattered. One could endure all manner of pain and stay inwardly serene. Christians supposedly sang while waiting for the lions to devour them in the Circus Maximus.

What more dramatic model of the Stoic being could there have been than Christ himself? Had Christ not allowed himself to be mocked, taunted, whipped? Had he not carried his own cross to Calvary and then refused to come down from that same cross when the challenge was given? Had he not forgiven his tormentors?

Stoicism remains as pervasive as ever and offers to many a genuine alternative to hedonism. In a period of ever accelerating rates of change, of densely packed urban centers in which violence has become a way of life, of depression in farm belts and neurosis in high rent districts, it is small wonder that many are asking less for pleasure than for inner peace. While the number of people making weekly pilgrimages to their analysts continually increases, one wonders whether some principles of Stoicism are not at work here also. After all, is not self-knowledge the whole point of psychoanalysis? Is it not the analyst's contention that, once people understand what is making them depressed, they will be able to transcend negative feelings? Is it not the analyst's promise that happiness is really within one's own power to create and preserve?

Assumptions of Stoicism

Like hedonism and Epicureanism, the stoic approach to happiness contains basic assumptions about the nature of existence. Stoicism cannot advocate the pursuit of pleasure in unlimited quantities because it assumes that (1) pleasure is not the purpose of life and (2) even if it were, the amount of pain in life far exceeds the pleasures we may chance to come upon. As a matter of fact, you would do well to remind yourself that *all* philosophies have underlying assumptions which need to be uncovered.

While Stoicism has undergone innumerable changes over the years, it remains staunchly rooted in the assumption that *the "rationality of mankind" is a meaningful phrase.* To control unpleasant emotions, to see through the causes of our unhappiness requires the ability to think straight, without the encumbrance of often indefinable feelings. One must be able to become detached from oneself, to view one's inner processes with dispassionate calm, seeing oneself virtually as if seeing another person altogether. It has long been a claim of the rationalists that reason is universal, shared by all who wish to employ it; hence it is possible to transcend the personal emotional states and ego-involvement which, so claim the Stoics, are the sources of unhappiness.

On the other hand, if a good deal of modern psychology is right and humankind is impulsive and discontinuous in its thought processes, if no such thing as universal reason exists, then the Stoic method of achieving happiness by coping intelligently with unhappiness may well be an illusion. Many psychologists would be quick to advise that it is dangerous to believe you have truly risen above your unhappiness by "merely" altering your feelings when the root causes may remain buried and continue to cause trouble.

A second profound assumption of Stoicism is one that made a good deal of sense to the Greeks and Romans, namely, that *events are never under human control anyway, therefore it is wise to adopt a philosophy of life which emphasizes the way people react to events.* There is a strongly fatalistic bent in Greek and Roman religions, a sense that the order of the universe requires that things be as they are, not as one would prefer them to be.

Christianity, which also found Stoicism very much to its liking, is not as clearly fatalistic. The freedom of individual will is central to many, though not all, of its interpreters. St. Augustine said God is omniscient, hence nothing can happen that is unknown to Him beforehand; at the same time God has given each of us the freedom to sin or not sin. Though we cannot understand how this can be, we can accept it on faith. St. Thomas Aquinas said that God, being all powerful, is free to allow *us* to be free. But John Calvin, a Protestant reformer, insisted that if God is omnipotent, it makes no sense to say that human beings control their own destinies.

In any event, a good many Christians are able to reconcile themselves to bitter events, like the accidental death of a young child, through profound faith in God's wisdom and justice. Whether people have the freedom to sin or be saved, it is a persistent characteristic of Christianity—and certainly an unbroken tradition in Judaism—to accept the "will of God" in cases of misfortune. No devout Jew or Christian believes in a universe which is free to go haywire, a universe in which everything happens by blind chance.

Hence the stoic creed operates successfully in a world in which the will of God is apparent. If one suffers inwardly because of what happens, it is clearly one's thinking, one's feelings that are wrong, not the nature of reality, not the way things tend to go. But if one has some misgivings about the will of God, or if one wonders why God should will so many disastrous events or whether God even exists at all, then one may well question the principles of Stoicism. If there is *no* universal order at all, then what is to prevent one from believing that events are as much under one's own control as anyone else's? If one accepts *full* responsibility for what happens to oneself, it is not always easy to maintain a stoic calm about mistakes and lost opportunities.

A third assumption behind Stoicism could be that *everyone experiences misfortune in equal amounts.* It is easier to cope with adversity when one is sure others must also do so than when one cannot help but feel that the good things in life are distributed unequally, or are thrown out for anyone to grab with the stronger, more ruthless individual getting more than his or her share. Yet a guarantee of universal suffering has never been implicit in fundamental Stoicism. The founder of the philosophy, Zeno, would have shaken his head emphatically if told that one of his students could accept unhappiness with inner calm so long as others were miserable too. He would surely have said that the whole point of Stoicism was to bear misfortune with quiet dignity no matter what good fortune others were receiving.

Aristotle: Happiness Is Not Pleasure

An assumption behind all of the philosophies we have considered thus far in this chapter has been that happiness is an actual state, an internal condition which can be felt, sensed, or in some way *known about*. It is in this respect akin to health. You are either healthy or not, and it is painfully apparent when you are not.

The appeal of the hedonist approach to the subject may perhaps be explained by the concreteness of the hedonist's definition of happiness. Happiness *is* equivalent to sensations of pleasure. There is nothing else it can be, hence there is absolutely no confusion over terminology.

Yet the belief that happiness is something that can be definitely and actively *experienced*—as opposed to some characteristic or condition of one's existence that can be *comprehended*—has been seriously challenged. In fact, no sooner was the hedonist philosophy advanced than it was given a thorough going-over by Aristotle, who rejected it completely as the true path to happiness.

Pleasure, a Limited Goal; Happiness, a Complete Goal

In his great work on the conduct of living, *The Nicomachean Ethics,* Aristotle agrees that pleasure must be counted as one of the good things in anybody's life. Obviously nobody hates to have it; people willingly seek it out, as much as they eagerly avoid its opposite, pain. But is pleasure to be regarded as the *highest* good?

Aristotle makes a trap of the hedonists' views in which to ensnare and refute their philosophy. One hedonist view which Aristotle addresses is "that any good thing . . . is made more desirable by the addition of pleasure." This, says Aristotle, is hard to deny. When you add pleasure to something good, the result is something even better. A example would be a group's getting together to celebrate a promotion received by one person and then drinking to the point of mellowness to enhance the occasion. It is obvious, according to Aristotle, that the sense of fellowship plus the drinking would be more enjoyable than the promotion by itself.

But then Aristotle cites an earlier Platonic argument: namely, that "if pleasure combined with something else is better than pleasure alone, it follows that pleasure cannot in itself be the supreme good." Using the example developed above, we could say that, if you gave the lucky person a choice between having only the pleasure of companionship and drinking or having the promotion as well, he or she

---

> **Montaigne**
>
> **If I had to live over again, I would live as I have lived. I neither complain of the past nor fear the future.**

would clearly choose the second alternative. (As a matter of fact, if having to choose between the promotion alone or the pleasure alone, he or she would no doubt forsake the pleasure!)

Another hedonist view which Aristotle singles out for analysis is that, since happiness is the highest good possible and no higher good than pleasure can be imagined, then pleasure and happiness must be the same. Aristotle agrees that happiness is clearly the reason for which people seek the good things in life, but *is not pleasure sought for the same motive?* That is, do not people desire pleasure because it gives them happiness to have it? If pleasure *makes* one happy, then it is a means, not an end. It is for the sake of happiness that pleasure operates. Hence the two must be distinct. If they were not, one would have to say that pleasure is desired for nothing except itself, but this, says Aristotle, is not true. If asked, people would always reply that pleasure leads to happiness.

> **If pleasure makes one happy then it is a means, not an end.**
>
> •
> •
> •

On the other hand, to what does happiness lead? That is, can we advance any particular reason for wishing to be happy? Do we not stare dumbfounded if we try to think of one? Does it not make perfectly good sense to say that we seek happiness for its own sake? May we say that of anything else? Aristotle's answer is: obviously not.

Every good thing in life is sought in order that, by possessing it, one may become happy. This is the case with pleasure, money, love, health, and so on. To test the validity of Aristotle's hypothesis, consider the absurdity of the following statement: I want to find love, but I do not want to be happy. Or: I want a good deal of money but for its own sake; I do not want to be made happy by having it.

That happiness is distinct from the things which make us happy is further indicated by the fact that *very often those things fail to do it.* How often one hears this: "I spent my life making a fortune; now I have it, and I am still not happy." Even the most dedicated hedonist would presumably reach a point at which she or he would admit that there were many pleasures not yet experienced. Therefore, to the question "Are you completely happy?" she or he would be forced to answer, "No." But if, as the hedonists contend, pleasure *is* happiness, then the cultivation of just one pleasure would be equivalent to full happiness, a position no hedonist could possibly take.

> •
> •
> •
> **"Every good thing is sought in order that, by possessing it, one may become happy."**

Yes, But What Is It?

To say that happiness must be distinct from the things we seek to achieve it does not define what it is. It is not money, not health, not love, not pleasure. Can it be a *thing* at all? Evidently not! For any *thing* we can think of would have to be in the same category as the other things with which happiness is sometimes identified.

Some people believe happiness to be a *state of euphoria*—a heightened sense of well-being, or at least one of not feeling pain, which appears to be easily worth achieving for its own sake. Yet it is still possible to separate this state from happiness itself, still possible to say that one, having reached euphoria, was not totally happy. Or else euphoria *did* produce complete happiness. In either case one is talking about cause and effect, and it is clear that cause and effect can never be identical.

There is, Aristotle says, one and only one category into which happiness can possibly fall, and that is *activity.* Of all human modes, activity is the only one that can be divided into (1) that in which one engages for the sake of something else, and (2) that in which one engages for no other reason. Since Aristotle has already concluded that happiness is a complete goal, self-sustaining and desirous of no further end beyond itself, it follows that for Aristotle happiness must be the highest form of human activity.

But what sort of activity is worth engaging in for its own sake? We engage in almost every task for the sake of some benefit we believe the completed task will offer us: money, some sort of improvement in our personal appearance or our surroundings, the satisfaction of having helped someone, and so on.

Aristotle concludes there is, however, one kind of activity which we prize for itself, and that is "conduct in accordance with virtue or excellence." Suppose, for example, you find you have lost or had stolen your wallet. It contains not only a considerable sum of money but all of your identification and credit cards. You expect never to see the money again, hoping only that the finder or thief will be charitable enough to return everything else. But instead, a package arrives in the mail, containing the wallet *with nothing missing,* and, most important, *no sender's name!* There is no way to reward the person; hence you recognize that the action was indeed performed "in accordance with virtue." It is not unlikely that you would applaud the action and find it had been worth doing for its own sake!

Thinking for no reason except thinking is another activity which Aristotle believed merits the designation of "happiness." As a matter of fact, Aristotle cites it as the "noblest" of the actions carried on for themselves, for it represents the exercise of the highest and best part of a human being: reason. While practical thinking requires that a problem be solved, the pure exercise of thought—what Aristotle calls "contemplation"—requires no stimulus or even conclusion. To speculate on the nature of things, the first cause of being, whether a higher power exists, the nature of good and evil, and so on, is to do something for which one needs no reward. Whether in our speculation we solve a problem or not, the exercise of reason is its own purpose and its own fulfillment.

To sum up, then, Aristotle believes happiness to be a way of behaving, of acting, which is carried on for virtuous or intellectual reasons, and no others. He excludes those actions which are carried on for personal gain or any other ulterior motive. Happiness is thus not a thing, yet it is always within one's grasp. It is not a state or condition, yet the happy person is always aware of his or her happiness. If we insist on putting happiness into a definite category, we could say it is a characteristic of rational people.

Some Implications of Aristotle's Theory

The most obvious and radical difference between Aristotle's approach to the subject of happiness and those of the hedonist school is that Aristotle does not believe happiness must be experienced. It is someone's characteristic or habitual way of living. That is, if you are a good person, if there is moral integrity in everything you do, and if you endeavor to be guided by reason in all of your thoughts, then it is appropriate to say that yours is a *happy life,* rather than to say you are happy.

Aristotle's theory implies no state of bliss, no surging emotions of joy or well-being, no euphoria, no sense of being "on top of the world." Not that these are bad things. They are pleasures and as such may be counted as good, but

---

Optimist
This is the best of all
possible worlds.

•

•

•

•

•

•

Pessimist
I know. That's what
bothers me.

they are not the highest good. One's life can be a happy one without them.

Thus it may be said that *happiness is a process rather than a product.* It is nothing to pursue, nothing to possess or fail to attain. Those persons who gnash their teeth at the thought of the happiness that has "passed them by" are deluded. They have been chasing a phantom. They have decided that their lives are not happy because they have not asked the right questions about the way they live. For Aristotle there are two fundamental questions whose answers will determine whether happiness is characteristic of anyone's life: "Am I basically a moral person?" and "Am I rational in my approach to life?"

Happiness has nothing to do with the way one *feels* at any given moment. You may have a toothache or indigestion, or be pining away for a lost love, and still know that your life is a happy one. You may lack beauty, money, position, status, or recognition, but not happiness. Happiness is not to be found, or taken away, or thrust upon you. It is not the result of amassing a fortune on a television game show, or taking that long awaited trip to Europe.

The tangible products we normally confuse with happiness may be desired for the sake of happiness, but Aristotle's point is that they are not essential to happiness. A sudden windfall or the flaring warmth of a newly experienced love may lead us into a state which we think must be happiness, but this state cannot last indefinitely, and we find ourselves once again "searching."

Health, ample means, friendship, and love relate to happiness in that, lacking them, we become obsessed with our feelings and therefore cannot operate with the rational integrity that is possible when our lives are not beset by obstacles. On the other hand, having made the discovery that products are not the same as happiness, it is possible to lack many products and yet not allow one's rational integrity to suffer. Feeling sorry for yourself because of the good things you have been denied is a good way to bar the door permanently against happiness.

Happiness: The Purpose of Life

Someone with no previous exposure to Aristotle's theory of happiness may initially feel letdown, have a sense of

---

W. S. Blount

He who has once been happy is forever out of destruction's reach.

disappointment. One would expect, after all, something more, something *gigantic* from one of the world's greatest philosophers. But really, one might well ask, what is in it for *me?* What specific advantage does this theory hold? What enticement does it offer? Happiness appears to be nothing that can be grasped, nothing there at all.

And yet the odd, unexpected aspect is that Aristotle found that this happiness, this process-not-product, was the key to understanding the whole mystery of existence. To Aristotle happiness was the purpose for which we are born.

The hedonists had never said that pleasure was the *purpose* of living. They had insisted only that pleasure was the greatest good life could yield. In fact, before Aristotle nobody had ever advanced the idea of purpose. Plato analyzed qualities and conditions, such as virtue and justice; Plato discussed the duality of matter and spirit and, above all, developed a complex theory of knowledge. But in all of the dialogues he wrote there is no analysis of life's *purpose.* It remained for Aristotle to invent *teleology,* the philosophy of purpose.

Aristotle did something else. He adopted the first major *developmental theory of existence.* In Platonism, each person is born complete: that is, each person contains the essence of humanity from the very beginning. All the knowledge human beings can ever possess is within the mind, and what we call growing up or developing was regarded by Plato as a process of discovering what one already has. In one of the most famous of the dialogues, the *Meno,* there is a segment in which Socrates, whom Plato uses as the spokesman for his ideas, demonstrates how a slave boy with no formal education is able to comprehend a complicated bit of mathematics because, presumably, he has innate knowledge of it.

Aristotle believed one could learn what did not know before. He believed people are born with an innate capacity for rational understanding, but that it takes experience to provide the mind with the material to be understood. In other words, two people of the same age could be worlds apart in intellectual achievement, in the actual amount of knowledge they had respectively accumulated.

From this fundamental split with the Platonic theory of knowledge, Aristotle continued to expand the notion of development. As he looked around at natural things, including

> **Happiness manifests itself as we develop toward our full potential. Happiness is actualizing that potential.**

animals lower than man, he recognized in development an apparently universal principle. In his school, which he called the Lyceum, he conducted the first natural science labs, and he and his students practiced dissection of both plant and animal life in order to test out the developmental hypothesis. This much seemed to be certain: everything *grew,* and not just randomly, but in accordance with some definite scheme, some design, which appeared to be the *natural order of things.* Of course, Aristotle was studying development only within a given species; he had no conception of evolution from one species to another.

But Aristotle began to speculate on the possible meaning of development. Why did species exist in this particular fashion? Why did they develop? His conclusion was that each natural thing, including a human being, grew towards a particular point which represented the perfection of its kind. Development, in other words, was not accidental, but always directional. Each thing comes into the world with—to use the technology of our own age—a kind of built-in *radar* which causes it to "know" what it wants to become, even though it lacks the formal knowledge of what this is. Each thing strives to reach its maximum *actualization.*

For human beings this actualization was evidenced by the perfection of humanity's two most distinguishing traits: virtue and reason. Since Aristotle defined happiness as the process of living in accordance with these traits, it followed that a completely virtuous and rational being—that is, a completely happy person—was at the same time the very apex of human development. In short, the human of the species had as its purpose in living the development of what we might call *the skill of being happy.*

Knowing this in advance, as it were, one could practice this skill until it was effortless, second nature, habitual. To always act with moral integrity, guided by the light of reason —hence not impulsively, emotionally, or selfishly—would be to take giant strides toward reaching the full flowering of human potential.

Since for Aristotle happiness was the very purpose for which we exist, it was also clear that the institutions of human society—in fact, human society itself—must exist for the same purpose. In his political writings, he characterizes the state as *existing to promote the happiness of its members.*

How would Aristotle view these?

It is not enough to succeed. Others must fail.
Gore Vidal

Tragedy is if I cut my finger. Comedy is if you walk into an open sewer and die.
Mel Brooks

Law, order, education, and every other function of the state have the same purpose. People must be protected from their baser natures in order that their higher potential may be realized, and this is the reason we have rules, enforcers, and penalties. We have schools in order that the mind can grow and the rational powers become stronger. (How different from some modern assumptions about the direct and exclusive relationship between education and jobs!)

The reason Aristotle, like Plato before him, did not favor democracy, or direct rule of the people, is that he did not believe the majority of people had sufficiently developed rational powers. He did not believe one could trust the majority to make sensible decisions, or to always act with moral integrity. Hence rulers were necessary, but rulers must never forget that their purpose was not to serve their own interests but rather to use their intellect to promote the happiness of their charges.

We have come a long way from Aristotle's fairly straightforward and uncomplicated model of the state. It seems clear that the contemporary state, regardless of its underlying political philosophy, must concern itself with many more issues than human happiness: poverty, disease, defense, and technology are just a few. One is often tempted to wonder whether the only purpose left is to keep things going as well as those who govern can do it and whether even this much purpose is often obscured.

Happiness and Impossible Dreams

Regardless of the political state to which one belongs, it is bound to happen that those who govern cannot possibly make decisions which always accord with one's own beliefs about how things should be done. In fact, to be human means often reaching certain conclusions about what ought to happen, only to discover one is wrong, that it has failed to happen.

It is also difficult to adopt Aristotle's theory as a personal guide for the conduct of life. Suppose one *were* to act with total integrity in every instance, doing only the rational thing, never the thing that might bring about the quickest profit. How long would it be before one realized that others were profiting from unscrupulous, underhanded actions which had no moral integrity about them? How long could one go on without complaining, or feeling sorry for oneself? Suppose one were never anything but completely honest and completely truthful with one's friends. How many friends would one have?

Aristotle's is an *uncompromising* approach. You do what reason dictates, and that is that. You never take what is not yours; you never lie, cheat on your income tax, or pretend to have done something you have not done (whether your job is at stake or not). It is theoretically possible to be living a happy life and never receive any material rewards. Sooner or later even the most determined Aristotelian might be tempted to think, "I deserve better than this; I will conduct myself as the others do."

There are vast numbers of people who do not compromise, however; who continue on resolutely no matter what life and other people do to them. It is to them that this section of the chapter is dedicated.

The Principle of the Thing

> It is theoretically possible to be living a happy life and never receive any material rewards.

There are people for whom happiness is the successful evasion of unhappiness, people who are miserable whenever they must lay aside their *code* and act out of other motives. Their approach to living is close to Aristotle's, except that they are acutely conscious of the code, whereas with Aristotle the good life is a matter of course. Reason is reason, and one does not make a celebrated cause out of it. The person being described in this section, however, is one who adheres to a particular principle, staunchly defending it, seeking to convert others, aware that the majority of people do *not* live by this code but is certain the world would be a far better place if they did. Aristotle was convinced that reason was universal, and the rational individual was neither a martyr nor a saint. The person who actively crusades on behalf of a cause he or she believes to be righteous and in the best interest of humanity is an idealist—and frequently *does* martyr him- or herself for this code.

Both literature and history are filled with the names and the deeds of idealists. Some, like Joan of Arc, Nathan Hale, Mohandas Gandhi, and Martin Luther King, Jr., have special importance for us; it is clear that we find idealism admirable, even if a little mysterious. We know that such people suffered martyrdom and much physical and emotional pain. Most of us doubt that we would be as resolute as they in similar circumstances. Yet, at the same time, there is always the assumption that idealism is worth the price. We assume that these rare personalities would have been unhappy abandoning their codes.

Living in accordance with principles that the world at large rejects is also recognized as being dangerous—sometimes fatal. Nonetheless it is a yardstick by which we evaluate human experience—and no doubt, secretly, ourselves. Whether this kind of idealism is workable or even meaningful in relation to the realities of human nature is not the point. Even the most unprincipled person often experiences an inner sense of unworthiness, no matter how successful his or her life may appear on the outside. Deep inside we strongly accept and endorse idealism, though we sometimes pity the idealist.

During the Vietnam war a great deal of publicity was given to Buddhist nuns and priests who set themselves on fire as a protest against oppression. Many persons might have asked themselves whether such extreme behavior would actually do anything constructive to put an end to oppression, but few could have condemned it. "I can't see that it does any good" is not the same as "It is not praiseworthy for human beings to engage in such nonsense." The latter response is rare, even among the most hardened realists.

The poet Alexander Pope once wrote: "Man never is, but always to be blest." Happiness is never achieved; it is *worked for.* This is the position taken by the idealist who places his or her code before all else. There can be no happiness in a world of corruption, compromise, greed, and selfishness, and there can be no happiness for one who sees clearly how

---

Stephen Crane

I saw a man pursuing the
 horizon;
Round and round they
 sped,
I accosted the man.
"It is futile," I said,
"You can never—" "You
 lie," he cried,
And ran on.

things *should* be and who does nothing at all to improve the situation.

Don Quixote and Sancho Panza

By far the most famous literary model of the noble idealist totally at odds with a corrupt world is the hero of Miguel de Cervantes' novel *Don Quixote,* composed between 1603 and 1614. The author, who lost a hand fighting in a war against the Turks and who also spent years in slavery after being captured by pirates, knew a good deal about codes, principles, and the harsh realities of life. His thoughts on the subject of idealism, as embodied in his great novel, are distinctly two-sided.

The original motivation behind the novel was to make fun of medieval romances. These works, constituting an entire school of "best sellers," depicted the fabulous exploits of brave knights and the pure and noble love they had for delicate, aristocratic ladies. Cervantes thought these works absurd and decided to do one of his own, only this time using a hero who was approaching senility and whose obsession for the literature of romance had made him insane. Everyone is familiar with some of the Don's misadventures, especially the duel with windmills, believed by the hero to be evil giants, and his endless quest of the lady Dulcinea, the epitome of womanly virtue and spiritual beauty, whose only drawback was that she existed only in the Don's mind.

Comic heroes, however, need to be offset and surrounded by some sanity; otherwise there would be no way of knowing them to be fools. Cervantes' brilliant ploy was to create Sancho Panza, an obese peasant who accepts the role of squire to Quixote's knight of La Mancha in order to protect the old man from both himself and the insensitive world about him. Sancho Panza is the realist and pragmatist, the person with no illusions about his own or others' noble potential.

Yet a curious thing happens as the novel develops. The author seems to make less fun of his hero as adventure succeeds adventure and to take his idealistic motives more seriously. The Don is continually endangered; the threats are very real, and, if the delusions are funny, the principles themselves are not. There is considerable debate among critics as to the full extent of Cervantes' involvement with his character and whether or not the work is to be considered ultimately a tragedy or the comedy originally intended. Nonetheless, it is impossible to read *Don Quixote* without viewing its protagonist as someone with a vision of a far better world than the one we inhabit.

A second curious happening is the gradual conversion of Sancho Panza from hardened realist to at least *semi*-idealist. Some of the Don's principles—fair play, justice, honesty, integrity—begin to rub off. Late in the novel Sancho conceives a utopian society of which he would like to be governor, and few readers ever come away believing Sancho's code of governing to be undesirable. When the hero lies on his death-bed and suddenly comes to his senses, totally renouncing the folly of his ways, it is Sancho who implores him to rise up in the full glory of his ideals, to do battle with evil and save the world.

Nor is Sancho's conversion a wild flight of literary fancy. The Don's brand of idealism, the need to live by a code of virtue, honor, and truth and to do everything in one's power to make the world a more desirable place, is a very real path taken by many. Without fanfare, without expecting miracles, thousands of people find happiness only in terms of working toward a better tomorrow. They do not give up because of the difficulty of the project. They campaign against pollution, fight for civil rights wherever these are denied, write letters to editors and legislators, volunteer for work in social agencies or hospitals, go door to door with pamphlets, and so on. There is never any doubt in their minds that a universal understanding of the phrase "better world" *does* exist and that, given their choice, the vast majority would prefer to be free to have all transactions fair and open, to know that honesty prevails and virtue is rewarded, and to sleep each night without having to lock the front door. Since there is such an understanding, it is, for them, pure hypocrisy to do anything else except dedicate their lives to the building if such a world.

In contrast to pure idealism is "realism". You see what ought to be, but you know it can never be. You are satisfied with very limited goals. You see no reason to devote your entire life to crusades which you believe are doomed before they start. Nobody really reads letters, nobody really listens to the ordinary person on the streets; power corrupts, and,

> **Marcus Aurelius**
>
> **How much time he gains who does not look to see what his neighbor says or does or thinks, but only at what he does himself, to make it just and holy.**

> **Shakespeare**
>
> **Cowards die many times before their deaths; The valiant never taste of death but once.**

since some will always seek power, there will always be corruption. While he was manager of the Brooklyn Dodgers, Leo Durocher summed up the Sancho Panza position most succinctly: "Nice guys finish last."

Of course, there is always some question about who is happier: idealists who are driven on by inspiring principles and noble goals, knowing they will never reach their destinations; or realists who recognize what humanity *could* be but are willing to settle for very much less. Idealists may have the satisfaction of knowing that their own motives are pure, but how do they tolerate what others do? Realists, for their part, seldom suffer the agony of disenchantment, but can they ever enjoy the luxury of hope?

If the formula for happiness lies in a choice between Don Quixote and Sancho Panza, are we then forced to conclude that there are drawbacks to either road and that consequently there can be no such thing as complete happiness? We must not forget that in the final episode of Cervantes' novel the two men switched positions, but for each one the new stance appeared as limited as the old one had been.

14

A MATTER OF LIFE OR DEATH

Overview

In *Zorba the Greek,* a very popular film of the 1960s, an idealistic young poet is asked by the hero what is probably the most frequently asked question in the history of the human race: "Why do people have to die?" The poet thinks for a minute and then, in a heartbroken sigh, answers: "I don't know." The angry Zorba, dissatisfied with the reply, comes back with yet another question: "What good are all your books if they cannot tell you that?" The poet thinks again, then says: "They are about the agonies of men who cannot answer such questions."

Humanity has been defined in many ways, but one recurrent definition is "the species that hates death and thinks about it long before it comes." Other animals love in season, store food in season, forage for food when necessary, kill to survive, and die when they must. The human species can

In the midst of life we are surrounded by death.
Ambrose Bierce

. . . those of us who think that death is an evil are in error.
Plato

If there be nothing after Now, And we be nothing anyhow, And we know that,—why live?
Edwin Arlington Robinson

And all our yesterdays have lighted fools
The way to dusty death.
William Shakespeare

Even so, I kept right on going on, a sort of human statement.
Anne Sexton,[2] "Live"

love any time at all (or never,) plan for food carelessly or not at all, dismiss future energy needs, capriciously steal or kill, or fearfully die many times before the physical event itself takes place.

Perhaps some day all people will learn not to kill for sport, not to solve their problems by that singularly human phenomenon called war; perhaps all people will learn how to live in tune with nature's rhythms—but the contemporary philosopher Joseph Wood Krutch predicts that these social ideals will never prevail. Nevertheless, there are some impediments to the art of being human which we are free to alter if we wish. One such behavior is the denial of life's potential because we hate the thought of dying.

This chapter points out first that negative attitudes toward death are not necessarily universal; that there seems to be a high correlation between an obsession with death and highly materialistic styles of life; that too many people fail to do much with their lives because of "death attitudes"—extensions of the fear of dying into all aspects of living, even those not directly connected with biological death; and that it is possible to adjust one's death attitudes and replace them with life-affirming images.

Cervantes

There is a remedy for all things but death, which will be sure to lay us out flat some time or other.

Attitudes Toward Death

The Greek slave Epictetus, who became a renowned Roman teacher, was especially concerned with the manner in which attitudes can make our lives happy or miserable.

He believed most people failed to realize that all problems begin and end with attitudes. For example, he observed that death in itself was not a terrible thing. What people really feared was the attitude that death was terrible. Rid yourself of the attitude, he advised, and the terror of death vanishes.

Since no one living has experienced death totally and finally—though many testimonies have been gathered from those who have hovered at the very brink, it seems reasonable that Epictetus was speaking wisdom. Everyone has an idea about what death must be like. Movies and television programs abound with images of violent and painful deaths; poetry and song tell of death in melancholy tones. On the other hand, there have been biblical movies in which

Thomas Hardy

"Come hither, Son," I heard Death say; "I did not will a grave should end Thy pilgrimage to-day, but I, too, am a slave!"

condemned Christians, their voices raised in song, wait almost joyously for the hungry lions to come charging into the Circus Maximus. Many accounts of the life of Joan of Arc have shown her walking exultantly toward the flames. The viewer, perceiving an actress smiling as pretend flames leap around her, might think, "No one can face death like that. It isn't human." But this is to project one's own attitudes toward death into the external world and to assume that there can be only one way to think about death.

The "knowledge" of what death is and what the experience of death must be like, stems from basic attitudes. And these attitudes are directly related to certain prevailing values, which are the concern of this section. It is possible that as your own values criss-cross and often oppose each other, your attitudes toward death can reflect the confusion.

Death and the Concept of Self

We have no proof that all people think or have thought about the "self" as many in modern Western society do. Most of us born and raised in reasonably large cities, within fairly small families (so that each new birth is an event of magnitude) have been accustomed to so much attention and conditioned to need so much esteem that we take it for granted that the preservation of the self is the number one priority in all the universe. The phrase "identity crisis" is so common today—as is the omnipresent line in television and movies "I've got to find out who I am!"—that it is hard for us to imagine living without this obsession with personal identity, and with the preservation of life in order for that identity to remain intact.

People in history who have willingly given up their lives for a cause are usually considered martyrs and honored accordingly. But the martyrdom is based on an assumption of the value the person condemned to death puts on his or her personal existence.

Socrates is a notable case in point. Found guilty of alleged crimes against the state, the philosopher was given a choice: death by poison, or a life in exile without the right to engage in free inquiry or philosophical discussion. Socrates chose death. Why? The answer, it seems, is that the activity of philosophy meant more to him than life. Without the activity there would be no point in living. The importance or

Emily Dickinson

Because I could not stop for death, He kindly stopped for me.

preservation of personal identity does not appear to have been the issue.

> *Some one will say: Yes, Socrates, but cannot you hold your tongue, and then you may go into a foreign city, and no one will interfere with you? Now I have great difficulty in making you understand my answer to this. For if I tell you . . . that I cannot hold my tongue, you will not believe that I am serious; and if I say again that daily to discourse about virtue, and of those other things about which you hear me examining myself and others, is the greatest good of man, and that the unexamined life is not worth living, you are still less likely to believe me.*

From these words attributed to Socrates in his speech to the court which condemned him, we sense the implication that those who supposedly could not understand would imagine death as being the worst possible fate, because they valued their own identities more than any activity such as the pursuit of truth. They could not imagine the importance of such an activity if they thought the philosopher could be bribed into renouncing it with something so unsatisfying as mere life. Some skeptical observers have pointed out that, since Socrates was already 75 years old, death would not have held the same terrors as it would for a 30-year-old philosopher. But perhaps they too are trying to transform personal assumptions into universal belief.

Assuming that Plato's portrait of Socrates is accurate, assuming that the philosopher *was* generally concerned with the mental act of reaching an understanding of certain absolutes like justice, virtue, and beauty, we do not detect any indication that Socrates was ever defensive or artificial. He always seems to be genuinely interested in seeking wisdom and not at all interested in making people feel sorry for him or afraid of him. On his final day, when he drinks the poison, surrounded by the young intellectuals who adore him, Socrates shows a singular absence of self-consciousness. He sounds willing to let go of his hold on his own identity. He does not say, "Remember always what I have taught you" or "Promise to keep going what I have begun."

Thus when Phaedo, one of the followers, observes that the master has drunk the poison "cheerfully," we have no reason to believe that Socrates was struggling to put on a brave act in front of his friends. And then there occurs a most telling statement:

And hitherto most of us had been able to control our sorrow; but now when we saw him drinking, and saw too that he had finished the draught, we could no longer forbear, and in spite of myself my own tears were flowing fast; so that I covered my face and wept, not for him, but at the thought of my own calamity in having to part from such a friend.

Phaedo weeps *but not for Socrates.* The young man's own identity is threatened by the imminent loss of a close and dear friend. Thus it is with many of us: the death of another self is inevitably measured in terms of one's own self. If you and I are close, inseparable, so that my own being is intricately tied up with yours, I cannot tolerate your passing. For it means the changing of my entire life. Nothing will ever again be as it was with me. My old self, in a real sense, is dead. Therefore I weep.

The point is not that the loss of close ones should not be mourned or that outward signs of grief and sincere and deep feeling for others should be concealed by civilized and sensitive human beings. The point here is that the acceptability of death—the tolerance we have for its intrusions—is correlated with the amount of attention given to one's sense of self. Where self is central, death seems to be regarded as a dreadful occurrence, an evil that plagues humanity. As the importance of self diminishes, the presence of death is less and less threatening.

It is at least possible to imagine two very dear friends, both of whom share pleasure in the same things. Perhaps they enjoy art, politics, sports, religion. They like to attend concerts, ball games, and the latest films. They enjoy trying subtle dishes at different restaurants. Neither suffers from an over-sized ego or a neurotic inner sense of inferiority, so that neither one needs the other's self as complement or reinforcement to his or her own. Each enjoys the other as a phenomenon, an important source of delight in a world of other delights, on the order of, though to a greater degree than, magnificent music.

It is possible to suppose that the death of one can be accepted by the other without its having a shattering effect, without its leaving a void in life that can never be filled. There is a certain rhythm to the existence of the mourner. There will be some grief—a normal and probably universal emotional response to death. But the stride will not break. Life will make the necessary adjustment—and move on. The

In Western culture the horror of death seems directly related to the importance attached to the self.

•

•

•

reason is that the one who is still alive is strong enough not to need a reinforcement of identity. As with Socrates, the activities rather than the concentration on self have been central in life, and will continue to be.

Insecure lovers sometimes test each other with questions like "If I should die, would you ever get over it?" Or "If I should die, would you ever love anyone else?" The expectation is usually "No. I'd be miserable forever, if I didn't have you!" A reply like "Surely you would want me to find someone else" would not be understood, or there would not have been a question to begin with.

One who is profoundly committed to Buddhist philosophy and to the practice of meditation is not likely to be overwhelmed by the thought of death—one's own or that of others. In Buddhism the self is regarded as not only unimportant, but nonexistent. One is not urged to deny the self, only to recognize it is an illusion. The Buddhist distinguishes between reality—that which is "out there," tangible and substantial—and thought. Everything that is not tangible and substantial, that is not *real,* is considered to be a thought. No distinction is made between an idea and an emotion. If it is going on inside, it is a thought. In Buddhism no thought really exists. Where is it found? Where does it go after it is forgotten? As a matter of fact, the Buddhist is not even interested in speculating on these points. Life should consist of appropriate actions with respect to the real world.

Thus it is clear for the Buddhist that the inner sense of "me" lacks substantial existence. During sitting meditation, identification with one's out-breath rather than one's thoughts causes the jangle known as "mind chatter" to become increasingly distant. In monastic forms of Buddhism, such as Zen, in which meditation sometimes lasts for an entire day and in which one might spend years without much contact with anyone else, the sense of self is said to virtually disappear. The point of monastic Buddhism is to become as large as experience itself, identifying with people and events, in terms of what is, not in terms of our responses and needs. Death for the Buddhist is simply another phenomenon, a thing that happens "out there." Death is therefore real, while the self is not. To think about the self, which is nonexistent, is for the Buddhist meaningless, if not mad.

The typical Western mind, however, views such attitudes

•

•

•

Cultures which do not think of the self as being the basic unit of existence seem less afraid of death.

with suspicion. An army colonel, interviewed shortly after his return from eight years in Vietnam, was asked for a brief profile of the Vietnamese—in particular, what it meant to ordinary citizens who lost their homes and possessions and saw members of their families killed before their very eyes. In the colonel's opinion, the Vietnamese did not respond like people in the West. They were far more stoic, far more reconciled to even the most horrendous of events. "These people," he added, "have never known anything but poverty and privation. Therefore they do not value life as we do."

Some Western observers believe that the Buddhist belief in the self-as-illusion makes sense in overpopulated countries in which social mobility is all but impossible. The army colonel went on to say that long hours of meditation in which the individual reaches a spacious emptiness work very well in countries with widespread unemployment and no hope of ever raising the ordinary individual to a position of dignity and recognition. With nothing to look forward to in life, he said, the average person in the East may as well take things as they come, even when they are disastrous.

The colonel perceived that the lives of only a few were valued in the East; consequently death was of no great concern. The reverse is frequently taken as a truth: that is, where the life of an individual seems to have more importance, death becomes a more sorrowful occasion. Surely we seem to pay extraordinary amounts of respect to fallen leaders, and Easterners appear to do likewise, a leader representing a self, a presence, of singular importance whatever the culture. The deaths of John F. and then Robert Kennedy, both in the 1960s, left for many a gaping void on the American political scene which has yet to be filled. It *does* seem that the more irreplaceable the departed self is seen to be, the less the death of a great person can be accepted with dispassionate calm.

Still, it cannot be said that our society attaches equal importance to every notable self. The death of Albert Einstein was marked in some quarters with due solemnity, but it was not a national event of singular magnitude. The death of popular singer Elvis Presley seemed far less acceptable to the vast majority of Americans. It could be said that Einstein was older, but age would not account for such a significant difference in public reaction.

Shakespeare

He was a man, take him for all in all, I shall not look upon his like again.

Hamlet—on his dead father

The importance of a departed self is possibly measured in terms of success, and success is measured in terms of notoriety, political stature, appearances in films and on television, and, of course, the amount of money one has made. The death of Howard Hughes, who had become legendary because of the undisclosed, and maybe unpronounceable, amount of his fortune, made headlines for months. If people did not exactly mourn, they still were fascinated by this unusual man. For the average American the passing of the well publicized Hughes seemed more significant than the passing of a neighbor down the street.

But what is being said? That as long as someone has not achieved great notoriety, his death may be tolerated and accepted? That if, for example, a factory worker or a kindergarten teacher dies, there is no special reason for mourning? Few would be content with such an implication, and there is no justification for it.

The way a nation buries its dead is indicative of its value system. Homage paid in our society to fallen leaders of high stature, wealth, and success (however measured) becomes the model by which *all* selves are regarded. Eulogies filled with exaggerated praise are delivered at graveside in our society no matter what the real achievements of the deceased were. The dead are treated *as though* they had made their mark. Indeed the eulogy can be the ultimate (and ironic) compensation for a life that was disappointing.

Most people in our society believe they must respond to a death as if it meant the loss of an irreplaceable individual. While homage to the dead may be appropriate (as a social ritual it has enormous value as a means of reinforcing a society's values), it is also true that the departed self is in no position to appreciate the honor. Therefore, in the opinion of many thanatologists (psychologists who specialize in counseling people having trouble reconciling themselves to their own approaching deaths or to those of loved ones), the concept of "singular loss" or of "an irreplaceable self" can make the living lose heart and believe that with the passing of the singular individual an era has ended. As the poet Wordsworth put the matter: ". . . there has passed away a glory from the earth." Such an attitude toward death—as that which causes unthinkable and irremediable damage—can cast a shadow over the ongoing, potentially productive life of any person. After all, one can ask, "Why bother,

> **The death of Elvis Presley seemed far less acceptable than the death of Einstein.**

when I know that death comes along to cut down even the most brilliant and successful?"

Lovers have been separated by death; parents have lost children long before the word "death" was ever mentioned in a home. To realize that life continues—that the irreplaceable being may, and perhaps ought to be, one day a fond but ever dimmer memory—is not necessarily to be unfeeling and callous.

Death and Religion

From the very beginning the history of human religion has been involved with the subject of death. While we cannot say for certain just how early individuals responded to the thought of death, it seems clear that some definite attitudes arose by the time a given religion had developed a view of the self in relation to what exists beyond the earth.

The Homeric religion of the early Greeks—with its Olympian gods—witnessed a sharp intensification of the concept of self. The immortal gods may have played cruel jokes on mortals and arranged some peculiar destinies for them, but mortals were always central to their plans (and schemes). Humans counted, and counted largely in the cosmos.

• *Glorious death* • The Homeric religion gave birth to the idea of glorious death. If men were not the equal of the gods, they were *nearly* so, and one way they could demonstrate their greatness was through valor on the battlefield. To die with honor was infinitely preferable to living as a coward. That glorious death could also be violent did not seem to matter.

Also of great importance was the fallen warrior's body, often burned on a huge pyre with his personal property. Those who were deemed to have died cowardly deaths, or who fought on the wrong side, had their bodies dishonored and denied proper burial, while their spirits were thought to wander forever in the underworld, never reaching a place of rest.

In contrast, the brave were thought to pass at once into the Elysian Fields, where their spirits would live in eternal bliss. Some believed that those who died gloriously experienced no physical death at all, no pain, regardless of the violence and bloodshed. The agony of dying was only for cowards.

While it was religion that created the Greek "geography

Shakespeare

Once more unto the breach, dear friends, once more, Or close the wall up with our English dead!

Henry V

of death," the visual imagery of a "beyond" separated from the world of the living by the River Styx, the idea of glorious death outlasted the Homeric gods. For the Spartans patriotism took the place of religion. One died bravely for one's country. Young men in Sparta were raised in the certainty that ultimate success would be a hero's death. The legendary Spartan mother, bidding farewell to her son, reminded him to return *"with* your shield or *on* it." How seriously the Romans ever took the gods and goddesses they inherited from the Greeks is questionable, but they clearly carried Spartan patriotism to extremes.

> Abraham Lincoln
>
> **The brave men, living and dead, who struggled here have consecrated it, far above our poor power to add or detract.**

Throughout human history, to the present moment, the ideal of glorious death has persisted. In the Middle Ages it was death in the Crusades, or death in the name and interest of one's land baron, or finally one's country. Every nation in Europe has its long list of great battles and its names of those who died glorious deaths. The United States continues to honor the heroes of the Revolutionary War. Both North and South acknowledge the greatness of those who died for either cause: to preserve the Union or to make possible the dream of the Confederacy. In fact, memoirs of Civil War times assert the respect both sides had for each other's bravery. Being unafraid to die the glorious death gave one a status that transcended battle lines in a society of gentlemen fighters.

The era of the second World War appears to have been the last stand of glorious death in the United States. There were few protest marches, few speeches urging young men to resist the draft. Rather, there was an intense unity, a pervasive conviction that it was a noble duty to sacrifice even life, if necessary, for the national good. Songs, poems, novels, and plays idealized singular acts of heroism and altruism on the battlefield.

If individual death in the interest of a cause greater than self did not matter, the same reasoning applied to the killing of others. It was not murder to shoot, stab, or blow up the enemy. It was a deadly game but with elements of honor, understood since the beginning of time.

At least, those were the ideals, not necessarily the truth. Even in Homer, in whose works *The Iliad* and *The Odyssey* one finds an epic picture of a human race rivaling the gods in glory, there occur some moments of doubt. In one scene of *The Iliad,* Menelaus, whose wife Helen has run off with Paris and thus started the Trojan War, finds an enemy warrior lying on the ground, wounded. He raises his lance for the expected kill, then hesitates. The stoic warrior at his feet looks up in confusion. Menelaus asks himself why he really *has* to kill this man who has done nothing to him. But in the long run the lance is thrust and the warrior allowed his glorious death. In this short encounter Homer has raised a big question: if the self is made to seem at least as important as the cause or the nation, does death become meaner, less noble?

> **World War II: a deadly game, but with elements of honor understood since the beginning of time.**

Certainly the mood of young America in the late 1960s was just that of Menelaus. What is so important about Vietnam that we must kill for it? they asked. Why should the United States be the conscience and protector of the whole world? In contrast, the 1960s stressed the importance of the solitary self: the drifter going down the road with his guitar; the motorcyclist who refused to take root anywhere; the ethnic minorities who were developing a strong self image. These individuals did not accept the idea of dying for an ill-defined cause. The right of a person not only to live, but to live in any manner he or she chooses, was paramount. For the rebellious youth of the 1960s, if glorious death existed at all, it was usually limited to the martyrdom of protesters who were beaten or shot by the police or the National Guard.

• *Fatalism* • In Western monotheistic society there exists a prominent attitude that, since God is all-powerful and all-knowing, the exact moment of each person's death, as well as the cause of it, must be known to Him in advance. St. Augustine in particular struggled with this question, concerned not with respect to death alone but with all of the evils which plague humanity. That is, God must know in advance about all events—good and evil—which befall humankind. The philosopher finally decided that God knows but does not have to will what happens. Indeed if God did plan in advance each person's destiny, then God could not hold anyone accountable for his or her sins. How could there *be* any sin? To solve the dilemma, St. Augustine maintained that each human being was given the gift of free will.

> John Milton
>
> **All is, if I have grace to use it so, As ever in my great Task-master's eye.**

Nonetheless, not everyone who accepts the one God of the Judeo-Christian tradition is inclined to accept that delicate balance between human free will and God's foreknowledge. For many, foreknowledge means advance planning. John Calvin (1509–1564), an extreme Protestant reformer upon whose views was founded the Puritan religion of the first American settlers, believed emphatically in predestination. Nothing else, for him, was compatible with God's omnipotence. A perfect being could not leave matters to chance and allow those he created to carve out their own destinies. The doctrine of predestination also extended to the afterlife. There was a heaven and there was a hell—everyone knew that. But only God knew the names of those destined for salvation and those destined for damnation. He believed the Catholic position—that humankind has free will to choose between right and wrong and thus has some control over reward or punishment in the next life—was untenable. Historians of Puritanism sometimes find themselves wondering why any Puritan ever went to church at all, since according to their beliefs nothing anyone did in this life could alter his or her eventual destiny.

The classic case for fatalism is made in The Book of Job, that extraordinary Old Testament work, which begins with an encounter between God and Satan. With some justifiable pride, God points to Job as a very model of the pious, humble, good man. With his characteristic cynicism, Satan reminds God that Job is good because God has showered him with a loving wife, with children, and with vast property holdings. Take it all away, Satan challenges, and see how pious Job will be. Accordingly, God allows Satan to inflict any sort of suffering on Job, short of allowing him to die.

Suddenly the good man is visited by a series of disasters. His sons are killed. He loses his livestock. His land becomes barren. Terrible boils break out on his body. Various friends come to see him, to offer him comfort, but all they can tell him is that he must in some way have offended God. His wife urges him to complain bitterly to God about the apparent injustice. But though he curses the conditions of his life, he maintains his famous patience for a very long while. Just as Job can stand his existence no longer, just as his patience is about to crack, God's voice comes thundering out of the whirlwind. Job is told in no uncertain terms that it is not his, nor any man's, right to question the workings of God. Since

---

Ecclesiastes

**Then shall the dust return to the earth as it was:
And the spirit shall return unto God who gave it.**

human beings did not create the earth, since they have no ultimate power, they must accept divine wisdom, no matter what happens to them. That is one ending, as written by one set of Biblical authors. According to an added version, what has been taken from Job is restored, and he is once again happy and rich. The moral: God gives and God takes away. Man accepts humbly both the good things and the bad. While many subsequent interpreters of *Job* view the work as a tragedy, others believe that it was intended to be a hard-nosed work of piety, underscoring that behind the worst life can offer, there still exists a divine reason for everything that happens.

The fatalism in *Job* is not simplistic. The work does not say that God keeps a chart on His wall with everyone's name on it, together with a time and a manner of death. *Job* is the supreme expression of divine providence. Its God is the loving God of Abraham and Jacob—the paternal, protective God. Bad as Job's lot seemed at the time, the reader was not supposed to question the wisdom of God. In fact, in *Job* the fear of God and the love of God are clearly the same thing.

Nonetheless, there exists a widespread fatalism with respect to death that combines monotheism with ancient religious beliefs. Even those who otherwise subscribe to the Augustinian doctrine of human free will can sometimes believe in fatalism. It comes and goes, as convenient. One can be a fatalist and still refuse to take unnecessary risks, such as not wanting to join a parachute jumping club or to ride a roller coaster standing up or to enter the Indianapolis 500. One might refuse to undergo a delicate operation with a 50/50 survival rate on the grounds that the odds are not favorable enough. But the same person who refuses risks for himself can say of the death of another, "His time came" or, in that unpleasant metaphor, "His number was up."

The fatalistic attitude is sometimes invoked in the always difficult task of explaining death to children. When grandparents die, a child is generally told that they have gone away or are now with God in heaven. But if, for example, the child's own mother should die, relatives have been known to "explain" the death in this way: "God so loved your mother that he wanted her to be with Him always, and so He took her up to heaven." Thanatologists who treat patients with severe death problems in accepting death, report that many adult anxieties have had their origins in

---

Fatalism survives, especially in the way death is explained to children.

The child is ready to cope with the idea of death when he or she understands the abstraction of time.

childhood ambivalent feelings toward a God who could be so cruel as to want to take a parent away.

Whether a purely fatalistic attitude toward death helps anyone is questionable. But one must always be cautious in using it to explain death to children. Very young people may be surprisingly able to handle the subject. Adults need to be sensitive to appropriate signs. One guideline suggested by thanatologists is that the child is ready to cope with the idea of death when he or she understands the abstraction of time. If the child has an idea of what "a lifetime" can mean, he or she will probably be able to comprehend the full import of the statement that a loved one has terminated that life-time. Too often, when adults try to help a child "cope" with death, they themselves are having problems accepting it.

An Afterlife

Religious people are reconciled to death in varying degrees because of a belief that life continues beyond the grave. Many persons facing death are known to experience a resurgence of religious faith, especially in an afterlife, whether or not such a belief has been an integral part of their lives before. But the average religious person, one who is not facing the end of his or her life, is likely to have only a vague conception of what "afterlife" really means.

When God speaks to Job out of the whirlwind, He promises the long-suffering man nothing. Faith is enough. That his possessions are to be restored, Job cannot know. That God is providential, the faithful must believe. No eternity of heavenly bliss is guaranteed. Throughout the Old Testament, either no material reward is deemed necessary for the faithful, or the reward of a good life spent in good deeds will be security and the love of one's fellows. The Old Testament Hebrews were a realistic people, oriented toward results. The afterlife is not precisely defined. The stress is on this life. Even Canaan, the land of milk and honey, the Promised Land, is real, a highly desirable fertile area where water is plentiful and crops can be raised.

In Christianity there appears to be a promised afterlife of some sort, but its exact nature is somewhat ambiguous. Christ on the cross is reported to have told the two thieves that they would be with him in Paradise, and Christians of course believe that Christ, after rising from the grave, did

> **An afterlife has not always been guaranteed. In *Job,* one of the great works in the Old Testament, God promises the hero nothing. Faith is enough.**

indeed ascend bodily and spiritually into what is called heaven. But it is not clear that this other world, this Paradise, is an actual place with a geography of its own. It is not certain that people will continue to exist as themselves, though in a spiritual form. Movies of the 30s and 40s frequently showed lovers reunited in the next world, looking exactly as they did in this world, except that their bodies were transparent. Christian clergy are usually reluctant to make definite promises to survivors, beyond the fact that those they mourn are better off now that they are with God.

One is tempted to wonder why the continuity of identity is so important to so many who profess religious faith. If the afterlife does indeed exist, it would appear to do so on a plane or in a dimension the living could not possibly comprehend. Whatever eternal joy is to be experienced could not possibly resemble any earthly joy, hence there appears to be no point in making promises to oneself about a literal place in which "spiritual bodies" with faces and names recognize each other, even to continuing the same family relationships they have enjoyed on earth.

Some religions, but not the major ones, guarantee literalistic afterlives. There is, for example, a bumper sticker which employs the language of real estate: HEAVEN IS A REAL PLACE—HAVE YOU RESERVED YOUR SPOT? During a tent revival meeting, a minister told the faithful that heaven is very much like earth. You need a house to live in when you get there, and that takes money. The money you place in the basket today is deposited in the fund reserving heavenly lots for the believers.

Major religions tend to concentrate on the judgmental aspect of the afterlife. The good are to be rewarded in "an eternity of bliss," while the bad are to be punished. Accounts of both rewards and punishments can be couched in very vivid language. Many cannot help visualizing "an eternity of bliss" and see it in terms of blazing light. But whatever afterlife may exist could not do so on any plane or in any dimension accessible to the human intellect; that is, heaven is beyond human conception because it is beyond human experience. Similarly, the thoughts of hell as a place of raging fires presuppose a body to experience pain. Obviously hell is as metaphoric as heaven. It has been stamped in the human imagination in the first part of Dante's *Divine Comedy*, "The Inferno."

Christ to the thief

Truly, I say to you, today you will be with me in Paradise.

Luke 23:43

Still, the metaphors have been with humanity for so long that no doubt many have come to fear death because of them. If you recognize that these metaphors are not realities, then you may fear, in Hamlet's words, the "undiscover'd country from whose bourn / No traveller returns. . . ." Whether the next world is called the Great Beyond or the Vast Abyss, the uncertainty probably causes as much anxiety for some as the possibility of there being nothing at all causes for others.

Thornton Wilder's (1940) play *Our Town* contains what could be some piercing insights. In the third and final act, the dead of Grover's Corners are seated at one corner of the stage, sitting in straight-backed chairs symbolic of their cemetery graves. At the other side of the stage the funeral of Emily, the play's heroine, is in progress. When the soul of Emily joins the other dead, she is comforted by being told that very soon she will begin to think less and less of her life on earth, and that after a while she will become indifferent to it.

In 1968 the late Bishop James A. Pike wrote a book called *The Other Side,* in which he describes his mystic quest of contact with his son Jim, who had committed suicide under the influence of drugs. Through the medium Arthur Ford, Bishop Pike supposedly reached beyond the barrier and recorded the words of his dead son, who speaks first of the afterlife, "a world where everybody is out to create a greater sense of love and harmony. A world in which music and color and poetry are all interwoven, making a majestic pattern. . . ." The son goes on to say he is trying to understand "to the point where I don't have to clutch at my identity so much . . . you see, we have to be selfless."

No doubt the major religions are concerned about those for whom the afterlife is an idealized version of this life on earth, a spiritual version of a material paradise, in which eternal bliss is something like being free of debt, not growing old, and never having to work for a living.

The Vale of Tears

During the Middle Ages, and no doubt with good cause, there arose a cynical view of life on earth, attended by religion's promise of relief from suffering beyond the grave. The average person was surrounded by death. Plague, pestilence, famine, and poverty comprised the human lot. Rituals

---

Visions of heaven and hell in the popular imagination have been strongly influenced by Dante's *Divine Comedy.*

Do you know how exciting it is to come back? To be dead—but we are not the dead ones, you are the dead ones, because you are only firing on two cylinders.

Reportedly spoken to Bishop James A. Pike at a séance

like the Dance of Death on All Hallow's Eve emphasized the stalking presence of phantoms from the grave, and little children played death games as they chanted death songs. One of these songs persists to this day.

> *Ring around the rosy,*
> *A pocket full of posies,*
> *Ashes! Ashes!*
> *All fall down.*

Carved death's heads, special baked goods in the shape of ghoulish figures all contributed to the omnipresent sense of mortality. While a casual glance might decide that medieval people were "morbid," second thoughts could tell a different story. For the long-suffering medieval peasant dragging his cart through the vermin-infested streets of overcrowded towns the thought of death may well have been the loner pleasure of his wretched life.

To this day in certain quarters there persists the belief that life is hell and death a welcome liberation. In rural Puerto Rico, for example, one can still run into festive celebrations held to mark the death of a child under the age of seven. The dead child is washed, dressed, then laid out on a table, surrounded by enough food and drink for days. Well-wishers come to visit the family and stay to feast and drink. The idea is that the greatest good to be experienced in life is to escape from it before one has reached the age of sin. The dead child's spirit is thought of as rejoicing in heaven without having had to suffer the pains of earth.

The New Orleans jazz funeral is well known. The body is accompanied to the cemetery by friends and relatives as well as a band playing a slow and mournful dirge. After the burial, when the soul of the deceased has by now risen above the sufferings of life, the mood changes. The band plays Dixieland, and the mourners strut and dance through the streets, drinking and carousing in their joy.

Hedonism and Death

By far the most difficult task of coping with death belongs to hedonistic societies—or members of those societies who subscribe consciously or unconsciously to the hedonist view of life.

Hedonism (see Chapter 13) is based on the assumption

that human beings are selfish, pleasure-loving animals. Since this is so, it is right and good that people should think primarily of their own comforts. Pleasure is defined in strictly physical terms, and in terms of the present. The memory or anticipation of pleasure does not count. Therefore, the good life for the hedonist is the active, unrelenting quest of more satisfying physical enjoyment.

Closely allied to physical sensation, for the hedonist, is the possession of objects, people, property, and money. If the possessions are not themselves a total pleasure, they are the means by which pleasure can eventually be obtained. Therefore acquisitiveness occupies all of the time not actively spent in enjoyable sensations.

The Greece of the third century B.C. as well as the Rome of the later empire (third and fourth centuries A.D.) is thought to have been an extremely hedonistic society. In both, a *carpe diem* ("seize the day") philosophy prevailed. This outlook is summed up in the perennial slogan "Eat, drink, and be merry, for tomorrow we shall die."

One view of history is that eras dominated by an intense hedonism tend to follow Golden Ages, eras of super achievement, when a culture is driven by the need to surpass all of the civilized glories that have ever existed on earth. For example, the Renaissance in Europe, extending from about the fourteenth through the sixteenth centuries, was followed by a period whose literature reflects a diminishing zeal for accomplishment and an increasing desire to relax and enjoy the pleasures which money and social rank made possible. The poems and plays of the seventeenth century show a preoccupation with the theme of love, especially sexual experience—the joys of the game, the seduction, the fulfillment, and moving on to new encounters, new conquests.

But in extolling the virtues of continual fun, seventeenth-century writers also incurred a debt: the continual recognition that the shadow of death was always there, ready to swoop down and spoil the party. Andrew Marvell, one exponent of seventeenth-century hedonism, summed up the mood of the period in a poem "To His Coy Mistress," the point of which is that the lady in question really should submit to the lustful desires of the poet rather than play a waiting game. Soon it will all be too late.

> But at my back I always hear
> Time's winged chariot hurrying near:
> And yonder all before us lie
> Deserts of vast eternity.
> Thy beauty shall no more be found;
> Nor, in thy marble vault, shall sound
> My echoing song: then worms shall try
> That long preserv'd virginity:
> And your quaint honor turn to dust;
> And into ashes all my lust.

Centuries before, the Greek philosopher Epicurus (see Chapter 13) had warned of the pitfalls of the hedonist

---

An intense preoccupation with physical pleasures may not be a celebration of life, but instead, an irrational flight from death.

Epicurus taught that for the dedicated hedonist life can never be long enough, and he or she is always cheated.

approach to life. If only pleasurable sensations count, he said, it becomes unthinkable to have a single moment without them. The onset of age and its attendant infirmities, culminating in the inevitable moment of death, are totally unpleasant for the hedonist, who must therefore spend much of his or her life in misery. It made more sense to Epicurus to expect more modest returns from life and not to require an indefinite supply of sensuous enjoyments.

If hedonist societies are death-fearing, they are also life-denying. One cannot really enjoy what one has with the specter of death always hovering in the background. To ease the anxiety caused by this specter, the hedonist often employs escapist strategies, such as alcohol or drugs. Those addicted to "chemical assistance" may think they are experiencing pleasure and making every moment count, but overwhelming evidence exists to show that the depression following temporary "highs" is always more profound than the one which preceded them. Suicide is frequently attempted, sometimes sucessfully, in the more extreme cases of depression.

In the opinion of many thanatologists, the United States as a society tends to be both life-denying and death-fearing. The symptoms are plainly there. Perhaps ours is not a *totally* hedonistic way of life. Perhaps the Puritan strain is still strong, so that "good hard work" (as opposed to leisure-time pleasure) is stressed in some quarters. But compared to most of the world's populations, citizens of the United States enjoy a high standard of living and require an inordinate amount of pleasurable sensation, an unmistakable sign of hedonistic tendencies.

Big cars	Ostentatious clothes
Water beds	Big-screen movies
Swimming pools	Lush stereo sounds
Massage parlors	Overeating
Promiscuity	Vicarious sex

Ours is a society with a low tolerance for pain, both emotional and physical. Psychiatrists and other therapists do a booming business. Books which massage the ego and soothe the reader wallowing in self-pity can catapult to the top of the best-seller list. Pharmaceutical companies grow rich from dispensing tranquilizers and pain-killers of sometimes alarming strength.

As in former times, the hedonist elements in our society cause death to loom as the most unacceptable pain in all the universe and, even worse, as the denial of sensation. Consequently, its presence is kept as low-key as possible. Euphemisms such as "pass away" or "pass on" are substituted for the verb "die." The livingroom wake, which is still found in many parts of Europe, Latin America, and rural areas of the United States, gives way to the funeral home viewing, limited to certain hours in the afternoon and evening. The dead are sometimes exhibited in "slumber rooms," in which theatrical lighting and make-up create a curious unreality which theoretically helps to cushion the full impact of loss.

Whether such strategies assist or hinder the process of recovering from death's visitations, the departed at any rate is none the worse for the experience! But in our society the denial of death extends to the person facing the end of his or her life, the terminally ill person, who has been trapped in what Dr. Carol Troescher, a well known thanatologist, has labeled the "Some Sooner" category.

Walls are built around the "Some Sooner" people, often as though they are suffering from a dreadful contagion which must infect all who come near. If visitors drop in at all, the subject of death is never mentioned. Small talk is dredged up from the scant resources of people's already depleted reservoir of inane trivia. The "conversation" is marked by frequent lapses into embarrassing silences. Thanatologists, if consulted at all on the "how to" of relating to the dying, normally recommend openness and honesty. When visitors feel very bad about what is happening to their friends, they should say so. The avoidance of any reference to death is a hopelessly artificial convention. Who could possibly think the dying person is not continually thinking about it?

> **Florence Nightingale once remarked that it is a sin to whisper in the room of a dying man.**

When an illness reaches the point at which hospitalization becomes necessary, both thanatologists and dying patients themselves report there are surprisingly few visitors any more, except for the immediate family. When people do come by, they seldom place themselves close to the bedside. Often they remain in the doorway. They avoid looking directly into the face of the person in the bed, nor do they ever touch either the face or the hands. Often, if two or more visitors appear at the same time, they will find an excuse to talk to each other, ignoring the dying patient altogether.

The reason seems to be that the person in the bed represents something with which the visitor cannot cope and is a visible reminder of the visitor's own mortality. Hence hospital sick rooms are denounced as "morbid" and "depressing."

Hospitalization itself has been challenged by Dr. Elisabeth Kübler-Ross, a Swiss-born psychiatrist and perhaps the world's leading authority on death and dying. Though Dr. Kübler-Ross owns that death has never been particularly pleasant for human beings, there are definite degrees of acceptance or rejection. She finds that affluent societies such as ours tend to be annoyed to revolted by the presence of death and wish to have as little to do with it as possible. Dying people, she contends, can usually fare much better at home than in the antiseptic atmosphere of a hospital room, where white screens hide unpleasant realities from healthy visitors and where doctors and nurses whisper *about* the patient's condition instead of speaking directly and openly *to* him.

In contrasting European with American ways of coping (or not coping) with death, Dr. Kübler-Ross indicates that "old-fashioned" customs like caring for the dying at home

> *are an indication of our acceptance of a fatal outcome, and they help the dying patient as well as his family. . . . If a patient is allowed to terminate his life in the familiar and beloved environment, it requires less adjustment for him. His own family knows him well enough to replace a sedative with a glass of his favorite wine; or the smell of a home-cooked soup may give him the appetite to sip a few spoons of fluid which, I think, is still more enjoyable than an infusion.[3]*

By analogy and because they represent an even more evident threat to the still healthy, the elderly of our society are also screened off, psychologically if not physically. In bleak surroundings, a widow or widower lives alone, without children or grandchildren to provide a home and loving attention. When the elderly become too infirm to care for themselves, they are generally transferred to nursing homes, which even under the best conditions cannot take the place of a family atmosphere. Appalling statistics show how quickly death comes to nursing home residents, especially when children live too far away for regular visits.

In other countries, as well as in rural areas of this country, the story is quite different. It is customary for several generations to live under the same roof; the grandparent or great-grandparent normally occupies a position of considerable respect and continues to "count" as a human being with authority and opinions worth heeding.

The elderly denizens of at least urban society seem to be forced into a game of perpetual youth. Thus it is that the game show host introduces the next contestant as being "80 years young!" The euphemism "senior citizen" replaces the words "old," or even "elderly." True, it can be argued that older people desire such euphemisms, but what else are they to do when everything around them stresses the importance of youth?

Death Attitudes

Death attitudes are conscious and unconscious negative assumptions about life in general, other people, and ourselves which underlie many of our actions. They underlie antisocial and self-destructive behaviors which reap no benefit for anyone, the person acting or the person acted upon. Their source may be the media around us, unfinished family business, early upbringing, unfortunate experiences in school, peer group influences, and a thousand other possible ways in which negativity can develop.

The man whose marriage proposals have been rejected by the first three women approached, may decide that he is unpleasant-looking, has a dull personality, is unintelligent, or is being punished by God for an unconfessed sin from his early childhood. He may believe no woman will ever have him because he is unworthy of woman's love. This is a death attitude—a private inner set of convictions which are all but unchangeable and which cause a person to die figuratively many times over before literal death comes.

Death attitudes do not relate directly to physical death, but their effects can so warp one's perceptions, so distort one's awareness of people and events that in extreme cases they can lead to suicide, either planned or unconscious. A recent case, which became celebrated among the medical

People sometimes feel embarrassed in face-to-face encounters with the dying. They don't know what to say.

•

•

•

The truth of one's feelings is usually appreciated:

"I am very unhappy because of what you must be going through."

faculty of a prominent university, involved a woman admitted to a hospital for treatment of what was thought to be a harmless leg infection. She remained there for six months, growing progressively weaker, losing 85 pounds though no signs of malignancy could be detected anywhere in her body. A psychiatric examination, administered while the woman was still relatively well, revealed a profound depression, induced by feelings of unworth, that became so massive her entire system absorbed the message and began to destroy itself.

Unworth and Symbolic Suicide

Fortunately, there are not many examples of the effects of "unworth" as extreme as the case cited above. But a negative self-concept can and does lead to many forms of symbolic suicide that can sap the energy not only of the victim of the delusion but of those around him or her.

The Rope Dancers, a brooding and disturbing play of the 1950s, concerned an extremely fastidious, Puritanic woman with a very rigid code of moral values, whose husband was an alcoholic and whose daughter, an only child, had been born with six fingers on one hand. The husband's condition was a result not of the child's affliction but of his wife's interpretation of it. The woman was convinced that her daughter's deformity was a hideous and socially unacceptable abnormality, and was not a natural accident, but the consequences of her own sin of lust during the night of the girl's conception. The morbid atmosphere of the house, from which the husband sought escape, was something the wife wanted, felt she deserved. Because of her unworth, she felt she must be forever denied happiness, and so, of course, her family was too.

Self-inflicted martyrdom is another form of symbolic suicide. There are people who will immediately volunteer for any task which appears distasteful or time-consuming or requiring of personal sacrifice. While others hem and haw and try to evade being asked, the martyr seizes almost gleefully upon the chance to overdo once more and draw from others the inevitable "Oh you poor thing. . . ." Unfortunately, the circle is a vicious one. The martyr, seeking acceptance in this destructive way, is doomed not to believe it, for his or her feelings of unworth run too deep. Not able

---

Death Attitudes:

"I'm too old to do that."

"What will they think of me?"

"Nothing ever turns out right."

Sophocles

Death is not the worst evil, but rather, when we wish to die and cannot.

to believe what others say of them, self-appointed martyrs wait desperately for the next opportunity to hold up the world, Atlas-like, on their own stooped shoulders.

In the opinion of many psychologists, compulsive gambling is another version of symbolic suicide. Those who wager large amounts on almost any chance happening—from the Kentucky Derby to the exact number of votes a candidate may earn—are said not to be people who desperately need money or who enjoy pitting their own intellect or intuition against reality, but who secretly hope they will lose the bet. Their sense of unworth drives them to play for high stakes, knowing deep down that statistics run high against them, ensuring they will lose.

Winning, for compulsive gamblers, is a source of momentary joy, because they experience a sudden flash of worth. They have successfully outwitted a system that is supposed to be unbeatable. But what do they do? Take their profit and leave? The answer is almost always that they bet again, usually risking even more money. Like the martyr, compulsive gamblers do not believe the signs that they are worthy of their success. The only recourse is to try once again—to lose. Should they be successful in losing, they may experience a sense of depression, but this generally takes the form of self-castigation: Why did you bet so much? Why didn't you quit while you were ahead? The symbolic beating administered by the self to the self is just treatment for a being which, in its own opinion, can never amount to anything, consequently deserves nothing but hatred.

Other forms of symbolic suicide include the obvious taking of unnecessary risks, such as driving at breakneck speeds, stunt flying, and the like. People who engage in such delightful pastimes are sometimes called "thrill seekers," but often such "thrills" consist of enjoying being punished for being the terrible creatures that only they know themselves to be. The world may be fooled, but the self-punishers are not.

Yet another vicious circle is created by the professional gloom-gatherer, the person followed by a private black cloud which rains only on her or him. So depressing is the company of such a person that few if any people solicit it. The gloom-gatherer receives few invitations. Sensitive to the slight, but recognizing deep inside how justified the slight really is, he or she may seize the chance for self-

---

Gambling is usually a self-destructive activity. The compulsive gambler is secretly hoping to lose.

punishment even more by confronting the source of rejection in hopes of being rejected once more: "I didn't mean to call at this time of night, especially when I know you're having a party, but I had to ask you about. . . ." The flustered party host at the other end of the line can stammer out a few apologies about "mislaid" invitations or coolly ignore the hints. Either response is enough to constitute the right upper-hook the gloom-gatherer is asking for.

Unworth and Symbolic Murder

There are two ways of dealing with one's feeling of unworth: self-destruction and destroying others. At almost any moment the self-hater may turn his or her venom away from the self, projecting it upon an unsuspecting world. If unable to punish the self because the threat of self-recognition is too great, he or she may easily find unworth outside the self. Other people may become symbolic versions of the self, but "their" unworth is easier to face.

Gossip about others is probably the most universal form of symbolic murder. The number of people who engage in it gives some indication of how widespread feelings of unworth really are. And the most prevalent form of gossip is, of course, the spreading of information, however accurate, about somebody else's scandal or misfortune—anything, really, that seems to guarantee a disaster for somebody else. Since everyone has some feelings of unworth, it is natural that everyone is capable of some gossip, but the degree to which one is passionately devoted to the sport offers some indication as to the seriousness of one's self-hatred.

The secret enjoyment of other people's unhappiness precludes any sincere feelings of compassion or altruistic desire to be of help. Only those whose sense of their own worth is secure are in any true position to be needed or to fulfill needs.

In more extreme forms, symbolic murder turns into stealthy manipulation of people and events in order to bring about the envied person's hoped-for misfortune. Letters are sent "from a friend" to the appropriately inappropriate parties. Casual remarks are dropped in full hearing of those most likely to initiate further gossip.

When any opportunity for such manipulation arises, almost everyone feels a compulsion to seize it. True, "normal"

La Rochefoucauld

People have an extraordinary ability to bear the misfortunes of others.

Symbolic Murders

"Go home. I don't mind staying late and missing dinner again."

"Hello. This is your mother. Remember me?"

"Darling, I loved your performance. I argued with everyone."

people stop short of wreaking real destruction upon others, but they seldom stop short of revealing something they have been asked to keep to themselves or, more common, wishing in that twilight border between the conscious and the unconscious that another will not receive a promotion or some honor for which he has been nominated.

Symbolic murder is easy enough to control and altogether stop. As soon as its causes are truly recognized, we can catch ourselves in the act of slipping in the symbolic dagger and laugh inwardly at our own absurdity. The trick is to know that one can be absurd and worthy at the same time.

Fear of Aging

Lying about one's age, dyeing one's hair, having a face lift (for those who can afford it), strenuously dieting, running—in general, being obsessed with the need to look, feel, and act young—all are symptoms of a death attitude that may *not,* after all, stem from the fear of death itself.

Everyone nurtures some fear of death. No thanatologist on earth would counsel people not to have such a fear or to suppress it when it shows up. It is part of being human to think of death as not being a particularly pleasant experience and to agree with what is written on W. C. Fields's tombstone: "On the whole, I'd rather be in Philadelphia."

Since everyone fears death to an extent but not everyone is obsessed with the pursuit of youth, it would seem to follow that the desperate (not the ordinary but the *desperate)* fear of aging stems from a different source. This, according to some thanatologists, is likely to be *a sense of failure.* One tries to deny to oneself or actually to cover up the telltale signs of age, not because life is so wonderful and every moment is precious, but because life is so unsuccessful that one cannot stand to think about how little time is left and how slim are the chances that success is ever going to be achieved.

In addition to everything else, ours is a success-oriented nation. The need not only to compete but to win is drummed into us almost from the beginning. True, slogans are flashed at us like ". . . it's how you play the game," but one cannot imagine many players being indifferent to winning.

To have won in some form of competition, to know that one is the best at something, is apparently not enough for

---

We are surrounded by:

"Number One" (almost anything)

The Top Forty

The Triple Crown

The Academy Awards

Tonys

Emmys

Grammys

The Ten Best Dressed . . .

The Pulitzer Prize

The Nobel Prize

Miss America, Ms. America, Mrs. America, Mr. America

Fortune 500 (top business executives)

Most Valuable Player Awards

Super Bowl

World Series

League Standings

Hall of Fame

Olympics gold, silver and bronze medals

Weekly TV ratings

---

most winners. Success must be marked by an external symbol: a newspaper headline, a wall plaque, a trophy, a medal, one's name engraved on the cup. Success in business means having gone up the ladder (see Chapter 3 for a fuller discussion of vertical imagery), and this form of winning also demands its symbols. It is not enough to have the power to effect significant changes in a company's product or policy. One must be *known* to have this power. Hence we crave a private office with a name on the door; a desk larger than the next person's, and at least one more window; a title, of course (never mind what it signifies, just as long as it is impressive); a prestige car; a big house in a prestige neighborhood; children attending prestige colleges; membership and offices in prestige organizations and so on.

Joe Namath

When you win, nothing hurts.

The reader may well argue "What's wrong with success?" The answer: nothing at all. Nor is there anything "wrong" with enjoying the good things success makes possible (except that big cars and big houses can be counterproductive to individual efforts at cutting down on the excessive use of energy). The real problem with success is that *by definition* it cannot be shared by all. No one can win a race unless somebody loses. No one can become president of the company unless there remain rank-and-file employees down below to comprise the company large enough to require a president.

What happens then is that people who continue not to win, not to be promoted, not to possess the symbols of power and status come to believe there is something wrong with them. The sense of failure grows, often deepened by feedback from others: "You've been with the company fifteen years, and where has it gotten you?" "I guess you were born to sit on the bench." "Are you *still* doing the same thing?"

If all of one's acquaintances were also "failures," the problem would shrink in size. But in the inevitable course of things, close friends begin to drift apart as one begins to move ahead of the other. Office executives rarely go to lunch with machine workers, no matter how inseparable they may once have been. In what we call a democratic society, work continues to be measured in other than human terms.

The spirit of competition may make for a healthy and free society in many respects, but being unsuccessful in the race can create a terrible self image unless one decides *in advance* that, if good things fail to happen, one will manage nicely anyhow. For the majority, however, adjustment to what is viewed as mediocrity does not come easily.

Vince Lombardi

Winning isn't everything. It's the only thing.

As age begins to manifest itself—graying of hair, crowsfeet around the eyes, the inevitable slowing down—the specter of failure can seem more and more grotesque and mocking. There is one inner sense of failure that almost everyone can share, even those who have achieved money, status, and power, and that is a suspicion that one is beginning to lose—or has already lost—his/her sexual attractiveness. Even if indifferent to not having the big car and the big house, it takes a superhuman effort to have no concern for physical good looks and the youth we believe to be indispensable to sexual success.

Where sex roles are defined by society and remain more or less rigid, as is indeed the case in nearly all Western cultures, women are expected to remain trim and youthful as long as possible, and men are expected to remain strong and sexually aggressive. The growing sense of personal inadequacy is experienced with particular intensity by the Western male, who can become preoccupied with maintaining an ability to "perform" as a sexual partner. If statistics from psychologists can be trusted, extraordinary numbers of aging males are afraid of impotency.

Knowing that people will pay a great deal of money to retain a youthful appearance, cosmetics manufacturers are sitting on top of one of the world's most lucrative empires. Despite the growing tendency among younger women to avoid make-up and keep a "natural look," sales of lipstick, rouge, mascara, eye shadow, foundation creams, and the like continue to grow year by year. Hair dyeing, which used to be a behavior exclusive to older women, is now shared by men. Both sexes have their faces lifted. Both sexes are now jogging and working out in gyms.

Again, one must be reminded that the *activity* of staying fit and youthful looking is not the issue. Fitness programs are, of course, to be recommended. Having a healthy outlook on death does not mean you should refrain from taking adequate measures to live as long and as happily as possible. The *real* issue here is the motivation. If you stay fit for the sake of health, fine. If you dye your hair or have a face lift out of an obsessive fear of aging and an obsessive dissatisfaction with life, you should recognize that the outward appearance will do nothing to ease the inner tension.

The Rules of Age

Not everyone struggles to maintain the look of youth. Overeating, another symptom of death attitudes, can make middle age hard to disguise. The sense of unworth previously discussed can convince a person that he or she will never be attractive anyway and must always be rejected, so why bother? In other words, we can find just as many people showing their age as hiding it. Is this a sign of adjustment to life's inevitable course? Not necessarily.

Whatever the physical appearance, some people, largely

out of social conditioning, develop a sense that there are rules governing each age, rules which decree which behaviors are appropriate or not. Thus it is all right for teenagers to get out on the dance floor and go through a variety of bodily contortions, but not for a 40-year-old. Swimming, surfing, and water-skiing are beach activities permissible for the young, but "unbecoming" to an older person. Young people have their kind of parties, while their parents have a different kind. Young people are not supposed to hang around with older people, and older people are segregated from the young.

Age barriers exist throughout our society, and they can be a fertile source of death attitudes. As activities and locations one by one become "unavailable," as membership cards in certain age groups expire, together with all of the rights and privileges, it becomes for some people a little like watching the lights go out in the stadium when the game is over. Gone are the crowds, gone is the excitement. What is left in life?

Clubs for the elderly, "leisure village" retirement communities catering to retired people bring a renewed sense of inclusion which can compensate for some of the *ex*clusion that has taken place. It should not, however, be *necessary* for people to remain mired in the customs, values, activities, the tribal rites, of any special age group. People should feel free to engage in whatever activities they have the time and energy for, without regard for "how it looks" and "what the others will say."

Priority Lists

Death attitudes apply not only to one's own life-denying behavior. They extend to our plans for other people's lives. Thus the son or daughter who is embarrassed because a parent comes into the forbidden party room and joins the crowd is being constrained by a rigid sense of what is appropriate for that parent. Everyone constructs priority lists. One such list is that of actions deemed acceptable in rank order. The parent may decide that number one on the list for the daughter is a good marriage to an attractive young man from a well connected family. The daughter may have different priorities. Perhaps number one on her list is being free of parental guidance or pursuing a career in baseball.

Most of us insist upon manipulating—or attempting to manipulate—the events and people around us, to bring reality

---

Benjamin Disraeli

Youth is a blunder; manhood a struggle; old age a regret.

Maurice Chevalier

Growing old isn't so bad when you consider the alternative.

Priority lists spring from an "If I had my way" approach to life. Wisdom springs from knowing when you don't have your way.

into closer conformity with our priorities. At one time or another each of us constructs a mental list of priority acquaintances, lovers, and marriage prospects. Somehow, circumstances "conspire" to rearrange our lists for us, for of course we have a talent for making our lists without consulting reality first. Perhaps the most precious list of all, the one we can least bear to see changed, is that which indicates the order in which we are willing to lose our loved ones to death.

For the young, grandparents come first, then parents, then siblings. Young people are often vague in placing themselves on the list, perhaps because in youth the death of oneself always appears less possible than the death of anyone else. As they grow older, people develop a clearer perspective about where they belong on the list. Thus parents imagine themselves as dying before their children. Because of the priority lists, society has developed the concept of "premature" and "untimely" death. Such inner documents make it doubly hard to adjust to sudden, accidental deaths and create a sense of unfairness when the priority list is violated.

Unpleasant as the brutal truth may be for many to face, the habit of listing can also make people feel negatively about those who "outlive their time." If grandfather is supposed to have died at a respectable age—say, 75—and is still here at 90, requiring care, those responsible for his well-being can easily harbor secret resentment at the "bad turn" life has given them. People sometimes tell an octogenarian, "You look so well for your age. I only hope I look as well as you . . . oh, but there's no chance *I'll* live that long." Perhaps such words are comforting to the octogenarian, but they can be a sign that the "well wisher" thinks *no one* should live beyond a certain age. No doubt the words could be reconsidered when the well wisher hits 79.

The plain fact of the matter is that no time clock exists in the natural world. Living systems go through cycles and inevitably die, and yes, certain *average* life spans can be computed. But averages are only ideas. They have nothing to do with all the possibilities. It could be wiser to keep as few lists as possible in the library of the mind.

Models of Life-Affirmation

If negative attitudes and internal imagery exist to dampen people's lives and cause them to "die" many times over before the actual and unique moment of true physical death, then it should follow—and it does—that positive attitudes and positive images are possible. One need only remember the advice of Epictetus the Stoic: "Death is not terrible, but the thought that death is terrible is a terrible thing." A more contemporary corollary: "We have nothing to fear but fear itself."

No one is talking here of shallow optimism, of spur-of-the-moment good feelings. The issue here is the profound realization that the potential for a productive, exciting life belongs to each of us. *We* control our attitudes —that is, we can if we allow ourselves to. Of course, others—society and the media—will influence those attitudes if we allow *them* to.

Life-affirmation, as opposed to death attitudes, is recognizing that real death happens only once and, in a sense, does not "happen" to us at all. We are no longer feeling sensation at the exact moment; for most people conscious sensation has terminated considerably before the stroke of death. Even in cases involving "sudden" death, such as a plane crash, there have been testimonies given just seconds before the end. Pilots of doomed planes have even spoken into tape recorders, indicating an unexpected sense of tranquility, sometimes even of exhilaration. Apparently, whatever force lies behind our lives makes it possible for them to end in a nontraumatic way. Death has been around for so very long it makes sense to suppose it "knows" how to manage by now.

The Phoenix

An ancient and enduring symbol of life-affirmation is that of the Phoenix, a mythological bird of rare and exotic plumage and supernatural powers. The Greek historian Herodotus reported that the Phoenix actually existed and was known to have visited the Egyptians every 500 years. The Roman belief was that each era bears witness to the birth of one and only one Phoenix bird, that it lives for a very long time and that, at the moment of its death, it generates a worm, which becomes the Phoenix for the next age.

Yet another version of the legend has it that the Phoenix is a bird from India which lives for 500 years and then flies to a secret temple, where he is burned to ashes upon the

---

Philippe Aries

When Launcelot . . . realized . . . he was about to die . . . he removed his weapons and lay down quietly upon the ground.

altar, only to rise from the ashes three days later, now young and resplendent.

In folklore, poetry, and song; in fiction, drama, and epic, the Phoenix has endured through time as a symbol of rebirth, new growth, regeneration, and redemption. Religions have counterpart symbols: gods who die or descend into the underworld, there to remain for a time, and then to rise, reborn and renewed.

The Phoenix has given structure to many masterworks, such as Dante's *Divine Comedy,* in which the poet, seeking a vision of God in Paradise, must first travel through the very depths of hell before his wish is granted. The Phoenix, whether consciously or not has suggested to many people certain ways of thinking about events. Thus does "I've been through hell" often preface an account of some happier turn of events, or at least invite the listener to effect a happy change for the sufferer through lavish sympathy or some other sign of affection. People say, "I'm going to pull myself out of this." Even the popular exhortation "Lift yourself up by your own bootstraps" has underlying innuendos of the Phoenix myth, for there exists within the bird the creative thrust to soar from its own ashes.

Nor is the Phoenix merely an empty symbol, a literary convention with no basis in reality. If we stop to think of it, the whole phenomenon of existence is Phoenix-oriented, not death-oriented.

Natural Cycles

In human negative thinking, death is final, the end, KAPUT! No such finality exists in the real world. Whether planned this way by a rational deity or evolved this way through some inner sense of order or simply by accident (though many of the greatest philosophers *and* scientists have a hard time believing so), the natural world seems "dedicated" to perpetuation and continuity. There seem to be cycles everywhere: the seasons, the ecosystem, the rhythm and balance of birth and death.

In one sense many things "die." By any kind of thumb except a green one, plants have a way of expiring when touched. Animal and human life ceases to exist *in a particular form.* But like plants, living things revert to the natural world and are caught up in the nitrogen cycle. If people were

---

A Death Model:

I've already taken the qualifying exam for the third time. Now I'm out for good. I'll never amount to anything.

•
•
•

•
•
•

A Phoenix Model:

I'm obviously not suited for that kind of work. Let me see . . .

willing to allow the bodies of loved ones to be placed beneath the ground without embalming and without caskets, the chemical process, not of disintegration but *re*integration, would begin to take place immediately.

Obviously this sense of "dying" is a human conception; to change form is not to die. It is alarming to realize how one-way-oriented humanity has become. All of nature appears to offer the cycle model, and yet we humans have created as many noncycles as we can think of. Individual and personal consciousness have been given such central importance in many cultures of the world that the loss of private awareness seems a disaster for which the physical facts of nature cannot compensate. In addition, with breathtaking ingenuity we have created non-biodegradable products (plastic milk cartons, for example). Instead of foreseeing a time when energy derived from fossil fuel must be exhausted, we embarked years ago upon a reckless depletion of the earth's fuel resources. So now we are facing the imminent *death of energy,* a condition not metaphoric but tragically real. It almost seems as though we have decided that, since we must perish as individuals, we may as well take everything with us.

The golden sun,
The planets, all the
  infinite host of heaven,
Are shining on the sad
  abodes of death,
Through the still lapse
  of ages.
    William Cullen Bryant

Cosmic Thoughts

We probably think on too small a scale, beginning with the obsession with ourselves. All you have to do is stand outside at night on a windy plain and look up at the awesome reaches of space, and the very idea of personal importance takes on a different perspective. Admittedly you face a giant step in moving outside self-preoccupation. But it can and does work.

For one thing, there is nothing to lose. Intelligence,

creativity, talent—whatever distinguishing characteristics go to make a person THAT person and no other, will still be there, no worse for the turning off of the spotlight. The depression that comes with aging and proximity to physical death can become minimal. After all, existence only seems assured for an indefinite length of time. If it ceases to matter *terribly* that one special existence is not assured indefinitely, then death as an idea begins to fade.

Recent scientific possibilities have suggested a stupendous change in the manner of thinking about existence. There actually *may* be principles at work which ensure the indefinite on-goingness of everything. One principle is the "big bang" theory, according to which the universe began from a huge explosion of a densely packed mass and is continuing to explode. The other principle is the "black hole" theory, according to which every bit of matter in the universe is being driven by the law of gravity down, down into another densely packed mass—as though driven by a cosmic garbage comprejssor.

The two principles, on the face of it, are contradictory. The big bang theory suggests indefinite expansion, the black hole theory, indefinite contraction. But some scientists are now speculating on the possibility that, as matter contracts through gravity and is compressed into such dense masses that it becomes invisible to us (hence "black holes" in space), the big bang continues to occur on the other side of the holes. That is, matter compresses indefinitely, only to re-explode indefinitely. If the relationship between the two principles proves to be accurate, then the universe becomes a perpetual cycle of expansion/contraction. The big bang seeks infinite explosion outward; the black hole seeks to lure all of matter back downward.

Whether we fully comprehend or accept such speculation is less important than the psychological effect of expansion/contraction internal imagery. If we begin to think in such terms, we begin to accept at least the possibility that existence is not a phenomenon which can cease. Personal death can seem dwarfed by the thought that the universe has caught hold of a built-in immortality process.

Life-Affirming Attitudes

Armed with legendary and scientific models, not to mention religious Phoenix symbols like "born again

---

John Keats

On the shore of the wide world I stand alone, and think Till love and fame to nothingness do sink.

baptism" or confession and absolution, one can set about making personal applications and developing "Phoenix strategies" which can combat the idea of premature death.

One can, for example, replace pyramids with circles as dominant inner images. In pyramid imagery, one visualizes oneself as rising through the ranks (of life, in one's job, etc.), reaching a peak or crest, and then being "over the hill." Whereas in circle imagery, one's life can be like a ferris wheel, rising, reaching a crest, going back down, and *then* starting up all over again.

You can consider you "lost" a job, or you can consider you are changing one phase of life, only to begin another. You can experience the end of love (the *death* of romance) or you can reach a new beginning, looking forward with excitement to the next love, which will inevitably come along. The great baseball catcher, Yogi Berra, once said, "It ain't over 'til it's over," a hopeful reminder for more than the last-inning scoreboard.

There are recycling, Phoenix-oriented ways of living each day, such as:

> rearranging the furniture
>
> changing routes going to or coming from
>
> deciding to do everything during one day in a totally different manner
>
> changing hair style
>
> buying a new outfit
>
> writing a long-delayed letter
>
> telephoning someone out of town
>
> walking out on a distasteful obligation

The sheer act of will involved, the realization that one is in control of one's internal imagery can be the beginning of a whole new way of living: living *without dying.*

But probably most important is the *forgiveness ritual,* which one can and should indulge in every so often. This ritual involves sitting quietly in a corner, concentrating very hard on all of the guilt one has accumulated, gathering up all of the negative thoughts one can possibly muster and compressing them into a tight ball, and then—calmly and deliberately—hurling the ball straight up toward the sky. It is possible to do this, to let the ball of guilt go where it may. It is even possible to imagine the ball of guilt suddenly transformed into a resplendent bird winging its way over a cloud, becoming lost in an obscure blue paradise, and never being heard from again.

Chapter 14 Footnotes

[1]"The Man Against the Sky" from COLLECTED POEMS of Edwin Arlington Robinson. Copyright 1916 by Edwin Arlington Robinson, renewed 1944 by Ruth Nivison.

[2]Anne Sexton, "Live," *Live or Die* (Boston: Houghton-Mifflin, 1966). © 1966 by Anne Sexton.

[3]Elisabeth Kübler-Ross, *On Death and Dying* (New York: Macmillan, 1969), p. 5.

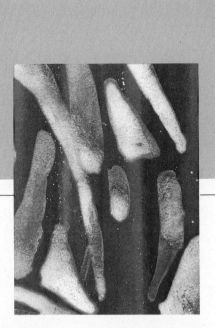

15 REMAINING ROADS TO FREEDOM

Overview

Thus far we the authors have attempted to steer as straight a course as possible through many issues raised in connection with the subjects "what it means to be human" and "how to practice the art of being human to the best of one's ability." Implicit in the determination not to be overwhelmingly one-sided about, say, the true definition of love or whether modern art is more or less satisfying than the art of the past, is an assumption on which the authors *do* take a definite stand: namely, that humanism means *making intelligent choices among significant options.*

Therefore, when it comes to the issue of the freedom to make such choices, humanism cannot be many-sided. It is fundamental to the humanism of any age that one must be free to go up or down the human ladder, free to develop one's human potential or allow it to lie dormant. Why praise poets, philosophers, artists, and scientists who have made notable contributions to the human cause unless these noteworthy individuals have been free not to be great, but instead chose to work tirelessly toward that greatness?

That freedom is, or should be, the basic human condition is also implicit in the attitude of Western tourists returning from a visit to India and reporting a sense of depression upon witnessing the poverty in the streets. "How can human beings live like that?" they ask, meaning that something should be done, that no one should have to remain a street beggar for his or her entire life. The natural horror we feel when reading accounts of Nazi atrocities inflicted on 7 million Jews, or the slaughter of innocent people in Uganda, surely implies the unshakeable conviction that human beings deserve far better fates and that *those who deny them such fates are that much less human.*

To suggest that these are matters of opinion, or subject to cultural relativity or political situations, is to throw the whole humanist perspective into a state of hopeless confusion.

On the other hand, there *are* those who insist that the humanist cause is a futile one, founded on a lie—the lie that

> human beings are really free, or
>
> they really want to be free, or
>
> being free, they tend to choose the better of two courses.

Why, for example, did the Nazis choose to murder seven million Jews? If they were free to not follow Hitler, why didn't they do so? If they became robots under Hitler's fiery oratory, then surely this suggests a basic weakness in the human fiber.

From Atilla the Hun to the most recent genocidal despots, history offers appalling examples of inhumanities inflicted on people by their own kind; if freedom is a natural human condition, the numbers who have chosen to ignore this must be reckoned with. At any rate, those who have freedom choose to deny it to others. Are the exploiters controlled by some base passion that may be "just as" fundamental to the human race as the urge to freedom?

Or is freedom merely the dream of those who find themselves oppressed?

Baron d'Holbach

In all this he always acts according to necessary laws, from which he has no means of emancipating himself.

Carlton Beck

Man is free. This is at once a heady luxury and also the source of his discontent.

It is necessary to confront these questions, for if there *is* no natural condition as freedom, then the humanist ideal is open to serious question. How is one to choose among significant alternatives if someone else sets up the confines within which one is forced to live?

Exploiters and Exploited: The View That Humans Are Naturally Aggressive

A number of philosophies dispute the idea that freedom, at least for all, is a natural human condition; philosophies draw parallels between the human kingdom and the animal kingdom, pointing to the fierce and bitter struggle for

survival which takes place in both. In nature, they say, no creature is free except to follow *its* nature, which is to be either the exploiter or the exploited.

Rousseau's Man with the Stick

> **If there is no natural condition as freedom, then the humanist ideal is open to serious question.**

One of the staunchest advocates of the philosophy of total and unlimited freedom for all was Jean-Jacques Rousseau (1712–1778), considered by many as the conscious architect of the French Revolution, by some as the indirect architect of modern society, and by at least one French historian as the one individual most responsible for all of the *evils* in that society.

In fanning the revolutionary flames beginning to sweep through a France becoming increasingly outraged at the decadence of the aristocracy and the gross injustices suffered by the common people, Rousseau constructed a mythical account of the origin of the species, to prove that freedom was both a natural condition and a natural right.

Called *A Discourse on the Origins of Inequality,* the myth draws a romantic picture of a lost Age of Innocence, when early people lived in peace and harmony, sharing the fruits of the abundant earth through a common realization that nature provided equal bounty for everyone. At this time no laws or government existed, because obviously law and government are not necessary when everyone is happy and there is no crime.

Then one day came the Man with the Stick, the first person to take it into his head to grab off more than his natural share of things, the first person to *abuse* nature's gift of freedom by putting it to his own advantage. With his stick he carved out a private piece of territory for himself.

> *The first man, who, after enclosing a piece of ground, took it into his head to say, "This is mine," and found people simple enough to believe him, was the true founder of civil society.*

The Man with the Stick was the founder of society because, by creating the model of the exploiter, by establishing for all time the inhuman alternative to natural freedom, he and his followers became an ever-present threat to the rights of the others and therefore had to be suppressed by the gradual development of law, government, and all other institutions dedicated to the curtailment, the limitation of rights.

Rousseau's position is clearly a revolutionary one. Revolution, even if violent, is a genuine alternative to exploitation and may often be the only means by which to deal with it. The first revolution would have been peaceful, however.

How many crimes, how many wars, how many murders, how many misfortunes and horrors, would that man have saved the human species, who pulling up the stakes or filling up the ditches should have cried to his fellows: Be sure not to listen to this impostor; you are lost if you forget that the fruits of the earth belong equally to us all, and the earth itself to nobody!

Rousseau profoundly believed that a violent revolution in France would rattle the corrupt air and, with its thunder and bloody rain, cleanse the country, and bring a new dawn of peace and prosperity. But what he does not explain in his myth is the origin of the Man with the Stick. What made this one man decide to become possessive? Or does the potential for exploitation lie deep within *every* member of that "innocent" society?

In asserting that repressive social institutions were the only logical way to deal with the exploiters, Rousseau made them seem inevitable, especially if the Man with the Stick was a typical human being with aggressive tendencies. How could one revolution crush forever all future Men with Sticks? In other words, what Rousseau did *not* do is explain how it would be possible to exist without the social institutions to deal with the exploiters. And what Rousseau did not know, because he died a decade before the Revolution, was that Napoleon would rise from the ashes of France and usher in a new age of exploitation, perhaps even more oppressive than the one it supplanted.

Rousseau's myth of the Age of Innocence has never been documented. We shall never know whether most people, left without law or government, would remain peaceful and willing to share the fruits of the earth with each other, or whether even more Men with Sticks would continue to arise and exploit the others. What does seem certain is that no revolution within human memory has been without its

Alexander Pope

Lo, the poor Indian!
  whose untutored mind
Sees God in clouds, or
  hears Him in the wind;
His soul, proud science
  never taught to stray
Far as the solar walk or
  milky way.

exploiters. History appears to demonstrate that the revolutionary leader, the fierce idealist who denounces the corruption wrought by the dehumanized institutions of society, generally becomes the next exploiter. In 1959 Fidel Castro led revolutionary forces in Cuba against what was condemned as a dictatorship, only to establish a totalitarian government, which curtailed freedom so that no new dictatorship might arise.

Nietzsche: Masters and Slaves

Friedrich Nietzsche, who was discussed in Chapter 6 in connection with the Apollo/Dionysus polarity, was more than concerned—he was *obsessed*—with the problem of the exploiter. For Nietzsche, no God imposed a definite meaning or purpose on life. Existence therefore belonged to the person who could define it and persuade others he or she was right. All values were relative, and the person who could convince everyone else of certain "truths" would prevail. Whether the truths were "true" or not did not matter, so long as people were willing to accept them.

Nietzsche thus divided society into two classes of people: masters and slaves. The masters were those who assumed they could prevail, and, in the absence of serious opposition, *did* prevail. The slaves were those who allowed it to happen, whose self-concepts were so low that they were willing to be exploited—would, in fact, *rather* be exploited than live in confusion, without guidelines or direction.

Nietzsche coined the label *übermensch,* or superman, to refer to the master who proved eminently successful in imposing his own vision of reality, his own value system, upon others. In his view, Jesus Christ was the very model of the superman. Nietzsche never for a moment believed that Jesus was a supernatural being, but he marveled at Jesus's ability to sway a crowd. Nietzsche saw that Jesus was able to convince millions that he was the son of God, sent down to earth by his father to redeem humankind. What concerned Nietzsche was not the authenticity of the claim, but the model that Jesus represented. It could be possible for someone equally visionary to rise up, step forward, and claim to be the vehicle of the Divine Voice.

Nietzsche also believed that people born into a "slave" background, that is, belonging to a group of people

---

John Dryden

I am as free as Nature
  first made man,
Ere the base laws of
  servitude began,
When wild in woods the
  noble savage ran.

having the slave mentality, would develop their parents' self-negation. People would not claim a right to freedom if all they ever heard in the home was that no one in the family deserved much of anything, and should be grateful for whatever charity those "better" than they (i.e., the "masters") wished to grant. For Nietzsche, the slave outlook valued virtues such as charity, love, altruism, caring, but the master outlook valued power, strength, cleverness, manipulation, and all of the characteristics which lent stability to the human enterprise. The "Master" honored traits that could restrain the impulses of the slave mentality.

Nietzsche believed no one was necessarily intended to be either a slave or a master. That is, human nature did not automatically place a person in one category or the other. But human nature *did* tend to narrow itself down to two alternatives. Nietzsche believed the choice was a matter of laziness versus aggressiveness. Some people had sluggish metabolisms perhaps, while others were hell-bent on bettering themselves no matter at whose expense. In any event, if Nietzsche is accurate, it seems clear that the urge for freedom is not shared by all. Some people are far happier allowing themselves to be led.

It's Easier to be Exploited

Nietzsche may have been right about a great many people who seem comfortable with a "slave mentality," who would rather be exploited than have to think for themselves or be in any position of power. Power, after all, dictates responsibility, creativity, vision. A position of lowly subservience seems easier, inevitable, suggesting no need for the energy or discipline required of those who want to better themselves.

To accept a status of inferiority implies no need to continue education, read books, or do anything else to broaden one's perspective. Instead, endless time can be spent standing around and complaining about working conditions, salaries, and those who appear to be receiving preferential treatment. After all, if the person complaining were suddenly wafted into power and had an obligation to improve things, he or she might decide that things were not so bad after all. So much better as far as *he* (or *she*)is concerned, that to remain a sunny, smiling slave, and have no obligation other than to complain seems to be a great option.

Karl Marx: The Determinism of Money

Not humanity, not nature, but money calls the turn—so believed Karl Marx (1818–1883), a German-born Jewish philosopher, who, in the opinion of many intellectual historians, singlehandedly altered the destiny of the human race. The ideas contained in the *The Communist Manifesto,* published in 1843 and authored by Marx and his colleague Friedrich Engels (1820–1895) changed the world.

Had it not been for Marx and Engels, there would be no Union of Soviet Socialist Republics today, no Peoples Republic of China; no Iron Curtain; probably no American involvement in Korea and Vietnam. Even Neil Armstrong's walk on the moon in 1970 and the entire space program were part of the American need to get to the moon before the Russians did.

So far, this book has been concerned with a number of polarities—opposite approaches, like Apollo and Dionysus, tragedy and comedy, faith and science, and so on. But no pair of opposites is more powerful than that of capitalism and socialism. They influence virtually every aspect of human life and have polarized the world. The fate of humanity may hinge on which philosophy more accurately reflects what people need, want, or will ultimately allow.

As a young intellectual Karl Marx fell under the strong influence of an earlier German philosopher Georg Wilhelm Friedrich Hegel (1770–1831), who had developed two massive theories pertaining to the workings of 1) the human mind and 2) history. Both theories were to be absorbed and then reinterpreted by Marx.

Hegel's logic is based on how the mind operates. Like everything else in nature, the mind seems to oscillate back and forth between poles, and to strive for a balance between them. First one begins with a *thesis,* the conviction that something is true. Immediately the thesis is countered by its own opposite, which Hegel called the *antithesis.* But the mind by nature cannot accept contradictions, so it automatically seeks a point midway between the two, called the *synthesis.*

Hegel called this method of thinking *the dialectic.* It does not work for all cases. One cannot reach a proper synthesis

---

George Bernard Shaw

We should have had socialism already, but for the socialists.

John F. Kennedy

Those who make peaceful revolution impossible will make violent revolution inevitable.

Thesis:

Only the Apollonian approach to life can work.

Antithesis:

Only the Dionysian approach can work.

Synthesis:

A combination of the Apollonian and Dionysian can work.

---

without starting out with a thesis statement that legitimately attracts its own opposite. The dialectic will not work, for example, for a conviction like "Death is not the end of one's being." Obviously such a belief is entertained through faith alone. If one has no faith, one cannot make the statement at all. It is meaningless, and as such, it can have no opposite. But there *is* an Apollonian approach to life through order and discipline. There *is* an opposite, and it must be considered; for everyone knows that many people do very well without order and discipline. The logician in this example has no choice but to admit that neither the Apollonian nor the Dionysian can work by excluding the other.

Hegel applied the dialectic method of thinking to his own theory of history, which he viewed as *the inevitable progress of humanity toward total freedom.* In the dialectic method, both poles—the thesis and the antithesis—are limited by what they say. If the thesis statement is positive, then it is limited by not including the negative. The same holds true in reverse for the antithesis statement. But the synthesis statement is therefore not limited, for it includes *both* the positive and the negative. Hegel saw human history as a continual shuttling back and forth between political and social systems, all of them limiting in some way. But inevitably he envisioned a world of people freed from all limitations.

Marx, much impressed by Hegel's logic and theory of history, refashioned both in his own terms. The result was *dialectical materialism,* the application of Hegel's principles to what Marx believed to be the concrete reality of human life, namely, economics. For Marx, the name of the game was money, not freedom; and the course of human history was the inevitable movement toward an *economic synthesis,* in which the balance of power was held neither by the bourgeoisie (thesis) nor the proletariat (antithesis), but belonged equally to all in the classless society.

Marx believed that capitalism, the inevitable outgrowth of humankind's natural competitive and aggressive tendencies, could maintain itself only through the exploitation of the working class. But unlike Nietzsche, who said that the exploited (slave class) accepted exploitation rather than do anything about it, Marx was convinced the exploited would rise up in revolution, overthrow the bourgeoisie, and pave the way for a utopian worker's paradise.

Contemporary Marxists often ignore a crucial point: Marx himself, logician that he was, had no choice but to prophesy the inevitable downfall of the classless society itself. For if there were a logic to history, if human beings were only puppets in the hands of vast economic forces beyond their control, why should history stop at any point? The cycle would have to repeat itself, as the classless society generated its own opposite, and a new synthesis was achieved. The current state of tension between the Soviet Union and the People's Republic of China may suggest a kind of thesis-antithesis conflict within the socialist world.

A crucial point of difference between Hegel and Marx—aside from the stress on economics—is the issue of freedom. It might seem obvious that a classless society would mean freedom for all, but it does not.

There is no true communism anywhere in practice on a large scale, no complete public ownership of all businesses and services. There is socialism, which is part public and part private ownership. When socialism prevails, the government becomes *all* powerful; otherwise the private sector might become *too* powerful. Governmental power in both Russia and China has silenced dissidents and strictly censored ideas conveyed in books and films. To have a worker's paradise, there must be strong enforcement from the top. Far from representing the synthesis Marx predicted, socialist governments exclude anyone with conflicting viewpoints. Private enterprise of a limited kind is permitted not because the government wishes to include an alternative economic system, but because total collectivism simply does not work. Even limited collectivism has to be controlled in order to work as well as it does.

Powerful government subsidy of the arts has resulted in

Marx

The freedom and independence of the worker during the labor process do not exist.

Lenin

When the state exists, there is no freedom. When there is freedom, there will be no state.

enviable achievements among socialist countries, where a great deal of money can be lavished on cultural activities. In the United States, opera, ballet, and theater have to fend for themselves, requesting donations from wealthy patrons. There are a few state opera and theater companies, but even this much subsidy could be taken away if the voters sought a referendum on the subject.

It is interesting to note, however, that the most clearly flourishing arts in socialist nations are musical. Since music is nonverbal and without words, it cannot tell the rest of the world anything negative about life on the other side of the curtain. But literature *can*. Perhaps this explains why only the approved writers remain subsidized and why so many disapproved writers are exiled.

In capitalist societies the usual argument against government subsidy of the arts is that money means control, and control can lead to censorship. Thus, in order to have free expression of *all* of the arts, the capitalist system works best, even though many artists who cannot achieve economic success must drop out of the race.

But the humanist who may long for some kind of government assistance in the development of the arts, who points out that the money allotted to the National Endowment for the Humanities, for example, is a comparatively small amount, is also likely to insist on freedom of thought and freedom of speech. Few, if any, humanists have ever come out in favor of the suppression of such freedoms, though there *have* been times when the whole truth may not have served the best interests of society. Nonetheless the humanist position has traditionally been a liberal one, willing to suffer the consequences of "too much truth" rather than to support the least denial of the right to cry out in protest, regardless of *whose* feathers are ruffled.

Winston Churchill

The inherent vice of capitalism is the unequal sharing of blessings; the inherent virtue of socialism is the equal sharing of miseries.

The Classical Position of Capitalism

Classically, the descendants of the first capitalists have argued that their lineage goes back to the missing link, to the first primates whose society ever had even a trace of organization. Their position has been and continues to be one of the acceptance and practice of what they consider basic human nature. Competitiveness and struggle, for them, represent nature's way of managing things human.

The humanist position has traditionally been a liberal one, willing to suffer the consequences of 'too much truth.'

B. F. Skinner

When I once asked a Russian economist why men will work when all food, clothing, and housing are free, he replied with a confident smile, 'for the common good,' but that is by no means certain.

The publication of Darwin's *Origin of Species* in 1859 gave capitalism a strong scientific boost, though that was hardly the work's intention. Spokespeople for the *laissez faire* theory of economics, whereby the government stays out of big business, often cited the "fair game" approach to business as a working out on the economic level of Darwin's law of natural selection, popularly known as the "survival of the fittest." That "the survival of the richest" may have had nothing to do with biology did not stop those who attempted to mix philosophy, science, and business.

Advocates of capitalist economy, who opposed Marxist views in the nineteenth century, said that a classless society was about as unnatural a thing as anyone could imagine. One response to Darwin's theory of natural selection was a movement known as Social Darwinism, which looked upon competition as natural and right. The English philosopher Herbert Spencer (1820–1903) developed a new system of morality he called *naturalistic ethics,* based on the contention that people must function not as spiritual creatures made and instructed by God, but as animals, children of nature, heeding natural instincts. Not only economic competitiveness but relative freedom in sexuality was sanctioned by this system.

General William S. Booth (1829–1912), founder of the Salvation Army, did not choose a military label and general style for his organization by accident. His own title came not from actual service to Her Majesty on the battlefield but from his fame as a revivalist, and perhaps his aggressiveness in saving souls. The fierce dedication of Booth and his loyal followers sprang from the profound conviction that in competitive society the devil was fighting for souls, just as everyone else was struggling for money. He believed that a certain number of souls inevitably went to the devil, for evil persisted. By the same token, a certain number of poor must always exist in any civilized society. In a book called *In Darkest England and the Way Out* Booth made an appeal for charity, but the work is virtually a defense of capitalist economy. It is inevitable, says Booth, that the rich should increase their wealth, but they should never forget those who are less fortunate. Booth equates charity with economic success, and economic success with God's bounty. Thus did the natural man of the Social Darwinists join forces with the Christian man of the Salvation Army.

Not long afterward John D. Rockefeller I said much the same thing. The economic struggle is right and natural, for it exists in a world under God's own providence. In his autobiography Rockefeller attributes all of his success to God's favor and implies that the philanthropy he practiced all of his life was one means of showing appreciation for that favor.

In 1959 a panel of economists hired by the Rockefeller Foundation to make an exhaustive study of the American system came up with the (expected) statement that economic success was and had always been a providential matter, placing spiritual obligations upon the fortunate.

A much earlier work by a German economist was *The Protestant Ethic and the Rise of Capitalism,* which placed the entire roots of the capitalist system in the Puritans' belief in predestination. As God had ordained which souls would be saved and which damned, so too, according to this version of Protestant thinking, must God have ordained who would succeed and who would fail in business. The free enterprise system was supposedly a divine ordinance, and governmental intervention a deliberate attempt to block God's work from getting done.

Winston Churchill

Some see private enterprise as a predatory target to be shot, others as a cow to be milked, but few are those who see it as a sturdy horse pulling the wagon.

. . . our Puritan ancestry has been one of the forces importantly involved in the evolution of the American social consciousness. This strain of self-imposed accountability has been a persistent note of our society. It has produced the recognition . . . that the ultimate justification of our economic system is measured not merely by the private pocketbook but by the general welfare.

Whether entirely justified or not, this interpretation of capitalism does remind us that no Christian religious sect has ever favored socialism as opposed to a free economy, and also that the charitable giving of money to righteous causes is expected of the successful man or woman. Perhaps it also explains a number of enduring proverbs:

The Lord helps those who help themselves.

Idle hands are the devil's workshop.

Waste not, want not.

A penny saved is a penny earned.

Never put off until tomorrow what you can do today.

Work, for the night is coming when men shall work no more.

Nothing succeeds like success.

The need to be charitable and kind, in appreciation of economic success, may have nothing to do with basic human nature, if the Social Darwinists are right. Capitalism may not have sprung from the Protestant Reformation, after all, but may have existed implicitly in human actions from the beginning.

Federal Bureaucracy and Freedom

Those who have made tremendous amounts of money and who have given the credit not to God but to their own ingenuity, do, however, sometimes argue that charity is possible only when government does not interfere with business. A federal reply is likely to be that one cannot count on business, no matter what it says. The many programs operated by the government depend upon heavy taxation to ensure enough funds for the general welfare.

The private citizen is often tempted to protest (and often does) that neither business nor the government is doing God's work or anybody's work except their own. Large corporations have so much power they can manipulate tax loopholes, leaving the ordinary worker to pay most of the bills.

And *that* Marx would have called exploitation. The private citizen, without being a Marxist, might well agree that he or she carries more than a fair share of the economic burden. The government, for its part, is likely to argue that certain inequalities are "built into" the system.

One reason for the long-suffering citizen's complaint that "I *thought* this was supposed to be a democracy," may lie in the very word "democracy" itself. Just as no true communism exists anywhere in the world, neither does pure democracy. For a democracy is *literally* government of, by, and for the people. It is not government through representation, nor does it include the necessary existence of a huge federal corporation with its thousands of employees, staggering payrolls, deficit spending, and inevitable bureaucracy.

Charles Reich's devastating attack on federal bureaucracy in *The Greening of America* (1970) made the sobering point that

Calvin Coolidge

The business of America is business.

the government *must* enter into partnerships with large corporations in order to feed itself. Any large organization, Reich maintained, becomes exploitative because of its very size. It scarcely matters whether Democrats or Republicans are living in the White House. The government's marriage to big business is too profound to be seriously affected by differing political philosophies. The federal government, according to Reich, has become an entity of its own, a living, breathing creature which will survive at all costs. Its original purpose—to serve the citizen—has been long since abandoned, and now the private citizen must really serve *it.*

Reich painted the federal system in bleak, pessimistic terms. Whether these are justifiable or not, the issue may well be not how democratic our society is, but how much or little the bureaucracy is doing to assist the people and causes which need help. In other words, the intelligent alternative to cries of exploitation and shouts of "undemocratic!" may be voter power—a sensitivity to what is happening in Washington, the writing of letters to legislators, even to the President, a continual feedback system from the private citizen to that vast, sprawling, ostensibly unknowable and unreachable thing, THE GOVERNMENT.

Not designed to exploit private citizens, the federal bureaucracy cannot function at the same time in everyone's best interest. Instead of bemoaning our insignificance, it may be wiser to remind ourselves that bureaucracy is not always willfully anti-individual and that the individual does have power. Witness the impact of Proposition 13 in California, when in 1978, contrary to the wishes of many politicians, the majority of voters put an end to escalating taxes. "Thirteen" suddenly became a verb and now describes the private citizen's capacity to effect governmental changes against government's will.

Other Limitations on Absolute Freedom

Even if the ideal society were through some miracle to take shape upon this earth, if people found themselves free to go anywhere, live anywhere, work as they wished without barriers from the socialist state, the federal government, or those who held the balance of economic power; if no known form of regulation or suppression existed . . . there are still those who say that absolute freedom would not prevail, because humanity cannot allow it to do so!

Character Consistency

For centuries philosophers have been engaged in a hot debate over whether humanity has freedom of the will. The Marxist view of history, for example, proclaims that one does not, that one is either the exploiter or the exploited, and that history will require the exploited to rebel, and the exploiter to fall.

Even those who do not think on such a grand scale often point out that freedom from the limitations of cause and effect would be madness, literally. For a person who does not react to a particular cause in an expected way is often thought to be insane, hence a danger to society.

For example, one person stops another in the street and strikes him in the face. The other person is "free" to respond but within certain limitations which are accepted and shared by all rational people. He may strike back. He may, because he is a pacifist, not strike back, but attempt to go his way without undergoing further harm. He may not use force himself, but call for a policeman to do it for him. He may "turn the other cheek," pointing out to his assailant the significance of the action. He may run away to avoid further trouble.

If the person struck should suddenly produce a sword and tell the assailant to kneel in front of him and be knighted for his good deeds, however, there is a good chance that he would be hauled away for observation. Such a response to the stimulus would clearly not fall within *any* meaningful category of behavior. Some philosophers who argue against the freedom of the will theory insist that only irrational people are free of known limitations. (But even the insane can be said to be limited by something in their past which has caused the deviation.)

Though the exact definition of "normal" may elude us, though many prefer the term "average," it seems likely that some minimum standard of rational behavior exists and that society requires it in order to exist. Dr. Thomas Szasz, a contemporary psychiatrist who has shocked his own profession by contending that real mental illness is an illusion,

Man's actions are best understood as determined when a person
objectively *observes his own functioning or when he attempts to*
observe other individuals and seeks reasons for their behavior. On the
other hand, belief in freedom is both necessary and possible . . . when
a person subjectively *experiences himself or empathetically*
experiences another person.

Bruce Shertzer and Shelly C. Stone

nevertheless admits that mental illness can be defined as behavior of which society disapproves. As we grow up, we are inevitably affected by society's do's and don't's, such as those of family, church, school, and so on. Adolescents are expected to be rebellious, but eventually everyone is expected to settle down and behave normally—that is, predictably, in accordance with basic rational standards.

Hence, say those philosophers who deny absolute freedom exists, each of us begins to develop a *character.* In the game of life each person's character amounts to a set of rules by which he or she is to be comprehended and dealt with. Not only does each person conform to the minimum standard of rational behavior, but he or she exhibits a personal pattern of characteristic behavior. Dependable people are counted on to be there on time, with work completed on schedule. Flighty, flustered, easily distracted people are not expected to be reliable. The eccentric are supposed to behave erratically to an extent, and no one is shocked when they do.

To be absolutely free means being unpredictable according to this theory. It is doubtful that anyone would wish to deal with the unpredictability. It would be hard to imagine the absolutely free person holding down a job or holding onto friends.

On the other hand, the *libertarians*—those who refuse to accept the idea that any limitations are "built in"—urge people not to be bound by their own characters, not to be unimaginatively predictable, but to always seek new opportunities for growth and change; to experiment with uncharacteristic behaviors whenever possible. After all, no one wants to acquire a hard and fast reputation for being always the same.

In the game of life each person's character amounts to a set of rules by which he or she is to be comprehended and dealt with.

Freud: The Unconscious and the Phantom Creatures

The libertarians urge
people not to be bound
by their own characters.

Theories of absolute freedom are not typical of the "mind science," psychology, which attempts to help people integrate their behavior by learning the causes of deviant, antisocial, or uncharacteristic actions. People go into therapy to find out why they do what they do. Sometimes it is to uncover the buried causes of feelings of depression or anxiety, sometimes to change destructive actions the patient seems unable to avoid. In any event, the controlling idea behind psychology has been that behavioral or emotional conditions have antecedents, which can be known. Few people would be satisfied with a therapist who, after listening, announced: "No one's behavior should be analyzed. You did what you wanted to do. That's all I know."

Though many, if not most, of his theories have been seriously questioned, the pioneer work of Sigmund Freud cannot be underestimated. There is little doubt that Freud's ideas have profoundly affected philosophy itself, especially in its efforts to establish a rational basis for believing in freedom of the will.

In Freud, the will is located only in the *conscious* ego and is a very superficial thing. One does something—say, checks into a hotel, requests a single room, is offered a double room, and "randomly" selects one of the two beds to occupy. The explanation for the choice, "Because I wanted to," is not that simple. The person in the hotel "wanted to" sleep in one bed rather than the other for reasons not consciously recognized.

The controlling idea
behind psychology has
been that behavioral or
emotional conditions
have antecedents, which
can be known.

Freud began his journey into what lies below conscious intelligence through early observations of certain physical ailments which could not be understood through any known physical causes. When he suspected that nonphysical (mental) reasons could lead to physical symptoms such as the loss of feeling in the legs and arms, Freud experimented with hypnosis, to help the patient discover forgotten incidents which explained present suffering. Freud's success with hypnosis encouraged him to abandon medicine as such and devote full time to investigations into what he was eventually to call the unconscious—that "region" in which we keep all of the memories we don't want or can't face, but which continue to haunt us by influencing our behavior in a thousand subtle ways.

The reason the unconscious has come into existence, the reason its "territory" grows so vast over the years, is that human society is basically an unnatural attempt to control or stifle natural drives and impulses. The child comes into the world, absolutely innocent of society and its demands. The child goes through three natural stages of early or infantile sexuality—stages which, according to Freud, are absolutely necessary: the oral phase, during which sexual stimulation is identified with the mouth (where breast feeding or the equivalent has taken place); the anal phase, during which erotic pleasure is transferred to the nether regions, whose activities suddenly assume great importance where once they were completely spontaneous and unheeded; and the phallic phase, during which the sex organs themselves assume their proper place as the zone of stimulation. Freud believed that the girl child developed feelings of inferiority during this stage. But as soon as the capacity for sexual excitement is discerned by the parents, restrictions are imposed: "Don't touch that" or "Don't ever let me catch you doing that" becomes a familiar warning.

Freud maintained that by the time society gets through molding us in its image (and remember he was writing for a highly suppressed Victorian society!), we have learned to conceal normal feelings. We have learned to be ashamed. We pretend much of the time that not only sexual appetites but all biological functions do not exist. Sexual maladjustment, however, is very much at the heart of most neuroses: the continual effort of society to control what was never meant to be held in check.

Since sexual appetites and sexual curiosity can seldom be in accord with the dictates of polite society, most people, according to Freud, go through life with buried guilt. Homosexuality may be unrecognized or deliberately suppressed.

All male children, Freud said, grow into adolescence with the buried guilt of *the Oedipus complex,* the normal sexual attraction toward the mother, aroused during the phallic stage of development. Girls develop Electra complexes: erotic feelings toward their fathers. These feelings are never fully brought into the open and analyzed, with the result that many people are doomed to seek not husbands or wives but parent substitutes.[1]

Freud's vision of the world was one of a vast population of neurotic people, sometimes brought to psychosis

Anatole France

A person is never happy except at the price of some ignorance.

(extremely deviant behavior rooted in highly complex unconscious causes), perpetually forced into a conformity which crushed their natural impulses. Almost nobody was truly happy, and as a result, the basic animal survival instinct was perverted in humans and became an unconscious death wish.

Freud taught that for most people the sex act itself was seldom a joyous, spontaneous celebration of life, but rather a desperate attempt to escape from depression and anxieties no one could account for but which were always present. Since the ego or conscious mind could not cope with anxiety, the sex act became the temporary and symbolic death of ego.

Thus our hypothetical gentleman, entering the double room at the hotel, might select the bed closest to the wall. (If the wall sloped down over the bed, the chances are even stronger that he would select it.) Freud explained that the death wish often shows itself in the desire to crawl into, snuggle up inside, or in some way to penetrate symbolic wombs. (Attics, sleeping bags, back seats of automobiles, tents, and the like all can represent symbolic wombs.)

But Freud was not without hope, bleak as his vision of the world may seem. He invented the science of psychoanalysis, through which troubled patients say whatever they think, freely associating one thing with another, regardless of how bizarre, and recounting dreams in as detailed a manner as possible. The aim of psychoanalysis is to assist patients in bringing the unconscious to light, to assist in coping with anxieties in a rational way.

Despite the criticism directed against Freud during the last two decades, psychoanalysis continues to be popular. Thousands see their analysts far more frequently than they do their family doctor or dentist. But Freudian analysts warn that the motivation for these visits may be the desire to find in the analyst a substitute parent and thus to retard self-awareness even further. Such a substitution may be useful in early analysis, when patients are encouraged to reveal more of themselves if the trust level is high.

From the statistics themselves—the sheer quantity of office visits to analysts each year—one could infer that Freud may have been on the right track. Whether all of his theories hold up or not, there seem to be a number of people who consider themselves disturbed and who seek someone to help them through the fog of their unsure identities. Free

---

Samuel Beckett

**We are all born mad.
Some remain so.**

agents in full control of their destinies are apparently a rare minority.

Skinner: It Isn't a Matter of Freedom

Freud made people aware that what they did was seldom a direct result of conscious thought or desire. If Freud showed that most people were not in control of their destinies, B. F. Skinner (b. 1904) has sought to radically alter the way people think about freedom. In effect, Freud said, "You can't be free until your conscious mind, ego, understands the source of your neurosis." Skinner, who calls himself an operant psychologist, says, "Let's reconsider what we think we are talking about when we say we want to be free."

Skinner's beliefs are rooted in a science barely getting under way in Freud's day: *behaviorism.* The central point of behaviorism is that human beings are behaving creatures. To understand people better and work to improve their lot, it is necessary to begin with what people actually *do,* not what they think, feel, or say.

Skinner has denied that the language of feeling or thought has a direct relationship to any observable reality. To say "I feel cheated," or "I want to be free" or, in the words of the popular song, "I want to be me" means nothing without accompanying action. What matters is not what people say about inner states, but what they do in response to an external stimulus.

Thus, if the shackled prisoner is suffering the pain and discomfort of solitary confinement and the guard threatens him with a nightstick, the prisoner may out of sheer desperation shout obscenities in the guard's direction. This, says Skinner, is concrete behavior, not the feeling "I want to be free."

By the same token, if the shackled prisoner is promised that he will be removed from solitary confinement and "allowed" to work on the rock pile so long as he refrains from future obscenities, he is very likely to accept the terms and avoid four-letter words. The "privilege" of working on the rock pile, in contrast to being in the dark and dingy cell, may well constitute an activity closer to "freedom" than the word or the so-called feeling.

Skinner calls freedom the effort to escape from the unpleasant consequences of certain actions. We slap at a

What matters is not what people say about inner states, but what they do in response to an external stimulus.

mosquito, about to attack, to avoid the annoying itching which will follow. A child who has thrown a tantrum and has been sent to bed without supper may cry loudly to escape hunger pangs. To have freedom there must be a condition acting as a stimulus to a response. No such "thing" as pure and absolute freedom exists or can be defined.

People, Skinner goes on, often identify the state of absolute freedom as one in which "aversive control" is absent: that is, if there is no apparent oppression, then people imagine themselves to be free. The literature of freedom, such as Rousseau's writings, which helped inspire the French Revolution, has always urged people to act against aversive control, against obvious forms of oppression. It either beckons followers, who have the false hope of believing society might be better organized but without controls, or else it fails to point out that there can be controls which appear less threatening but which nevertheless also condition people's behavior.

The fact is, Skinner tells us, there is no way to escape all forms of control. If humanity can be said to have a nature, it lies in *the capacity to be conditioned.* Everything we do is the result of a reinforcement of behavior. Those actions which are followed by pleasant consequences tend to be repeated; those followed by unpleasant or painful consequences tend to be avoided.

Even aggression and exploitation, which Marx implied were basic to human nature, are forms of behavior induced by external circumstances. Aggression is one way of escaping negative reinforcement (an unpleasant consequence). If one acts first, then one escapes being acted *upon.* One may exploit others as long as possible to escape controls one may have experienced in the past but not want to see in the present. Aggressors or exploiters may imagine themselves to be free, but they have simply not understood the forces that are conditioning their particular behavior.

Victims of aggression or those who are exploited are better off than those being conditioned by nonaversive, nonthreatening controls, says Skinner. The obvious victims are either rescued eventually by some freedom movement, or they themselves rise up and rebel. (Or else they prefer to be victims). The ones who are really in bad shape are the "happy slaves"—people who are molded by hidden controls and don't know it; people who believe themselves to be free.

According to proponents of behaviorism, if humanity can be said to have a nature it lies in the capacity to be conditioned.

•
•
•

•
•
•

According to the opponents, conditioning reduces human dignity and diminishes the contributions of great artists, writers, and philosophers.

The literature of freedom has been designed to make men 'conscious' of aversive control, but in its choice of methods it has failed to rescue the happy slave. [2]

Skinner is aware that his outlook is often rejected by the humanists, for whom (as was pointed out in the Overview to this chapter) the question of freedom is likely to be the most important single issue, the thing that clearly distinguishes human beings from other animals. Skinner says the desire to hold fast to this ancient and honorable abstraction "freedom" is tied in with the belief that human dignity is lost if it is shown that humanity is not nor ever can be considered free. For what happens to the great artists, writers, and philosophers if they were only products of conditioning forces?

We are not inclined to give a person credit for achievements which are in fact due to forces over which he has no control. [3]

But, argues Skinner, "dignity" has no meaning as an absolute abstraction. People do not vibrantly experience an inner something called "dignity" at the thought of being free. Like every other human condition, dignity is a very specific response to a particular kind of stimulus: it is the positive reinforcement given to one who has behaved properly or who has performed some achievement deemed notable. Dignity = praise. Dignity = recognition. Robbing someone of his dignity is taking away recognition he believes is rightfully his.

Praise and recognition represent very positive reinforcements and, as such, are among the most pervasive of conditioning forces. Moreover, we may push Skinner's idea even further and point out that, to win praise and recognition, some people would do just about anything required of them. Many have forgiven their own lapses of artistic or intellectual integrity because the stakes were high enough. How many writers and composers have said a fond farewell to the novel in the closet or the sonata in the piano bench in exchange for fame and fortune in films or television?

Now a case could be made for the contention that dignity *is* personal integrity and that the person who holds fast to this dignity, in this sense of the word, is indeed free. One could cite the example of Vincent Van Gogh, an artist who received virtually no praise or attention for any of his work, except from his brother Theo. Far from doing everything in his power to win recognition, Van Gogh continued to paint exactly as he wished. There never was any doubt in his mind concerning his mission as an artist. He wanted to move people, to touch them in a very special kind of way. He was often discouraged by his obscurity, but it is probable that he never lost faith in the way he painted. One could say that Van Gogh possessed both artistic dignity and creative freedom.

A Skinnerian could counter by pointing out that Van Gogh's genius was nurtured by the very absence of recognition, the lack of positive reinforcement. Can anybody say for certain that the artist's style was not in some sense a response to critical indifference, not in some sense the result of a decision to paint as eccentrically (for his time) as possible? The "freedom" of artistic expression which some might claim for Van Gogh may have been, in reality, a positive response to negative conditions. Can anybody say for certain that a critically acclaimed Van Gogh would have remained the same person, felt the same emotions, and continued to express himself on canvas in the same style?

Hence Skinner's title for his most comprehensive work: *Beyond Freedom and Dignity* (1971). We need, says Skinner, to take broad terms that mean very little in themselves and redefine them in strictly behavioral language. We need to concentrate on creating what Skinner calls a "technology of behavior." Since people are going to be conditioned anyway, the focus should be on the good controls that *can* exist.

> *The problem is to free men, not from control, but from certain kinds of control, and it can be solved only if our analysis takes all consequences into account.*[4]

Skinner is a kind of modern utopian thinker, believing that eventually an ideal society can be designed in which people develop to the maximum of their abilities through carefully preplanned reinforcements. In such a society there would be no crime, no aggression, no exploitation. If it could ever come about, this society could well be closer to the humanist's dream than any that has yet existed.

But *can it come about?* Humanists do not question Skinner's motives, but they do show some concern for methods. A "technology of behavior" sounds too precise, too clinical for most humanists, who keep asking about the behavioral technicians, the engineers of this utopia. When these people realize how much power they have, what will stop them from using those very aversive techniques which Skinner wants to eliminate?

Then too, the humanist does not cherish the thought of giving up the "human mystery"—the haziness about creativity, genius, and human potential which keeps us from knowing too much about what we are doing. Do we wish, asks the humanist, to avoid doing those very things which lead to human milestones? After all, what if Van Gogh had lived in Skinner's behaviorally engineered society? He might have filed a petition against public indifference, been given a stipend by the Minister of Culture, and perhaps never painted again. Is this what we want?

Sociobiology: It's All in the Family

Mention must be made of a very new science, more recent even than Skinner's brand of behaviorism, than operant conditioning. According to sociobiology, which views social behavior in biological rather than purely cultural terms, genetics is the key to understanding much of what we do.

Sociobiologists hold that since human beings are essentially genetic systems, they are motivated by the identical concerns which are programmed by nature into the single gene: survival and reproduction. Whatever is true for the single gene is also true for the entire person. Self-interest forms the basis of all our actions: that is, the genes must survive and multiply. We choose companions and make all decisions solely in genetic terms.

For example, people tend to favor family members in their dealings. One is less likely to sell a junk car to a brother or sister than to someone outside the family circle, however close a friend that person may be. Brothers and sisters have close genetic ties, and therefore they translate into self-interest to us. Fathers and mothers have even closer genetic ties; hence they mean our self-interest even more. We do things for father and mother without even thinking we are making a sacrifice because the closer the genes, the less true sacrifice is involved.

People fall in love to ensure genetic propagation. In the

Carl Sagan

It is precisely our plasticity, our long childhoods, that presents a slavish adherence to genetically pre-programmed behavior in human beings more than in any other species.

days before sophisticated contraceptives and birth control devices, women tended to fall in love less readily and willingly—that is, they were able to control their sexual appetites more easily—because of the risk of making a "genetic investment" in a particular young man. Men were more easily stimulated because they made no genetic investment unless there were a father lurking about the front door with a shotgun. Nowadays, say the sociobiologists, people feel freer to enjoy sex without having to fall in love—that is, the genetic investment has become more a matter of deliberate choice. But nonetheless, it is this, and nothing else, which determines whether "true love" is indeed present.

"I am not ready to get married" means "I am not yet prepared for a genetic investment." But sooner or later the need for such an investment may arise. Many sociobiologists contend that those who argue that the desire for motherhood or fatherhood is not basic to human nature, who say they are content to be together and enjoy each other without wishing to reproduce, are only channeling genetic self-interest in other directions. For example, there are "substitute families." Those who decline motherhood or fatherhood may go into social work or join volunteer groups such as the Peace Corps working for the "family of humanity." Some have adopted war orphans or the offspring of unwed parents. Even the commune has been one sort of substitute family—often lasting until members discover that in the absence of true genetic self-interest communal living can lose its charm.

The impact of sociobiology has not yet begun to be felt, but already an organization has been formed, primarily composed of humanists, who object violently to its premises. One objection is that sociobiology absolutely denies the possibility of free choice in the matter of social relationships or of deeds we choose to perform. The humanist prefers to believe that an individual may pursue genetic self-interest if she or he wishes, but is not constrained to do so. Sociobiology tends to find "genetic symbolism" in all deeds.

Altruism, for example, which has always meant a concern for another for the other's sake, becomes, in sociobiology, an extension of genetic self-interest. A mother may sacrifice for her children, but she does so only because the children mean the propagation of her own genes—her own survival, in other words. She might even face death to save her child, but not to save a total stranger. If she does sacrifice in the interest of another's child, the sacrifice is only an extension of her role as a mother. The sacrifice represents "genetic symbolism." By the same token, a soldier might die to save his batallion, but only after this has become a substitute family.

The concern for the future—whether it is a father buying ample life insurance for his family's "welfare" or an artist's desire to create as much as possible for as long a time as may be possible—is in reality the need to know that one's genetic (actual or symbolic) lineage will continue.

Why, ask the sociobiologists, do so many persons become depressed when they realize that they are both childless and "the last of their line"? Why do so many childless couples seek to adopt children? Is it not that, lacking real genetic survival, people despair and are willing to settle for whatever they can get?

Does anybody have or want to have children for the sake of the children? Parents may tell their children that they have sacrificed a great deal in order to "bring them into the world," but, except for the very religious, one can scarcely imagine parents actually believing that unborn children were waiting in line somewhere, hoping for birth. Parents, according to sociobiology, are serving their own needs by giving birth. It is imperative both that they reproduce their genes and *that they be known for an ability to do so.*

One may argue that it is commonplace for a young man or woman to grow so alienated from the family circle that escape becomes vital. Sociobiology, however, warns of pervasive guilt feelings resulting from the breaking of family ties.

The humanist prefers to believe that an individual may pursue genetic self-interest if he wishes, but he is not constrained to do so.

If sociobiology is right, then one may have to accept genetic self-interest as a fact of life and realize that one's ability to make a free choice is always going to be limited by genetic considerations. One may choose a marital partner despite parental objection because genetic reproduction hinges on the marriage. Sociobiology tells us we can virtually predict our decisions in almost every instance according to how our genetic self-interest will fare.

The Possibilities for Freedom

Humanism, as pointed out at the beginning of this book, is the capacity for making a free choice among significant options. One says to oneself, "I am here, and I may do this, or I may do that, or perhaps I shall do neither." The determinant is always the extent to which one will grow because of the choice, the extent to which one's potential will become that much more liberated. Humanism hates apathy and a refusal to grow when the opportunity is there. Humanism thrives on the variety of choices provided to human beings —and on the individual's ablilty to discern these choices.

The question now is whether, with all of the impressive arguments which can be posed against the idea of freedom, the humanist must conclude that he or she is a passive entity: either an exploiter or the exploited by nature, a conditioner or the conditioned by circumstance—but in no case, free to make a choice out of an act of will.

A few words remain to be said on the question of freedom.

Will

The issue of freedom has much to do with the will. For centuries philosophers asked, "Is the will free?" More recently, they have asked, "Is there such a thing as the will?" B. F. Skinner, for example, argues that the will cannot be detected, cannot be felt. One cannot say "I have free will" with reference to a specific sensation or emotion. The will, whether free or not, may be only a word.

A German philosopher of the last century, Arthur Schopenhauer (1788–1860) was concerned with the problem of whether the will existed. After much deliberation he came to a most interesting conclusion. Stand, he said, in front of a mirror. Observe yourself. Then think that you would like to raise your left arm. Decide that you *want* to raise the arm. Then do it. There is no doubt that anyone who followed those instructions would see his arm being raised (assuming no physical impediment, of course). The final observation is that of *the will objectified.* One instant the desire to raise the arm is locked inside the mind, the consciousness. The next instant, it is visibly present in the action perceived in the mirror.

Schopenhauer's simple experiment can be repeated in thousands of different ways, and in each case one experiences the will. At this very moment the reader may decide to stand up or not, turn on the television set or not, hum a few bars of a song or not. One can experience a direct sense that what one is *not* doing is a deliberate act of omission.

Humanism is the capacity for making a free choice

The unfree choice is to be either an exploiter or the exploited by nature, a conditioner or the conditioned by circumstance.

When Skinner tells us we cannot feel the will, he *may* mean that most people do not bother to focus their thoughts on the will. At any given moment they cannot say whether they are doing what they have willed to do or are not doing what they have willed not to do.

The student in the classroom, told to close his books in preparation for a surprise quiz, may groan and feel at that instant like a slave, a prisoner. He may feel he would rather be at the beach, at the movies, driving his car. Instead of groaning, however, he has the option of saying to himself: "I do not will that I must take a test this morning." If the proposition sounds reasonable—that is, not absurd—the student has confirmed the existence of his will. He is withholding his will. If the will were merely an illusion, he could have no rational opinion about the test. It could not be an unpleasantness, an imposition upon him, unless there were other occasions upon which he could say, also quite reasonably: "I will that I am doing this. . . ."

Consciousness of will could, conceivably, make a difference in the matter of whether everything we do is the result of some previous cause, as the behaviorists tell us. By focusing the attention on a particular action or omission of an action, one can decide whether one has freely chosen this kind of response to whatever caused the action (or its absence). One can decide that a different response would have been more appropriate, a response that *might* have been made.

It may well be that the behaviorists are not allowing intelligence to play a significant enough role in the determination of actions. It may well be that people can slow down their rate of response and make themselves less susceptible to external influences over which they themselves exercise no control. A long chain of cause and effect may lead us into a moment of choice, but who is to say that one cannot become acutely conscious of possibilities and do the thing that seems most in accord with one's will?

Regret and Relief

The American philosopher William James (see Chapter 8 for a discussion of James's psychological approach to religion) reviewed the case for pure determinism as set forth by

> **Thoreau**
>
> **I know of no more encouraging fact than the unquestionable ability of man to elevate his life by a conscious endeavor.**

European philosophers and concluded they were wrong. In fact, James developed a theory he pointedly called *indeterminism,* which presents the world as a random collection of chance happenings. Determinism, for James, was too coldly logical. Cause A leads to Effect A. Determinism made people seem like well-run, well-oiled machines. James said, on the contrary, people were indecisive, unpredictable, exactly the opposite of machines.

Regret, he added, was a universal phenomenon. At any given moment people are able to think back over a hundred choices they wish they had not made. But at the same time, regret could not be meaningfully experienced unless there existed an opposite, satisfaction, which gave regret its identity. In other words, within the random collection of happenings, people sometimes make what they consider the right move and many times make what they consider the wrong move. If everything were predetermined—that is, if the will were not free—looking backward could not reveal missed chances, roads not taken, opportunities wasted. We could not see them unless they had existed, though we may have been blind to them at the moment of choice. How often does the murderer think back and realize that he did not *have* to carry a pistol with him for the confrontation with his enemy? For James, hindsight was proof that genuine alternatives always exist.

If we were to extend the philosophy of indeterminism, we could say that another revealing exercise (similar to the hand in the mirror) is to sit back and think of all of the terrible things one might have done last week but refrained from doing:

> had a confrontation with a friend that could have threatened the relationship
>
> lied about something that would have involved a whole series of other lies
>
> dropped a course in an impulsive moment, a course that is required for graduation
>
> taken a chance and driven the old car with two bald tires

There is yet another opposite of regret, and that is *relief.* Again it is a matter of intelligence, of focusing the attention on the vital matters. One is not aware of relief unless one

People are able to think back over a hundred choices they wish they had not made.

That we can say we have made many mistakes is an admission that we know ourselves to be free agents.

surveys the wrong moves that might have been made, but were not.

Our lives are probably split down the middle, with good moves on one side and bad moves on the other. That we can say we have made many mistakes is an admission that we know ourselves to be free agents. That we have sometimes chosen wisely seems to back up the claim.

Long Black Coats and Horse-Drawn Buggies

In a modest-size New Jersey town, adjacent to a race track, discotheques, drive-in movies, and not far away from the gambling casinos of Atlantic City, where once a year the Miss America beauty pageant is held, dwells a small colony of Chassidic Jews. They inhabit tiny apartments in two blocks of "residence halls" located on a main highway that carries motorists to the Jersey shore. The male members of this tiny community wear long black coats, regardless of the season, black hats, and beards. The female members do not wear make-up and have their hair covered at all times. The male children wear skull caps, even when out playing.

Motorists, tourists, and passers-by are inclined to stare at these people, who go about their business without the least trace of self-consciousness. The synagogue is the center of their adult lives, together with a meeting house, where they get together on days other than the Sabbath. The children go to a special school, where they are taught the principles and moral precepts of their religion. Nonetheless, one would imagine that the environment would bring a good deal of pressure to bear on the young and the newly married. Don't the women see cosmetic advertisements? Do the youth not know there are movies and TV programs? And a weekend disco blaring from the lobby of the Holiday Inn one short block away? Yet even the teenagers in the community can be seen quietly walking in the footsteps of their elders.

In Pennsylvania, not far from the crowded city of Lancaster, with its shopping malls and night life, live the Amish. They use no electricity, hence none of the appliances most people find indispensable. They drive about in horse-drawn buggies. Young people cannot telephone each other, nor can they step out for a casual date. As with the Chassidic Jewish women, make-up is taboo. But the Amish women may not even wear short dresses. No Amish people may be

> **The survival intact of cultures totally alien to their environment testifies to the power of group will.**

photographed; consequently, when they die, they leave behind no record of how they looked. At the same time, the Amish are concerned with wealth derived from farming, but there is very little they would allow themselves to buy with their money.

While some rebellion probably takes place in both colonies, the survival intact of cultures totally alien to their environment—indeed to the prevailing lifestyle of the entire country—no doubt testifies to the power of *group will.* One *can* say that the young people are conditioned by the elders, but models of alternate, and perhaps more attractive, modes of living are surely plentiful. One cannot imagine that those who do not rebel are miserable at their lot. Those who shake their heads and say, "Poor souls! They just don't know any better," may well be talking of themselves. To follow one mode of life, when others are possible, is to exercise a conscious freedom.

Often those who advance the argument that people are not free agents do so because what they observe around them may not always represent what they themselves would do; hence it strikes them that free choice could not have entered the picture.

Self-Imposed Limitations

The Stoic teacher Epictetus once advised his students to sit and refuse food the next time they attended a banquet. Such advice was part of Stoic training, for the Stoic philosophy is built on the idea that one can be happy, can cope with life's horrors by controlling one's attitudes. An opinion about what happens is unnecessary; events cease to be either good or evil. To refrain from eating at a banquet, therefore, meant that one was in control of appetite. If something so basic as appetite were within one's power to manage, why not everything else? To convert hunger into an attitude and to refuse to hold the attitude—that is, refuse to allow hunger to enter the consciousness—was true liberation.

The Stoic teachings are among the most enduring influences on the humanist's methods of achieving a clear sense of freedom. One does exactly the reverse of what he might think "freedom" entails. Instead of running about wildly doing whatever comes into the head, one willfully sets up certain parameters—which include limitations—within

---

Wordsworth

Nuns fret not at their convent's narrow room; And hermits are contented with their cells.

If you can keep your head while all about are losing theirs, you simply do not understand the situation.

Popular Wall Placard

which to operate. These, of course, are changed as the situation demands.

People who jog know all about the relationship between freedom and limits. They will tell you about a consciousness of freedom in running, pushing against the wind, and feeling their arms and legs equal to the demands made by the will. For the runner, in contrast to what Skinner has said, *does* feel his or her will. When there is a sharp incline, the runner must draw upon reserve strength. On the downward slope, the runner knows that power may once more be conserved. If one is running against others in a race and there is a need to win, one accelerates; if there is only the need to complete the course, one adopts a more leisurely pace.

The vivid experience of will does not happen all of a sudden. In the beginning, jogging is a distinct effort, accompanied by pain and soreness. There is the inevitable shortening of breath, the pulling of muscles, the labored breathing, the tendency to overheat rapidly. In the beginning one stops running for the slightest excuse. After a time one sets a goal: to the end of the road and then back. If one is developing into a runner, the self-imposed limit is crucial. Gradually the "required" distance is lengthened. Nothing on earth, including wind and rain, will deter most runners from completing their course. The ultimate sense of liberation—the experience of floating on a cloud that all runners know about occurs only when and if the runner has been faithful to the limitations imposed by the inner self.

Consider the case of a student who has felt he absolutely "must" attend a certain baseball game. The home team will or will not win the title this night. One can talk in Skinnerian terms about the whole history of baseball as a conditioning factor in Western culture. One can point to the machismo image of sports in molding the male personality. To love baseball is to accrue to oneself positive points toward masculinity. (By the same token, one would suppose, females may be conditioned to like baseball because of the long struggle for sexual equality.) But in addition to the possible cultural influences, there exists the undeniable fact that the student has experienced positive rewards from frequent attendance at ball games—that *he likes baseball.*

This   same   student   tends   to   be   average,   but   not distinguished, in his classroom performances. He wants to graduate from college, to have the degree so that he may do better financially than he believes he would without proof of a college education. He has never been particularly motivated to pursue learning in any field for its own sake. He has always done what was necessary to earn an honorable, passing grade in every course.

Tomorrow he must hand in a term paper in the last course he needs to pass for graduation. All other examinations are over. The student has already written a brief and generally superficial paper, one which he knows might have been better but will no doubt satisfy the professor enough to ensure a decent grade. He can forget the paper and enjoy the ball game. There simply are not enough rewards for staying home and making the paper longer, more detailed, more thorough: *a better paper.*

The Skinnerian psychologist would probably bet money on the student's "inevitable" choice of the ball game. And indeed most people in this student's situation might do the predictable thing. But it is not impossible for a human being to do the unpredictable thing by a personal act of will. It is not impossible to imagine the student's deciding that *for once in his life* he will hand in a piece of work that represents the best he can do, not the minimum for "getting by."

If the student foregoes the game, giving up the certain rewards of the ball game for the uncertain reward of a potential achievement in which he may be able to take pride, he will be doing something which, in Skinner's theory, is uncharacteristic of human beings: namely, erecting an obstacle which need not have been erected so that it may (by no means certainly) be overcome. The student would have shared an experience similar to that of the non-eater at Epictetus' banquet and the jogger who refuses to stop until he has reached the end of his route. *He would have transferred the reward system from a definite external to an indefinite internal source.*

To argue that no such student would do this is to argue without foundation. It could happen. There is nothing in the cosmic scheme of things to prevent its happening. Indeed amazing reversals of character and sudden spurts of growth are probably accounted for in this very manner.

To do what one does not have to do may be where freedom really begins. Whatever grade the student may receive for his efforts, the opportunity is there for him to experience

---

Merry Haber

There are only a few things we 'must' do. One of them is to blink when someone blows air on our eyes. Most of the other 'musts' are 'wants.'

It is not impossible for a human being to do the unpredictable thing by a personal act of will.

a true sense of having deliberately broken an old pattern of behavior. All of us have such opportunities, provided we take the time to become acutely conscious of what these patterns are.

The numbers of people who want to break old patterns and assert their wills may be limited, but this is only to say that not everyone is free. Nobody ever said the definition of freedom must apply to all people. Skinner is probably right, up to a point. But then William James is also right, up to a point. Freudian therapy too may be highly accurate for some kinds of problems.

The humanist, however, derives a measure of satisfaction from the knowledge that no one has yet been shown to have said the final word for every person on this earth. This knowledge in itself constitutes a road to freedom.

> **To do
> what one does not have
> to do
> may be where freedom
> really begins.**

Chapter 15 Footnotes

[1]Oedipus was the Greek mythological hero who saved Thebes from destruction, became King, and then married the former King's widow. This woman, it turns out, was his natural mother. Electra was the daughter of Agamemnon, who returned from the Trojan War, only to be slain by his wife and her lover.

[2]B. F. Skinner, *Beyond Freedom and Dignity* (New York: Bantam/Vintage, 1972), p. 37.

[3]*Ibid.*, p. 41.

[4]*Ibid.*, p. 39.

16

THE CRITICAL THINKER

Overview

Inevitably, humanists become critics: of themselves, others, works of art, what's happening around them and, as much as they know of it, the world. Humanists—the people who practice the art of being human—learn that it is essential to go outside the self, to rise above the personal concerns that, for far too many people, constitute the "all" of existence. It was long ago said that the Greeks possessed an uncanny ability to "see things steadily and see them whole." Whether this statement accurately describes an entire culture or not, the observation applies to the fully actualized humanist of any time and any place.

To say that one ought to become a critic in the broadest sense of the term is not meant to imply that one strives to be negative, to tear down rather than build up. Criticism, in the true sense of the word, is not limited to finding faults. It can involve praise of the highest order—or a refusal to put *any* label on the object of criticism until all of the returns are in. Criticism essentially means careful analysis leading to an evaluation. It is the condition, the state of mind, which should precede choices and actions. It is the opposite of going through life with total spontaneity, of making all decisions intuitively (though it is important that we listen to what intuition tells us).

In its more formal aspects, criticism is associated with literature and the arts. A professional critic is someone paid to read, view, or listen and present an informed opinion. Society absolutely needs such people. Critics are to plays and concerts what medical specialists are to designated parts of the body. Professional critics are paid to discern things with cool detachment before making up their minds and to give us the benefit of their expertise.

The humanist learns from the professional critic some tricks of the trade. He or she comes to recognize the importance of cool detachment, but the humanist applies the skill to all aspects of living, not just to literature and the arts. Like the professional critic (who may be a humanist too), the humanist neither likes nor dislikes, approves nor disapproves until there are substantial reasons for choosing. The humanist comes to an event as the professional critic comes to the play—quietly, unassumingly, slipping into a customary chair, waiting for the spectacle to begin. Humanists keep their eyes and ears open, their minds clear and finely tuned to the occasion.

Feelings enter into evaluations, even for the most coolly detached, but they never dominate. Like intuitions, emotions should be heeded, but put in proper perspective. Often the feeling "there is something about this person that I cannot quite trust" will turn out to have been right on target from the outset; but just as often one needs to control or temper an impulsive opinion.

Criticism, then, is an activity of the mind which carefully defines, describes, and analyzes something—a movie, an event, a presidential decision, a daughter's desire to move into her own apartment. It probably should be but often is not the mental activity in which people enjoy engaging more than in any other. Its rival activities include constant complaining; the suspicion that the troubles of the world derive

Criticism is not limited to finding faults.

Humanists keep their eyes and ears open, their minds clear . . .

from plots and conspiracies; skill in vindicating oneself at all times and at all costs; the tendency to form conclusions at once, refusing to be led astray by facts; and the tendency to fall immediately into line with the other person's viewpoint.

Critical thinking, in turn, is the ongoing process of criticism. It is the disposition of the mind to behave in a certain way: that is, to define, describe, and analyze as accurately, as fairly, as dispassionately, as possible. It is a lifelong commitment. It is the fertile context within which a specific act of criticism takes place.

Critical thinkers quickly become known, become identified as people whose opinions can be trusted. Many times over they have demonstrated a knack for hitting the situation squarely between the eyes, commenting clearly on what is taking place, assessing the matter reasonably, and making a memorable pronouncement on the subject.

It is not at all difficult to distinguish critical from noncritical thinkers. The latter take things literally and fail to move on quickly to the next step. They have a hard time figuring out why people say what they say. They are not aware of what we might call *the shape of experience.* The morning after a party, noncritical thinkers cannot put it into some sort of perspective. Critical thinkers, on the other hand, will tell you concisely just what happened and what it felt like to be there.

Critical thinking is not an exact science. But it has identifiable characteristics. It has goals. There are certain ways of achieving it, ways that can be articulated. The purpose of this chapter is to systematize these ways as much as possible.

Thinking About Thinking

For all practical purposes, brain is mind.

The first step in becoming a critical thinker is to develop some idea of what you mean by thinking. Since thinking is a process that "happens" or "takes place" in the mind, the definition of the process depends upon what you imagine or see when you talk about the mind.

For centuries, speculations about the mind belonged exclusively to the domain of philosophy. Few could have suspected that psychology, an actual *science* of the mind, would one day come into being. Where once it was believed by many that the mind was a spiritual, or at least nonmaterial, entity, floating somehow within but not connected to the body, many more now take for granted that all functions of mind (from daydreaming and nightdreaming to the most complex series of interweaving ideas) are functions localized in the brain. Take away the brain and the mind disappears. One may include the nerve centers and the five senses themselves to form a complex construct which can be called the mental *system,* but the brain is known now to be the crucial element. For all practical purposes, the brain *is* mind.

At the same time, not everything about the human brain is known for certain. Scientists know what it looks like, and California anthropologist Ralph Holloway, by making plaster casts of primitive brains based on indentations found inside ancient skulls, has constructed a reputable theory of the brain's evolution. The theory includes a description of the relationship between the brain of Homo sapiens and the brains of direct ancestors and distant relatives. But there are still many things about the brain, as it currently exists, which elude exact knowledge.

Left Hemisphere, Right Hemisphere

It is known, for example, that the brain is divided into two clearly separated halves, or hemispheres. A few years ago psychologists advanced the theory that the two hemispheres represent two diametrically opposite aspects of human thinking. The left hemisphere seems to handle abstractions, concepts, and all forms of symbolism, including language. The right hemisphere seems to handle intuition and creativity, as well as ideas which cannot readily be verbalized—things we "just know" but cannot explain why or how. Some believe that when we dream we are under right-hemispheric control, while our waking, conscious life is governed by the more disciplined, structure-conscious left hemisphere. Of course, we find ourselves slipping into the right hemisphere at a moment's notice, as when we lean back and start daydreaming or let our thoughts wander. Often we catch ourselves and go back to conscious thought without remembering very clearly what we felt or saw during the lapse.

Some maintain that the first few moments after the alarm clock has sounded, when we lie there in bed slowly becoming oriented to waking reality, offer a rare opportunity to sense the right hemisphere in action. If we try, we can sometimes catch hold of the last fading phantom from the dream world. Sigmund Freud believed that even the most puzzling and bizarre of dreams had a meaning which could be interpreted and verbalized, that dreams were ways employed by the unconscious mind to bring to light truths about ourselves we dared not face consciously.

Many right-hemisphere theorists, however, believe dreams are a good deal more complicated than that and serve a variety of functions. As a matter of fact, they contend human culture is so left-hemisphere oriented, and understands so little about the other hemisphere, that the full picture of the human brain has yet to be drawn. Perhaps what we call thinking is a conscious sequence of interconnecting ideas and conclusions occurring in the left hemisphere, and what can be called *knowing* is an unconscious, sudden "flash" in the right. Surely, all of us have had the experience that is usually verbalized as, "I know what it means, but I can't say it." The left hemisphere, which is language-oriented, naturally thinks in words. But who is to say that all knowledge must be translatable into language?

In any event, if the left/right hemisphere division holds, we may say that whatever happens in the right side does so without any particular guidance. The right hemisphere does its work all the time and probably does it with great efficiency. Hunches, intuitions, sudden insights are continually popping up, and they no doubt serve us well. Can you imagine what it would be like to have to sit down and analyze every move we made in life?

Left	Right
Logic	Intuition
Speech	Nonverbalism
Mathematics	Music
Reading	Experience
Concern for time	Independence of time
Stress on individualism	Empathy with others

According to this concept of the brain, the right hemisphere needs no monitoring, no "training". Despite the fact that our culture is considered left-hemisphere dominant—with logic, science, and language enjoying the highest of reputations—it is *that* hemisphere and not the right which has trouble performing its function. Our culture traditionally and historically applauds the logical, the scientific, and the linguistic, yet popular culture (television, movies, glossy magazines, and so on) does not. Extremely logical and verbal people are rarely treated so sympathetically, are seldom considered so important and newsworthy as people with complicated emotional problems. Newscasting continues to report on summit meetings or presidential energy proposals, but a good deal of attention is paid to divorce, crime, and disasters.

If the left/right hemisphere model is an accurate one, we may think of each of us as being two kinds of people. Each of us is thoughtful critic and impulsive adventurer rolled into one. But the thoughtful critic often sits there, woebegone, in his left-hand chair, wishing to be heard—wishing in vain.

Old Brains, New Brains

Another brain model is that described by philosopher/scientist Carl Sagan *(The Dragons of Eden).* [1] In this model there is a three-part division to the brain. The bottom and middle sections are survivors of millions of years of evolution and can be called the old brains. The topmost section, or new brain, is most advanced in Homo sapiens—humanity in its present form. Higher primates, like chimpanzees, have the new brain in a less complex form.

The oldest brain is sometimes referred to as *reptilian;* it once belonged to early inhabitants of planet Earth. These creatures needed a brain to process information delivered by the sense of sight as they foraged about for food and shelter. They needed to be alert to danger, to the possibility of encountering creatures larger than they. Hence this oldest brain developed survival techniques, including aggression ("Get them before they get you"), what Robert Ardrey has called the "territorial imperative" ("This area is mine, so keep off!"), and an insistence upon and respect for hierarchy, or chain of command ("If you want to last, you'd better take orders from me, because I'm capable of killing you").

As time went on and *mammals* began to evolve, a new kind

of brain was needed to process information passed on from the sense of hearing. The new order of species was at first quite small in size and would not have had much of a chance against the dinosaurs and other large reptiles without an acute capacity for hearing threatening sounds from a considerable distance. In addition, the mammals could only travel about at night, when the reptiles were sleeping, so *their* brain developed extraordinary insights and intuitions of both danger and safety. This brain came to value all those things associated with shelter, including the family instinct, togetherness, early forms of love, and even charity and self-sacrifice.

Despite their size and fearsome appearance, the great reptiles could not survive. Earth leadership passed into the keeping of the mammals, and clearly brains, not brawn, assumed priority. The reptiles that remained became smaller, while the mammals grew larger. Today, whales, especially dolphins, exhibit versions of this middle brain, and examples of their intelligence, as well as of their "tender" qualities, have been eminently documented.

With the coming into being of the higher primates, including Homo sapiens, over a multi-million year span, the topmost brain evolved. Its unique specialty has been to handle the ever more complex problems of a socialized animal. The "simpler" problems, such as where to nest or where to best forage for food undetected by larger animals, were superseded by questions of communication, leadership, interpersonal relationships, revolution, and above all, developing the best methodology for getting jobs done. Jane Goodall, famous for her observations of chimpanzees, notes that all of these needs can be found in chimp behavior. Chimps engage in something approximating human forethought. They plan, they even scheme. On one occasion Goodall observed an actual revolution, when a gang of chimps, apparently as a result of a careful plan, "jumped" an undesirable (antisocial) chimp and killed him. (Human beings also make elaborate plans for killing other human beings.) At any rate, the top brain, or new brain, became skilled at adaptation and survival through planning and, eventually, conceptualizing. These things required the development of the elaborate communication system we call language. (By the way, chimps do not have much to do with spoken language, but they can and do understand sign language.)

Characteristics of the Reptilian Brain:

aggression

territory

chain of command

ritual

resistance to change

•

•

•

•

•

•

Characteristics of the Mammalian Brain:

insights

intuitions

shelter

family

charity

self-sacrifice

The main point of the triple-brain theory is that the old brains were not phased out, but rather added to! This means that traces of both reptilian and early mammalian brains remain with us, and that the human brain, capable of intellectual operations we have yet to understand in full, is of far more recent origin, and less at home in the cranium than the others which, having been around for eons, "know the ropes."

Within the context of this theory, the thoughtful critic resides in the topmost brain. Thoughtful critics are relatively new at the business of surviving within and coping with a continually shifting environment. Their problems, too, are vastly more intricate than those of their remote ancestors. They must pay heed to both sensory information *and* abstract thought. They are called upon to make momentous decisions which sometimes involve hundreds or thousands of lives. Not only that, but the work of conscious, sustained thought can be difficult, taxing, exhausting. It may take another million years for the topmost brain to perform as efficiently as the computer, whose functions represent the brain's own but in a perfected form.

If Computers Can, Why Can't I?

There are computers which in a few seconds can solve math problems that may have eluded staff mathematicians at leading universities for years. There are computers which project the winner of a presidential election with the barest fraction of returns in; computers which can diagnose an illness that once required the consultations of five physicians, design a house, write a story, compose a symphony, offer psychological counseling, and, perhaps some day, will be able to tell research scientists which proposed cure for cancer will really work.

In inventing the computer, modern science studied the workings of the human brain, or at least that portion of the brain which stores information and memories and is able to make connections between thoughts that are logically related. Modern science has been able to reproduce those workings with such increasing accuracy that the inevitable next step (already taken, one hears) is a computer which connects up electrical circuits, becomes aware that it has done so, finds the language to explain the process, and

---

Top Brain:

conscious sustained thought; ability to abstract and synthesize.

The computer works better at those tasks for which it is designed.

speaks to the baffled human who has pushed the button!

Now, of course, the obvious question is this: if science can make a machine work so well, why can't our natural brains do it? The answer is not, "They can, but we may as well let the machine do the work." Intellectual achievement is a source of pride. The computer is not analogous to the power-propelled lawn mower, which makes mowing easy and pleasant but which is not essential. But the computer *has* become indispensable, mainly because the individual brain cannot match its swiftness. After all, the brains which program it have been able to work out the problems at their own pace! The computer, in short, works better at those tasks for which it is designed than the brain does.

If the computer has learned from the real brain, however, may not the real brain reverse the process, study the computer, and learn to imitate its process? What, for example, of the computer's exquisite dedication to its labors? Who enjoys "thinking" as much as the computer does? Who would continue intellectual efforts day and night without food or sleep? Who prefers thought to any sensual pleasure imaginable? Who is never known to procrastinate in performing a purely mental task?

Merle L. Meacham

In a few minutes a computer can make a mistake so great that it would take many men many months to equal it.

Bottom Brain Thoughts

What shall we have for supper tonight?

Can we afford to pay the rent?

I was here first.

I'll get to the top if it takes me ten years.

How much does he earn?

Who does she think she is?

Who's in charge here?

I am in charge here.

Now that I'm the manager, I'll need a larger house.

Borrowing from the triple-brain model discussed in the preceding section, one can say that an advantage "enjoyed" by the computer is not having legacies from the old brains with which to contend. It has no reptilian brain messages urging the body to be food-conscious, aggressive, defensive of territory; and it is not impressed by rank and status.

Nor does the computer possess, unless so programmed, the middle brain, with its overwhelming concern for family ties and caring for others. True, a machine that reaches out to stroke one in sympathy might be reassuring, but sympathy does not produce facts, figures, and percentages.

Middle Brain Thoughts

Be home by ten.

Don't go out with him; he's not for you.

Married ten years and only one child?

She's old and helpless; we have to take her in.

I don't quite trust him; he has shifty eyes.

I like him, he speaks my language.

It can be argued that most of our days are devoted to problems of a "lower" order, which is to say that similar problems have been around for millions of years. They are not unimportant; obviously they are vitally related to survival. But they do not represent the full extent of what can concern a human being. If they did, the topmost brain would never have been needed.

As things stand now, it looks as though the majority of us use the topmost brain strictly when necessary: to get through a math assignment; to plan some strategies for getting by next year, with not one but two children in college now; to compose a business letter demanding "in a nice way" satisfaction from the store "or else." Sustained sequences of concentrated thought—the computer's specialty —are avoided whenever possible. They are difficult for us. After all, *some* people are planning, arranging, formulating the rules. *We* don't have to worry about those things.

The majority of us use the topmost brain strictly when necessary.

Computers "think" for no reason and to no purpose. It is we who have the purposes. The computer would just as soon run through its operations, rather than have its current turned off. Perhaps, in inventing the computer, human beings could have in some way instilled a reinforcement system, caused the computer to weigh the prospects when asked to perform a task, made it possible for the computer to choose whether to think or not to think. But such a built-in program would have made little sense except as an exercise in computer technology.

By contrast, human beings generally require a specific reason for engaging in their kind of sustained, critical thinking: planning, speculating, pondering, wondering, reaching conclusions, analyzing conclusions, changing course and trying another line of thought. Moreover, one often resents having a reason to think, preferring activities—really *pass*ivities—which are less trouble. Do people sit by the hour and watch television because of the active pleasure, or because passivity in itself is sought? In bygone days, the days of the old brains, creatures could curl up and sleep when not required to look for food and shelter, care for their young, or worry about reproduction. A certain amount of good old days must remain with us.

Computers are not sidetracked. They do not seize any opportunity whatever to avoid conscious thought. Computers do not walk around aimlessly, look out the window, go to the refrigerator, or reread the morning's mail. They do not allow nerves or emotions to cloud their issues. They stay on course.

The moral is not that we should pattern ourselves after the computer, though we may want to reconsider the perpetually scornful references to machines, such as "He's a regular machine" and "There's something wrong; I seem to be going mechanically through the day." Humanism has been anti-machine for a very long time, and it is second nature for humanists, old and new, to insist that human beings are not reducible to so many mechanical parts, that human beings have mysterious qualities which elude analysis.

> No doubt a human being is a whole that equals far more than the sum of its components.

No doubt a human being is a whole that equals far more than the sum of its components. Einstein was more than a complex brain. At the same time, we do not want to allow the "human mystique" to serve as an excuse for allowing many of the new brain's amazing powers to go to waste. There are times when we need to try the process of sustained thought, not for any practical purpose, but for the sake of using what is there; otherwise, why *is* it there?

Carl Sagan's *The Dragons of Eden,* which offers, in addition to the three-part brain model, speculations on the present nature and the possible future of human intelligence, underscores the necessity for visualizing and encompassing the full scope of the brain. Accepting the triple-brain model with some modifications of his own, Sagan believes that the possibilities of the new brain are virtually unlimited. He believes that a time will come—and not too far off—when the entire nature of this universe will lie within human comprehension, when human beings will, in fact, have caught up with their own machines:

> *. . . we can imagine a universe in which the laws of nature are immensely more complex. But we do not live in such a universe. Why not? I think it may be because all those organisms who perceived their universe as very complex are dead.* [2]

In other words, Homo sapiens not only survived but rose to a position of eminence because of the steady growth of its higher mental capacities. At the present moment in human history, critical thinking—the capacity for long periods of sustained thought not immediately related to a food-and-shelter or even a human relationship problem—is no doubt the highest of these capacities. The reason? Critical thinking will enable humanity not only to comprehend its universe to a point at which it no longer seems very complex, as Sagan points out, but to take charge of, or at least become a partner in, its own further development.

Every reader who is out there at this very moment, looking at these words, is a representative of the human species. Every reader possesses the faculty of critical thought and has the potential to take himself or herself who knows how far?

The critical thinkers are the people who will come up with the ideas, who will persuade others, who will be nature's collaborators. Those who hang back, who allow their most precious gift to grow rusty from want of care, may well have to follow another person's lead. The day may come when they find themselves trapped in a job or a lifestyle not of their own choosing and definitely not to their liking.

If so, it would be their own fault.

Mind Play

When the average person comes home from a day's work, he or she is likely to seek out what is popularly called recreation or leisure-time fun. Reading a book, having a serious conversation on some important issue which does not have to do with dinner or television, or reaching for *The New York Times* Crossword Puzzle is probably not the average person's idea of fun. In our society, fun almost always means activity that pointedly does *not* require thought. Serious thinking is usually equated with hard work, and hard work is almost automatically excluded from the domain of fun.

Why this aversion to thinking, when hard work is traditionally something of which the worker is proud? A person who has built a house by hand—that is, without dividing the labor among professional contractors—is never ashamed of the feat. Is "hard" thinking only good insofar as it yields a tangible product? A house is literally a *solid* achievement. Algebra homework can be held in the hand, can be seen as well as touched. A committee's long-range plan of urban renewal may one day result in beautiful shopping malls, a rapid transit system, national publicity. Yet spending time deep in thoughts that have no real tangible payoff—except in and for themselves—goes against the cultural grain.

Now, of course, the question inevitably arises: why *bother* with "idle" thinking? What is wrong with having fun that excludes thought? What is so special, so essential about the act of thinking?

The answer lies in a combination of two factors. First, humanity has proved itself worthy of survival and further development almost exclusively through brain power. While physical activity is very important, one must admit that humankind does not fare well in strictly physical comparisons with other species. Elephants are stronger, monkeys are more agile, and gazelles run faster. Birds probably have a cleaner accident record than most airlines—but birds did not invent machines to make up for what they could not do themselves.

Second, that marvelous brain power which has carried humankind this far is still a relatively recent arrival on the scene. Many things about the mind work efficiently without conscious effort on our part. We learn to walk and speak long before we know precisely what it is we are doing. Stroke victims often bounce back with astonishing rapidity, their brains transferring certain functions from damaged areas to still healthy ones. But highly conscious, concentrated, sustained thought does not happen except through an act of will. The critical faculty does not yet take care of

Arnold Toynbee

To be able to fill leisure intelligently is the last product of civilization.

No Inflation Here:

"A penny for your thoughts."

itself, though in persons who enjoy thinking, it probably springs to life readily, without excessive goading. In short, the brain needs exercise just as much as muscles do.

What is the brain made of? Photographs and models reveal a sponge-like mass. This "sponge" is comprised of billions of neurons, or nerve cells, which are joined together by tiny connectors. A thought takes place when electrical impulses travel from certain neurons to other neurons via these connectors. Something like an electrical circuit is set up. A simple act of thought would be free association. The teacher in front of the room is reading Somerset Maugham's short story "Red," and you might remember that your first date had red hair. A more complicated act of thought would be a circuit composed of neurons related only through what we would call logic. The brain is adept at free associations, less so at logical thought. Hence, daydreaming is easier than concentrated thought.

Creating new thought circuits is distinctly pleasurable to the brain. After all, it lives for no reason other than to have its neurons connected. People who play bridge, chess, Scrabble, or Botticelli (a complicated question and answer game that fully taxes one's memory) know about the pleasure that comes from mind play. They will tell you that a brilliant chess move, or scoring a lot of points in a Scrabble match by coming up with bizarre words unfamiliar to the other players, can be as satisfying as winning at tennis or golf (though neither of these sports is without its intellectual elements).

The brain that has had a great deal of practice finds the task of making thought circuits more and more pleasant, until there comes a point at which the task comes under the heading of fun and relaxation. People who work under a good deal of mental pressure often entertain themselves in their leisure moments by punning, making witty observations, solving puzzles.

A double Nobel Prize winner (for both chemistry and peace) is Linus Pauling, who testifies to the delight he takes in mind play. Even when he is not in the laboratory, he is continually thinking, turning over possibilities, looking for connections. When asked once how it was possible for one person to distinguish himself in so many ways, he answered simply: "That's easy. You have to have a lot of ideas, and then throw away all the bad ones."

The average person may suppose that unreflective leisure-time amusements such as movies, television, and sports offer the body a positive, good, much-needed rest. But in fact such "rest" may be harmful to the brain. Looking for hours at images on a screen or players on a field can cause a jam-up inside the brain. The brain may be receiving too many stimuli without time to sort them out. It may decide to give up, to let sensory data keep coming in, and never to process anything. This is known as surrendering to passive experience, which is somewhat analogous to driving around the corner for a newspaper, rather than walking.

An unwillingness to embark on mind play may stem from:

the fear of failing at it

the work ethic of our society which cries, "Useless!"

the selling job done by the media

not liking yourself, not wanting to spend time with yourself

Roadblocks to Critical Thinking

Obstacles to Critical Thought

lack of positive reinforcement from society

bad self-image

guilt

emotions

fear of thinking

The preceding section dealt with some current models—visualizations—of how the brain is structured. None has been proved completely valid, at least to everyone's satisfaction. Proponents of the hemisphere theory, who maintain that the left side of the brain is conceptually and symbolically oriented and the right side is intuitively oriented, have been challenged by those who maintain that both hemispheres can be shown to have duplicate functions, that if the left hemisphere is damaged, the right hemisphere will take over. Stroke victims can lose the ability to talk, and regain it several weeks later.

On the other hand, one can say that the brain *does* control language, conceptualization, as well as intuition. The model itself may not matter, so long as we grasp what the brain actually does. Aggressiveness and the "territorial imperative" may or may not stem from a so-called reptilian brain, but it is hard to deny that these traits exist within most people, at least at some points in their lives.

What happens if you find yourself in a doctor's waiting room with a long stretch of time before you and nothing but old magazines to occupy your time?

Is it possible to find something to do?

Try the Alphabet Game. Identify celebrated names that begin with the same letter: Alan Alda, Binnie Barnes, Betty Boop, Carol Channing, Donald Duck.

The list can be limited to entertainers, fictional characters, sports figures, the living, or the deceased.

Cities work very well. How about two-syllabled, first-accented cities like Houston, Phoenix, Boston? Or, even harder, three-syllabled, first-accented cities like Utica or Buffalo? Or cities whose names have Indian origins like Chattahoochee, Tallahassee, Wichita?

You can make up your own rules. The time will pass rapidly, and your brain will be eternally grateful.

How about picking a subject—any subject—and writing down everything you know about it? Two things will happen. You will find out how much you really *do* know about a good many subjects, and you will discover any number of subjects about which you know nothing. You may find some new intellectual interests.

Thinking about thinking, and if possible trying to visualize the thinking process in terms of left and right, of old brains and new brains, or of thought circuits, is a helpful first step toward becoming a critical thinker. There even is a current theory that one can communicate with the brain and ask it to work harder, to concentrate better.

But before this communication can take place, we need to define and assess some possible obstacles to serious thought.

The Social Context

One such obstruction might be a threatening external environment, which seems to make unreasonable demands on our powers of thought, demands we feel unable to meet. The boss says: "All right. Where is that report? It was due last Friday." We panic inwardly. We had imagined dashing it off in an hour or two. Now we become defensive: "It's not my

Student to teacher:

"I'll read that, but how much extra credit will I get for it?"

•

•

•

•

•

•

Family friend to student:

"And what are you studying to be?"

fault. The deadline was never made clear to me." The boss: "It's essential that I have it. Please put it on my desk by 9:00 tomorrow morning." Whatever the boss's actual tone may have been, chances are good that we shall feel intimidated. Ours is a society which places a high premium on producing to order, *on schedule.* Our educational system has long stressed the importance of deadlines. Testing is usually conducted under highly mechanized, time-conscious circumstances. "Do not open the test booklet until the signal is given. Work rapidly. When time is called, put down your pencils, and close your books at once!"

It is therefore inevitable that we devise a roadblock of our own: procrastination. Everyone knows what it is like to be faced with a task that is going to require sustained thought, such as planning a term paper, writing a speech, or composing a business letter. Are there not a hundred ways to avoid getting down to business? Eyestrain, "Let's see what's in the refrigerator," uncommon domesticity: "Think I'll straighten the room up first." To procrastinate is to perpetuate the assumption that sustained thinking is going to hurt.

But even if we disclaim the notion of its hurting, there remains the undeniable fact that our society tends to withhold positive reinforcement for original feats of thought. Maintaining schedules and meeting deadlines are important, but far too often the external demands outweigh the originality of the content, the logic of the internal structure, the integrity of the thinking. There are penalties for being late, but not necessarily rewards for being profound.

In fact, it is often to one's disadvantage to be pegged as a loner who spends a good deal of time in thought. People tend to distrust continual thinkers. Or, to change the emphasis slightly, few are ever rejected for their unwillingness to think. The rewards for intellectual laziness exceed the penalties by far. It seems to be easier to find friends when one has nothing of importance to say than when one wants to pursue intensive thought.

Most parents want their children to "get a decent education," to graduate from high school and, usually, college, and then to "find a good job." Once these goals have been reached, it is the rare parent who asks: "Do you keep up with your reading? Have you written anything interesting lately? Have you had any unusual insights?"

Generally Rewarded

being reliable

obeying orders

getting the job done on time

doing the job properly

not complaining

offering limited suggestions

Generally Unappreciated

doing the job in a novel way

devising a plan no one asks for

taking too much time, but coming up with a large result

continually questioning the guidelines

Poor Self-Concepts

A *chronic* unwillingness to embark upon bold mental adventures no doubt springs from the poor self-concept with which most of us start out in life and which some of us never manage to transcend. We are smaller than our parents; we never seem to do anything right. We feel, as a recent and perceptive book indicated, "not OK." It is a rare person who can dissolve all of the inhibitions caused by feelings of unworthiness, unintelligence, and not being able to succeed at anything. Childhood memories of being shushed whenever we ventured a suggestion, of being smiled at condescendingly whenever we tried to be creative, remain with us, to a greater or lesser extent, throughout our lives.

The child who is raised as the apple of the doting family's eye may be just as hapless, for this child quickly recognizes what he must do or say to win instant approval. Dare he risk the loss of his smiling audience by doing or saying strange and perhaps unrecognizable things?

The self-concept needs continual care and nurturing. It is a fragile entity and can go to extremes at almost a moment's notice. It can wallow in fantasies of unworthiness ("Nobody likes me, I can see it in their eyes every time I enter the room"), or it can rise defensively to heights of imperiousness ("I don't care what they say, I'm better than anyone else"). Both extremes make critical thinking impossible, for the essence of careful, precise thought is the ability to survey a situation calmly and clearly and *not* in terms of vested self-interest.

At first glance one might be tempted to suppose that people with low opinions of themselves need to have their egos inflated. Nothing could be less desirable. Critical thinking, the skill of observing how things are with a minimum of self-interest getting in the way, is the better antidote. It is astonishing how many people think they are observing and commenting upon the course of life without ever knowing that they are looking at and speaking about *themselves.* The person who says, "Sure! As soon as I change traffic lanes, I get behind a line of parked cars," may think he is making a pronouncement on universal injustice, but he is only reinforcing his own poor self-concept through self-pity. "It only rains on weekends" may sound like humorous cynicism, but it can also conceal a pitiful lack of faith in oneself that blinds one to real possibilities. In any event, "Now that I'm here, everyone will go home" is usually not a tragic self-realization, but immature self-indulgence.

One reason for such self-indulgence, self-preoccupation, is lingering guilt over real or imagined past misdeeds. There is only a short hop from "Who am I to expect good things?" to "I don't *deserve* any." Guilt may be one of the most unnecessary emotions human beings can experience. It stands to reason that if one *has* committed a misdeed and agrees with the judgment of religion or society that it should be punished, one ought to take the punishment and move on. Oftentimes, however, guilt is induced by standards of society, family, school, or peer group with which one may *not* be in agreement but which nonetheless starve an already puny self-image. Guilt often comes about from a withdrawal of positive support, so that, instead of inquiring into the reason for the change or ignoring it altogether, one supposes one has in some way *earned* the rejection. On the other hand, the withdrawal of support can be a sign that one has behaved in certain undesirable ways that need to be duly investigated. One should never laugh off the possibility, but one should not burden oneself with unresolved, often unexpressed, guilt either.

Profound cases of guilt involve broken promises (when death intervenes to make real or imagined restitution impossible) or serious violations of a family or religious code, causing a permanent breach (marrying outside the faith;

Groucho Marx

I wouldn't join a club that would have me as a member.

having an abortion; being homosexual). It is not easy to tell oneself one has no need of guilt feelings when the scars run deep. Still, it *is* possible for people to take periodic inventory of their guilts and often to forgive themselves completely. It is sad to wait year after lonely year for a letter to come. There has to be a time when, all reasonable channels having been tried, one's only recourse is to open the window and let the guilt go.

Emotions and Thought

Unnecessary guilt is a feeling that has not been subjected to cool, rational analysis. We may say that any feeling that dominates us to the point of inhibiting the ability to see things clearly is a roadblock to critical thought. There are those who extol the virtues of feeling and downgrade the benefits of reason to such an extent that they regard extremes of emotionalism as automatically desirable. "Let it all out" is a familiar enough exhortation, and while emotional release is sometimes a needed preliminary to reestablishing inner equilibrium, it is true that the need to feel can become an obsession.

Feeling and thought are often regarded as identical phenomena. Casual conversation confuses the issue by generally making no distinction between them. Many statements begin with either "I think" or "I feel," and listeners seldom differentiate. The real damage comes from the fact that, since feelings come more easily than sustained thoughts, "I think" tends to mean "I feel" but is not recognized as being outside the province of critical thought. "I think" statements are often mistaken for informed opinions when all the while they are expressions of emotions, as in "I think all feminists must be bored housewives."

But it is ironic that, in recent years, feelings have so risen in acceptability, even in academic circles, that the burden of proof continues to remain on the side of thinking anyway. In other words, it is becoming unnecessary to disguise feeling statements with the prefix "I think." Overt thinkers have to prove themselves over and over. They are sometimes viewed with automatic suspicion: they are the developers of deadly weapons; the designers of concentration camps; the ones who use language to mislead the less-than-verbal. It is

Thomas Gray

Thought would destroy
  their paradise.
No more; where ignorance
  is bliss,
'Tis folly to be wise.

risky to admit that one attempts to be rational in matters which require rationality, for this can be construed as inhuman, sterile, cruel, and arrogant.

Other Fixed Notions

I Know, Because:

I've *been* there

I feel it in my bones

you can tell by looking at him

I once met a man who . . .

I Believe It Is So, Because:

I've read widely on the subject

I've thought the matter over for some time

a number of competent authorities have offered evidence

The advocates of feeling [over thought] often take the position that experience supersedes logic. People who have *been* there, done the work, or mingled with the workers assume that their views are more reliable than those of people who base their opinions upon common sense. But surely it is not necessary to be poor to have a rational belief concerning the welfare system; it is not necessary to be a member of a minority group to comprehend discrimination. True, views based on no experience whatever can be questioned, but at the same time experience is not helpful if it is not itself subjected to careful scrutiny.

Yet another roadblock to critical thought is the deep-rooted conviction that one is going to fail at any project requiring the use of brain power. Some people eagerly accept challenges; many—perhaps the majority—prefer to surrender before they start.

You just happen to be visiting in a city where the seventh and deciding game of the World Series is to be played. The media announce in no uncertain terms that the game is an assured sellout. You mention to friends that, having never actually been present for such a game, you would like to try your luck at getting in. They stare at you as if you had taken leave of your senses. There is no way of doing it, they say; forget it. What do you do? Devise some scheme of proving them wrong, or decide it is not worth risking their scorn if you *should* fail?

Critical thinking is sometimes akin to what has been termed "positive thinking," except that the latter phrase, as popularly used, tends to suggest that courage is the important ingredient. The courageous thinker who defies popular opinion and does finally get into the World Series game needs a good bit of luck on his or her side. The critical thinker who does the same thing has made certain advance computations: not everyone who holds a ticket is going to make it to the stadium; extra tickets will be on sale; some will be going for outrageous prices; statistics almost guarantee that there will have to be some few sellers who, left with only one ducat, will take a reasonable offer. The critical thinker has also determined how much he would be willing to pay relative to how badly he wants to see the game. If all prices exceed his degree of enthusiasm, he will conclude that seeing the game is not, after all, worth the cost.

Finally, the noncritical person is likely to be overpowered by the complexity of a problem. The critical thinker has learned how to break it into small components which can be dealt with methodically. The noncritical thinker is usually discouraged at the very outset when a problem appears to require more than one step.

Those who would laugh at the mere mention of getting into the World Series game may be reacting to the complicated dimensions of the task. They have trouble with distance vision and see only a gigantic fence covering the horizon. "No way" has become part of the folk lore of a defeated people, a cynical rejection of the yellow brick road that led to the palace of Oz. But the adventurous critical thinker does not see fences. He or she sees the steps of a puzzle, and sets about to put them in order and to go through them calmly. What is the best and fastest way to reach the stadium? Where shall I park so I can leave in case I decide not to buy a ticket? Where are the sellers likely to be standing? What are the proper stance and facial expression for one who wishes to give the appearance of merely casual interest? Taking the world in bite-sized pieces keeps us from going under and it may be the only recourse for sensible people, as the rate of change continues to accelerate. The critical thinker knows that the pace at which he or she goes is *not* beyond his or her control.

To sum up, the main roadblocks to the practice of critical thinking are: the expectation that sustained thought is going to be difficult and painful; the association of "serious" thought with work and school deadlines, and never with the built-in rewards of the process itself; the tendency to procrastinate; the withholding of praise for those who like to think; an impoverished self-concept, which keeps insisting you have nothing important to think or say; accumulated guilt, which prevents you from recognizing your own worth as an individual; the expectation that you are going to fail at any project involving mental agility and cleverness; and the fact that feelings are often elevated to a position of superiority over thoughts.

Literalists and Figuratists

Human nature is often cloudy, often contradictory, often impossible to read. People do not fall readily into categories, and it is not fair to insist upon hard and fast distinctions. Critical thinkers do not consistently maintain such a role. Sometimes they like to let their feelings take them where they will. Sometimes they become discouraged by a thought circuit that seems to be getting nowhere. But people who make up their minds to adopt the critical approach to living *do* acquire certain definite characteristics, and so do those who choose not to.

In this section we are concerned with the way in which critical thinkers tend to use language. Critical thinkers are

> **Galileo**
>
> **I do not feel obliged to believe that that same God who has endowed us with sense, reason, and intellect has intended us to forego their use.**

highly figurative in their speech, while others are quite literal in both their communication and their understanding.

On Being Literal

The literal mind avoids or does not see the general principle but concentrates on specific examples. There are times and places for being specific rather than general, for being concrete rather than abstract, but the following conversation shows what happens when one is narrowly specific at the wrong moment.

A: *I wish life would provide experts. I'd love to have someone whom I could ask important questions: where to live, whether to change jobs, what school is best, what suntan lotion to use.*

B: *My dermatologist gave me the name of a good suntan lotion. Just a minute. I have the name written down.*

A is making the rueful observation that there is no certainty, that in a philosophical sense we are all alone. This is the general principle behind the observation. *B* hears only the examples, but not the random nature of them. *B,* who is not accustomed to hearing or discussing principles, is unaware that *A* is not interested in suntan lotion no matter what his actual words may have been.

Consider still another imaginary conversation.

Mother: *I find the only safe topic with my teenage son is something noncontroversial. I can't talk about his car, expenses, girlfriends, or his plans for school and a career. I know he's interested in baseball, so this morning I mentioned how well the Dodgers are doing. I told him they were six games ahead, and he corrected me. Ten games! It gave him a chance to explain something to me, and it worked. At least we didn't fight this morning.*

Friend A: *I know, the only safe topic in our house these days is the new television lineup.*

Friend B: *The Dodgers are twelve games ahead.*

Which friend is the literalist? More important, by what process did either reply come to be what it is?

Friend *A* listened to what was being said by the mother. Friend *A* heard the general principle: since it is difficult to communicate with the younger generation on one's own terms, it is wiser to adapt oneself to *its* terms. Knowing the point of the observations, Friend *A replied in kind.*

Friend *B,* on the other hand, is probably not in the habit of listening very carefully to begin with. Literalists are literalists because they see object by object, hear sound by sound, but are unaware of wholes, of what was alluded to earlier in this chapter as *the shape of experience.* Their own conversation tends to be tedious, except perhaps to other literalists, because they themselves do not speak to the large or significant issues, the principles. Or if they attempt to, they tend to bog themselves down in a quagmire of boring details, until at some point they have forgotten the original principle.

Literalists often change the subject without realizing they have done so. Since they have not grasped the true subject to begin with, they will often hang on the very last thing that has been said and take it to what they consider the next logical step.

A: *The problem of capital punishment torments me. I see no easy solution. On one hand, the planned and deliberate taking of a human life disturbs me, but on the other, I object to the tax dollars it takes to support a murderer for life. I honestly don't know which side to be on.*

B: *And another thing, there's all this coddling of prisoners and giving into their constant demands for better living conditions.*

B has heard bits and fragments of *A.* He has picked up, "I honestly don't know," and taken it to signal the end of *A*'s time on the floor. Now it is his turn to speak. "And another thing" is a giveaway, an indication of a clear misconstruction of *A*'s entire argument. He imagines *A* has reached a conclusion.

A critically thinking *B* would be very likely to respond in one of the following manners:

"I don't know either" OR

"I don't think a human life and tax dollars are on the same plane" OR

"If we use tax dollars not merely to support but to rehabilitate, I believe the possible benefits to society would be worth the expense" OR

"I believe killing is wrong, no matter who is doing it. I think we have to solve the problem from that point on."

Literalism *also* stems from self-preoccupation. Literalists are too busy waiting for their turn to speak, too busy thinking of what *they* might say to hear what others are saying. Even a transition like, "I have nothing to contribute to this discussion; may we turn to another?" gives evidence of the critical mind at work, and assuming that *A* is typically a critical thinker, is easier to deal with.

". . . one must become able to transcend the narrow confines of a self-centered existence and believe that one will make a significant contribution to life—if not right now, then at some future time."[3]
Bruno Bettelheim

Literalism is not always a sign of a nonthinking person. Some very bright people have proved incapable of moving from dead center in any conversation. One reason may very well be a humorless approach to life, a belief that mind play is childish, that all thought and discussion not directly related to action or the making of money should be avoided. Such people are used to working with the concrete realities of each moment and adjust their responsiveness to experience accordingly. Life is detail after detail. They are often not so much blind to general principles as impatient over wasting time. Sometimes they enjoy discrediting those who are not dedicated to "important" matters but spend their time idly chatting about books or world affairs which obviously have nothing much to do with making a living.

Recognizing Contexts

No one goes through life completely isolated. One cannot live on an island and never have contact with others. Therefore, everything we say or do occurs within a context—a framework of circumstances and relationships. The figuratist perceives context; the literalist seldom does.

Enter a room, and you are in the midst of a context. Who is present? What are they talking about? What precisely is going on? What relationship do you have with each of these people? The figuratist seldom barges into the midst of the conversation or ventures an opinion before he or she has formed a perception of the total context. The literalist almost always reacts to random stimuli, since he or she is in the habit of responding to parts, never wholes.

The literalist seldom seeks a perspective on world events. He or she is likely to have some interest in national problems, more in state issues, much more in matters relating to the city and, above all, the neighborhood. Characteristic of this person, once again, is self-centeredness. The closer the problem comes to home, the greater the involvement. Such imbalance is a basic cause of operating without a true context.

Each day can be divided into contexts. One usually awakens to the family setting—to a family context. There is always unfinished business, some ongoing problem, some existing network of relationships. The nature of the context changes constantly, so one must keep tuned in. Family contexts are easily ignored, especially if one is abnormally self-centered. That is, an issue involving the whole family can immediately be translated into "How am I affected?" How often does one really look at and listen to close family members? How often does one ask, "I wonder if Brother (Sister, Mom, Dad) perceives the problem as I do?" One believes that, because of the peculiar nature of the family circle, one is exempt from having to view family matters objectively.

Some contexts happen without warning, and the literalist is caught napping. A chance remark, a quick reply, the exchange of glances between two other people—and a context is set up. Anthropologist Gregory Bateson laments that too many live in terms of "pieces," but "the pieces of . . . patterns are not the patterns."

One example he uses is the prosecution of an offender for alleged "criminality." What, after all, *is* criminality? It is a type of behavior for which one may be held responsible and made to pay a penalty. But, in Bateson's opinion, the specific behavior in question is only a piece of the pattern, not the entire pattern. Later, when the offender is released from prison, he is determined to "work the pattern with more skill, so as not to get caught. For thousands of years people have tried to punish pieces of the pattern."

Bateson reports that once, after a lecture on contexts, a hostile student came up and asked him, "How do you weigh a context?" (The young man was implying that contexts are subjective matters and have no real validity.)

The literalist reacts to random stimuli—parts, never wholes.

•

•

•

•

•

•

The secret of figuratism is knowing what is appropriate to think and say about a given phenomenon.

So, as I'm talking, I put my hand in my pocket, dig out a nickel, and as he comes up, I reach out and give it to him. He automatically takes it. He then gets very angry: "Why did you give me a nickel?" My message has no context. Finally, after he controls himself, he reaches in his pocket and gives me a dime.[4]

The literalist would never have given Bateson a dime, nor would the literalist even comprehend the reason for the exchange of coins. The figuratist would know to look beyond the coin to the significance of the entire transaction, to realize that Bateson was creating a context and the student was quick to fit himself into it.

Almost anything declares a possible context:

The curbside mailbox left unstraightened for years.

The tiny restaurant which has no menu.

People who wash their cars every morning.

"May we look forward to seeing you at this year's Policeman's Ball?"

Eleven "For Sale" signs on the same block.

32 registered for the course; 16 took the final exam.

Contexts exist whether recognized or not. Almost any remark one makes contains assumptions, expectations, objectives. Read the following statements carefully, and develop a context for each one. What is the speaker really concerned about? What is really being said?

"Let's invite Nicki for Fred."

"You'll appreciate your college education more if you find a part-time job."

"When you were in India, what did you learn about the people, or more important, what did you learn about yourself?"

"The new neighbors kept me up all night with their wild party. I've lived in this section for years."

"Mother's Day came and went, without even a lousy card from my son."

"If God had intended woman to be man's equal, He would have made her so."

"I'm afraid health food addicts get sick from not having chemicals or additives in their diets."

Which of the above statements was made by the figuratist? That is, which statement contained a craftily concealed context which was obviously of the speaker's devising and therefore under his or her control? The other statements probably contain unconscious assumptions, hence exist in contexts of which the speaker is not aware.

Linguistic Tip-Offs

Figuratists are so called because their language gives them away. It is colorful and imaginative, nonliteral. Their language declares their independence of the details. Instead of telling you everything that happened, the figuratist sums it all up in a few bold strokes.

Don't look back. Something may be gaining on you.
Satchel Paige

The law, in its majestic equality, forbids the rich as well as the poor to sleep under bridges.
Anatole France

The difficult we do right away; The impossible takes a little longer.
Business sign

Literalists frequently mix their metaphors. The literalist says, "People walk all over me, but I'm putting my foot down!" *(Unaware of whose foot is down.)* The figuratist is likely to reply, "If people walk all over you, make sure you have a good strong mattress." And the literalist is likely to add, "I buy almost everything at Sears."

The secret of figuratism is knowing what is appropriate to think and say about a given phenomenon. When the state representative reports to a group of his constituents, all teachers, that his bill for a higher educational budget was defeated because "the conservatives literally emasculated me," the figuratist raises a curious eyebrow. The speaker is not thinking of what he is saying; how well is he handling his job up there in the capital?

Figuratists are particularly skilled at trapping literalists in their own webs. Woe to the careless person who tries to wii a round!

Parent: *You're foolish to go to the dog races so much. Don't you know you win one night and lose it all back the next?*

Offspring: *Okay. I'll go every other night.*

Lady Bracknell: *Do you smoke?*

Jack Worthing: *Well, yes, I must admit I smoke.*

Lady Bracknell: *I am glad to hear it. A man should always have an occupation of some sort.*

When it is appropriate—and it is not always appropriate —figuratists operate from general principles rather than a long string of specific instances. It strikes the figuratist as a banal waste of time to bore friends with a blow-by-blow description of all the incompetents met during the course of a single day. He or she may ignore the matter altogether on the grounds that everyone is familiar with the existence of incompetence at every turn, or may quietly observe, "I did a bit of shopping today and was pleased to see that standards of incompetence are being met in every store." End of subject.

Literalists relive their days over and over because they never stray very far beyond their own egos. They bring everything down to the personal level and for this reason cannot see general principles. If they do discover a general principle, it is usually that people and events are conspiring against them. They are fearful of being objective, of seeing things as they are, for, if the literalist lets go, he or she might not find his way back home!

Figuratists, on the other hand, are free spirits, not easily threatened by situations, not easily cowed by other people. They do not have to talk about themselves all the time because they are not insecure about their own worth. At the same time, they save themselves from arrogance by the very fact that they *do* attempt to be objective about all things, including themselves. They make mistakes like anyone else, but do not hide guiltily from them. They may even joke about them.

Literalists talk too much, as a rule, and the ironic reason

"Business is business'

"Family is family"

"Boys will be boys"

"Love is sometimes only a one-night stand"

Nobody can be a critical thinker all the time. There are times when only the hard details matter.

Mechanic: *"The distributor cap is cracked, the points are worn, and the rotor needs replacing. As a matter of fact, the points should be gapped with a gauge; the dwell should be checked with a tach, and the timing needs resetting. The gap should be set at 35, the rpm at 750, and the timing at 6 degrees before top dead center."*

Bewildered: *"Why doesn't the car run?"*

is their poor opinions of themselves. A literalist may cover up for his fright by over-explaining, hoping to win every listener over to "his side," though he cannot always articulate exactly what that "side" may be.

Figuratists give their listeners credit for a certain amount of knowledge and understanding. They do not talk compulsively, but communicate for the direct purpose of communicating. Therefore they see no need to fill in the background. They speak and reply as close to the point as possible.

For this reason the figuratist knows that speaking generally or using figures of speech is not always what the situation requires. Would you like to think that the following exchange could take place between a commercial pilot and an air controller?

Pilot: *Mid-Western Flight 73 approaching the landing field. Are we clear? Come in, tower.*

Tower: *Some people never come out of the clouds no matter what happens.*

Oscar Wilde

"In this world there are only two tragedies. One is not getting what one wants, and other other is getting it"

"Put all your eggs in one basket and—WATCH THAT BASKET."

Mark Twain

One of the problems with popular catch phrases is that they were once fresh and clever, but have totally outworn their usefulness. Figuratists avoid clichés and would rather speak simply and directly. They would infinitely prefer "Let's begin" to "Let's get crackin'." They would never say, "Different strokes for different folks," or "That's the way the cookie crumbles." In a meeting with educators they would never speak of "teaching the whole child." In such circumstances specifics are needed, not vague generalities. To be able to distinguish between cliché principles and relevant generalizations is part of the critical thinker's skill.

The Art of Critical Thinking

It is risky to provide a "how to" manual on the subject of critical thinking, but from the descriptions that have been given of both critical and noncritical approaches to living, it is possible to draw certain inescapable conclusions. Here follows a set of guidelines that are not infallible but should not lead you seriously astray either.

Understand and Respect Your Mind

One would think nothing could be easier than this first step, yet for many it is next to impossible. It is necessary to have both time and silence in order to become friends with one's mental processes. A half-hour or, better still, an hour each day should be set aside for allowing the mind to do its job. (It is fascinating to observe its workings.) People should take a long walk if convenient, or even just sit in one place and do nothing but let the mind exercise itself.

I will confront these shows of the day and night,
I will know if I am to be less than they,
I will see if I am as majestic as they,
I will see if I am not as subtle and real as they,
I will see if I am to be less generous than they,
I will see if I have no meaning, while the houses and ships have
   meaning,
I will see if the fishes and birds are to be enough for themselves, and I
   am not to be enough for myself.
   Walt Whitman

The first thing one notices is that the mind will daydream. It will appear to be running wild—very much like an active and exuberant dog that has been penned up in the house all day and is suddenly set free. Thoughts will tumble over thoughts. The mind circuits will be lighting up all over the place. It is highly desirable to let this happen. After all, if the mind did not need such exercise, it would not engage in it.

After a time the racing will subside, and more stable patterns of thinking will begin to develop. A sorting-out process can now take place. Some of these patterns will be familiar themes but now vividly experienced: old worries, old guilt feelings, anxieties over tasks that need completion. Unless one is determined to get beyond this barrier, one may easily surrender and find oneself trapped in a dead end. The trick is not to evaluate the familiar themes, not to apply them to oneself; the trick is to take note of them and to remain neutral. The feeling of power that sweeps over one is astonishing!

People tend to respect the product of visible work more than the product of invisible thoughts.

A danger at this stage, however, is in becoming overly affected by external pressures: to believe one is wasting time, not getting done what must be done, not advancing one's cause. Ours is a society very much work-oriented. People tend to respect the product of visible work more than the product of invisible thoughts.

The senses, of course, are always functioning, delivering stimuli. Concentrated thought requires silence and looking inward; it has to continually struggle against the lures, the immediate rewards of things outside us. For some unaccountable reason this appears to be a rule: *time spent responding to external stimuli never seems as wasted as time spent in the company of one's thoughts.*

But for our purposes, with due regard to what has just been said and to much that has been left unsaid (and with the indulgence of those who will at first be inclined to dissent), *we shall consider mind chiefly as conscious knowledge and intelligence, as what we know and our attitude toward it—our disposition to increase our information, classify it, criticize it, and apply it.* [5]

James Harvey Robinson

Besides, since visible work gets positive reinforcement in our society, it is tempting to suppose that one has done "enough" when such work has been completed. One is entitled to "relaxation." which generally means giving oneself over to sensory stimuli. There is a prevalent fear, a phobia against thinking: an absolute certainty that thinking will mean one has yielded up one's right to play after a hard day's work. Few consider thinking to be play. Yet the critical thinker knows it can be.

What must be stressed is that the fears and phobias are enemies, not friends. They are not on our side. They keep us from doing what we are by nature equipped to do: THINK.

Work is not unimportant. Work is necessary. But there is no reason to put a label on it, no reason certainly to stamp it as the highest good and as a genuine alternative to thinking. You can think while working if the job is a monotonous one. You may also have a job that requires thought. If so, there is no reason to tell yourself that this is all the thought you need for the day. The notion of "well deserved relaxation" is a myth—and a culturally dangerous one at that. It produces a nation of machines that switch themselves on "when it counts" and turn themselves off when the environment is making no further demands.

Of course, nobody is implying that the critical approach to life means continual *intensive* thought. Once the mind has been trusted, once it has become a friend, it is always going to be there; and the critical thinker can watch television, go to the movies, listen to music, or just sit and talk with friends—can do everything his or her noncritical counterpart does, but with one difference: he or she is perceptive, responsive, *aware.* He or she realizes this state of awareness is the greatest form of "relaxation" there is.

Become Neutral toward the Environment

This does not mean being indifferent to energy and pollution problems. It means not allowing your personal environment to turn you into a machine. It means:

not becoming rigid over deadlines
not allowing yourself to feel neglected by friends
not harboring grudges and other irrational forms of malice
not believing the environment is hostile and threatening
not skulking around in corners because of your "inadequacy"
not imagining everyone is laughing at your "unworthiness"

People who create an image of their environment remain self-centered. They want to put the greatest amount of distance between themselves and everything else. It becomes impossible then to look objectively at the shape of experience.

Perceptive, critical, aware people do not have to be self-centered. They have thought things through; they know where they stand, and that is that. They can devote themselves to the basic art of seeing what is all around them.

Someone will ask, "Yes, but how do I stop feeling threatened by my environment? Just telling myself not to be threatened doesn't work." One recourse is to adopt the manner of someone who is liberated from such feelings of being trapped, to stop saying the things that give you away. Sooner or later, if you have stopped personalizing everything, bringing every subject back to your own interests, you are bound to feel fewer and fewer of the emotions which provoke the sense of being trapped in an unfriendly world. The less you think of your own security in this world, the more reality oriented you become, the fewer reasons you will have for being *in* secure. Just remember this: nobody has time to be looking at you every minute or talking about your blunders; since this is true, nobody is thinking "blunder" but you yourself!

Listen More, Talk Less

The noncritical person has a hard time sizing up situations, getting the point of what is happening, and observing general principles at work behind specific circumstances. One reason is an inability or unwillingness to listen carefully to what people are saying—or to read carefully what people are writing.

We allow our ideas to take their own course, and this course is determined by our hopes and fears, our spontaneous desires, their fulfillment or frustration; by our likes and dislikes, our loves and hates and resentments. There is nothing else anything like so interesting to ourselves as ourselves. [6]
James Harvey Robinson

During a conversation a person will be thinking ahead to what he will say when it is his turn to speak. Perhaps an amusing story will occur to him, a joke he has just heard the day before, and he is anxious to tell it to the others. He may impose the joke on the group whether the moment is appropriate or not. He is forever changing the subject, not having followed the thread of the conversation to begin with. He is so immersed in his own problems, his own worries and fears, or so anxious to impress others with some good fortune that has befallen him, that often his sole concern is to talk as frequently and as long as possible.

We do not, of course, know what goes on in other people's heads. They tell us very little, and we tell them very little . . . We find it hard to believe that other people's thoughts are as silly as our own, but they probably are. [7]
James Harvey Robinson

The compulsive need to talk and not listen, however, does not always erupt into overt speech. Another noncritical person can be shy and introverted, so fearful of being rejected by others that he or she does not dare say much of anything. But one's reticence does not mean one is listening. It is possible to carry on internal dialogs with oneself.

A well known entertainer, on in years but still popular, died suddenly and unexpectedly of a heart attack while in Europe. Two of his friends, also famous entertainers, were asked for comments.

One said: "I feel crushed, abandoned. I idolized him. I used him as a model. I would never have become successful had it not been for his encouragement. Life for me will never be the same without him."

The other said: "He changed the entire history of popular songs. He introduced a style of singing that countless have imitated. He was the first performer to use the microphone instead of merely standing behind it. He created a sound that will probably never be forgotten."

Such egocentricity is particularly unfortunate since it can solidify a poor self-concept, whereas looking long and hard at what people are doing and listening carefully to what they are saying very often causes one to recognize that others have their problems also. The expectation of how others are reacting or are going to react to one's comments is usually woven out of fantasy.

Situation	Impulsive Noncritical	Delayed Critical
People are talking about a book you have not read.	"I think they're show-offs; they probably haven't read it either."	"What is the book basically about?"
You discover that the number of burglaries in your neighborhood has tripled.	"Thank God my house has been spared!"	"Perhaps I should get an estimate on a security system."
You read that two small Third-World countries control much of the earth's supply of energy.	"What's that got to do with me?"	"Why is our country not developing new energy sources? How may I show my concern?"

It is surely ironic that unassertive, unassuming people often give the impression of needing to have their egos built up, while the cool and confident critical thinker is often identified as an egotist. This is precisely what the critical thinker is *not.* The person who is *unsure* of him- or herself, who is defensive, is the person who must always personalize whatever happens, *whether he or she does so openly or not.* You cannot become a critical thinker until you learn that impulsive, self-centered responses are not the only ones that can be made. A rule of thumb is to delay *reacting.* Whenever a comment is called for or whenever you think something to yourself, you should pause, contemplate what the comment or thought is likely to be, and then not go through with it if a more sensible alternative presents itself.

. . . the word "criminal" is not only on a much higher level of abstraction than "the man who spent three years in the penitentiary," but it is . . . a judgment, *with the implication "He has committed a crime in the past and will probably commit more crimes in the future." The result is that when John Doe applies for a job and is forced to state that he has spent three years in the penitentiary, prospective employers . . . may say to him, "You can't expect me to give jobs to criminals!"*[8]
S. I. Hayakawa

Personalizing what happens and what others say is usually a cover-up for a lack of perception. One may have become so accustomed to leap without looking or listening that one is easily confused by events. One manipulates them inside one's own brain so that they seem not to be confusing. "Oh, I see what that's all about," or, "Nobody can fool me on that one." Another ploy is to force someone else to support one's manipulations: "Am I right? Wouldn't you have done the same thing. Sure you would!" Other people, perhaps involved in their own personalizations, may offer positive support just to avoid having to figure out the situation for themselves.

The roots of imperception lie buried in the childhood of most of us. One should think back to dinner table talk. Was it full of silly little details, such as "Who spilled the salt?" or "Finish every mouthful of that meat, or you'll get no ice cream"? Or were real *subjects* discussed?

Once there were two performers opening in new plays on the same night. After the performances both entertained friends and fans in their dressing rooms.
One performer asked: "How was I?"
The other performer asked: "How was it?"

Parents often make the mistake of supposing that children are immature and can thus be dealt with in any way that suggests itself at the moment. Many parents do not bother to prepare their children to assume the rules of responsible, critical adults. If the family watches a television show together, is it talked about afterwards? Or does this happen: "Turn off the set and march right up to bed?" If a bedtime story is read, does the parent show an obvious desire to turn out the light and leave the room, or is the story discussed? It is a sad fact of human experience that little of general, impersonal concern is mentioned within the family circle.

Most of us grow up, as Paul Goodman put it, "absurd." Most of us grow up any way we can. There is very little we can do about how we grew up. But we *can* decide it is high time to start thinking, to start examining, our remarks and our thoughts for the amount of personalizing and the lack of general awareness we will find. It is possible to make the conscious decision to be otherwise. The very best starting place is silence and a determination to hear and notice more.

WELCOME TO REALITY

Chapter 16 Footnotes

[1](New York: Ballantine Books, 1977).

[2]Carl Sagan, *The Dragons of Eden,* (New York: Random House, 1977) p. 242.

[3]Bruno Bettelheim, *The Uses of Enchantment: The Meaning and Importance of Fairy Tales* (New York: Alfred A. Knopf, Inc., 1976) pp. 3–4.

[4]Gregory Bateson, interviewed by Daniel Goldman, "Breaking out of the Double Bind," *Psychology Today* (August 1978), p. 51.

[5]James Harvey Robinson, *The Mind in the Making* (New York: Harper & Row, 1950), p. 36.

[6]*Ibid.,* p. 38.

[7]*Ibid.,* p. 37.

[8]S. I. Hayakawa, *Language in Thought and Action* (New York: Harcourt, Brace, Jovanovich, 1978), p. 191.

INDEX

82 83 84 85 9 8 7 6 5 4